PASS THE TOEIC® TEST

NEW EDITION Advanced Course

MILES CRAVEN

REGISTER

Use the code below to register your copy of **Pass the TOEIC Test**.

Your registration code **GLOB-3007-2019**

After you register, you will be able to

- take one complete online TOEIC Practice Test absolutely free.
- download the complete Audioscript and Answer Key.
- download the full Audio program.

How to register

1. Go to **www.pass-the-toeic-test.com**.
2. Click "Register your book code here".
3. Register, using your registration code from above.

YOUR *FREE* ONLINE TOEIC® PRACTICE TEST

After you register, you will receive an e-mail with your access code.

1. Go to **www.pass-the-toeic-test.com**.
2. Click TOEIC PRACTICE TESTS.
3. LOG IN with your email address and password.
4. Choose Practice Test 1, and enter your access code.

First Press ELT

Pass the TOEIC® Test Advanced Course
Miles Craven

© 2020 First Press ELT
Published by First Press ELT

First Press ELT is an innovative provider of English language teaching solutions, whose registered office address is Normans Corner, 41 Church Lane, Fulbourn, Cambridgeshire, CB21 5EP, United Kingdom.

Series Editor: Helen Ambrosio
Contributing Editors: Mariel deKranis, Berta de Llano, Elaine Langlois, Tony Garside
Development Editor: William Calabretta
Recording Manager: Phil Lee
Cover/Interior Design: Hart McLeod Ltd.
Web Design: WebSanity
Contributing Authors: Susan Purcell

The author would like to thank the many professionals who have given their time and contributed greatly to the development of this project. In particular, thanks must go to the hundreds of teachers and students who have participated in interviews, focus groups, piloting and reviewing stages. Thanks also to all those involved in the editorial, production and design stages, especially to Jo Barker, Graham Hart and all at Hart McLeod, Gerald Thulbourn at www.websanity.co.uk, everyone at CityVox and John Marshall Media New York, Chris Ambrosio, Charlotte Aldis, Mitsuyasu Miyazaki, Li-ling Lee, An-Jean Jiang, Tzyhrong Wu, Julie Middleton at Studio Cambridge, and all at The Møller Centre, Cambridge for their assistance. A special thanks to Jessica Craven for her help and support, and to Duncan Prowse for his kind advice and expert guidance. Finally, the author would like to thank Berta de Llano for all her hard work, dedication, and professionalism pushing this new edition to completion.

Visit the website that accompanies this course at **www.pass-the-toeic-test.com**.

Photo Credits

The publisher would like to thank the following for their permission to reproduce Photographs: p3, p7, p9, p10 (bottom), p11, p12 (top/middle), p14, p15, p18 (top), p20, p116 (bottom), p344, p346 (bottom), p386 (top), p387 (bottom), p388 ©Contributors/Miles Craven: p10 (top), p12 (bottom), p16, p19 (top), p115 (bottom), p386 (bottom), p387 (top) ©The Moller Centre: p3, p18 (bottom), p19 (bottom), p115 (top), p116 (top), p117 (top), p117 (bottom), p345, p346 top, ©Thinkstock.co.uk.: p93, p283, p286, p351, p380, p422 ©Shutterstock

Cover image: © Shutterstock

ISBN: 978-1-908881-08-3
TOEIC® is a registered trademark of Educational Testing Services (ETS).

CONTENTS

Scope and Sequence

Listening Comprehension

Reading

Grammar and Vocabulary Part 5 and Part 6

Part 5   Incomplete Sentences

Part 6   Text Completion

Part 7   Reading Comprehension

INTRODUCTION

Guide to the TOEIC® Test

TOEIC stands for Test of English for International Communication. The TOEIC test measures your ability to understand and use English across a wide range of business, travel, and work scenarios. Nearly eight million people take the TOEIC test every year. It is an increasingly popular way to assess English proficiency in the world of work.

The test is divided into two main sections: Listening Comprehension and Reading. There are 100 items in each section, and all the items are multiple choice. The test takes two hours to complete.

In 2016, some sections of the TOEIC test were revised for test-takers in Japan and South Korea. From 2018 these changes came into effect worldwide. The chart below shows the changes in the revised TOEIC test:

TOEIC Test before 2018		TOEIC Test revised	
Listening Comprehension 45m	Questions		Questions
Part 1: Photographs	10	Part 1: Photographs	6
Part 2: Question-Response	30	Part 2: Question-Response	25
Part 3: Short Conversations 10 conversations 3 questions per conversation	30	Part 3: Short Conversations 13 conversations 3 questions per conversation	39
Part 4: Short Talks 10 talks 3 questions per talk	30	Part 4: Short Talks 10 talks 3 questions per talk	30
Total	100	Total	100
Points	495	Points	495
Reading 75m			
Part 5: Incomplete Sentences	40	Part 5: Incomplete Sentences	30
Part 6: Text Completion 3 texts with 4 questions per text or 4 texts with 3 questions per text	12	Part 6: Text Completion 4 texts with 4 questions per text	16
Part 7: Reading Comprehension 7–10 single passages 2–5 questions per passage 4 double passages 5 questions per set	28 20	Part 7: Reading Comprehension 10 single passages 2–4 questions per passage 2 double passages 3 triple passages 5 questions per set	29 10 15
Total	100	Total	100
Points	495	Points	495
Total TOEIC Score	990	Total TOEIC Score	990

TOEIC Scoring

You cannot fail the TOEIC test. Your "raw" scores are converted into a test score of between 5 and 495 per section. This gives a total TOEIC score of between 10 and 990. Your TOEIC score is valid for two years.

Your Score on the TOEIC Test

Don't expect to score a maximum 990! Be realistic with your aims. Your target should be to reach the highest score that you are able to achieve. There are three levels in the course. This is the *Advanced Course*. After completing all the exercises in this book you should be able to score around 900 on the TOEIC test. Of course, if you study hard your score may be a lot higher than 900.

About this Course

Pass the TOEIC Test New Edition is fully revised and updated to reflect the latest changes to the TOEIC test. The exercises provide authentic, up-to-date language practice and skills development for each part of the test.

Each part is organized in a similar way

Overview	This opening section gives you a preview of what to expect in the test.
Improve Your Performance	Here you practice the language and skills you need to do well in each part. This material forms the basis of your preparation. Work through these exercises and you will improve your score. Identify any weaknesses you may have and work hard to overcome them.
Steps to Success	This section helps you develop your test-taking skills, giving you detailed guidance on how to attempt each type of question.
Strategy Review and Tips	This reviews the best strategies to use for each part of the test, and gives you some advice other test-takers have found useful.
Review Test	This final section is a complete test for each part. Your performance on this test will help you assess your progress.

Assessing your progress

As well as the complete *Review Test* at the end of each part, *Pass the TOEIC Test* includes other tests to help boost your score.

Mini Tests	Regular Mini Tests give you authentic test practice specific to each language point or skill.
Listening Comprehension Test	A complete Listening Comprehension Test assesses your ability on the Listening section of the test.
Reading Test	A complete Reading Test assesses your ability on the Reading section of the test.
Practice Tests	Two full-length Practice Tests at the back of the book evaluate your performance across both the Listening and Reading sections of the test. You can use the *Score Conversion Chart* to get an approximate indication of your TOEIC score.

Additional features

Grammar and Vocabulary	These handy sections focus on the grammar and vocabulary you need to progress successfully through this level.
Essential Vocabulary	This is a comprehensive list of words and phrases used in this level.
Understanding Accents and Spoken English	This provides practice recognizing the various accents used in the test, and understanding features of connected speech. This will help to improve your listening comprehension.

Online Support

You will find a lot of additional TOEIC preparation exercises and activities on the website that accompanies this course. Go to **www.pass-the-toeic-test.com** to:

- find out more about *Pass the TOEIC Test*
- get information and advice on taking the TOEIC test
- read useful *Study Tips* for ideas on how to improve your Listening and Reading skills
- download the *Audio Program*
- download the *Answer Key* and *Audioscript*
- see a *Word List* of the most common words and phrases used in the book
- try the useful *Worksheets*, giving you further practice in the language and skills you need to succeed in the TOEIC test.

To access the full range of *Worksheets*:

1. Go to **www.pass-the-toeic-test.com**.
2. Click **FREE ACTIVITIES**.
3. Choose a Worksheet.

Online TOEIC Practice Tests

Go to **www.practice-the-toeic-test.com** for authentic TOEIC test practice. Each full-length Practice Test follows the format of the TOEIC test and gives you authentic practice that will help you:

- improve your timing
- develop your test-taking skills and strategies
- boost your confidence
- identify areas for improvement
- increase your TOEIC score.

After each test, you will see an estimated TOEIC score. You can review your answers, listen again, and see full explanations.

At the front of this book you have a unique registration code that allows you to take one online TOEIC Practice Test *absolutely free*. Simply follow the instructions to claim your free test.

LISTENING COMPREHENSION

Guide to the Listening Test

The first section of the TOEIC® test is Listening Comprehension. In this section, the test focuses on how well you understand spoken English. There are four parts in this section.

Part 1: Photographs   6 questions
Part 2: Question-Response   25 questions
Part 3: Short Conversations   39 questions
Part 4: Short Talks   30 questions

You will have 45 minutes to complete this section of the TOEIC test.

Directions are given for each part. You need to mark your answers on the separate Answer Sheet provided.

> **QUICK CHECK**
>
> How many parts are there in the Listening Comprehension section of the TOEIC test?
>
> How many questions are there?
>
> How much time do you have to complete the Listening Comprehension section?
>
> Where do you mark your answers?
>
> **1 MIN**

Guide to this section of *Pass the TOEIC Test*

The Listening Comprehension section of *Pass the TOEIC Test* is divided into the same four parts as the TOEIC test. Each part begins with an *Overview*, which gives one or more examples and explains the main challenges you will face. You then study important skills and useful language in *Improve Your Performance*. In *Steps to Success* you practice special strategies for taking each part of the test, before *Strategy Review and Tips* summarizes key guidance and gives useful advice. Finally, you put everything into practice in a *Review Test*.

For all *Examples*, the gender and accent of each speaker is given using these abbreviations:

[M-Am] American man   [F-Am] American woman
[M-Br]   British man   [F-Br]   British woman
[M-Au] Australian man   [F-Au]   Australian woman
[M-Cn] Canadian man   [F-Cn] Canadian woman

The gender and accent of every speaker for every recording is given in the *Audioscript*.

This part of the TOEIC® test consists of six black-and-white photographs. For each photograph, you will hear four short statements. You must choose the statement that best describes what you see in the photograph.

The purpose is to find out how well you relate what you *hear* with what you can *see*. Photographs often involve an individual or group of people, but they sometimes feature a scene or an object instead. Most statements describe the general context, or the more obvious features of the photograph, but some statements focus on smaller details or objects that are less prominent.

Importantly, the statements are spoken only once. There is a short pause between items, but there are no pauses between the statements that describe each photograph, and they are not written in your test book. You only have one chance to process the information you hear.

> ## QUICK CHECK
>
>
>
> 1 MIN
>
> How many photographs are there in this part of the TOEIC test?
>
> How many statements are there for each photograph?
>
> How many times do you hear each statement?
>
> As well as photographs of people, what other types of photographs are there?
>
> Is there a pause between the statements you hear that describe each photograph?
>
> What do most of the statements tend to focus on?

1 EXAMPLE

Look at the photograph and listen to the four statements.

[M-Am]

(A) A man's pointing to some plastic cups on the desk.

(B) A man's giving a presentation to a small group of people.

(C) Some office furniture has been rearranged for display.

(D) The audience is applauding a product demonstration.

The best description of the picture is statement (B), "A man's giving a presentation to a small group of people." You should mark answer choice (B).

(A) ● (C) (D)

Answer choice (A) is partly true. There are some cups on the desk, but none of the men are pointing at them. Answer choice (C) incorrectly interprets the situation. We can see some furniture, and this might be in an office, but there is no indication it has been *rearranged*, or that the furniture is *for display*. Answer choice (D) also confuses the context. This might be a product demonstration, but the audience is not applauding.

REMEMBER *On the actual test, you will hear but NOT see the four answer choices.*

Challenges

Part 1 presents few problems for advanced TOEIC test-takers. Most statements tend to be short and use fairly simple grammatical structures. In many cases, it is not unusual for all four of the statements that describe a photograph to begin with the same subject (*He's*, *There's*, *A woman is*, *People are*, etc.). Many statements use the present simple or present continuous tense. They are therefore generally easy to understand, so you should aim to achieve a high score on this part of the test.

However, there are a number of ways that the difficulty level of statements in Part 1 can be increased, and it is useful to be aware of them.

▶ Length

Some statements can be a few words, but others are much longer. Longer statements have more information to process, and there is more scope to be misled by distractors.

▶ Subject

While many statements start with the same subject (*She's*, *A man is*, etc.), sometimes you will hear different subjects for up to four of the statements. This means you need to think quickly.

▶ Grammar

The level of grammatical complexity may be higher in some statements than others. Typically, the more challenging statements will use the passive.

▶ Vocabulary

You may also hear uncommon or specialized vocabulary that you do not know.

▶ Pace

You need to think quickly and mark your answer right away. You won't be able to remember the statements after you hear them, and you have little time to reflect.

▶ Aural distractors

Incorrect statements may include words that sound the same as, or similar to, something you can see in the photograph. You may also hear words that relate to what you see, but confuse the context or are only partially correct.

It is these more complex statements that you will focus on in the following sections.

IMPROVE YOUR PERFORMANCE

In this section you will practice ways to improve your score on Part 1 of the TOEIC® test.

These are the exercises you will cover:

Previewing Photographs ▷ learning how to quickly and effectively preview different types of photographs

Avoiding Errors ▷ identifying incorrect statements, and understanding why they are incorrect

As you work through *Improve Your Performance*, try to identify any weaknesses you have, and focus on the areas you need to improve.

Previewing Photographs

In Part 1 of the TOEIC test there is a short pause of a few seconds between each question. You should use this time to *preview* the photograph. This means looking quickly at the photograph to find out as much information as you can.

Most photographs feature one or more people. However, sometimes you will see a photograph of a scene, or an object.

How to preview Part 1 photographs

Photographs of people

STEP 1 Look at the photograph from a "general" perspective. Ask yourself:

Where is this?

What is happening?

STEP 2 Look more closely at the people. Ask yourself:

Who are these people? What is their job? What is their relationship?

What are they doing?

Photographs of a scene

STEP 1 Look at the photograph from a "general" perspective. Ask yourself:

Where is this?

What can you see?

STEP 2 Look more closely and notice any details. Ask yourself:

What is in the foreground? What is in the background?

What is significant about this scene?

Photographs of an object

STEP 1 Look at the photograph from a "general" perspective. Ask yourself:

What is it?

Where is it?

STEP 2 Look more closely and notice any details. Ask yourself:

What is it made of?

What is it used for?

Note: Sometimes there may be several objects.

2 For each photograph, you will hear four statements. Listen and choose the statement: (A), (B), (C), or (D), that best describes the photograph. Use the time before you hear the statements to quickly preview each photograph.

1.

2.

3.

Score .... /3

Avoiding Errors

In Part 1, you need to listen carefully and quickly identify whether the statements you hear accurately describe what you can see in the photographs. An incorrect answer choice is known as a distractor. To maximize your score on this part of the test, you need to be familiar with the types of distractors commonly used. This will help you avoid unnecessary mistakes.

There are three main types of distractors that are intended to confuse you.

Incorrect interpretations

Statements often include one or two things you can see in the photograph, but nevertheless they misinterpret the situation. For example, a photograph shows a line of cars parked outside a building, but the statement you hear says "The cars are stuck in traffic." Alternatively, a statement might refer to something you *associate* with what you can see. For example, a photograph shows a man looking around a shoe store, but the statement you hear says "The man is trying on some shoes." In both examples, the statements misinterpret the situation. This is the most common type of distractor.

 Immediately after you hear each statement, always ask yourself if it describes *what you actually see.*

Partially true statements

Some statements may include just *one* detail that is incorrect. For example, a photograph shows a vase of flowers on top of a coffee table, but the statement you hear says "There's a vase of flowers next to the table." In this case, the preposition "next to" is incorrect. In other cases, it may be a verb, an adjective, or a noun that is incorrect.

 Pay particular attention to key words (nouns, verbs, adjectives, and prepositions).

Similar-sounding words

Occasionally, statements try to trick you by using words that sound similar to something you see in the photograph. For example, a photograph shows two people meeting in a park, but the statement you hear says "They're eating in a park." The words *eating* and *meeting* sound similar.

 Make sure you listen closely to every word.

Photograph 1

Exercise A 3 Quickly preview this photograph.
You will hear eight statements. Listen carefully and
check (✓) *Correct* or *Incorrect* for each statement.
Try not to be misled by distractors.

1. Correct ☐   Incorrect ☐
2. Correct ☐   Incorrect ☐
3. Correct ☐   Incorrect ☐
4. Correct ☐   Incorrect ☐
5. Correct ☐   Incorrect ☐
6. Correct ☐   Incorrect ☐
7. Correct ☐   Incorrect ☐
8. Correct ☐   Incorrect ☐

Exercise B 3 Listen again to the statements.
For each incorrect statement, check (✓) the
type of distractor used.

	1	2	3	4	5	6	7	8
Incorrect interpretation								
Partially true statement								
Similar-sounding word								
Correct								

Photograph 2

Exercise A 4 Quickly preview this photograph.
You will hear eight statements. Listen carefully
and check (✓) *Correct* or *Incorrect* for each
statement. Try not to be misled by distractors.

1. Correct ☐   Incorrect ☐
2. Correct ☐   Incorrect ☐
3. Correct ☐   Incorrect ☐
4. Correct ☐   Incorrect ☐
5. Correct ☐   Incorrect ☐
6. Correct ☐   Incorrect ☐
7. Correct ☐   Incorrect ☐
8. Correct ☐   Incorrect ☐

Exercise B 4 Listen again to the statements.
For each incorrect statement, check (✓) the type
of distractor used.

	1	2	3	4	5	6	7	8
Incorrect interpretation								
Partially true statement								
Similar-sounding word								
Correct								

Photograph 3

Exercise A 5 Quickly preview this photograph. You will hear eight statements. Listen carefully and check (✓) *Correct* or *Incorrect* for each statement. Try not to be misled by distractors.

1. Correct ☐   Incorrect ☐
2. Correct ☐   Incorrect ☐
3. Correct ☐   Incorrect ☐
4. Correct ☐   Incorrect ☐
5. Correct ☐   Incorrect ☐
6. Correct ☐   Incorrect ☐
7. Correct ☐   Incorrect ☐
8. Correct ☐   Incorrect ☐

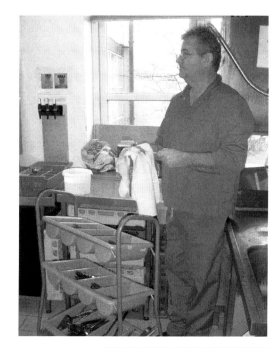

Exercise B 5 Listen again to the statements. For each incorrect statement, check (✓) the type of distractor used.

	1	2	3	4	5	6	7	8
Incorrect interpretation								
Partially true statement								
Similar-sounding word								
Correct								

Photograph 4

Exercise A 6 Quickly preview this photograph. You will hear eight statements. Listen carefully and check (✓) *Correct* or *Incorrect* for each statement. Try not to be misled by distractors.

1. Correct ☐   Incorrect ☐
2. Correct ☐   Incorrect ☐
3. Correct ☐   Incorrect ☐
4. Correct ☐   Incorrect ☐
5. Correct ☐   Incorrect ☐
6. Correct ☐   Incorrect ☐
7. Correct ☐   Incorrect ☐
8. Correct ☐   Incorrect ☐

Exercise B 6 Listen again to the statements. For each incorrect statement, check (✓) the type of distractor used.

	1	2	3	4	5	6	7	8
Incorrect interpretation								
Partially true statement								
Similar-sounding word								
Correct								

Photograph 5

Exercise A 7 Quickly preview this photograph. You will hear eight statements. Listen carefully and check (✓) *Correct* or *Incorrect* for each statement. Try not to be misled by distractors.

1. Correct ☐   Incorrect ☐
2. Correct ☐   Incorrect ☐
3. Correct ☐   Incorrect ☐
4. Correct ☐   Incorrect ☐
5. Correct ☐   Incorrect ☐
6. Correct ☐   Incorrect ☐
7. Correct ☐   Incorrect ☐
8. Correct ☐   Incorrect ☐

Exercise B 7 Listen again to the statements. For each incorrect statement, check (✓) the type of distractor used.

	1	2	3	4	5	6	7	8
Incorrect interpretation								
Partially true statement								
Similar-sounding word								
Correct								

Photograph 6

Exercise A 8 Quickly preview this photograph. You will hear eight statements. Listen carefully and check (✓) *Correct* or *Incorrect* for each statement. Try not to be misled by distractors.

1. Correct ☐   Incorrect ☐
2. Correct ☐   Incorrect ☐
3. Correct ☐   Incorrect ☐
4. Correct ☐   Incorrect ☐
5. Correct ☐   Incorrect ☐
6. Correct ☐   Incorrect ☐
7. Correct ☐   Incorrect ☐
8. Correct ☐   Incorrect ☐

Exercise B 8 Listen again to the statements. For each incorrect statement, check (✓) the type of distractor used.

	1	2	3	4	5	6	7	8
Incorrect interpretation								
Partially true statement								
Similar-sounding word								
Correct								

9 For each photograph, you will hear four statements. Listen and choose the statement: (A), (B), (C), or (D), that best describes the photograph. Do not be misled by incorrect interpretations, partially true statements, or similar-sounding words.

1.

Ⓐ Ⓑ Ⓒ Ⓓ

2.

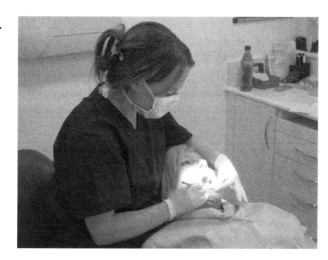

Ⓐ Ⓑ Ⓒ Ⓓ

3.

Ⓐ Ⓑ Ⓒ Ⓓ

Score .... /3

STEPS TO SUCCESS

This section presents an effective, step-by-step approach to use when answering questions on Part 1 of the TOEIC® test. The steps shown here are designed to help you maximize your score on this part of the test.

 Quickly preview the photograph to get a general idea of the context.
Ask yourself:
Where is this?
What is happening?

2 Examine the photograph in more detail. Ask yourself more questions, depending on the type of photograph.
- For a photograph involving people, ask yourself:
  Who are these people? What is their job/relationship?
  What exactly are they doing?
- For a photograph of a scene, ask yourself:
  What is in the foreground / background? What is significant about this scene?
- For a photograph of an object, ask yourself:
  What exactly is it? What is it made of/used for?

3 Listen carefully to *all four* statements. As you listen, eliminate any statements you are sure are incorrect. To help you eliminate incorrect statements:
- listen closely for key words
- ask yourself if what you hear describes exactly what you can see
- be wary of incorrect interpretations and partially true statements
- watch out for words that sound similar to things and activities you can see in the photograph.

 Mark your answer. Then immediately move on and preview the next photograph.

Practice 1

STEP 1 ▶ Quickly preview the photograph. Note your answers to these questions.

Where is this? ....

What is happening? ....

STEP 2 ▶ Look at the photograph in more detail.

Who are these people? ....

What is their relationship? ....

What exactly are they doing? ....

STEP 3 ▶ 🔊 10 Listen to four statements about the photograph. As you listen, eliminate any statements you are sure are incorrect.

(A) [ ] eliminate   [ ] consider

(B) [ ] eliminate   [ ] consider

(C) [ ] eliminate   [ ] consider

(D) [ ] eliminate   [ ] consider

STEP 4 ▶ Select the one statement that best describes what you see in the photograph.

Mark your answer.   Ⓐ   Ⓑ   Ⓒ   Ⓓ

Practice 2

STEP 1 Preview the photograph. Note your answers to these questions.

Where is this? ....

What is happening? ....

STEP 2 Look at the photograph in more detail.

Who are these people? ....

What is their relationship? ....

What exactly are they doing? ....

STEP 3 🔊 **11** Listen to four statements about the photograph. As you listen, eliminate any statements you are sure are incorrect.

(A) [ ] eliminate   [ ] consider

(B) [ ] eliminate   [ ] consider

(C) [ ] eliminate   [ ] consider

(D) [ ] eliminate   [ ] consider

STEP 4 Select the one statement that best describes what you see in the photograph.

Mark your answer.   (A)   (B)   (C)   (D)

STEP 1 Quickly preview the photograph. Note your answers to these questions.

Where is this? ....

What is happening? ....

STEP 2 Look at the photograph in more detail. What can you see? Make a list of prominent objects, and note their location.

Objects:

..........bottles..........

....

....

....

Locations:

..........in the center of the table..........

....

....

....

STEP 3 **12** Listen to four statements about the photograph. As you listen, eliminate any statements you are sure are incorrect.

(A) [ ] eliminate   [ ] consider

(B) [ ] eliminate   [ ] consider

(C) [ ] eliminate   [ ] consider

(D) [ ] eliminate   [ ] consider

STEP 4 Select the one statement that best describes what you see in the photograph.

Mark your answer.   (A)   (B)   (C)   (D)

STRATEGY REVIEW AND TIPS

Strategy Review Listening Test – Part 1

Remember, in the test…

Quickly preview each photograph before you hear the statements. Ask yourself where it is and what is happening. For any people you see, ask yourself who they are, what they are doing, etc. Some statements might focus on small details, so notice what the people are wearing, and also try to identify any objects you think might be significant.

Listen carefully to all four statements before marking your answer.

While you listen, eliminate any answers that you are sure are wrong.

If you are not sure which answer choice is correct, decide quickly. Choose an answer from the remaining possible choices, and move on.

As soon as you mark your answer, preview the next photograph.

TIPS *Here is some advice that people taking the TOEIC test have found useful for this part. Choose the tips you like, and try to use them.*

"Don't waste time worrying about answers once you have marked them. You won't be able to remember the statements anyway, so go straight on and preview the next photograph."

Andi Osmani

"Remember that most statements describe the general context. Just keep looking at the photograph and find the one statement that actually describes what you see."

Shik Gwon

"If you hear a word you don't know, don't assume the statement is correct. However, after you've heard all four statements if you are still not sure which answer is correct, then choose the one with the word you don't know."

Naoko Iwata

Review Test

 Directions: For each question, you will hear four statements about a photograph. Listen and select the one statement: (A), (B), (C), or (D), that best describes the picture. Then mark your answer. You will hear the statements only once.

1.

Ⓐ   Ⓑ   Ⓒ   Ⓓ

2.

Ⓐ   Ⓑ   Ⓒ   Ⓓ

3.

Ⓐ Ⓑ Ⓒ Ⓓ

4.

Ⓐ Ⓑ Ⓒ Ⓓ

5.

Ⓐ Ⓑ Ⓒ Ⓓ

6.

Ⓐ Ⓑ Ⓒ Ⓓ

Score .... /6

EXTRA PRACTICE ONLINE

Go to **www.pass-the-toeic-test.com** for advice and useful exercises to help improve your score on Part 1 of the TOEIC test.

▶ Similar-sounding Words
▶ Homophones
▶ Recognizing Context

PART 2 QUESTION-RESPONSE

There are 25 items in this part of the TOEIC® test. Each item consists of a question, or sometimes a statement, followed by three responses. You must listen carefully and choose the most appropriate response.

The purpose is to test how quickly and accurately you can respond to what you hear. There are no photographs to look at or answer choices to read, which makes this a "pure" listening challenge. You have to listen intently to the recording and quickly select the correct response to each question or statement. You will hear each item only once. There is a short pause between each item, but there are no pauses between the responses you hear that follow each question or statement.

QUICK CHECK

How many items are in this part of the TOEIC test?

Does every item start with a question?

How many responses follow each question or statement?

Are the questions or statements repeated?

Is there a pause between the responses to each question or statement?

In what ways is this a "pure" listening challenge?

1 MIN

▶ OVERVIEW

◄14 EXAMPLE

You hear: [M-Am]   Would you mind helping me finish this report?

You then hear: [F-Cn]   (A) That's very kind of you.

                            (B) I thought you would.

                            (C) No, not at all.   Ⓐ Ⓑ ●

The best response to the question "Would you mind helping me finish this report?" is answer choice (C), "No, not at all." You should mark answer choice (C).

> Answer choice (A) assumes the question is an offer, whereas it is a request. Answer choice (B) is an illogical response, repeating *would*, and using a word that sounds similar to a word in the question (*thought* sounds similar to *report*).

REMEMBER *On the actual test, you will hear but NOT see each question or statement and the three answer choices.*

Challenges

In Part 2, the questions and statements, as well as the answer choices that follow them, are fairly short, and for the most part they use language that you will be familiar with. However, there are a number of reasons why even the most advanced test-takers risk losing points on this part of the test.

▶ Concentration
It can be hard to keep your focus when listening to 25 items in rapid succession, especially toward the end. Maintaining focus is possibly the most difficult challenge that test-takers face in Part 2.

▶ Language level
Although the items are short, their level of grammatical complexity can vary considerably. You may also hear words and expressions you are unfamiliar with.

▶ Aural distractors
Incorrect answer choices may include words that sound the same as a word in the question or statement (e.g., *fare* and *fair*), or words that sound similar (e.g., *report* and *thought*). You may also hear the same word (e.g., *hard*), but with two different meanings (e.g., *rigid* and *difficult*). These traps are very easy to fall into if your mind wanders and you temporarily lose concentration.

▶ Variety
You never know what type of question you will hear next, or whether the item will start with a statement instead of a question. Occasionally, responses can be questions, too! This constant variety means that you have to think quickly the entire time.

▶ Pace
As there is no pause between responses, and only a short pause between items, you need to mark your answer almost immediately. If you don't act decisively and mark your answer choices right away you can find yourself "falling behind" the recording.

IMPROVE YOUR PERFORMANCE

In this section you will practice ways to improve your score on Part 2 of the TOEIC® test.

These are the exercises you will cover:

Question Types ▶ recognizing *Wh-* questions, *Yes/No* questions, choice questions, tag questions, negative questions, embedded questions, and statements

Avoiding Errors ▶ identifying incorrect answer choices, and understanding why they are incorrect

As you work through *Improve Your Performance*, try to identify any weaknesses you have, and focus on the areas you need to improve.

Question Types

In Part 2 of the TOEIC test, the majority of questions you hear begin with *What*, *When*, *Where*, *Who*, *Whose*, *Why*, *Which*, and *How*. Recognizing each type of *Wh-* question can help you identify the correct response, so it is especially important to pay attention to the beginning of each question.

Exercise A 15 Listen to each *Wh-* question and write the *first word* you hear.

1. ....   5. ....
2. ....   6. ....
3. ....   7. ....
4. ....   8. ....

Exercise B 16 Listen again to the questions and choose the correct response: (A), (B), or (C).

1. (A) (B) (C)   **3.** (A) (B) (C)   **5.** (A) (B) (C)   **7.** (A) (B) (C)
2. (A) (B) (C)   **4.** (A) (B) (C)   **6.** (A) (B) (C)   **8.** (A) (B) (C)

Other types of questions you may hear in Part 2 of the TOEIC test include:

Yes/No questions	– can be answered *Yes*, *No*, *I don't know*, or with a statement
Choice questions	– ask about alternatives or preferences
Tag questions	– added to the end of a statement to make a question
Negative questions	– begin with a negative
Embedded questions	– questions contained within a question

You may also hear statements, in place of questions, for some items.

Exercise C 17 Listen and check (✓) each question type you hear.

	1	2	3	4	5	6
Yes/No question						
choice question						
tag question						
negative question						
embedded question						
statement						

Exercise D 18 Listen again to each question or statement and choose the correct response: (A), (B), or (C).

1. (A) (B) (C)   **3.** (A) (B) (C)   **5.** (A) (B) (C)
2. (A) (B) (C)   **4.** (A) (B) (C)   **6.** (A) (B) (C)

Questions with *What*

Questions beginning with *What* may ask about a specific activity, idea, or problem, but there are multiple possibilities (*What size/color, What time, What type/kind of, What will/did/would/have, What's the matter with*, etc.) so you need to listen closely to the context.

19 Read each question and think of some possible responses. Then listen and choose the correct response: (A), (B), or (C).

1. What would you think if I offered you a raise?   (A) (B) (C)
2. What's showing at the movie theater tonight?   (A) (B) (C)
3. What issue is the staff most concerned about?   (A) (B) (C)
4. What's happened to Sarah from human resources?   (A) (B) (C)
5. What kind of restaurant would you like to go to?   (A) (B) (C)
6. What's the best way to clean this carpet?   (A) (B) (C)
7. What caused the heating pipes to burst?   (A) (B) (C)
8. What did the bank say when you asked for a loan?   (A) (B) (C)

Questions with *When* or *Where*

Questions beginning with *When* often ask about the day, date, year, or time something happened, or is due to take place. Questions beginning with *Where* generally ask about a location or position.

20 Read each question and think of some possible responses. Then listen and choose the correct response: (A), (B), or (C).

1. When can we expect another delivery?   (A) (B) (C)
2. Where's the summit being held?   (A) (B) (C)
3. Where have you put the first aid kit?   (A) (B) (C)
4. When will we get to the consulate?   (A) (B) (C)
5. When's the best time to call?   (A) (B) (C)
6. Where can I get my car serviced?   (A) (B) (C)
7. Where would you like me to sit?   (A) (B) (C)
8. When should I empty the recycling bin?   (A) (B) (C)

MINI TEST Questions with *What, When,* or *Where*

21 You will hear ten questions that begin with *What, When,* or *Where*. Each question is followed by three responses. Listen and choose the correct response: (A), (B), or (C).

1. (A) (B) (C)	**4.** (A) (B) (C)	**7.** (A) (B) (C)	**10.** (A) (B) (C)
2. (A) (B) (C)	**5.** (A) (B) (C)	**8.** (A) (B) (C)	
3. (A) (B) (C)	**6.** (A) (B) (C)	**9.** (A) (B) (C)	Score .... /10

Questions with *Who*, *Whose*, *Why*, or *Which*

Questions beginning with *Who* often ask about a name, group, or job title. Questions beginning with *Whose* ask about possession. Questions beginning with *Why* ask about a reason, and those beginning with *Which* ask about a specific choice or clarification.

22 Read each question and think of some possible responses. Then listen and choose the correct response: (A), (B), or (C).

1. Why was the accountant here so early this morning? Ⓐ Ⓑ Ⓒ
2. Whose proposal did the chairman accept? Ⓐ Ⓑ Ⓒ
3. Which report is Dr. Klysters referring to in his article? Ⓐ Ⓑ Ⓒ
4. Who agreed to give them a 10 percent discount? Ⓐ Ⓑ Ⓒ
5. Why won't these security updates download properly? Ⓐ Ⓑ Ⓒ
6. Who's going to clear away this mess? Ⓐ Ⓑ Ⓒ
7. Whose office is across the hall? Ⓐ Ⓑ Ⓒ
8. Which way around does this lid go? Ⓐ Ⓑ Ⓒ

Questions with *How*

Questions beginning with *How* have multiple possibilities (*How much/many*, *How about*, *How often*, *How soon*, *How big/far/long*, etc.) so you need to listen closely to the context.

23 Read each question and think of some possible responses. Then listen and choose the correct response: (A), (B), or (C).

1. How long is the carnival in town? Ⓐ Ⓑ Ⓒ
2. How soon can you start work? Ⓐ Ⓑ Ⓒ
3. How often should the oil be changed? Ⓐ Ⓑ Ⓒ
4. How far into the future do these projections go? Ⓐ Ⓑ Ⓒ
5. How did you manage to get back-stage passes? Ⓐ Ⓑ Ⓒ
6. How serious are your symptoms? Ⓐ Ⓑ Ⓒ
7. How do you deal with hecklers during a talk? Ⓐ Ⓑ Ⓒ
8. How much weight can this steel beam hold? Ⓐ Ⓑ Ⓒ

MINI TEST Questions with *Who*, *Whose*, *Why*, *Which*, or *How*

24 You will hear ten questions that begin with *Who*, *Whose*, *Why*, *Which*, or *How*. Each question is followed by three responses. Listen and choose the correct response: (A), (B), or (C).

1. Ⓐ Ⓑ Ⓒ	4. Ⓐ Ⓑ Ⓒ	7. Ⓐ Ⓑ Ⓒ	10. Ⓐ Ⓑ Ⓒ
2. Ⓐ Ⓑ Ⓒ	5. Ⓐ Ⓑ Ⓒ	8. Ⓐ Ⓑ Ⓒ	
3. Ⓐ Ⓑ Ⓒ	6. Ⓐ Ⓑ Ⓒ	9. Ⓐ Ⓑ Ⓒ	Score .... /10

Yes/No Questions

Questions that can be answered *Yes* or *No* often begin with a form of the verb *be* (*Is*, *Were*, etc.) or an auxiliary verb (*Did*, *Have*, etc.). They may also form part of a request, offer, or invitation (*Could you*, *May I*, *Would you like to*, etc.). A variety of responses is therefore possible (*I think so*, *Not yet*, *I'm not sure*, etc.).

25 Read each question and think of some possible responses. Then listen and choose the correct response: (A), (B), or (C).

1. Did you get the key from reception?   (A) (B) (C)
2. Would you like help planning the gala dinner?   (A) (B) (C)
3. Could I get your opinion on this draft proposal?   (A) (B) (C)
4. Have you been to see Dr. Walters yet?   (A) (B) (C)
5. Is the committee going to reconvene next week?   (A) (B) (C)
6. Does this latest analysis match up with your data?   (A) (B) (C)
7. May I have a word with you in my office?   (A) (B) (C)
8. Are you aware that this is a restricted area?   (A) (B) (C)

Choice Questions

Some questions involve choosing between two possibilities. For example, the question might be *Would you like coffee or tea?* Often, one of the alternatives is repeated in the response; for example, *Tea would be fine*. However, some responses require you to think more carefully; for instance, *I'm not thirsty*.

26 Read each question and think of some possible responses. Then listen and choose the correct response: (A), (B), or (C).

1. Shall we take the bus to get to the stadium, or the tram?   (A) (B) (C)
2. Will you check these expense reports, or shall I?   (A) (B) (C)
3. Should the brochure be 16 or 24 pages?   (A) (B) (C)
4. Would you like me to close the door or leave it open?   (A) (B) (C)
5. Can you give me a ride to the station, or should I call a cab?   (A) (B) (C)
6. Are you flying business or first class this time?   (A) (B) (C)
7. Do you want a cold drink or something hot?   (A) (B) (C)
8. Are you employed here full-time or part-time?   (A) (B) (C)

MINI TEST *Yes/No* Questions and *Choice* Questions

27 You will hear ten *Yes/No* questions and *Choice* questions. Each question is followed by three responses. Listen and choose the correct response: (A), (B), or (C).

1. (A) (B) (C)   4. (A) (B) (C)   7. (A) (B) (C)   10. (A) (B) (C)

2. (A) (B) (C)   5. (A) (B) (C)   8. (A) (B) (C)

3. (A) (B) (C)   6. (A) (B) (C)   9. (A) (B) (C)   Score .... /10

Tag Questions

Tags are added to the end of a statement to make a question. Positive tags (e.g., *is he?* or *are there?*) are added after a negative statement, and negative tags (e.g., *didn't she?* or *wasn't it?*) come after a positive statement. Sometimes you may hear other expressions (e.g., *right?* or *OK?*) which also function as tags.

28 Read each question and think of some possible responses. Then listen and choose the correct response: (A), (B), or (C).

1. You will be here in time for the conference call, won't you?   Ⓐ Ⓑ Ⓒ

2. The new vice president isn't that charismatic, is he?   Ⓐ Ⓑ Ⓒ

3. We see Tina about any overtime payments, don't we?   Ⓐ Ⓑ Ⓒ

4. There are some employee manuals in the boardroom, aren't there?   Ⓐ Ⓑ Ⓒ

5. You can't speak Spanish, can you?   Ⓐ Ⓑ Ⓒ

6. Tuesday's the day we leave for Paris, isn't it?   Ⓐ Ⓑ Ⓒ

7. You don't want to work late tonight, do you?   Ⓐ Ⓑ Ⓒ

8. Mr. Williams used to work for Jarvis Associates, didn't he?   Ⓐ Ⓑ Ⓒ

Negative Questions and *Embedded* Questions

For questions that begin with a negative (e.g., *Didn't* or *Weren't*) the response can be either positive or negative. Questions contained within a question (e.g., *Do you know if* or *Can you tell me how*) can be answered in various ways.

29 Read each question and think of some possible responses. Then listen and choose the correct response: (A), (B), or (C).

1. Don't you want to take a break?   Ⓐ Ⓑ Ⓒ

2. Can you tell me where I can find a replacement bulb for this lamp?   Ⓐ Ⓑ Ⓒ

3. Does anyone know whose umbrella this is?   Ⓐ Ⓑ Ⓒ

4. Haven't they started setting up the stand yet?   Ⓐ Ⓑ Ⓒ

5. Do you know why there's such a high dropout rate for our internship program?   Ⓐ Ⓑ Ⓒ

6. Won't you be coming to the annual meeting?   Ⓐ Ⓑ Ⓒ

7. Is someone going to find out when the flight from Kansas gets in?   Ⓐ Ⓑ Ⓒ

8. Didn't the electrician get back to us with a quote?   Ⓐ Ⓑ Ⓒ

MINI TEST *Tag* Questions, *Negative* Questions, and *Embedded* Questions

30 You will hear ten *Tag* questions, *Negative* questions, and *Embedded* questions. Each question is followed by three responses. Listen and choose the correct response: (A), (B), or (C).

1. Ⓐ Ⓑ Ⓒ   4. Ⓐ Ⓑ Ⓒ   7. Ⓐ Ⓑ Ⓒ   10. Ⓐ Ⓑ Ⓒ

2. Ⓐ Ⓑ Ⓒ   5. Ⓐ Ⓑ Ⓒ   8. Ⓐ Ⓑ Ⓒ

3. Ⓐ Ⓑ Ⓒ   6. Ⓐ Ⓑ Ⓒ   9. Ⓐ Ⓑ Ⓒ   Score .... /10

Statements

Now and then in Part 2 of the TOEIC test you will hear a statement, rather than a question. There are many different types of statements (e.g., announcements, exclamations, suggestions, and requests), with a wide range of possible responses.

Exercise A 31 For each statement you will hear six responses. Listen carefully and mark each response ✓ (correct) or ✗ (incorrect).

1. Don't forget to tell Linda when the press release is ready.
   1. ☐   2. ☐   3. ☐   4. ☐   5. ☐   6. ☐

2. What a difference it makes to have a professionally designed brochure!
   1. ☐   2. ☐   3. ☐   4. ☐   5. ☐   6. ☐

3. Come back and see me in two weeks if the pain isn't any better.
   1. ☐   2. ☐   3. ☐   4. ☐   5. ☐   6. ☐

4. Let's reschedule the brainstorming session to next Monday.
   1. ☐   2. ☐   3. ☐   4. ☐   5. ☐   6. ☐

5. It looks like Mr. Tanaka wants to relocate back to Tokyo.
   1. ☐   2. ☐   3. ☐   4. ☐   5. ☐   6. ☐

6. I'd appreciate it if you could put this issue on the front burner.
   1. ☐   2. ☐   3. ☐   4. ☐   5. ☐   6. ☐

Exercise B 32 Read each statement and think of some possible responses. Then listen and choose the correct response: (A), (B), or (C).

1. That's a very astute observation.   Ⓐ Ⓑ Ⓒ
2. I've never eaten here before.   Ⓐ Ⓑ Ⓒ
3. The server's been acting up ever since the upgrade.   Ⓐ Ⓑ Ⓒ
4. Our success rate from cold-calling is around 15 percent. Ⓐ Ⓑ Ⓒ
5. We're here for the energy assessment training.   Ⓐ Ⓑ Ⓒ
6. I wish they wouldn't let people in after the movie has started. Ⓐ Ⓑ Ⓒ
7. What an amazing presentation that was!   Ⓐ Ⓑ Ⓒ
8. Let's take a taxi back to the office.   Ⓐ Ⓑ Ⓒ

MINI TEST Statements

33 You will hear ten *Statements*. Each statement is followed by three responses. Listen and choose the correct response: (A), (B), or (C).

1. Ⓐ Ⓑ Ⓒ	4. Ⓐ Ⓑ Ⓒ	7. Ⓐ Ⓑ Ⓒ	10. Ⓐ Ⓑ Ⓒ
2. Ⓐ Ⓑ Ⓒ	5. Ⓐ Ⓑ Ⓒ	8. Ⓐ Ⓑ Ⓒ	
3. Ⓐ Ⓑ Ⓒ	6. Ⓐ Ⓑ Ⓒ	9. Ⓐ Ⓑ Ⓒ	Score .... /10

Avoiding Errors

In Part 2, you need to listen carefully to each question or statement and quickly identify the correct response. To help you avoid unnecessary mistakes, you need to be familiar with the types of distractors commonly used in incorrect responses.

Incorrect inferences

Responses often include a word or phrase that links logically or linguistically back to the question or statement, but nevertheless results in an illogical response. For example, you hear the statement "Some new people have moved in next door" followed by the response "I preferred the old one." This response relates the words *old* and *new*, but the subject and context don't match.

Repeated words

Incorrect responses sometimes repeat a word or phrase that you hear in the question or statement. For example, you hear the question "Did anyone call while I was out?" followed by the response "Yes, I'll call them now." Repeated words may also include words with multiple meanings. For example, you hear the statement "Ted's going to run the workshop." followed by the response "Yes, he likes to run." This statement and response use two meanings of the verb *run*.

Homophones

An incorrect response may include a word that sounds identical to something you hear in the question or statement. For example, you hear the statement "Dr. Mendoza will be visiting for a week" followed by the response "She's feeling very weak."

Answers a different question

Sometimes a response answers a different question from the one asked. For example, you hear the question "Where will the reception be?" followed by the response "At five o'clock, I think." This response answers the question *When*, not *Where*.

Wrong subject

Some responses include an incorrect subject. For example, you hear the question "Can you check this report?" followed by the response "He's already done it." This response uses the subject *He*, not *I*.

Wrong tense

Some responses include an incorrect tense. For example, you hear the question "Will you be working tomorrow?" followed by the response "No, I didn't."

Similar-sounding words

Responses often use words that sound similar to something you hear in the question or statement. For example, you hear the statement "I think the train leaves at eight" followed by the response "No, the training's at nine."

To confuse you further, incorrect responses can combine more than one distractor. Remember also that a response can itself be a question.

 TIP Immediately after you hear each response, always ask yourself if it *makes sense*.

Exercise A 34 For each question or statement, you will hear five responses. Check (✓) any correct responses. For each incorrect response, check (✗) the type of distractor.

1. You haven't seen the stapler anywhere, have you?

	1	2	3	4	5
Wrong subject					
Repeated word					
Correct					

2. Why did you decide to start your own business?

	1	2	3	4	5
Incorrect inference					
Answers a different question					
Correct					

3. A one-hour consultation will cost $200.

	1	2	3	4	5
Wrong tense					
Similar-sounding word					
Correct					

4. Did you hear that Jean passed her driving test?

	1	2	3	4	5
Incorrect inference					
Homophone					
Correct					

5. How often are inspections carried out at the plant?

	1	2	3	4	5
Repeated word					
Answers a different question					
Correct					

Exercise B 35 You will hear ten questions or statements. Each question or statement is followed by a single response. Listen carefully and check (✓) *Correct* or *Incorrect* for each response.

1. Correct ☐   Incorrect ☐
2. Correct ☐   Incorrect ☐
3. Correct ☐   Incorrect ☐
4. Correct ☐   Incorrect ☐
5. Correct ☐   Incorrect ☐
6. Correct ☐   Incorrect ☐
7. Correct ☐   Incorrect ☐
8. Correct ☐   Incorrect ☐
9. Correct ☐   Incorrect ☐
10. Correct ☐   Incorrect ☐

Exercise C 35 Listen again and note the type of distractor used for each incorrect response.

1. ....
2. ....
3. ....
4. ....
5. ....
6. ....
7. ....
8. ....
9. ....
10. ....

MINI TEST Avoiding Errors

36 You will hear ten questions or statements, each followed by three responses. Listen and choose the correct response: (A), (B), or (C). Do not be misled by distractors.

1. (A) (B) (C)   4. (A) (B) (C)   7. (A) (B) (C)   10. (A) (B) (C)

2. (A) (B) (C)   5. (A) (B) (C)   8. (A) (B) (C)

3. (A) (B) (C)   6. (A) (B) (C)   9. (A) (B) (C)   Score .... /10

STEPS TO SUCCESS

This section presents an effective, step-by-step approach to use when answering questions on Part 2 of the TOEIC® test. The steps shown here are designed to help you maximize your score on this part of the test.

1 ▷ Listen carefully, especially to the first word or phrase, and pick out any key words.

2 ▷ Quickly identify the type of question (*Wh-*, *Yes/No*, etc.).

> **REMEMBER** Sometimes you will hear a statement instead of a question.

3 ▷ Listen carefully to each answer choice, and immediately eliminate any responses you are sure are incorrect.

> **REMEMBER** To help you eliminate incorrect responses:
> - ask yourself if each response is *logical* (i.e., that it matches the question type)
> - ask yourself if each response is *plausible* (i.e., that the subject and tense fit)
> - do not be misled by incorrect inferences
> - be wary of words that are repeated, or sound the same as or similar to a word in the question/statement

4 ▷ Mark your answer.

Practice 1

37 You will hear three questions, each followed by three responses. Listen and practice Steps 1–4 for each question.

Question 1

STEP 1 ▶ Listen carefully to this question. Pay particular attention to the beginning.

STEP 2 ▶ Quickly identify the question type, and any key words.

STEP 3 ▶ Listen to the responses. Eliminate any you are sure are incorrect.

(A) [ ] eliminate   [ ] consider

(B) [ ] eliminate   [ ] consider

(C) [ ] eliminate   [ ] consider

STEP 4 ▶ Mark your answer.   Ⓐ   Ⓑ   Ⓒ

Question 2

STEP 1 ▶ Listen carefully to this question. Pay particular attention to the beginning.

STEP 2 ▶ Quickly identify the question type, and any key words.

STEP 3 ▶ Listen to the responses. Eliminate any you are sure are incorrect.

(A) [ ] eliminate   [ ] consider

(B) [ ] eliminate   [ ] consider

(C) [ ] eliminate   [ ] consider

STEP 4 ▶ Mark your answer.   Ⓐ   Ⓑ   Ⓒ

Question 3

STEP 1 ▶ Listen carefully to this question. Pay particular attention to the beginning.

STEP 2 ▶ Quickly identify the question type, and any key words.

STEP 3 ▶ Listen to the responses. Eliminate any you are sure are incorrect.

(A) [ ] eliminate   [ ] consider

(B) [ ] eliminate   [ ] consider

(C) [ ] eliminate   [ ] consider

STEP 4 ▶ Mark your answer.   Ⓐ   Ⓑ   Ⓒ

Practice 2

38 You will hear three questions, each followed by three responses. Listen and practice Steps 1–4 for each question.

Question 1

STEP 1 Listen carefully to this question. Pay particular attention to the beginning.

STEP 2 Quickly identify the question type, and any key words.

STEP 3 Listen to the responses. Eliminate any you are sure are incorrect.

(A) [ ] eliminate   [ ] consider
(B) [ ] eliminate   [ ] consider
(C) [ ] eliminate   [ ] consider

STEP 4 Mark your answer.   Ⓐ   Ⓑ   Ⓒ

Question 2

STEP 1 Listen carefully to this question. Pay particular attention to the beginning.

STEP 2 Quickly identify the question type, and any key words.

STEP 3 Listen to the responses. Eliminate any you are sure are incorrect.

(A) [ ] eliminate   [ ] consider
(B) [ ] eliminate   [ ] consider
(C) [ ] eliminate   [ ] consider

STEP 4 Mark your answer.   Ⓐ   Ⓑ   Ⓒ

Question 3

STEP 1 Listen carefully to this question. Pay particular attention to the beginning.

STEP 2 Quickly identify the question type, and any key words.

STEP 3 Listen to the responses. Eliminate any you are sure are incorrect.

(A) [ ] eliminate   [ ] consider
(B) [ ] eliminate   [ ] consider
(C) [ ] eliminate   [ ] consider

STEP 4 Mark your answer.   Ⓐ   Ⓑ   Ⓒ

Practice 3

39 You will hear three statements, each followed by three responses. Listen and practice Steps 1–4 for each statement.

Statement 1

STEP 1 ▶ Listen carefully to this statement. Pay particular attention to the beginning.

STEP 2 ▶ Quickly identify the question type, and any key words.

STEP 3 ▶ Listen to the responses. Eliminate any you are sure are incorrect.

(A) [ ] eliminate   [ ] consider
(B) [ ] eliminate   [ ] consider
(C) [ ] eliminate   [ ] consider

STEP 4 ▶ Mark your answer.   (A)   (B)   (C)

Statement 2

STEP 1 ▶ Listen carefully to this statement. Pay particular attention to the beginning.

STEP 2 ▶ Quickly identify the question type, and any key words.

STEP 3 ▶ Listen to the responses. Eliminate any you are sure are incorrect.

(A) [ ] eliminate   [ ] consider
(B) [ ] eliminate   [ ] consider
(C) [ ] eliminate   [ ] consider

STEP 4 ▶ Mark your answer.   (A)   (B)   (C)

Statement 3

STEP 1 ▶ Listen carefully to this statement. Pay particular attention to the beginning.

STEP 2 ▶ Quickly identify the question type, and any key words.

STEP 3 ▶ Listen to the responses. Eliminate any you are sure are incorrect.

(A) [ ] eliminate   [ ] consider
(B) [ ] eliminate   [ ] consider
(C) [ ] eliminate   [ ] consider

STEP 4 ▶ Mark your answer.   (A)   (B)   (C)

STRATEGY REVIEW AND TIPS

Strategy Review Listening Test – Part 2

Remember, in the test…

Listen particularly closely to the beginning of each question or statement. Recognizing the type of question (*Wh-*, *Yes/No*, etc.) can help you predict possible responses.

Listen carefully to all three responses. Immediately eliminate any answers that you are sure are wrong.

If you are not sure which answer is correct, mark whichever remaining answer choice seems the most rational.

Decide quickly! There is only a short pause of a few seconds between each question. Never leave an answer choice blank.

Maintain concentration all the way through. Don't let your mind wander!

TIPS *Here is some advice that people taking the TOEIC test have found useful for this part. Choose the tips you like, and try to use them.*

"Sometimes the correct responses are not so obvious. You might have to think about the context and make inferences. For example, you might hear *Why did you drive to the theater?* and the correct response is *The forecast was for rain*." *Eduardo Sanchez*

"I noticed that sometimes even though the tense or subject might be different, it's still the correct response. For example, the question might be *The board meeting is next Tuesday, isn't it?* and the response is *Nobody's mentioned it to me*." *Jean Laurent*

"The best tip I know is to stare at A, B, and C for each item on the answer sheet the whole time. It helps me concentrate. I never look up during this part." *Manish Seth*

"As I listen, I keep my pencil over the letter of the response I think is correct. When I've heard all three responses, I mark the option my pencil is over." *Atsuko Shinohara*

Review Test

40 Directions: Listen to these questions and statements. After each question or statement, you will hear three responses. Select the most appropriate response: (A), (B), or (C). Then mark your answer. You will hear each question or statement, and the responses, only once.

1. Mark your answer. (A) (B) (C)
2. Mark your answer. (A) (B) (C)
3. Mark your answer. (A) (B) (C)
4. Mark your answer. (A) (B) (C)
5. Mark your answer. (A) (B) (C)
6. Mark your answer. (A) (B) (C)
7. Mark your answer. (A) (B) (C)
8. Mark your answer. (A) (B) (C)
9. Mark your answer. (A) (B) (C)
10. Mark your answer. (A) (B) (C)
11. Mark your answer. (A) (B) (C)
12. Mark your answer. (A) (B) (C)
13. Mark your answer. (A) (B) (C)
14. Mark your answer. (A) (B) (C)
15. Mark your answer. (A) (B) (C)

16. Mark your answer. (A) (B) (C)
17. Mark your answer. (A) (B) (C)
18. Mark your answer. (A) (B) (C)
19. Mark your answer. (A) (B) (C)
20. Mark your answer. (A) (B) (C)
21. Mark your answer. (A) (B) (C)
22. Mark your answer. (A) (B) (C)
23. Mark your answer. (A) (B) (C)
24. Mark your answer. (A) (B) (C)
25. Mark your answer. (A) (B) (C)

Score .... /25

EXTRA PRACTICE ONLINE

Go to **www.pass-the-toeic-test.com** for advice and useful exercises to help improve your score on Part 2 of the TOEIC test.

▶ More Homophones
▶ Words with Different Meanings
▶ Making Inferences

PART 3 SHORT CONVERSATIONS

This part of the TOEIC® test consists of thirteen short conversations. After each conversation, you will hear three questions. There are four answer choices for each question, and you must choose the correct answer from the four choices. Although the questions and the answer choices are printed, you cannot read the conversations.

The purpose is to test your listening comprehension. You need to show you can understand short spoken exchanges that cover a wide variety of workplace and general situations. Questions will test your understanding of the main ideas as well as specific details, and will sometimes require you to make inferences. You will hear each conversation, and the three questions that follow each conversation, only once. There is a pause of eight seconds after each question.

NOTE

- Most conversations are between two people, and there are four "turns" (i.e., each person speaks twice). However, for some conversations speakers can have up to four or five "turns" each. This doesn't mean the conversations are much longer; each person has more "turns", but each "turn" is shorter.

- Conversations are designed to showcase natural English in a variety of business-related settings. They feature a range of formal and informal language, contractions (*I'd* rather than *I would*), fillers (*Ah, Um*, etc.), incomplete sentences, and other features of conversational discourse.

- One conversation is between three speakers.

- For some questions, you need to make inferences based on what you hear. These questions often test your knowledge of colloquial language and idioms.
  For example, *What does the woman mean when she says, "Let's pull out all the stops"?* [This phrase means *make a great effort to do something well and succeed*.]

- Other implied meaning questions test your ability to understand context.
  For example, *Why does the man say, "If you wouldn't mind"?* [He could be accepting an offer, or making a request, depending on the context.]

- Three conversations include a graphic (e.g., a label, map, flyer, etc.). One question requires you to study the graphic to find the information you need.

  For example, you see a simple pricelist, and the question is: *Look at the graphic. What did the man buy?* You will not hear the item, but the man may say *"I'll have one of those, please."* and the assistant responds *"That'll be $3.50."* The only item on the pricelist costing $3.50 is a notepad.

QUICK CHECK

How many questions are there in this part of the TOEIC test?

How many conversations are there?

Do any conversations feature more than two speakers?

What kinds of graphics are sometimes used?

What do implied meaning questions test?

Do all the conversations include a graphic?

How much time do you have between each question?

Are the conversations repeated?

1 MIN

OVERVIEW

EXAMPLE 1 - a typical conversation

Most conversations are between two speakers. Each speaker has two "turns".

[M-Am] OK, so of the three we've finally managed to short-list, who do you think we should take on? I'd say it's a pretty close thing, actually.

[F-Br] Yes, I agree. They all have their strengths. I thought that Frances Chivers came across very well, which is critical of course, but perhaps she lacks the knowledge of the market we need right now. I mean, she's keen all right, but she's only been in the business 18 months. We can't afford to make any mistakes.

[M-Am] Hmm. And I'd say Frank Lee is the strongest on paper, but he's changed companies almost every two years, which does worry me a little. He has the experience, though.

[F-Br] That's basically what it boils down to, isn't it? But for my money, Laura Hofmann proved she has good contacts with all our major clients, and she has a strong track record. I'd say you give her a call and make an offer.

1. Who most likely are the speakers?
   (A) Client service analysts
   (B) **Human resources managers**
   (C) Market researchers
   (D) Finance directors

   The speakers are discussing the suitability of three job candidates. Of the four answer choices, this is the only option that directly relates to recruitment.

2. What does the woman imply?
   (A) The budget is too small.
   (B) Mistakes have been made.
   (C) **Ms. Chivers is inexperienced.**
   (D) The market is strong.

   Referring to Ms. Chivers, the woman says *perhaps she lacks the knowledge of the market we need* and points out that *she's only been in the business 18 months*.

3. According to the woman, what should the man do?
   (A) **Contact Ms. Hofmann**
   (B) Return some money
   (C) Wait for an offer
   (D) Call important clients

   The woman refers to Ms. Hofmann's *good contacts* and *strong track record*, adding that the man should *give her a call*.

REMEMBER *On the actual test, you will hear but NOT see each conversation.*

42 EXAMPLE 2 - a longer conversation

This example shows a conversation between two speakers where each speaker has more than two "turns". Notice Question 3, which is an example of an implied meaning question.

[M-Am] Oh no! Is that the time? It's nearly 5 o'clock already.

[F-Cn] It can't be! It only feels like an hour since we had lunch.

[M-Am] Time flies, all right. Well, I suppose I'd better get going.

[F-Cn] Surely you're not leaving already? We haven't finished reviewing these student assignments.

[M-Am] It'll have to wait. The Dean asked me to drop these letters off at the post office on my way home. It closes at five thirty, so I have to get a move on.

[F-Cn] Hmm. Sooner you than me. It'll take ages to get there in this traffic.

[M-Am] Tell me about it!

1. Where do the speakers most likely work?

  (A) At a delivery firm

  (B) **At a university**

  (C) At a driving academy

  (D) At a research agency

> The woman mentions *student assignments*, and the man refers to the *Dean*. We can deduce they work at a university.

2. Why is the man concerned?

  (A) His wristwatch is malfunctioning.

  (B) The sales figures are overdue.

  (C) **He has to be somewhere urgently.**

  (D) Some packages have been damaged.

> The man wants to take some letters to the post office. The time is *nearly 5 o'clock* and the post office *closes at five thirty*. He has to *get a move on* (meaning *hurry*) as he is worried about arriving late.

3. What does the woman mean when she says, "Sooner you than me"?

  (A) She thinks the packages should have been sent earlier.

  (B) She wants the man to leave work before her.

  (C) **She does not envy the man the task.**

  (D) She wants to share the responsibility.

> Here, *sooner* is used meaning *rather*. The woman would rather the man (not her) take the letters to the post office, as getting there may *take ages*.

> **REMEMBER**   *On the actual test, you will hear but NOT see each conversation.*

43 **EXAMPLE 3 - a conversation between three speakers**

This example shows a conversation between three speakers. Notice Question 3, which is an example of an implied meaning question.

[F-Am]   Hey, where have you two been? It's two-thirty! I've been here on my own since one.

[M1-Am] Sorry. We bumped into James Richter from British Airways, in the Main Hall. He'd just finished a presentation.

[M2-Br] Yeah, we had a lot of catching up to do. You know he's their new Marketing Director now?

[M1-Am] And he was saying they're looking for an agency to run their next big brand campaign. TV, radio, online… the lot! We set up a meeting for next Tuesday.

[F-Am]   Hmm. Well, <u>I suppose that's OK</u>. But, it's been really busy on the stand. I've handed out almost all our flyers and brochures. I need a break!

[M2-Br] OK, well why don't you take five. We'll carry on from here.

1. Where most likely are the speakers?

    (A) In an office
    (B) At a hotel
    (C) **At a trade show**
    (D) At an airport

> The woman mentions she's been busy *on the stand*, handing out *flyers and brochures*. The men refer to *the Main Hall*, and *a presentation*. We can deduce they are at a trade fair.

2. What can be inferred about the men?

    (A) They are old friends.
    (B) **They work together.**
    (C) They are usually reliable.
    (D) They know many people.

> One man says *We set up a meeting* with Mr. Richter, and later adds *We'll carry on from here*. This suggests the men are coworkers.

3. What does the woman mean when she says, "I suppose that's OK"?

    (A) She is granting the men permission.
    (B) She approves of a decision the men have taken.
    (C) **She accepts the men's excuse.**
    (D) She is doubtful the men are telling the truth.

> The woman asks the men why they are late. They explain they met an important client and have arranged a meeting. This phrase indicates the woman accepts their explanation for being late.

> **REMEMBER**   *On the actual test, you will hear but NOT see each conversation.*

44 EXAMPLE 4 - a conversation including a graphic

This example shows a conversation including a graphic. Notice Question 2, which requires you to relate the information you see in the graphic to what you hear in the conversation.

[M-Am] Hey Susan. How much do you think a taxi ride to Folsom Field will cost?

[F-Cn] Depends how far it is. From here… what do you think?

[M-Am] It's not in the downtown area, for sure. Four miles? Maybe more?

[F-Cn] Well, it's definitely less than five, because I took a taxi to the university yesterday and that was over five miles. It cost a fortune. The stadium is closer than that, for sure.

[M-Am] Hmm. OK, well I'll need something for food and drink when I'm there, so I guess I'd better get some more money first. Is that an ATM over there?

Distance	Flat rate
Downtown	$8
Up to 5 miles	$15
5–8 miles	$22
8–10 miles	$28

1. Where does the man want to travel to?
   (A) A country park
   (B) A shopping mall
   (C) **A sports arena**
   (D) A college campus

> The man wants to go to *Folsom Field.* The woman later refers to this as a *stadium*. (A) confuses *Field* with *country park*. (B) is not indicated. (D) relates to where the woman went yesterday.

2. Look at the graphic. How much will the taxi fare cost?
   (A) $8
   (B) **$15**
   (C) $22
   (D) $28

> The man says the stadium is *not in the downtown area*, and the woman says it is *definitely less than five* miles. We can see from the graphic that the cost *Up to 5 miles* will be $15.

3. What will the man do next?
   (A) **Withdraw some cash**
   (B) Have something to eat
   (C) Telephone for a taxi
   (D) Look for a sign

> The man needs money *for food and drink* and sees an *ATM*. We can deduce he will withdraw some cash. He plans to eat (B) at the stadium later. He will take a taxi (C) after he gets *some money first*. He is not looking for a sign (D), but spots an ATM.

> **REMEMBER** *On the actual test, you will hear but NOT see each conversation.*

Challenges

In Part 3, there are some distractors (similar-sounding words, partially true statements, etc.) as in Parts 1 and 2, but the main challenge you face is to study the questions and answer choices *before* you hear each conversation, so you know what to listen for. Then, while listening to each conversation, you need to maintain concentration and try to understand the context and substance of what you hear, as well as remember key details. For three conversations, you also need to refer to information contained in a graphic (list, chart, etc.). Here are some factors to be aware of on this part of the test.

▶ **Length**
The conversations you hear can vary in length and some can be rather long. Clearly, the longer the conversation the more information you need to process and remember.

▶ **Language level**
The complexity of the sentence structure and grammar can vary considerably. You may also sometimes hear words and expressions you do not know, such as specialized vocabulary, unusual meanings of common words, and idiomatic usage.

▶ **Question types**
The questions test your ability not just to understand the main ideas and details, but also to make inferences. Sometimes you may need to connect two or more pieces of information in order to identify the correct answer.

▶ **Answer choices**
Some answer choices can be quite short, while others are longer. The longer answer choices take more time to read, and therefore to process.

▶ **Repetition**
The more difficult conversations involve less repetition of ideas and less paraphrasing. This means you may only get one chance to identify the information you need to answer a question correctly.

▶ **Sequencing**
In the majority of cases, the information you need to answer each of the three questions is in the same order in the conversation. However, sometimes this is not the case, and you might find that the information for the third question actually comes in the middle of the conversation, or even at the start.

▶ **Bunching**
To further increase the challenge, a conversation may occasionally "bunch" key information. This means that the information you need to answer not just one but two questions can come very close together, or even within the same sentence.

▶ **Graphics**
Conversations that have a graphic add an extra layer of complexity, as you need to study both the question and the information in the graphic while you listen.

▶ **Three speakers**
The conservation with three speakers adds an additional challenge, as the speakers can change more frequently and there is a third accent to process.

IMPROVE YOUR PERFORMANCE

In this section you will practice ways to improve your score on Part 3 of the TOEIC® test.

These are the exercises you will cover:

Question Types	recognizing main idea questions, detail questions, and inference/implied meaning questions
Understanding Inference and Implied Meaning	listening for information that is not directly stated
Conversations Including a Graphic	relating what you hear with information you can see in a simple graphic (e.g., a chart, map, etc.)
Previewing Short Conversations	practicing how to quickly and effectively preview questions, answer choices, and graphics

As you work through *Improve Your Performance*, try to identify any weaknesses you have, and focus on the areas you need to improve.

Question Types

Main Idea Questions

In Part 3 of the TOEIC test, the first question that follows each conversation often tests your ability to understand the main ideas. Questions that ask about main ideas in a conversation focus on the *people*, *topic*, *location*, and *activities*.

People	*Who are the speakers?* *Who is the man talking to?* *What is the woman's occupation?*
Topic	*What is the subject of the conversation?* *What are the man and woman discussing?* *What is the woman talking about?*
Location	*Where most likely are the speakers?* *Where does this conversation take place?* *Where does the woman probably work?*
Activities	*What is the man doing?* *What are the speakers doing in the lobby?*

- As you listen, ask yourself:
  Who is speaking?
  What are they talking about?
  Where are they?
  What are they *doing*?
- You do not need to understand every single word in a conversation in order to understand the main ideas.

Detail Questions

The majority of comprehension questions in Part 3 test your ability to identify and understand important details. Questions that ask about details in a conversation may focus on a variety of points, such as *times, reasons, feelings, requests, offers, advice, suggestions, problems, plans,* and *opinions*.

Times	*When does the seminar begin? How long will the promotion last?*
	How often are trainees assessed? How soon will the package be delivered?
Reasons	*Why does the man have to work late? Why is the discount no longer available?*
Feelings	*What does the woman find surprising? How does the man feel about the situation?*
Requests	*What does the woman ask the man to do?*
Offers	*What does the man offer to do?*
Advice	*What does the woman advise the man to do?*
Suggestions	*What does the man suggest the woman do next?*
Problems	*According to the conversation, what is the problem? What is the woman concerned about?*
Plans	*What does the woman plan to buy? What will the man probably do next?*
Opinions	*What do the speakers think of the new laser printer?*
	What is the woman's opinion of the safety regulations?

 • As you listen, ask yourself: *What information am I listening for?* Try to pick out any key words or phrases that might relate to the information you need.
• Focus only on the information you need to answer each question.

Inference/Implied meaning Questions

Some questions test your ability to infer a speaker's *attitude*, or make *deductions* based on what you hear.

Attitude	*How does the woman probably feel?*
Deductions	*What does the man imply (about...)? What is probably true about...?*

You also need to show your understanding of language in context, and colloquial (i.e., informal/idiomatic) phrases.

Context	*Why does the man say, "Are you sure about that"?*
Phrases	*What does the woman mean when she says, "Keep your chin up"?*

 • As you listen, notice how the speakers' stress and intonation can reflect their mood.
• Try to think "behind" the words and draw conclusions from what you hear.

45 Practice listening to identify people, times, and offers. Listen to these conversations and choose the most appropriate answer: (A), (B), (C), or (D), for each question.

1. Who most likely are the speakers?
   (A) Delivery drivers
   (B) Account managers
   (C) Mail room clerks
   (D) Sales representatives

2. When did the man send the report?
   (A) Earlier that day
   (B) Two days ago
   (C) Last week
   (D) A month before

3. What does the woman offer to do?
   (A) Send a document
   (B) Finish the chores
   (C) Share the work
   (D) Tell a colleague

4. Look at the graphic. How much will the jacket cost?
   (A) $40
   (B) $36
   (C) $30
   (D) $20

5. When does the special discount period end?
   (A) Today
   (B) This weekend
   (C) At the end of the month
   (D) On the first of next month

6. What does the man offer to do?
   (A) Reduce the purchase price
   (B) Check the availability of another offer
   (C) Authorize a free gift coupon
   (D) Guarantee the best deal available

1. (A) (B) (C) (D)				**3.** (A) (B) (C) (D)				**5.** (A) (B) (C) (D)			
2. (A) (B) (C) (D)				**4.** (A) (B) (C) (D)				**6.** (A) (B) (C) (D)			

Score .... /6

46 Practice listening to identify topics, reasons, and advice. Listen to these conversations and choose the most appropriate answer: (A), (B), (C), or (D), for each question.

1. What are the man and woman discussing?
   (A) A job interview
   (B) A planning meeting
   (C) A performance appraisal
   (D) A strategy seminar

2. Why is the man concerned?
   (A) He has to go on a business trip.
   (B) He expects to lose his job.
   (C) He failed to win a contract.
   (D) He did not meet some goals.

3. According to the woman, what should the man do?
   (A) Prepare in advance
   (B) Manage his time well
   (C) Warn some coworkers
   (D) Key in all the answers

---

4. What is the subject of the conversation?
   (A) A visit to a farm
   (B) A factory tour
   (C) A college reunion
   (D) A museum trip

5. What does the man mean when he says, "It was a real eye-opener"?
   (A) It was a very beautiful display.
   (B) He learned something new and surprising.
   (C) He could not believe what he saw.
   (D) He felt shocked and disappointed.

6. What does the man advise the woman to do?
   (A) Return with her students
   (B) Order more samples
   (C) Take an advanced class
   (D) Ask for extra assistance

1. Ⓐ Ⓑ Ⓒ Ⓓ 3. Ⓐ Ⓑ Ⓒ Ⓓ 5. Ⓐ Ⓑ Ⓒ Ⓓ
2. Ⓐ Ⓑ Ⓒ Ⓓ 4. Ⓐ Ⓑ Ⓒ Ⓓ 6. Ⓐ Ⓑ Ⓒ Ⓓ

Score .... /6

47 Practice listening to identify locations, feelings, and suggestions. Listen to these conversations and choose the most appropriate answer: (A), (B), (C), or (D), for each question.

1. Look at the graphic. Which room is the man talking about?
(A) Eisenstein
(B) Martingale
(C) Livingstone
(D) Beaufort Suite

Harriot Conference Center	
Room	Capacity (max)
Eisenstein	45
Martingale	22
Livingstone	30
Beaufort Suite	50

2. How does the man most likely feel?
(A) Excited
(B) Amused
(C) Embarrassed
(D) Anxious

3. What does the woman suggest the man do?
(A) Exchange rooms
(B) Try to be honest
(C) Check the program
(D) Organize things better

4. Look at the graphic. Where is the woman flying to?
(A) New York
(B) Sydney
(C) Los Angeles
(D) London

Flight Departures	Time: 17:00
Status	Destination
Last call	New York
Gate closing 17:20	Sydney
Gate closing 17:30	Los Angeles
Wait in lounge	London

5. What does the woman dislike?
(A) Moving offices
(B) Taking long journeys
(C) Answering questions
(D) Being kept waiting

6. What does the man suggest?
(A) Calling a coworker
(B) Sending an e-mail
(C) Checking the itinerary
(D) Reviewing security

1. Ⓐ Ⓑ Ⓒ Ⓓ   3. Ⓐ Ⓑ Ⓒ Ⓓ   5. Ⓐ Ⓑ Ⓒ Ⓓ
2. Ⓐ Ⓑ Ⓒ Ⓓ   4. Ⓐ Ⓑ Ⓒ Ⓓ   6. Ⓐ Ⓑ Ⓒ Ⓓ

Score .... /6

48 Practice listening to identify activities, requests, and problems. Listen to these conversations and choose the most appropriate answer: (A), (B), (C), or (D), for each question.

1. Look at the graphic. On which day does the conversation take place?
   (A) Tuesday
   (B) Wednesday
   (C) Thursday
   (D) Friday

2. What does the man ask the woman to do?
   (A) Call again next week
   (B) Try to book online
   (C) Wait until Thursday
   (D) Go back at 4:00 P.M.

3. What is the woman's problem?
   (A) She cannot find her patient number.
   (B) She is locked out of her home.
   (C) She is unable to register for a service.
   (D) She does not have enough time.

4. What are the speakers doing?
   (A) Stacking some boxes
   (B) Delivering some packages
   (C) Organizing stationery
   (D) Preparing a mass mailing

5. What does the woman ask the man to do?
   (A) Calculate the potential profit
   (B) Weigh each item carefully
   (C) Keep count of their progress
   (D) Number the items in order

6. What is the man concerned about?
   (A) Completing the task in time
   (B) Arranging a collection
   (C) Forgetting to meet a client
   (D) Correcting a document

WESTDALE MEDICAL CENTER		
	AM	PM
Monday	Dr. Patel	Dr. O'Brien
Tuesday	Dr. O'Brien	Dr. Wilson
Wednesday	Dr. Patel	Dr. O'Brien
Thursday	Dr. Wilson	Dr. Patel
Friday	Dr. O'Brien	Dr. Wilson

1. Ⓐ Ⓑ Ⓒ Ⓓ
2. Ⓐ Ⓑ Ⓒ Ⓓ
3. Ⓐ Ⓑ Ⓒ Ⓓ
4. Ⓐ Ⓑ Ⓒ Ⓓ
5. Ⓐ Ⓑ Ⓒ Ⓓ
6. Ⓐ Ⓑ Ⓒ Ⓓ

Score _____ /6

49 Practice listening to identify plans, opinions, and inferences. Listen to these conversations and choose the most appropriate answer: (A), (B), (C), or (D), for each question.

1. What will the woman do this afternoon?
   (A) Visit a real estate agency
   (B) Request some information
   (C) View a commercial property
   (D) Check out of a hotel

2. What does the man think of the woman's plan?
   (A) It should not be a main priority.
   (B) It might take longer than expected.
   (C) It could be very expensive.
   (D) It will be difficult to achieve.

3. What does the woman imply?
   (A) Granville Street is a popular location.
   (B) There is no time for explanations.
   (C) She cannot meet a deadline.
   (D) There are only a few places left.

4. What is the woman's opinion of the show?
   (A) It was well produced.
   (B) It was unremarkable.
   (C) It lasted too long.
   (D) It was a good value.

5. What does the woman imply about their seats?
   (A) They were very close together.
   (B) They were uncomfortable.
   (C) They were the only ones available.
   (D) They were too low down.

6. What does the woman mean when she says, "Rather you than me"?
   (A) She does not want to join the rewards program.
   (B) She thinks the man has received preferential treatment.
   (C) The man has more points than she thought.
   (D) She is glad the show has finished.

1. Ⓐ Ⓑ Ⓒ Ⓓ   3. Ⓐ Ⓑ Ⓒ Ⓓ   5. Ⓐ Ⓑ Ⓒ Ⓓ
2. Ⓐ Ⓑ Ⓒ Ⓓ   4. Ⓐ Ⓑ Ⓒ Ⓓ   6. Ⓐ Ⓑ Ⓒ Ⓓ

Score .... /6

Understanding Inference and Implied Meaning

Some conversations test your ability to make inferences and understand things that are not *directly* stated.

Listening "behind" the words

You hear …	Meaning
Do you need your car tomorrow?	The speaker might like to borrow the car.
I was wondering when you'd get here.	The speaker could be annoyed the person is late.
I can't get this window to open.	The speaker wants some help to open the window.
You don't want to leave yet, surely?	The speaker feels it is too early to leave.
Is that the best you can do?	The speaker is unhappy with the quality of work.
You're not still doing that report, are you?	The speaker thinks the report has taken too long.

Exercise A1 Read the request and the responses. What do you think each speaker means? Check (✓) your answers.

Could you please help me with the filing?

	No	I'd rather not	Yes
1. I have a meeting in two minutes.	[ ]	[ ]	[ ]
2. There isn't so much, is there?	[ ]	[ ]	[ ]
3. Why not?	[ ]	[ ]	[ ]
4. Can't Joseph help you instead?	[ ]	[ ]	[ ]
5. It won't take long, will it?	[ ]	[ ]	[ ]
6. Many hands make light work!	[ ]	[ ]	[ ]
7. I'm flat out right now.	[ ]	[ ]	[ ]
8. Filing's not my strong suit, I'm afraid.	[ ]	[ ]	[ ]
9. I thought you'd never ask.	[ ]	[ ]	[ ]

Expressions in context

Exercise A2 Read the dialogs. What do you think the expressions with *get* mean?

1. Man: It's hopeless. We've lost all the data and the system is crashing.

   Woman: Oh, get a grip, will you? Let's think this through.

2. Man: The train leaves at 4 o'clock.

   Woman: It's 3:30 now. We'd better get a move on.

3. Man: You need to finish that report, and then get straight on with the accounts.

   Woman: I wish you'd get off my back. I'm doing my best.

4. Man: Guess what? We got the Levenshulme contract!

   Woman: Get out of here! No way!

5. Man: Do you think we'll get the loan?

   Woman: Get real, Peter. The bank will never agree to lend us $500,000.

Exercise A3 50 Listen to these dialogs. Why does each speaker say, "All right"? Write the number of each dialog (1-5) next to the correct function.

___ to comfort someone

___ to accept an apology

___ to get someone's attention

___ to agree to a request

___ to accept a suggestion

Idiomatic language

Exercise A4 Match each expression (1-8) with a meaning (a-h).

You hear...

1. Come off it!
2. By all means.
3. Check this out.
4. Don't bet on it.
5. Any luck?
6. I'm all ears.
7. All in good time.
8. It's about time.

Meaning

a. Did you succeed in what you wanted to do?
b. You have my complete attention.
c. Wait and try to be patient.
d. It has taken longer than expected.
e. Take a look at this.
f. I strongly disagree/object.
g. You have my permission.
h. It is not likely to happen.

MINI TEST Understanding Inference and Implied Meaning

51 Practice listening for inference and implied meaning. Listen to these conversations and choose the most appropriate answer: (A), (B), (C), or (D), for each question.

1. What does the woman mean when she says, "So what?"?
   (A) She cannot see the relevance.
   (B) She did not understand.
   (C) She has heard enough.
   (D) She is not interested.

2. Where most likely is the conversation taking place?
   (A) In a sports store
   (B) At a marketing agency
   (C) At an outdoor event
   (D) In a coffee shop

3. What does the man imply about Mr. Mitchell?
   (A) He is a professional climber.
   (B) He may help to boost sales.
   (C) He likes using their products.
   (D) He attends many conferences.

4. What can be inferred about the man?
   (A) He does not have a very good salary.
   (B) He is thinking about leaving the company.
   (C) He is worried about his retirement plans.
   (D) He wants advice on an important decision.

5. What does the woman mean when she says, "What?"?
   (A) She did not hear the man clearly.
   (B) She is not sure she understood.
   (C) She is surprised at what she heard.
   (D) She does not believe the man.

6. Who most likely is the woman?
   (A) A financial advisor
   (B) A coworker
   (C) A salesperson
   (D) A senior manager

7. What do the women imply about the cafeteria?

    (A) It is very expensive.

    (B) The service is slow.

    (C) The quality is poor.

    (D) It is not very convenient.

8. What does the man mean when he says, "It's hard to say"?

    (A) He is unsure how many visitors will come.

    (B) He is not permitted to give an answer.

    (C) He is confused by the arrangements.

    (D) He is unable to express how he feels.

9. How do the speakers feel?

    (A) Exasperated

    (B) Dissatisfied

    (C) Disappointed

    (D) Apprehensive

10. What can be inferred about Harry?

    (A) He has a very serious illness.

    (B) He fulfils a managerial role.

    (C) He is one of a team of workers.

    (D) He is usually very punctual.

11. What does the woman mean when she says, "It's not the end of the world"?

    (A) The man is overreacting.

    (B) The problem is easily solved.

    (C) It is not a serious issue.

    (D) It is less important than it was.

12. Where do the speakers most likely work?

    (A) At a pharmacy

    (B) At a delivery company

    (C) At a bakery

    (D) At a warehouse

1. Ⓐ Ⓑ Ⓒ Ⓓ	4. Ⓐ Ⓑ Ⓒ Ⓓ	7. Ⓐ Ⓑ Ⓒ Ⓓ	10. Ⓐ Ⓑ Ⓒ Ⓓ
2. Ⓐ Ⓑ Ⓒ Ⓓ	5. Ⓐ Ⓑ Ⓒ Ⓓ	8. Ⓐ Ⓑ Ⓒ Ⓓ	11. Ⓐ Ⓑ Ⓒ Ⓓ
3. Ⓐ Ⓑ Ⓒ Ⓓ	6. Ⓐ Ⓑ Ⓒ Ⓓ	9. Ⓐ Ⓑ Ⓒ Ⓓ	12. Ⓐ Ⓑ Ⓒ Ⓓ

Score .... /12

Conversations Including a Graphic

Conversations that include a graphic (e.g., a map, schedule, list, etc.) test your ability to relate the information you hear with the answer choices you read and the information you see in the graphic.

Types of graphic

There are many types of graphic you will encounter. For example:

1. a directory, list or calendar, showing people, departments, phone numbers, etc.

Personnel	Extension
Sandy Kline	221
Bob Statham	249
Gerry Connors	322
Mel Leeson	389

2. a simple map, graph, or chart.

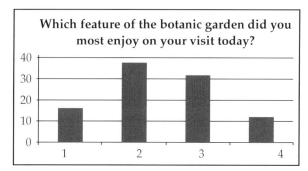

3. a timetable, showing bus/train times and destinations, flight information, etc.

Departures		
Flight	Gate	Destination
AE53	44	Boston
YH8	17	Washington
BA901	23	Seattle
CN377	15	Miami

4. an agenda, plan, or schedule (e.g., for a movie theater) showing performances and times, speakers and activities, rooms and functions, etc.

Harriot Conference Center	
Room	Capacity (max)
Eisenstein	45
Martingale	22
Livingstone	30
Beaufort Suite	50

5. an advertisement, coupon, menu, price list or other type of promotional material.

STOCK ITEM

Vermont Sweater

Reference number	Color	Size
5225	Brown	XL
5219	Green	XL
2525	Red	XL
2519	Blue	XL

Tips

- These questions always begin *Look at the graphic*.
- Identify the type of graphic (a schedule, map, etc.)
- Quickly notice any numbers, dates, names, prices, etc.

Warning!

The information you hear may differ from what you see in the graphic. For example, you see a flight departures board with a list of gate numbers and destinations, but in the conversation the speakers say the gate number for their flight has changed.

52 Practice listening for conversations that include a graphic. Listen to these conversations and choose the most appropriate answer: (A), (B), (C), or (D), for each question.

1. Who are the speakers?
   (A) Outdoor instructors
   (B) Maintenance staff
   (C) Sales assistants
   (D) Office cleaners

Department	Floor
Gardening	4
Technology	3
Furniture	2
Kitchenware	1

2. Look at the graphic. Where is the woman at the moment?
   (A) 4th Floor
   (B) 3rd Floor
   (C) 2nd Floor
   (D) 1st Floor

3. What will the woman probably do next?
   (A) Help to move some furniture
   (B) Make her way to the next floor
   (C) Clear away some equipment
   (D) Complete the task she is working on

4. What is the woman going to do next week?
   (A) Visit her family
   (B) Host some guests
   (C) Dine with the man
   (D) Travel on vacation

Top restaurants in Monterey

Restaurant	Type of cuisine	Reviews
Luigi's	Italian	****
Thai Palace	Thai	*****
Taj Mahal	Indian	****
Yoyo Sushi	Japanese	***

5. Look at the graphic. Which restaurant are they talking about?
   (A) Luigi's
   (B) Thai Palace
   (C) Taj Mahal
   (D) Yoyo Sushi

6. What does the man imply?
   (A) It may be difficult to book a table at short notice.
   (B) The food is not as good as some people say.
   (C) He ate there and was unhappy with his meal.
   (D) He advises against going to the new restaurant.

1. (A) (B) (C) (D)
2. (A) (B) (C) (D)
3. (A) (B) (C) (D)
4. (A) (B) (C) (D)
5. (A) (B) (C) (D)
6. (A) (B) (C) (D)

7. Why is the man calling?

(A) To report an accident at work

(B) To ask for an insurance quote

(C) To make a claim on a policy

(D) To request an official document

Carlton Insurance Office Directory	
Department	Extension number
Commercial	225
Public Liability	238
Automobile	242
Health	256

8. Look at the graphic. Which extension will the man be put through to?

(A) 225

(B) 238

(C) 242

(D) 256

9. What does the woman imply?

(A) The man needs a case number.

(B) She cannot provide further help.

(C) The fire was started deliberately.

(D) The policy is no longer valid.

10. Why does the woman talk to the man?

(A) To ask him to finish

(B) To take his order

(C) To give him the bill

(D) To offer him a drink

Day	Opening times
Monday – Wednesday	8:00 A.M. – 6:00 P.M.
Thursday	8:00 A.M. – 8:00 P.M.
Friday	8:00 A.M. – 7:00 P.M.
Saturday	9:30 A.M. – 6:00 P.M.
Sunday	Closed

11. Look at the graphic. On which day does this conversation take place?

(A) Wednesday

(B) Thursday

(C) Friday

(D) Saturday

12. What does the woman ask the man to do?

(A) Clean the table where he is sitting

(B) Come back later in the day

(C) Take his cup to a particular place

(D) Wait at the counter to be served

7. (A) (B) (C) (D)   9. (A) (B) (C) (D)   11. (A) (B) (C) (D)

8. (A) (B) (C) (D)   10. (A) (B) (C) (D)   12. (A) (B) (C) (D)

Score .... /12

Previewing Short Conversations

Before you hear each conversation, you should quickly read the questions and answer choices and study the graphic if there is one, so that you know what information you need to listen for. This is called *previewing*. The more effectively you preview the higher your score will be on this part of the test.

You need to answer the questions *while you are listening*. After each conversation, the three questions are read aloud. You should not wait and listen to these questions. Instead, you should use this time—24 seconds in total—to *preview the next item*.

How to preview Part 3 short conversations

STEP 1 Preview the graphic (if there is one)

Notice the type of graphic (a list, coupon, map, etc.) and study the information it contains. Look for key details (numbers, names, dates, etc.).

Ask yourself where might you read this? What is its purpose?

Express Mail International Postage rates			
Weight not over (lb.)	Zone 1	Zone 2	Zone 3
2	$20	$28	$35
4	$25	$34	$39
6	$30	$40	$50
8	$35	$44	$59
10	$40	$58	$72
Zone 1 = US Zone 2 = Europe Zone 3 = Asia			

Graphic

a shipping price list.

STEP 2 Preview the questions

Read each question and identify exactly what information you need to listen for. Notice the first word, and any key words that follow.

Information needed

1. Where does the woman most likely work?   *location*

2. When will the package to Singapore arrive?   *time/date*

3. Look at the graphic. How much will the package to Hong Kong cost to send?   *price*

Preview the answer choices

Quickly read the answer choices to get an idea of the situation. Notice any key words, and ask yourself what they tell you about the context.

1. Where does the woman most likely work? Ⓐ Ⓑ Ⓒ Ⓓ
   (A) At a post office
   (B) In a mail room
   (C) At a packaging plant
   (D) In a bookstore

2. When will the package to Singapore arrive? Ⓐ Ⓑ Ⓒ Ⓓ
   (A) By the end of the week
   (B) In three to five days
   (C) In six to ten days
   (D) At the end of the month

3. Look at the graphic. How much will the package
   to Hong Kong cost to send? Ⓐ Ⓑ Ⓒ Ⓓ
   (A) $39
   (B) $50
   (C) $59
   (D) $72

Possible context

mailing a package?

53 Listen to the conversation and choose the most appropriate answer: (A), (B), (C), or (D), for each question.

Previewing – Conversation 1 – a typical conversation

Exercise A For each question, highlight the first word and any key words. Then note the information you need to find.

Information needed

1. Why is the man calling? ....

2. What did the woman do last week? ....

3. What area does the man work in? ....

Exercise B Quickly read these answer choices and note what they tell you about the possible context.

1. Why is the man calling?   Ⓐ   Ⓑ   Ⓒ   Ⓓ
   (A) To report a change in policy
   (B) To ask about an order
   (C) To update a staff member
   (D) To confirm travel plans

2. What did the woman do last week?   Ⓐ   Ⓑ   Ⓒ   Ⓓ
   (A) She went on a business trip.
   (B) She visited a client.
   (C) She took a vacation.
   (D) She applied for a job.

3. What area does the man work in?   Ⓐ   Ⓑ   Ⓒ   Ⓓ
   (A) I.T. support
   (B) Customer service
   (C) Human resources
   (D) Product development

Possible context

....

54 Listen to the conversation and choose the most appropriate answer: (A), (B), (C), or (D), for each question.

Previewing – Conversation 2 – a typical conversation

Exercise A For each question, highlight the first word and any key words. Then note the information you need to find.

<u>Information needed</u>

1. Where does this conversation take place? ....

2. What does the woman suggest? ....

3. What does the man plan to do? ....

Exercise B Quickly read these answer choices and note what they tell you about the possible context.

1. Where does this conversation take place?   Ⓐ Ⓑ Ⓒ Ⓓ
   (A) At a restaurant
   (B) At a hotel
   (C) At a theater
   (D) At a museum

2. What does the woman suggest?   Ⓐ Ⓑ Ⓒ Ⓓ
   (A) Changing the date
   (B) Making a cancellation
   (C) Coming back later
   (D) Trying again in two weeks

3. What does the man plan to do?   Ⓐ Ⓑ Ⓒ Ⓓ
   (A) Speak with the manager
   (B) Consult his associates
   (C) Alter his travel plans
   (D) Choose an alternative route

<u>Possible context</u>

....

55 Listen to the conversation and choose the most appropriate answer: (A), (B), (C), or (D), for each question.

Previewing – Conversation 3 – a conversation with three speakers

Exercise A For each question, highlight the first word and any key words. Then note the information you need to find.

<u>Information needed</u>

1. What are the speakers concerned about? ....

2. How long have they been in their current premises? ....

3. What does the woman recommend they do? ....

Exercise B Quickly read these answer choices and note what they tell you about the possible context.

1. What are the speakers concerned about? (A) (B) (C) (D)
   - (A) The quality of renovation work
   - (B) The terms of their lease
   - (C) The amount of rent they pay
   - (D) The condition of the building

2. How long have they been in their current premises? (A) (B) (C) (D)
   - (A) Six months
   - (B) One year
   - (C) Three years
   - (D) Five years

3. What does the woman recommend they do? (A) (B) (C) (D)
   - (A) Renegotiate the lease
   - (B) Look for alternative premises
   - (C) Complain to the landlord
   - (D) Wait and see what happens

<u>Possible context</u>

....

56 Listen to the conversation and choose the most appropriate answer: (A), (B), (C), or (D), for each question.

Previewing – Conversation 4 – a conversation including a graphic

Exercise A Notice the type of graphic and study the information it contains. Where might you see this? What is its purpose?

Destination	Flight	Time of departure
Atlanta	AA425	17:30
New Orleans	DL572	17:45
Detroit	DL901	19:15
Cleveland	AA225	19:50

<u>Graphic</u>

....

Exercise B For each question, highlight the first word and any key words. Then note the information you need to find.

<u>Information needed</u>

1. How long will the woman's trip last?

....

2. What does the woman suggest about the upcoming audit?

....

3. Look at the graphic. Where is the woman flying to?

....

Exercise C Quickly read these answer choices and note what they tell you about the possible context.

1. How long will the woman's trip last?   Ⓐ Ⓑ Ⓒ Ⓓ
   (A) Five days
   (B) One week
   (C) Almost two weeks
   (D) Exactly two weeks

2. What does the woman suggest about the upcoming audit?   Ⓐ Ⓑ Ⓒ Ⓓ
   (A) It will be no different to previous audits.
   (B) She is looking forward to it very much.
   (C) It could last longer than expected.
   (D) She suspects the figures may be inaccurate.

3. Look at the graphic. Where is the woman flying to?   Ⓐ Ⓑ Ⓒ Ⓓ
   (A) Atlanta
   (B) New Orleans
   (C) Detroit
   (D) Cleveland

<u>Possible context</u>

....

57 Listen to the conversation and choose the most appropriate answer: (A), (B), (C), or (D) for each question

58 Listen to these conversations and choose the most appropriate answer: (A), (B), (C), or (D), for each question. Answer the questions *while you are listening*. After each conversation, immediately look ahead and use the time to preview the next conversation. Quickly preview the first conversation (Questions 1–3) now.

1. What is the man asking about?
   (A) A financial product
   (B) An item of lost property
   (C) Internet advertising
   (D) Flexible payment plans

2. What does the man want to do?
   (A) Withdraw some money
   (B) Arrange a delivery
   (C) Take early retirement
   (D) Confirm some information

3. What does the woman ask the man to do?
   (A) Fill out an application
   (B) Study some forms
   (C) Wait for a short time
   (D) Correct a document

4. What does the woman ask the man to do?
   (A) Arrange an appointment
   (B) Make a recommendation
   (C) Confirm a reservation
   (D) Request a meeting

5. What does the woman imply about Franco's pizzeria?
   (A) It is overpriced.
   (B) It is unwelcoming.
   (C) It is too far away.
   (D) It is unhygienic.

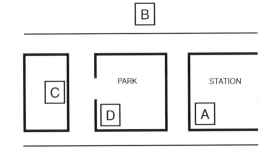

6. Look at the graphic. Where will the woman most likely decide to go?
   (A) Building A
   (B) Building B
   (C) Building C
   (D) Building D

1. Ⓐ Ⓑ Ⓒ Ⓓ   3. Ⓐ Ⓑ Ⓒ Ⓓ   5. Ⓐ Ⓑ Ⓒ Ⓓ
2. Ⓐ Ⓑ Ⓒ Ⓓ   4. Ⓐ Ⓑ Ⓒ Ⓓ   6. Ⓐ Ⓑ Ⓒ Ⓓ

7. Who most likely is the woman?

    (A) A new employee

    (B) A store manager

    (C) A job candidate

    (D) A shopper

8. What are the speakers mainly discussing?

    (A) Work skills

    (B) Store policies

    (C) Hiring practices

    (D) Working benefits

9. What is suggested about the woman?

    (A) She does not have a job.

    (B) She wants to change jobs.

    (C) She was recently promoted.

    (D) She has just graduated.

---

10. What are the speakers discussing?

    (A) A business seminar

    (B) A grant application

    (C) A marketing campaign

    (D) A bid for a contract

11. Who most likely is Mr. Nichols?

    (A) A business advisor

    (B) An employee at Petersons

    (C) A college administrator

    (D) A senior lecturer

12. What is the man concerned about?

    (A) A deadline for a proposal

    (B) A rival company

    (C) The company's reputation

    (D) A sports competition

7. Ⓐ Ⓑ Ⓒ Ⓓ   **9.** Ⓐ Ⓑ Ⓒ Ⓓ   **11.** Ⓐ Ⓑ Ⓒ Ⓓ

8. Ⓐ Ⓑ Ⓒ Ⓓ   **10.** Ⓐ Ⓑ Ⓒ Ⓓ   **12.** Ⓐ Ⓑ Ⓒ Ⓓ

Score .... /12

STEPS TO SUCCESS

This section presents an effective, step-by-step approach to use when answering questions on Part 3 of the TOEIC® test.

The steps shown here are designed to help you achieve the highest possible score when you take the test.

1 Preview the questions and any accompanying graphic. Make sure you know exactly what information you need to listen for (e.g., *Where* – a location, *Why* – a reason, *When* – a time, etc.).

> **REMEMBER** Question types will cover a range of main ideas, details, and inferences.

2 Preview the answer choices. Use the key information to get a general idea of the context. Ask yourself: *Where could this be? Who are the speakers? What are they talking about?*

> **REMEMBER** You must be quick. Do not read every word. Just focus on the key words.

3 Listen carefully to the conversation. As you listen, study the questions and answer choices, and any graphic. Remember, for questions with a graphic you need to link what you hear with the information you see. Eliminate any answers you are sure are incorrect.

> **REMEMBER** Always try to mark your answers as you listen. Do not wait until the conversation has finished.

4 As soon as the conversation finishes, quickly mark any remaining answers, and move on to preview the next item.

> **REMEMBER** Never leave a question unanswered. You will not have time to return, and will not be able to recall the details if you do.

1. Why is the woman calling?

(A) To report a problem with her computer

(B) To withdraw from a commitment

(C) To give some technical advice

(D) To apologize for a mistake

2. What is implied about the woman's computer password?

(A) The man has used it before.

(B) It relates to the woman's surname.

(C) It allows access to the O drive.

(D) Someone has recently changed it.

3. What will the man do in the afternoon?

(A) E-mail a report

(B) Leave work early

(C) Give a presentation

(D) Call a coworker

1. Ⓐ Ⓑ Ⓒ Ⓓ
2. Ⓐ Ⓑ Ⓒ Ⓓ
3. Ⓐ Ⓑ Ⓒ Ⓓ

STEP 1 ▶ Preview the questions.

Question 1: main idea [ ]   detail [✓]   inference [ ]

Need to listen for: ....reason...

Question 2: main idea [ ]   detail [ ]   inference [ ]

Need to listen for: ....

Question 3: main idea [ ]   detail [ ]   inference [ ]

Need to listen for: ....

STEP 2 ▶ Quickly preview the answer choices.
Possible context ....

▶ **REMEMBER**   *On the actual test, you cannot mark the test paper, or make notes. You should quickly preview the questions and answer choices silently to yourself.*

STEP 3 ▶ 59 Listen to the conversation. As you listen, look at the questions and answer choices above. For each question, eliminate any answer choices you are sure are incorrect and mark your answer as soon as you can.

STEP 4 ▶ When the conversation finishes, immediately mark any remaining answers.

1. Where does the woman most likely work?

(A) At a supermarket

(B) At a department store

(C) At a security company

(D) At an office supplies store

2. What is the problem?

(A) A product is out of stock.

(B) A file has been misplaced.

(C) An item cannot be found.

(D) A coworker is missing.

Everything 4 Business
Vancouver Megastore

ZONE 1	ZONE 2
Aisles 1–5	Aisles 6–10

ZONE 3	ZONE 4
Aisles 11–15	Aisles 16–20

3. Look at the graphic. Where does the woman suggest the man go?

(A) Zone 1

(B) Zone 2

(C) Zone 3

(D) Zone 4

1. Ⓐ Ⓑ Ⓒ Ⓓ

2. Ⓐ Ⓑ Ⓒ Ⓓ

3. Ⓐ Ⓑ Ⓒ Ⓓ

STEP 1 Preview the questions and the graphic.

Question 1:　main idea [ ]　　　　detail [ ]　　　　inference [ ]

Need to listen for:...

Question 2:　main idea [ ]　　　　detail [ ]　　　　inference [ ]

Need to listen for:...

Question 3:　main idea [ ]　　　　detail [ ]　　　　inference [ ]

Need to listen for:...

Graphic　　　　...

STEP 2 Quickly preview the answer choices.

Possible context　..

>**REMEMBER**　*On the actual test, you cannot mark the test paper, or make notes. You should quickly preview the questions and answer choices silently to yourself.*

STEP 3 **60** Listen to the conversation. As you listen, look at the questions and answer choices above, and study the graphic. For each question, eliminate any answer choices you are sure are incorrect and mark your answer as soon as you can.

STEP 4 When the conversation finishes, immediately mark any remaining answers.

1. What are the speakers mainly discussing?

(A) Reports of a serious traffic accident

(B) Arrangements for a colleague's visit

(C) An important customer's travel plans

(D) Problems with public transportation

2. What does the woman decide to do?

(A) Reschedule a meeting

(B) Drive to Los Angeles

(C) Contact the sales manager

(D) Book a hotel room

3. What time does the man intend to meet Mr. Potter?

(A) At 10:00 A.M.

(B) At 1:00 P.M.

(C) At 4:00 P.M.

(D) At 5:30 P.M.

1. (A) (B) (C) (D)

2. (A) (B) (C) (D)

3. (A) (B) (C) (D)

STEP 1 Preview the questions.

Question 1: main idea [ ]   detail [ ]   inference [ ]

Need to listen for:..

Question 2: main idea [ ]   detail [ ]   inference [ ]

Need to listen for:..

Question 3: main idea [ ]   detail [ ]   inference [ ]

Need to listen for:..

STEP 2 Quickly preview the answer choices.

Possible context ....

REMEMBER   *On the actual test, you cannot mark the test paper, or make notes. You should quickly preview the questions and answer choices silently to yourself.*

STEP 3 **61** Listen to the conversation. As you listen, look at the questions and answer choices above. For each question, eliminate any answer choices you are sure are incorrect and mark your answer as soon as you can.

STEP 4 When the conversation finishes, immediately mark any remaining answers.

1. Where do the speakers most likely work?

   (A) At a taxi service

   (B) At a car rental agency

   (C) At a tour company

   (D) At a public transportation agency

Customer	Complaint
Margaret de Carle	The air-conditioning did not work.
Ashley Walsh	The seats were uncomfortable.
Cameron Bronstein	The driver did not arrive on time.
Brenda Brady	There were long traffic jams.

2. According to the man, what has Mrs. Jackson done?

   (A) Left a message

   (B) Asked for a reduction

   (C) Decided to call back

   (D) Authorized a discount

3. Look at the graphic. Who will the woman now call?

   (A) Margaret de Carle

   (B) Ashley Walsh

   (C) Cameron Bronstein

   (D) Brenda Brady

1. Ⓐ Ⓑ Ⓒ Ⓓ
2. Ⓐ Ⓑ Ⓒ Ⓓ
3. Ⓐ Ⓑ Ⓒ Ⓓ

STEP 1 ▶ Preview the questions.

   Question 1: main idea [ ]   detail [ ]   inference [ ]

   Need to listen for:..

   Question 2: main idea [ ]   detail [ ]   inference [ ]

   Need to listen for:..

   Question 3: main idea [ ]   detail [ ]   inference [ ]

   Need to listen for:..

   Graphic   ....

STEP 2 ▶ Quickly preview the answer choices.

   <u>Possible context</u> ....

REMEMBER *On the actual test, you cannot mark the test paper, or make notes. You should quickly preview the questions and answer choices silently to yourself.*

STEP 3 ▶ 62 Listen to the conversation. As you listen, look at the questions and answer choices above, and study the graphic. For each question, eliminate any answer choices you are sure are incorrect and mark your answer as soon as you can.

STEP 4 ▶ When the conversation finishes, immediately mark any remaining answers.

Strategy Review and Tips

TIPS *Here is some advice that people taking the TOEIC test have found useful for this part. Choose the tips you like, and try to use them.*

"At the beginning of Part 3, you don't need to listen to the directions. You should know what to do. Use the time to look ahead and preview the first few conversations."

Shino Matsuhiro

"By the middle of this part, it's easy to get tired and lose concentration. Just keep on your toes and think of nothing else except the conversation you are listening to."

Marguerite Bosquet

"For conversations with a graphic, I preview the graphic carefully first, and then look at the questions and answer choices as I listen."

Marta Diaz

"You have to keep your mind thinking on two levels: the general level of who are they and where are they, and then the detail of what exactly they are saying."

Pak Dong-Sun

"Make sure you keep all three questions in your mind as you listen. The answers could come up in any order."

Jorge Lopez

Review Test

Directions: You will hear thirteen conversations. For each conversation, read the three questions and the four answer choices that follow each question. Select the most appropriate answer: (A), (B), (C), or (D). Then mark your answer. You will hear each conversation only once.

1. Who is the man talking to?
   (A) A medical doctor
   (B) A physical therapist
   (C) A sports psychologist
   (D) A fitness instructor

2. What does the woman imply about the man's injury?
   (A) It is showing signs of improvement.
   (B) It must have happened very recently.
   (C) It requires an urgent operation.
   (D) It will take a long time to heal.

3. What will the man probably do next?
   (A) Start treatment
   (B) Contact a specialist
   (C) Enter a competition
   (D) Return home

4. What is the man doing?
   (A) Using a calculator
   (B) Working on a spreadsheet
   (C) Taking measurements
   (D) Lining up some figures

5. Where do the speakers most likely work?
   (A) At a bank
   (B) At an accountant's office
   (C) At a newspaper
   (D) At a college

6. What does the woman recommend that the man do?
   (A) Improve his skills
   (B) Train harder
   (C) Attend a lecture
   (D) Sign some documents

7. Who most likely is the woman?
   (A) A company accountant
   (B) A financial advisor
   (C) A bank manager
   (D) A payroll clerk

8. What is suggested about the man's company?
   (A) It has a poor credit history.
   (B) It has disappointing sales.
   (C) It has expanded too quickly.
   (D) It has been mismanaged.

9. What is the man concerned about?
   (A) The recent weather conditions
   (B) The safety of his property
   (C) The repayment of a loan
   (D) The development of the company

10. Where does the conversation most likely take place?
    (A) At a tram stop
    (B) On a train platform
    (C) At a ticket office
    (D) On a street corner

11. What does the woman plan to do?
    (A) Take a long walk
    (B) Visit a friend
    (C) Travel on vacation
    (D) Go to the theater

12. What is probably true about the woman?
    (A) She has just passed an exam.
    (B) She will return in the afternoon.
    (C) She has a map with directions.
    (D) She likes to wear simple clothes.

1. (A) (B) (C) (D)   4. (A) (B) (C) (D)   7. (A) (B) (C) (D)   10. (A) (B) (C) (D)
2. (A) (B) (C) (D)   5. (A) (B) (C) (D)   8. (A) (B) (C) (D)   11. (A) (B) (C) (D)
3. (A) (B) (C) (D)   6. (A) (B) (C) (D)   9. (A) (B) (C) (D)   12. (A) (B) (C) (D)

13. Why is the man calling?
    - (A) To arrange a delivery
    - (B) To cancel a meeting
    - (C) To place an order
    - (D) To make a complaint

14. What will happen next Monday?
    - (A) Mr. Macintyre will visit an important client.
    - (B) The XR20 labeling machine will be installed.
    - (C) Engineers from Dawsons will carry out a repair.
    - (D) Sun Valley Foods will take delivery of a new machine.

15. What is suggested about the XR20 labeling machine?
    - (A) It is not economical to use.
    - (B) It has not been very reliable.
    - (C) It cost a lot of money to purchase.
    - (D) It operates at a slow speed.

16. What are the speakers discussing?
    - (A) Vacation entitlement
    - (B) Leisure preferences
    - (C) Working from home
    - (D) Employment legislation

17. What will the man probably do in the summer?
    - (A) Go to work in the USA
    - (B) Travel around Europe
    - (C) Try to take two weeks off
    - (D) Keep working right through

18. How does the man feel about the situation?
    - (A) He needs more time to decide.
    - (B) He thinks it is unhealthy.
    - (C) He finds it hard to believe.
    - (D) He expects to get used to it.

19. What does the man want to do?
    - (A) Scan a picture
    - (B) Print a document
    - (C) Save a file
    - (D) Send a fax

20. What does the woman suggest?
    - (A) Contacting her personal assistant
    - (B) Finding the maintenance engineer
    - (C) Using the computer at reception
    - (D) Asking a member of the board

21. When will the board meeting begin?
    - (A) In a few minutes
    - (B) In 30 minutes
    - (C) In an hour
    - (D) In two hours

22. Who most likely is the woman?
    - (A) A box office clerk
    - (B) A travel agent
    - (C) A hotel concierge
    - (D) A theater actor

23. What does the man imply?
    - (A) He would prefer to see a comedy show.
    - (B) He will be happy with almost anything.
    - (C) He is not interested in a standard musical.
    - (D) He wants seats that have good views.

24. Why does the woman say, "it'll be luck of the draw, I'm afraid"?
    - (A) The man needs to enter a prize drawing.
    - (B) The show the man sees depends on availability.
    - (C) She cannot guarantee to get tickets.
    - (D) She feels sorry the man is out of luck.

13. Ⓐ Ⓑ Ⓒ Ⓓ 16. Ⓐ Ⓑ Ⓒ Ⓓ 19. Ⓐ Ⓑ Ⓒ Ⓓ 22. Ⓐ Ⓑ Ⓒ Ⓓ
14. Ⓐ Ⓑ Ⓒ Ⓓ 17. Ⓐ Ⓑ Ⓒ Ⓓ 20. Ⓐ Ⓑ Ⓒ Ⓓ 23. Ⓐ Ⓑ Ⓒ Ⓓ
15. Ⓐ Ⓑ Ⓒ Ⓓ 18. Ⓐ Ⓑ Ⓒ Ⓓ 21. Ⓐ Ⓑ Ⓒ Ⓓ 24. Ⓐ Ⓑ Ⓒ Ⓓ

25. What does the man want to do?
- (A) Rent a large tent
- (B) Stage a rock concert
- (C) Buy camping equipment
- (D) Build a home extension

26. What does the woman mean when she says, "better to be safe than sorry"?
- (A) Safety is the most important thing.
- (B) It is wise to take precautions.
- (C) A decision must be taken quickly.
- (D) Sometimes no apology is necessary.

27. Why might the cost increase?
- (A) It is a customized service.
- (B) A company logo is required.
- (C) Certain features are extra.
- (D) The floor might need to be raised.

28. Who is the man talking to?
- (A) An immigration official
- (B) A police captain
- (C) A security guard
- (D) A customs officer

29. What does the woman ask the man to do?
- (A) Mind the counter
- (B) Unpack a bag
- (C) Open a suitcase
- (D) Check in quickly

30. Why is the man concerned?
- (A) He has lost some luggage.
- (B) He is behind schedule.
- (C) He has the wrong information.
- (D) He needs to wait for someone.

Menu

Drinks	
Hot	$3.00
Cold	$2.50

Sandwiches	
Tuna salad, cheese	$4.00
Turkey, chicken salad	$4.50

31. What will the woman do straight after paying?
- (A) Eat her sandwich
- (B) Make a phone call
- (C) Go to the end of the counter
- (D) Return to her workplace

32. What is implied about the woman?
- (A) She rarely orders food.
- (B) She often skips lunch.
- (C) She is late for a meeting.
- (D) She feels very hungry.

33. Look at the graphic. How much will the woman pay?
- (A) $5.50
- (B) $6.50
- (C) $7.00
- (D) $7.50

25. Ⓐ Ⓑ Ⓒ Ⓓ **28.** Ⓐ Ⓑ Ⓒ Ⓓ **31.** Ⓐ Ⓑ Ⓒ Ⓓ
26. Ⓐ Ⓑ Ⓒ Ⓓ **29.** Ⓐ Ⓑ Ⓒ Ⓓ **32.** Ⓐ Ⓑ Ⓒ Ⓓ
27. Ⓐ Ⓑ Ⓒ Ⓓ **30.** Ⓐ Ⓑ Ⓒ Ⓓ **33.** Ⓐ Ⓑ Ⓒ Ⓓ

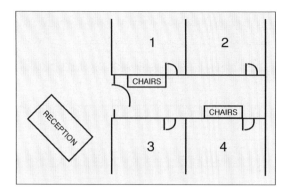
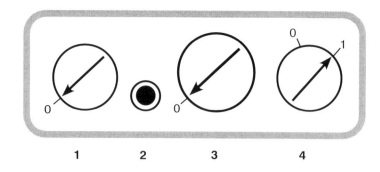

34. Who most likely is the woman?
(A) A medical doctor
(B) An office receptionist
(C) A nursing assistant
(D) A hearing specialist

35. When will the man probably go in to see the doctor?
(A) In 20 minutes
(B) In 30 minutes
(C) At 2:30 P.M.
(D) At 3:00 P.M.

36. Look at the graphic. Which is Dr. Williams' office?
(A) Office 1
(B) Office 2
(C) Office 3
(D) Office 4

37. Why is the woman calling?
(A) To ask for instructions
(B) To report a fault
(C) To confirm check in
(D) To make a complaint

38. Look at the graphic. Which dial should the woman turn?
(A) Dial 1
(B) Dial 2
(C) Dial 3
(D) Dial 4

39. What does the man ask the woman to do?
(A) Phone him again if necessary
(B) Wait until 12 o'clock
(C) Try to reset the system
(D) Contact him in 20 minutes

34. Ⓐ Ⓑ Ⓒ Ⓓ   **37.** Ⓐ Ⓑ Ⓒ Ⓓ
35. Ⓐ Ⓑ Ⓒ Ⓓ   **38.** Ⓐ Ⓑ Ⓒ Ⓓ
36. Ⓐ Ⓑ Ⓒ Ⓓ   **39.** Ⓐ Ⓑ Ⓒ Ⓓ   Score ..../39

EXTRA PRACTICE ONLINE

Go to **www.pass-the-toeic-test.com** for advice and useful exercises to help improve your score on Part 3 of the TOEIC test.

▶ Occupations

▶ Activities

▶ Word Families

This part of the TOEIC® test consists of ten short talks. After each short talk, you will hear three questions. There are four answer choices for each question, and you must choose the correct answer from the four choices. Although the questions and the answer choices are printed, you cannot read the short talks.

The purpose is to test your listening comprehension. You need to show you can understand a variety of short talks, such as advertisements, public announcements, news bulletins, etc. You will hear each short talk, and the three questions that follow each short talk, only once.

The short talks are all given by a single speaker and there is an introductory statement that specifies the type of talk.

NOTE

- Some questions require you to make inferences. Questions involving implied meaning test your knowledge of context, and vocabulary function. For example, *What does the man mean when he says, "I've been meaning to ask"*?

- Two talks include a graphic (e.g., a price list, agenda, map, etc.). One question requires you to relate the information contained in the graphic to what you hear.

- Speakers sometimes use idiomatic and colloquial language e.g., *Get out of here!*, *You can say that again!*, etc.

- After each short talk, you will hear the three questions. There is a pause of eight seconds between each question.

> **QUICK CHECK**
>
> How many questions are there in this part of the TOEIC test?
> How many short talks are there?
> How much time do you have between questions?
> How many short talks include a graphic?
> What kinds of graphics are used?

1 MIN

OVERVIEW

64 **EXAMPLE 1 - a typical short talk**

[M-Am] Good afternoon, folks. I'm Larry Brockman and you're listening to *The World of Business* right here on WKR-FM. Our guest for today's program is Daniel Sandown, entrepreneur, retail guru, and of course best known as founder of Dan's Delis. In just a few moments, he's going to talk to us about what it takes to start your own business, so if you want to ask a question or indeed just share your experiences, call 555-0120 now. Once again, that's 555-0120. Call us. We're live on-air. But before we hear how Dan's Delis came to be the phenomenal statewide success it is today, first let's go to our very own Trisha Wilson to hear the latest market news, starting with all the inside gossip about movers and shakers here in North Carolina. Over to you, Trisha.

1. What is indicated about Dan's Delis?

(A) It is an international company.

(B) **It has stores across North Carolina.**

(C) It was founded very recently.

(D) It is a popular franchise.

> The speaker mentions the *statewide success* of Dan's Delis, and later reveals the location as *here in North Carolina*.

2. Who most likely is Trisha Wilson?

(A) A local entrepreneur

(B) A radio show host

(C) **A business reporter**

(D) A company executive

> The speaker introduces Trisha Wilson as *our very own*, suggesting she works for the radio station. She will speak about *market news* and *inside gossip*, indicating she is a reporter.

3. What will listeners hear next?

(A) The story behind a successful retail business

(B) An advertisement for a moving company

(C) An interview with Daniel Sandown

(D) **News of leading local businesspeople**

> The speaker says listeners will hear Trisha Wilson next, who will start by giving news on the *movers and shakers* across the state.

REMEMBER *On the actual test, you will hear but NOT see each short talk.*

65 EXAMPLE 2 - a short talk including a graphic

This example shows a short talk including a graphic. Notice Question 2, which is an example of an implied meaning question.

[M-Cn] Ladies and gentlemen, thank you for coming this evening to see the four winners in the Young Musicians of the Year competition receive their prizes. To remind you, the categories were piano, string instruments, woodwind, and brass. Each winner will receive an equal share of the prize money, donated by our generous sponsors and supporters. We thought last year's total prize pot of $8,000 was incredible, but this year's is even larger, at $10,000. This competition wouldn't be possible without the generous backing of music-lovers like you, so please do continue to show your support. A collection will be made at the end of the evening. But before we award the prizes, let's hear our four winning musicians. They're all equal winners, so I'm going to introduce the performers in alphabetical order by surname. Please welcome our first soloist.

Young Musicians of the Year

Renate Schultz, *trumpet*

Henry Murphy, *piano*

Lydia Kerry, *cello*

Charles Thomas, *flute*

---

1. How much money will each prize-winner receive?
   - (A) $2,000
   - (B) **$2,500**
   - (C) $8,000
   - (D) $10,000

> The speaker says this year's prize money is *$10,000*. There are *four winners* who will receive *an equal share*. (A) is a quarter share of last year's prize pot. (C) was the total prize money last year. (D) is the total prize pot this year.

2. Why does the speaker say, "please do continue to show your support"?
   - (A) Fewer people than expected have purchased tickets.
   - (B) He wants the audience to give a round of applause.
   - (C) Support for the competition has been declining.
   - (D) **He is encouraging further financial donations.**

> The speaker has just referred to *generous backing* (meaning, *financial support*), and continues by mentioning a *collection* to be made later. The other answers refer to other contexts and other senses of "support."

3. Look at the graphic. Which instrument will be played first?
   - (A) Trumpet
   - (B) Piano
   - (C) **Cello**
   - (D) Flute

> The speaker says he will *introduce the performers in alphabetical order by surname*. From the graphic, we can see that K is the first surname when spelled alphabetically. Lydia Kerry plays the cello, a string instrument.

REMEMBER *On the actual test, you will hear but NOT see each conversation*

Challenges

In Part 4, it is essential to preview the questions and answer choices *before* you hear each short talk. This helps you focus on the information you need while you listen. For two short talks, you also need to refer to information contained in a graphic (list, chart, etc.). Here are some factors to be aware of on this part of the test.

▶ Length

The short talks in Part 4 are longer than the conversations in Part 3. The longer the short talk, the more information you need to process and remember.

▶ Fatigue

Listening closely for an extended period can be tiring. By the time you reach Part 4, you will have been listening intently to the recording for over half an hour. It can be easy to lose concentration, and for your attention to wander.

▶ Variety

The short talks you hear cover a wide range of different genres, which change one after the other. As you listen, you need to quickly understand the context behind each short talk.

▶ Language level

The more difficult short talks include complex grammar and specialized vocabulary you may not be familiar with, alongside idiomatic and colloquial expressions.

▶ Question types

Questions test your ability to understand the main ideas and details, as well as to make inferences. You may need to connect two or more pieces of information in order to identify the correct answer.

▶ Answer choices

Answer choices can vary in length. Longer answer choices take more time to read.

▶ Repetition

Part 4 short talks involve limited repetition of information and ideas. Miss one word, and you may not be able to identify the correct answer.

▶ Memory

As you listen to each short talk, you need to remember as much as you can. You might find that the information you need to answer the first question only comes at the end of the short talk.

▶ Bunching

Key details you need can come very close together, or even within the same sentence. While you are marking your answer for one question, you may miss the information you need to answer the next question.

▶ Graphics

Short talks that have a graphic add an extra layer of complexity, as you need to study both the question and the information in the graphic while you listen.

Improve Your Performance

In this section you will practice ways to improve your score on Part 4 of the TOEIC® test.

These are the exercises you will cover:

Question Types	recognizing main idea questions, detail questions, and inference/implied meaning questions
Short Talks Including a Graphic	relating what you hear with information you can see in a simple graphic (e.g., a chart, map, etc.)
Previewing Short Talks	practicing how to quickly and effectively preview questions and answer choices

As you work through *Improve Your Performance*, try to identify any weaknesses you have, and focus on the areas you need to improve.

Question Types

Main Idea Questions

In Part 4 of the TOEIC test, the first question that follows each short talk often tests your ability to understand the main ideas. Questions that ask about main ideas in a short talk focus on the *speaker*, *topic*, *audience*, *location*, and *purpose* of the talk.

Speaker	*Who most likely is the speaker?*
	What area of business does the speaker work in?
Topic	*What is the message mainly about?*
	What is the speaker announcing?
	What is the news broadcast about?
Audience	*Who is the intended audience for this talk?*
	Who most likely are the listeners?
Location	*Where is this announcement being made?*
	Where most likely does the speaker work?
Purpose	*What is the main purpose of this talk?*
	What is the purpose of the telephone message?

TIPS
- As you listen, ask yourself:
  Who is the speaker?
  What is the speaker talking about?
  Who is the speaker talking to?
  Where is this taking place?
  What is the *aim* of the talk?
- You do not need to understand every single word in a short talk in order to understand the main ideas.

Detail Questions

As for Part 3, most questions in Part 4 test your ability to identify specific information and understand important details. Questions that ask about details in a short talk may focus on a variety of points, such as *times, reasons, feelings, requests, advice, problems, suggestions, sequences, plans,* and *opinions*.

Times	*On which day does the promotion end? When should Mr. Harper arrive at the factory? How many years has the speaker worked at PBD Engineering?*
Reasons	*Why does the message suggest applying online? Why is a full risk assessment needed?*
Feelings	*What does the woman find surprising? How does the man feel about the situation?*
Requests	*What is Gary Fielding asked to do? How are listeners invited to respond?*
Advice	*What does the speaker recommend that listeners do?*
Problems	*What is the caller concerned about? What is the cause of the problem?*
Suggestions	*What does the speaker suggest listeners do?*
Sequences	*According to the speaker, what will happen after lunch? What will listeners hear next?*
Plans	*What does the speaker say she will do? According to the e-mail, what will Jamie do later?*
Opinions	*What does the speaker think of the venue?*

- The statement at the start of each short talk tells you the genre.
- As you listen, ask yourself: *What information am I listening for?* Try to pick out any key words or phrases that might relate to the information you need.

Inference/Implied Meaning Questions

Some questions test your ability to understand things that are not directly stated. You need to infer a speaker's attitude, or make deductions based on what you hear.

Attitude	*How does the speaker probably feel (about…)?*
Deductions	*What does the speaker imply (about…)? Which of these statements is probably true?*

You also need to show your understanding of language in context, and colloquial (i.e., informal/idiomatic) phrases.

Context	*Why does the speaker say, "I'm sorry to bother you"?*
Phrases	*What does the speaker mean when he says, "That's neither here nor there"?*

- As you listen, notice the speakers' stress and intonation. The way a word or phrase is spoken can tell you a lot about the speaker's feelings and attitude.
- Draw conclusions by thinking about the meaning "behind" the words you hear.

66 Practice listening to identify speakers, opinions, and inferences. Listen to these short talks and choose the most appropriate answer: (A), (B), (C), or (D), for each question.

1. Who most likely is the speaker?
   (A) A painter
   (B) An art critic
   (C) A museum guide
   (D) An auctioneer

2. What does the speaker say about Claud Bergerac?
   (A) He used the same technique throughout his lifetime.
   (B) He was more famous in his youth.
   (C) His son was also a talented artist.
   (D) His work has been copied many times.

3. What does the speaker imply?
   (A) Some listeners may be familiar with the artist.
   (B) Bergerac was married several times.
   (C) *The Waiter* was painted in the early 1900s.
   (D) Experts cannot agree on certain facts.

4. Look at the graphic. How many staff will be affected by the relocation to Manchester?
   (A) 14
   (B) 26
   (C) 34
   (D) 97

5. What is the speaker's opinion of the restructuring plan?
   (A) It is essential to the company's future.
   (B) It may take longer than predicted.
   (C) It will be inexpensive to implement.
   (D) It should not cause any disruption.

ARK Industries		
	Location	No. of staff
Customer Care	Stockport	14
Main office	Leeds	26
Warehouses	Stoke Bradford	34
Factories	Harlow Crewe Halifax	97

6. What does the speaker imply?
   (A) There will be significant staff reductions.
   (B) A three-shift system is not necessary.
   (C) The company will lose important business.
   (D) Some listeners may not approve of the plan.

1. Ⓐ Ⓑ Ⓒ Ⓓ   3. Ⓐ Ⓑ Ⓒ Ⓓ   5. Ⓐ Ⓑ Ⓒ Ⓓ
2. Ⓐ Ⓑ Ⓒ Ⓓ   4. Ⓐ Ⓑ Ⓒ Ⓓ   6. Ⓐ Ⓑ Ⓒ Ⓓ

Score .... /6

MINI TEST Locations, Reasons, and Requests

67 Practice listening to identify locations, reasons, and requests. Listen to these short talks and choose the most appropriate answer: (A), (B), (C), or (D), for each question.

1. Where is this announcement being made?
- (A) At a bus station
- (B) At a ferry terminal
- (C) At a train station
- (D) At a truck stop

2. Why has the 8:53 service been canceled?
- (A) There is a mechanical fault.
- (B) The station has been closed.
- (C) It was a temporary service only.
- (D) There has been a serious accident.

3. What are passengers to Maybridge asked to do?
- (A) Wait at the entrance until further notice
- (B) Use an alternative means of transportation
- (C) Make their way to another destination
- (D) Take the 8:59 service to Charlesville

4. Look at the graphic. On which floor is the speaker's office?
- (A) Floor 1
- (B) Floor 2
- (C) Floor 3
- (D) Floor 4

5. Why is the speaker leaving the company?
- (A) He is moving away from the area.
- (B) He is going to take early retirement.
- (C) He has accepted another job.
- (D) He has been dismissed.

6. What are listeners asked to do?
- (A) Stay behind and work late
- (B) Try to keep as warm as possible
- (C) Take up an outdoor sport
- (D) Help themselves to refreshments

Harpers Associates	
Department	**Floor**
Sales & Marketing	1
Research	2
Operations	3
Human Resources	4

1. (A) (B) (C) (D)   **3.** (A) (B) (C) (D)   **5.** (A) (B) (C) (D)

2. (A) (B) (C) (D)   **4.** (A) (B) (C) (D)   **6.** (A) (B) (C) (D)

Score .... /6

MINI TEST Purpose, Problems, and Suggestions

68 Practice listening to identify the purpose, problems, and suggestions. Listen to these short talks and choose the most appropriate answer: (A), (B), (C), or (D), for each question.

1. What is the purpose of the message?
   (A) To request a quote
   (B) To place an order
   (C) To ask for information
   (D) To check delivery times

2. What is the speaker concerned about?
   (A) Forgetting instructions
   (B) Losing a client
   (C) Missing a call
   (D) Finding a fault

3. What does the speaker suggest that Miriam do?
   (A) Contact a coworker
   (B) Call him next week
   (C) Leave the office
   (D) Confirm a phone number

4. What does the woman mean when she says, "it's time to wrap things up now"?
   (A) The meeting has lasted too long.
   (B) Preparations need to be made.
   (C) She wants to conclude the event.
   (D) Some items need to be protected.

5. What problem does the speaker mention?
   (A) Some people have not signed a form.
   (B) The attendance list has been lost.
   (C) An important deadline might be missed.
   (D) The next event is oversubscribed.

6. What does the speaker suggest listeners do?
   (A) Register for the September meeting
   (B) Remember to put up some signs
   (C) Hand out promotional leaflets
   (D) Enjoy their annual leave

1. (A) (B) (C) (D)   3. (A) (B) (C) (D)   5. (A) (B) (C) (D)
2. (A) (B) (C) (D)   4. (A) (B) (C) (D)   6. (A) (B) (C) (D)

Score .... /6

MINI TEST Audience, Advice, and Plans

69 Practice listening to identify the audience, advice, and plans. Listen to these short talks and choose the most appropriate answer: (A), (B), (C), or (D), for each question.

1. Who is the speaker addressing?
- (A) Recruiting agents
- (B) Job seekers
- (C) Employers
- (D) Workers

2. What is scheduled to take place next week?
- (A) A special promotion
- (B) A job fair
- (C) An office renovation
- (D) A new competition

3. What does the man imply when he says, "So what are you waiting for"?
- (A) Waiting in line is not necessary.
- (B) Listeners should take action right away.
- (C) Some people are hesitating.
- (D) There is no excuse for further delay.

4. Who most likely are the listeners?
- (A) Tour leaders
- (B) Hotel managers
- (C) City officials
- (D) Travel agents

Morning Program

10-11 A.M	Planning to succeed	Green Room
11-12 P.M.	Time management	Side Suite 2
12-1 P.M.	Getting it right!	Seminar Room 4
1-2 P.M.	Lunch	Main Hall

5. What does the speaker advise listeners to do?
- (A) Book accommodations well in advance
- (B) Consider the needs of their customers
- (C) Go sightseeing on a local tour bus
- (D) Prioritize families with young children

6. Look at the graphic. Where should listeners go after lunch?
- (A) Green Room
- (B) Side Suite 2
- (C) Seminar Room 4
- (D) Main Hall

1.	Ⓐ	Ⓑ	Ⓒ	Ⓓ	**3.**	Ⓐ	Ⓑ	Ⓒ	Ⓓ	**5.**	Ⓐ	Ⓑ	Ⓒ	Ⓓ
2.	Ⓐ	Ⓑ	Ⓒ	Ⓓ	**4.**	Ⓐ	Ⓑ	Ⓒ	Ⓓ	**6.**	Ⓐ	Ⓑ	Ⓒ	Ⓓ

Score .... /6

MINI TEST Topics, Times, and Sequences

70 Practice listening to identify topics, times, and sequences. Listen to these short talks and choose the most appropriate answer: (A), (B), (C), or (D), for each question.

1. What is the speaker announcing?
   (A) Changes to a schedule
   (B) A program of events
   (C) Reports of a robbery
   (D) The contents of a show

2. When will Graham Edwards be interviewed?
   (A) At 7:00 A.M.
   (B) At 7:15 A.M.
   (C) At 7:30 A.M.
   (D) At 8:00 A.M.

3. What will listeners hear next?
   (A) A weather forecast
   (B) A celebrity interview
   (C) The latest news
   (D) A traffic report

4. What is the message mainly about?
   (A) A fashion show
   (B) A special promotion
   (C) An annual celebration
   (D) A store's anniversary

5. What are customers encouraged to do after lunch?
   (A) Go to the main entrance
   (B) Have coffee in the cafeteria
   (C) Attend an in-store event
   (D) Pick up a red star sticker

6. When does the *Fashion in Philly* gala most likely end?
   (A) Today
   (B) Monday
   (C) Saturday
   (D) Sunday

1. (A) (B) (C) (D)   3. (A) (B) (C) (D)   5. (A) (B) (C) (D)
2. (A) (B) (C) (D)   4. (A) (B) (C) (D)   6. (A) (B) (C) (D)

Score .... /6

Short Talks Including a Graphic

Short talks with a graphic (e.g., a chart, or schedule) test your ability to relate what you hear with the information you see in the graphic. While you listen and read the question and answer choices, you also need to study the graphic.

The types of graphics you will see in Part 4 are similar to those in Part 3; a building directory, floor plan, schedule, price list, order form, map, meeting agenda, advertisement, timetable, etc.

BUS	DEPARTURE TIME
X5	12:00 P.M.
Skyliner	12:15 P.M.
Central	12:30 P.M.
City Express	1:15 P.M.

STOCK ITEM

Vermont Sweater

Reference number	Color	Size
5225	Brown	XL
5219	Green	XL
2525	Red	XL
2519	Blue	XL

TRAVEL ADVENTURES

Discover Mexico *All-inclusive packages* **Flights + hotel**	Price
Cancun ----- 13 nights, 4★ hotel	$3,450
Riviera Maya ----- 11 nights, 3★ hotel	$2,650
Puerto Vallarta ----- 11 nights 4★ hotel	$2,699
Acapulco ----- 13 nights, 3★ hotel	$2,950

KENT COLLEGE LIBRARY

	Reading Room	
[West Entrance] **2**	**West Room 4**	**Study Area 3**
	Front desk 1 [Main Entrance]	

Tips

- These questions always begin *Look at the graphic*.
- Identify the type of graphic (a program, timetable, etc.).
- Quickly identify the key information (places, names, numbers, etc.).

Warning!

The purpose of a talk is sometimes to notify of changes to a schedule, or plan. For example, the graphic shows a personal work calendar with dates and times of meetings, but the speaker is calling to leave a message about a change of venue.

MINI TEST Short Talks Including a Graphic

71 Practice listening to short talks that include a graphic. Listen to these short talks and choose the most appropriate answer: (A), (B), (C), or (D), for each question.

1. Which exhibit is the speaker planning to see tomorrow?
   (A) Indian fabrics
   (B) Watercolor paintings
   (C) French portraits
   (D) Eastern art

2. Where does the speaker suggest meeting?
   (A) At the main entrance
   (B) In the museum's garden
   (C) At a side entrance
   (D) At a nearby restaurant

3. Look at the graphic. On which day is this phone call made?
   (A) Wednesday
   (B) Thursday
   (C) Friday
   (D) Saturday

Waterside Art Museum	
Opening times	
Sunday	9 A.M. – 4 P.M.
Monday	Closed
Tuesday	10 A.M. – 5 P.M.
Wednesday	10 A.M. – 5 P.M.
Thursday	10 A.M. – 5 P.M.
Friday	10 A.M. – 8 P.M.
Saturday	10 A.M. – 5 P.M.

4. What is the purpose of the talk?
   (A) To apologize to one of the speakers
   (B) To announce the next presentation
   (C) To report a change in schedule
   (D) To ask listeners for assistance

5. What problem does the speaker mention?
   (A) Audio-visual equipment is malfunctioning.
   (B) Technicians are still working in the Annex.
   (C) Mr. Larssen was not happy with his room.
   (D) There is an electrical fault in part of the facility.

6. Look at the graphic. What time will Nils Larssen's session begin?
   (A) 13:30
   (B) 13:45
   (C) 14:00
   (D) 14:15

Session	Speaker	Time	Room
Should I follow my passion?	Candice Moreno	10:30	Meeting room 2
Coffee break 11:30			
Prepare your elevator pitch	Miguel Lopez	11:45	Meeting room 2
Lunch and networking 12:45			
Optimize your social media presence	Nils Larssen	13:45	Annex
Coffee break 14:45			
Boost your creative thinking	Adriana Lowe	15:00	Meeting room 2

1. Ⓐ Ⓑ Ⓒ Ⓓ 3. Ⓐ Ⓑ Ⓒ Ⓓ 5. Ⓐ Ⓑ Ⓒ Ⓓ
2. Ⓐ Ⓑ Ⓒ Ⓓ 4. Ⓐ Ⓑ Ⓒ Ⓓ 6. Ⓐ Ⓑ Ⓒ Ⓓ

7. What can be inferred about William Barclay?
   (A) He was late checking in.
   (B) He has been reported missing.
   (C) He canceled his booking.
   (D) He may miss his flight.

8. What will happen in five minutes' time?
   (A) The gate will open.
   (B) Staff will shut the plane doors.
   (C) Boarding will commence.
   (D) The flight will depart.

9. Look at the graphic. Which gate should Mr. Barclay go to?
   (A) 18
   (B) 15
   (C) 22
   (D) 12

Flight number	Destination	Gate number
UA459	Minneapolis-St. Paul	18
AC455	Milwaukee	15
AC445	Minneapolis-St. Paul	22
UA344	Milwaukee	12

10. Who most likely is the speaker?
    (A) A park ranger
    (B) A gardener
    (C) A tree surgeon
    (D) A schoolteacher

11. Look at the graphic. Next to which tree are the listeners standing?
    (A) Oak
    (B) Maple
    (C) Birch
    (D) Pine

12. What does the speaker imply?
    (A) Listeners should proceed carefully.
    (B) There will be a difficult climb.
    (C) The area is known for accidents.
    (D) Some trees are hard to find.

Tree	Fruit/Seed
Oak	Acorn
Maple	Samara
Birch	Catkin
Pine	Cone

7. Ⓐ Ⓑ Ⓒ Ⓓ
8. Ⓐ Ⓑ Ⓒ Ⓓ
9. Ⓐ Ⓑ Ⓒ Ⓓ
10. Ⓐ Ⓑ Ⓒ Ⓓ
11. Ⓐ Ⓑ Ⓒ Ⓓ
12. Ⓐ Ⓑ Ⓒ Ⓓ

Score .... /12

Previewing Short Talks

Exactly as for Part 3, in Part 4 you need to preview the questions, answer choices, and any graphic *before* you hear the recording, so that you know what information to listen for. The more effectively you can preview the higher your score will be on this part of the test.

You need to answer the questions *while you are listening*. After each short talk, the three questions are read aloud. You should not wait and listen to these questions. Instead, you should use this time—24 seconds in total—to *preview the next item*.

How to preview Part 4 short talks

STEP 1 **Preview the graphic (if there is one)**

Notice the type of graphic (a chart, label, graph, etc.) and study the information it contains. Look for key details (numbers, names, dates, etc.).

Ask yourself where might you read this? What is its purpose?

Clarkson College Library	
Department	Extension
HR Systems	3589
User Admin	7845
Service Center	8708
WiFi Support	5623

Graphic

a department contact list

STEP 2 **Preview the questions**

Read each question and identify exactly what information you need to listen for. Notice the first word, and any key words that follow.

Information needed

1. Who most likely are the listeners?   *audience*

2. What does the speaker recommend that listeners do?   *advice*

3. Look at the graphic. What extension should listeners call if they have difficulty with online access?   *number*

Preview the answer choices

Quickly read the answer choices to get an idea of the situation. Notice any key words, and ask yourself what they tell you about the context.

1. Who most likely are the listeners?   (A) (B) (C) (D)
   (A) Graduate students
   (B) Library employees
   (C) Visiting scholars
   (D) Faculty professors

2. What does the speaker recommend that listeners do?   (A) (B) (C) (D)
   (A) Return in three days
   (B) Share their knowledge
   (C) Leave quietly
   (D) Adhere to the rules

3. Look at the graphic. What extension should listeners   (A) (B) (C) (D)
   call if they have difficulty with online access?
   (A) 3589
   (B) 7845
   (C) 8708
   (D) 5623

Possible context
_____at_a_library?_____

🔊72 Listen to this short talk and choose the most appropriate answer: (A), (B), (C), or (D), for each question.

Previewing – Business Talks

Business talks often cover the start or end of presentations, meetings, speeches, conferences, seminars, or lectures. Some examples of common scenarios are welcoming new employees, giving or accepting an award, making a retirement speech, outlining a schedule of events, giving a tour of a city, factory, or facility, thanking people for attending an event, and concluding a meeting.

Exercise A For each question, highlight the first word and any key words. Then note the information you need to find.

Information needed

1. Who is the speaker addressing? ....

2. What does the speaker imply about the event? ....

3. How many minutes will the Fast Pitch session last? ....

Exercise B Quickly read these answer choices and note what they tell you about the possible context.

1. Who is the speaker addressing? Ⓐ Ⓑ Ⓒ Ⓓ
   (A) Company employees
   (B) Business executives
   (C) Restaurant staff
   (D) Marketing managers

2. What does the speaker imply about the event? Ⓐ Ⓑ Ⓒ Ⓓ
   (A) It takes place every month.
   (B) It is becoming more popular.
   (C) It will last for over an hour.
   (D) It follows a traditional format.

3. How many minutes will the Fast Pitch session last? Ⓐ Ⓑ Ⓒ Ⓓ
   (A) 2
   (B) 3
   (C) 10
   (D) 20

Possible context

....

73 Listen to this short talk and choose the most appropriate answer: (A), (B), (C), or (D), for each question.

Previewing – Recorded Announcements

Recorded announcements often include recorded messages, automated telephone menus, and voicemail messages. Some examples of common scenarios are out-of-hours messages at a medical practice, company on-hold messages, and personal or work-related messages left by callers on an answering machine.

Exercise A For each question, highlight the first word and any key words. Then note the information you need to find.

Information needed

1. Why would a caller hear this message? ....

2. What kind of organization has been reached? ....

3. What number should callers press to ask about a bill? ....

Exercise B Quickly read these answer choices and note what they tell you about the possible context.

1. Why would a caller hear this message?   Ⓐ Ⓑ Ⓒ Ⓓ
   (A) The offices are currently closed.
   (B) Nobody is available to answer the call.
   (C) Dr. Hartington is speaking on another line.
   (D) An incorrect number has been dialed.

2. What kind of organization has been reached?   Ⓐ Ⓑ Ⓒ Ⓓ
   (A) A medical practice
   (B) A community hospital
   (C) An emergency department
   (D) An outpatient clinic

3. What number should callers press to ask about a bill?   Ⓐ Ⓑ Ⓒ Ⓓ
   (A) 0
   (B) 3
   (C) 5
   (D) 6

Possible context

....

74 Listen to this recorded message and choose the most appropriate answer: (A), (B), (C), or (D), for each question.

Previewing – Advertisements

Advertisements often cover commercial radio and television messages promoting products or services. Some examples of common scenarios are radio ads endorsing products or promoting stores and companies, ads for local sports events or tourist attractions, ads for travel or transportation services, and ads giving details of job opportunities.

Exercise A For each question, highlight the first word and any key words. Then note the information you need to find.

Information needed

1. What is being advertised? ....

2. What is mentioned about the cost? ....

3. Why are listeners encouraged to call customer service? ....

Exercise B Quickly read these answer choices and note what they tell you about the possible context.

1. What is being advertised?   Ⓐ Ⓑ Ⓒ Ⓓ
   (A) A party planning service
   (B) An outdoor activity center
   (C) An amusement park
   (D) A family camping trip

2. What is mentioned about the cost?   Ⓐ Ⓑ Ⓒ Ⓓ
   (A) There is a 20 percent discount.
   (B) The amount charged may vary.
   (C) Food and drink is included.
   (D) Families qualify for a discount.

3. Why are listeners encouraged to call customer service?   Ⓐ Ⓑ Ⓒ Ⓓ
   (A) To request further details
   (B) To make a reservation
   (C) To discuss their requirements
   (D) To ask for a quotation

Possible context

....

75 Listen to this advertisement and choose the most appropriate answer: (A), (B), (C), or (D), for each question.

Previewing – Public Announcements

Public announcements cover announcements made at small and large public venues, such as department stores, conferences, transportation centers, and outdoor events. Some examples of common scenarios are in-store promotions, passenger announcements at train or bus stations, in-flight announcements, and public notices broadcast at sporting events.

Exercise A For each question, highlight the first word and any key words. Then note the information you need to find.

Information needed

1. Who is probably speaking? ....

2. What is the main purpose of the announcement? ....

3. What does the speaker mean when he says,
   "I'll see if I can make it up during the flight"? ....

Exercise B Quickly read these answer choices and note what they tell you about the possible context.

1. Who is probably speaking? Ⓐ Ⓑ Ⓒ Ⓓ
   (A) A flight engineer
   (B) An air steward
   (C) An airline captain
   (D) A chief purser

2. What is the main purpose of the announcement? Ⓐ Ⓑ Ⓒ Ⓓ
   (A) To advise on safety procedures
   (B) To prepare passengers for takeoff
   (C) To apologize for a setback
   (D) To report a change of schedule

3. What does the speaker mean when he says, Ⓐ Ⓑ Ⓒ Ⓓ
   "I'll see if I can make it up during the flight"?
   (A) The flight may arrive on time.
   (B) Further checks may still be needed.
   (C) Compensation can be provided.
   (D) He intends to issue an apology.

Possible context

....

76 Listen to this announcement and choose the most appropriate answer: (A), (B), (C), or (D), for each question.

Previewing – News, Weather, and Traffic Reports

These short talks include radio broadcasts, news reports, and public information bulletins. Some examples of common scenarios are the beginning or end of current affairs shows, extracts from guest interviews, news summaries and updates, emergency bulletins, weather forecasts, and road traffic reports.

Exercise A For each question, highlight the first word and any key words. Then note the information you need to find.

<u>Information needed</u>

1. Who is Gareth Bowers? ....

2. What kind of company is Denton? ....

3. Why are police investigating Arco TX? ....

Exercise B Quickly read these answer choices and note what they tell you about the possible context.

1. Who is Gareth Bowers?   Ⓐ   Ⓑ   Ⓒ   Ⓓ
   - (A) Chairman of Eastport Resources
   - (B) A high-ranking politician
   - (C) A public relations consultant
   - (D) A senior business executive

2. What kind of company is Denton?   Ⓐ   Ⓑ   Ⓒ   Ⓓ
   - (A) An energy supplier
   - (B) A vehicle manufacturer
   - (C) A mining company
   - (D) A banking corporation

3. Why are police investigating Arco TX?   Ⓐ   Ⓑ   Ⓒ   Ⓓ
   - (A) Arsonists are suspected of causing disruption.
   - (B) Financial accounts may have been altered.
   - (C) Workers have been injured in a dispute.
   - (D) Faulty equipment has caused an accident.

<u>Possible context</u>

....

77 Listen to this news report and choose the most appropriate answer: (A), (B), (C), or (D), for each question.

Previewing – A Short Talk Including a Graphic

Exercise A Notice the type of graphic and study the information it contains. What is its purpose?

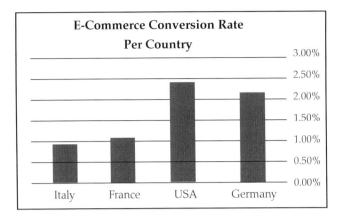

Graphic

....

Exercise B For each question, highlight the first word and any key words. Then note the information you need to find.

Information needed

1. What is indicated about the e-commerce conversion rate?   ....

2. What does the speaker imply?   ....

3. Look at the graphic. Which country will listeners hear about next?   ....

Exercise C Quickly read these answer choices and note what they tell you about the possible context.

1. What is indicated about the e-commerce conversion rate?   Ⓐ Ⓑ Ⓒ Ⓓ
   (A) It has changed a lot in Europe recently.
   (B) It is much lower than expected.
   (C) It can depend on geographic location.
   (D) It is higher for people using mobile devices.

2. What does the speaker imply?   Ⓐ Ⓑ Ⓒ Ⓓ
   (A) The situation is more complex than initially thought.
   (B) European countries are in competition with the USA.
   (C) The main markets are all performing in a similar way.
   (D) Performance data can be difficult to predict.

3. Look at the graphic. Which country will listeners hear about next?   Ⓐ Ⓑ Ⓒ Ⓓ
   (A) Italy
   (B) France
   (C) USA
   (D) Germany

Possible context

....

78 Listen to this short talk and choose the most appropriate answer: (A), (B), (C), or (D) for each question.

79 Listen to these short talks and choose the most appropriate answer: (A), (B), (C), or (D), for each question. Answer the questions *while you are listening*. After each short talk, immediately look ahead and use the time to preview the next short talk. Quickly preview the first short talk (Questions 1–3) now.

1. Look at the graphic. On which floor does Ms. Jarvis most likely work?
   (A) Ground
   (B) First
   (C) Second
   (D) Third

Hanko Logistics	
Department	**Floor**
Finance	Ground
Human Resources	First
Operations	Second
Legal	Third

2. What does the speaker say about Ms. Jarvis?
   (A) She is new to the area.
   (B) She is a valued customer.
   (C) She is very experienced.
   (D) She lives in Toronto.

3. What are listeners asked to do next?
   (A) Introduce themselves
   (B) Justify their opinion
   (C) Complete a questionnaire
   (D) Give a presentation

4. Who is the speaker?
   (A) A meteorologist
   (B) An atmospheric scientist
   (C) A weather researcher
   (D) An environmental statistician

5. According to the speaker, which city will experience the lowest temperatures?
   (A) Kansas City
   (B) Boston
   (C) Phoenix
   (D) Seattle

6. What does the speaker say about the weather in northern California?
   (A) It has been unseasonably wet and chilly.
   (B) Conditions are very different from the Southwest.
   (C) Winds and hail may cause damage to property.
   (D) It will become less muggy over time.

1. Ⓐ Ⓑ Ⓒ Ⓓ   3. Ⓐ Ⓑ Ⓒ Ⓓ   5. Ⓐ Ⓑ Ⓒ Ⓓ
2. Ⓐ Ⓑ Ⓒ Ⓓ   4. Ⓐ Ⓑ Ⓒ Ⓓ   6. Ⓐ Ⓑ Ⓒ Ⓓ

7. Who most likely is the speaker?
    (A) A travel sales executive
    (B) A tourist information clerk
    (C) A tour services manager
    (D) A business travel consultant

8. What does the speaker want Mr. Travers to do?
    (A) Confirm a booking
    (B) Place a deposit
    (C) Mail a document
    (D) Respond quickly

9. How long does Mr. Travers probably intend to be away?
    (A) About one week
    (B) 12 days
    (C) Over two weeks
    (D) One month

10. What kind of organization has been reached?
    (A) An energy supplier
    (B) A train operator
    (C) A telecommunications firm
    (D) An engineering company

11. According to the message, what is the cause of the problem at Langton?
    (A) An electrical fault
    (B) Urgent repair work
    (C) A power outage
    (D) A fault on the line

12. What are customers in Cobar asked to do?
    (A) Call customer service
    (B) Ask for an engineer
    (C) Wait until 3:00 P.M.
    (D) Check their equipment

7. Ⓐ Ⓑ Ⓒ Ⓓ   9. Ⓐ Ⓑ Ⓒ Ⓓ   11. Ⓐ Ⓑ Ⓒ Ⓓ

8. Ⓐ Ⓑ Ⓒ Ⓓ   10. Ⓐ Ⓑ Ⓒ Ⓓ   12. Ⓐ Ⓑ Ⓒ Ⓓ

Score .... /12

STEPS TO SUCCESS

This section presents an effective, step-by-step approach to use when answering questions on Part 4 of the TOEIC® test.

The steps shown here are designed to help you achieve the highest possible score when you take the test. By following these steps, you should be able to maximize your score on this part of the test.

1 ▶ Preview the questions and any accompanying graphic. Make sure you know exactly what information you need to listen for (e.g., *Who* – the speaker/audience, *Where* – the location, *How long* – a period of time, etc.).

> **REMEMBER** Question types will cover a range of main ideas, details, and inferences.

2 ▶ Preview the answer choices. Use the key information to get a general idea of the context. Ask yourself: *Who is speaking? What are they speaking about? Who are they speaking to?*

> **REMEMBER** You must be quick. Do not read every word. Just focus on the key words.

3 ▶ Listen carefully to the short talk. As you listen, study the questions and answer choices, and any graphic. Remember, for questions with a graphic you need to link what you hear with the information you see. Eliminate any answers you are sure are incorrect.

> **REMEMBER** Always try to mark your answers as you listen.

4 ▶ As soon as the short talk finishes, quickly mark any remaining answers, and move on to preview the next item.

> **REMEMBER** Never leave a question unanswered. You will not have time to return, and will not be able to recall the details if you do.

1. Where would this announcement most likely be heard?

(A) At an ice-hockey arena

(B) At a football stadium

(C) At a shooting range

(D) At a baseball park

2. According to the speaker, what are spectators forbidden from doing?

(A) Taking photographs

(B) Obstructing the exits

(C) Asking for autographs

(D) Recording the event

3. What are some spectators asked to do?

(A) Move to a different area

(B) Find their seats quickly

(C) Contact security personnel

(D) Prepare to vacate the venue

1. (A) (B) (C) (D)

2. (A) (B) (C) (D)

3. (A) (B) (C) (D)

STEP 1 ▶ Preview the questions.

Question 1: main idea [✓] detail [ ] inference [ ]

Need to listen for:......*location*......

Question 2: main idea [ ] detail [ ] inference [ ]

Need to listen for:......................

Question 3: main idea [ ] detail [ ] inference [ ]

Need to listen for:......................

STEP 2 ▶ Quickly preview the answer choices.

Possible context ....

> **REMEMBER** *On the actual test, you cannot mark the test paper, or make notes. You should quickly preview the questions and answer choices silently to yourself.*

STEP 3 ▶ 🔊 80 Listen to the announcement. As you listen, look at the questions and answer choices above. For each question, eliminate any answer choices you are sure are incorrect and mark your answer as soon as you can.

STEP 4 ▶ When the announcement finishes, immediately mark any remaining answers.

1. What is the speaker announcing?

  (A) A series of layoffs

  (B) A restructuring plan

  (C) A departmental review

  (D) An important new contract

2. What does the speaker mention about Mr. Cranshaw?

  (A) He recently visited the company.

  (B) He has been spreading rumors.

  (C) He works at the main office.

  (D) He has gone abroad on vacation.

3. Why might some employees decide to contact their line managers?

  (A) To request a pay raise

  (B) To ask for a transfer

  (C) To claim a reward

  (D) To make a suggestion

1. (A) (B) (C) (D)

2. (A) (B) (C) (D)

3. (A) (B) (C) (D)

STEP 1 ▶ Preview the questions.

  Question 1: main idea [ ] detail [ ] inference [ ]

  Need to listen for: ....

  Question 2: main idea [ ] detail [ ] inference [ ]

  Need to listen for: ....

  Question 3: main idea [ ] detail [ ] inference [ ]

  Need to listen for: ....

STEP 2 ▶ Quickly preview the answer choices.

  Possible context ....

▶ **REMEMBER** *On the actual test, you cannot mark the test paper, or make notes. You should quickly preview the questions and answer choices silently to yourself.*

STEP 3 ▶ **81** Listen to the short talk. As you listen, look at the questions and answer choices above. For each question, eliminate any answer choices you are sure are incorrect and mark your answer as soon as you can.

STEP 4 ▶ When the short talk finishes, immediately mark any remaining answers.

Practice 3

1. Who most likely is the speaker?

   (A) An engineering student

   (B) An academic coordinator

   (C) A college professor

   (D) A research associate

2. According to the message, why is Mr. Bryce unable to take the call?

   (A) He is out of the office for the day.

   (B) He is taking a vacation in Europe.

   (C) He is attending a presentation.

   (D) He is at an international conference.

3. What should callers with urgent inquiries do?

   (A) Leave a voicemail message

   (B) E-mail Chris Bryce's secretary

   (C) Ask for a different department

   (D) Speak to an administrative assistant

   1. Ⓐ Ⓑ Ⓒ Ⓓ
   2. Ⓐ Ⓑ Ⓒ Ⓓ
   3. Ⓐ Ⓑ Ⓒ Ⓓ

STEP 1 ▸ Preview the questions.

   Question 1: main idea [ ]   detail [ ]   inference [ ]

           Need to listen for:...

   Question 2: main idea [ ]   detail [ ]   inference [ ]

           Need to listen for:...

   Question 3: main idea [ ]   detail [ ]   inference [ ]

           Need to listen for:...

STEP 2 ▸ Quickly preview the answer choices.

   <u>Possible context</u> ....

   > **REMEMBER** *On the actual test, you cannot mark the test paper, or make notes. You should quickly preview the questions and answer choices silently to yourself.*

STEP 3 ▸ ⏸ 82 Listen to the message. As you listen, look at the questions and answer choices above. For each question, eliminate any answer choices you are sure are incorrect and mark your answer as soon as you can.

STEP 4 ▸ When the message finishes, immediately mark any remaining answers.

Practice 4

1. What is the purpose of the call?

   (A) To ask for information

   (B) To respond to an inquiry

   (C) To confirm a decision

   (D) To report a problem

2. Look at the graphic. Which make of printer does the listener most likely have?

   (A) HP

   (B) Lexmark

   (C) Canon

   (D) Brother

3. What will the speaker do next?

   (A) Make a purchase

   (B) Ask for advice

   (C) Keep browsing

   (D) Leave the store

OFFICE EXPRESS SUPERSTORE
STAR BUYS! This month…
great deals on ALL printer cartridges!

		Regular price	Mad March price!
HP	10 x black ink C345	$69.99	$47.95
Lexmark	4-pack 150XL color	$89.99	$60.49
Canon	T63 Tri-Color pack of 2	$28.95	$15.95
Brother	PGI SuperG color x 5	$74.99	$49.99

1. Ⓐ Ⓑ Ⓒ Ⓓ
2. Ⓐ Ⓑ Ⓒ Ⓓ
3. Ⓐ Ⓑ Ⓒ Ⓓ

STEP 1 ▸ Preview the questions.

Question 1: main idea [ ]   detail [ ]   inference [ ]

Need to listen for:...

Question 2: main idea [ ]   detail [ ]   inference [ ]

Need to listen for:...

Question 3: main idea [ ]   detail [ ]   inference [ ]

Need to listen for:...

Graphic   ....

STEP 2 ▸ Quickly preview the answer choices.
Possible context   ....

▸ **REMEMBER** *On the actual test, you cannot mark the test paper, or make notes. You should quickly preview the questions and answer choices silently to yourself.*

STEP 3 ▸ 83 Listen to the voicemail message. As you listen, look at the questions and answer choices above, and study the graphic. For each question, eliminate any answer choices you are sure are incorrect and mark your answer as soon as you can.

STEP 4 ▸ When the voicemail message finishes, immediately mark any remaining answers.

Strategy Review and Tips

Strategy Review Listening Test – Part 4

Remember, in the test…

Before each short talk begins, quickly preview the questions (and graphic, if there is one). Make sure you know what information you need to listen for. Study the answer choices to get a general idea of the context.

During each short talk, listen and study the questions and answer choices, plus any graphic. Eliminate any answer choices you think are wrong. Mark any correct answer choices as soon as you identify them.

After each short talk finishes, immediately mark any remaining answers. If you are not sure, don't waste time. Decide quickly! Then go straight on to preview the next short talk.

TIPS *Here is some advice that people taking the TOEIC test have found useful for this part. Choose the tips you like, and try to use them.*

"Concentrate 100 percent on everything that the speakers are saying, and don't get distracted. You will feel tired, but this is the final part of the listening section so keep focused."
Nicole Lombard

"When I'm listening to a short talk, I imagine the words printed on a sheet of white paper. I think it helps."
Michael Cheong

"Remember that the answer to the first question might only come at the end of a talk. Don't read the first question and focus only on that. You should be listening for the answers to all three questions."
Gustavo Espinoza

"Where there is a graphic, you need to look at the graphic and the answer choices simultaneously. Keep flipping back and forth as you listen."
Dominik Glik

"Never leave a question unanswered. You should always make a guess. If I'm not sure, I look to see if one of the answer choices is much longer than the rest, and choose that. If there isn't a longer answer choice, I choose C because I think that is the most common correct answer."
Kaya Yamaguchi

Review Test

84 **Directions:** You will hear ten short talks given by a single speaker. For each short talk, read the three questions and the four answer choices that follow each question. Select the most appropriate answer: (A), (B), (C), or (D). Then mark your answer. You will hear each short talk only once.

1. What is being advertised?
   (A) A vintage car race
   (B) An outdoor event
   (C) A music festival
   (D) A family fun day

2. Who is Heather Jarvis?
   (A) A presenter
   (B) A singer
   (C) An actress
   (D) A dancer

3. What does the speaker imply?
   (A) Tickets are limited.
   (B) The event lasts one day.
   (C) The show starts at 3:00 P.M.
   (D) Parking is free of charge.

4. What is indicated about Hayfield Dental Practice?
   (A) It opens at 8:00 A.M. on weekdays.
   (B) There is an emergency clinic every Tuesday.
   (C) It is closed on Friday afternoons.
   (D) It is sometimes open after 5:00 P.M.

5. Why does the message suggest visiting a website?
   (A) To view available services
   (B) To make an appointment
   (C) To check the latest offers
   (D) To confirm directions

6. According to the recording, what should callers do next?
   (A) Schedule a visit
   (B) Call back later
   (C) Leave a message
   (D) Continue to hold

7. What type of radio show is this?
   (A) A music show
   (B) A documentary
   (C) A reality show
   (D) A talk show

8. Who is Dr. Farah?
   (A) A healthcare practitioner
   (B) A welfare manager
   (C) A social scientist
   (D) A medical doctor

9. When will the show end?
   (A) At 2:15 P.M.
   (B) At 2:20 P.M.
   (C) At 2:45 P.M.
   (D) At 3:00 P.M.

1. Ⓐ Ⓑ Ⓒ Ⓓ				**4.** Ⓐ Ⓑ Ⓒ Ⓓ				**7.** Ⓐ Ⓑ Ⓒ Ⓓ			
2. Ⓐ Ⓑ Ⓒ Ⓓ				**5.** Ⓐ Ⓑ Ⓒ Ⓓ				**8.** Ⓐ Ⓑ Ⓒ Ⓓ			
3. Ⓐ Ⓑ Ⓒ Ⓓ				**6.** Ⓐ Ⓑ Ⓒ Ⓓ				**9.** Ⓐ Ⓑ Ⓒ Ⓓ			

10. Where is this announcement being made?
    (A) On the street
    (B) On a train
    (C) On a bus
    (D) At a visitor center

11. What does the speaker ask listeners to do?
    (A) Keep to the schedule
    (B) Check their watches
    (C) Wait at the entrance
    (D) Return at 11:00 A.M.

12. What does the woman mean when she says, "It's going to be a full day"?
    (A) Everyone should have an enjoyable time.
    (B) The itinerary is very busy.
    (C) Listeners will have no time to relax.
    (D) There are many hours of daylight ahead.

13. Who is the speaker most likely talking to?
    (A) University students
    (B) I.T. professionals
    (C) Computing enthusiasts
    (D) Research analysts

14. What is the purpose of this talk?
    (A) To compare technologies
    (B) To advise on programming
    (C) To share research data
    (D) To promote a product

15. How long will the talk last?
    (A) Half an hour
    (B) 60 minutes
    (C) Until 2:00 P.M.
    (D) All afternoon

16. What is the main purpose of this telephone message?
    (A) To apologize for an error
    (B) To ask for information
    (C) To thank a customer
    (D) To offer a reward

17. What kind of business is Tysons?
    (A) A takeout restaurant
    (B) A supermarket chain
    (C) A department store
    (D) A local greengrocer

18. What is the cause of the problem?
    (A) A product has been mislabeled.
    (B) Goods have been incorrectly packaged.
    (C) A storage container has been lost.
    (D) Some dairy produce has gone missing.

10. (A) (B) (C) (D)   13. (A) (B) (C) (D)   16. (A) (B) (C) (D)
11. (A) (B) (C) (D)   14. (A) (B) (C) (D)   17. (A) (B) (C) (D)
12. (A) (B) (C) (D)   15. (A) (B) (C) (D)   18. (A) (B) (C) (D)

19. What is this news broadcast mainly about?
- (A) The progress of an ongoing court case
- (B) An inquiry into illegal trading activity
- (C) The collapse of a major hedge fund firm
- (D) A boardroom feud at a financial company

20. What is scheduled to happen next month?
- (A) The C.E.O. of Brinton International will resign.
- (B) $300 million will be returned to investors.
- (C) Several executives will face questioning.
- (D) A senior executive will be sent to prison.

21. According to the speaker, what will Mr. Heston most likely do?
- (A) Apologize in court
- (B) Issue an appeal
- (C) Contest the charges
- (D) Change his legal team

22. Who most likely is the speaker?
- (A) A training manager
- (B) A call center agent
- (C) A Mirabel employee
- (D) A meditation expert

23. What does the speaker say will happen at midday?
- (A) The workshop will end.
- (B) Sam will join the company.
- (C) A delivery will arrive.
- (D) There will be a test.

24. What does the woman imply when she says, "It's taken a big chunk out of my budget"?
- (A) Her budget has recently been cut.
- (B) The workshops are very expensive.
- (C) More resources are urgently required.
- (D) Damaged items need to be replaced.

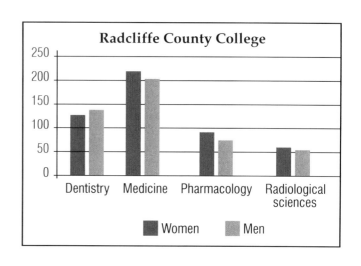

Radcliffe County College

25. Which group is the speaker talking about?
- (A) College applicants
- (B) Graduates
- (C) Freshmen
- (D) Drop-outs

26. Look at the graphic. Which major will the speaker discuss next?
- (A) Dentistry
- (B) Medicine
- (C) Pharmacology
- (D) Radiological sciences

27. What does the speaker anticipate may happen?
- (A) The number of students who drop out may fall.
- (B) Some departments may struggle to attract students.
- (C) The percentage of male students could increase.
- (D) College faculty will overturn a key decision.

19. Ⓐ Ⓑ Ⓒ Ⓓ   **22.** Ⓐ Ⓑ Ⓒ Ⓓ   **25.** Ⓐ Ⓑ Ⓒ Ⓓ
20. Ⓐ Ⓑ Ⓒ Ⓓ   **23.** Ⓐ Ⓑ Ⓒ Ⓓ   **26.** Ⓐ Ⓑ Ⓒ Ⓓ
21. Ⓐ Ⓑ Ⓒ Ⓓ   **24.** Ⓐ Ⓑ Ⓒ Ⓓ   **27.** Ⓐ Ⓑ Ⓒ Ⓓ

28. Where is this talk taking place?

(A) On a tour bus

(B) Inside a café

(C) Outside a large house

(D) In a travel agency

29. Look at the graphic. Which property is the speaker referring to?

(A) Devonshire Hall

(B) Raleigh Manor

(C) Marlborough Abbey

(D) Wellington Court

30. What does the speaker recommend the listeners do?

(A) Walk around the gardens

(B) Purchase a brochure

(C) Book a guided tour

(D) Visit the terrace

Great Houses of Britain

Name of property	Year the property was built
Devonshire Hall	1863
Raleigh Manor	1701
Marlborough Abbey	1790
Wellington Court	1835

28. Ⓐ Ⓑ Ⓒ Ⓓ

29. Ⓐ Ⓑ Ⓒ Ⓓ

30. Ⓐ Ⓑ Ⓒ Ⓓ   Score .... /30

EXTRA PRACTICE ONLINE

Go to **www.pass-the-toeic-test.com** for advice and useful exercises to help improve your score on Part 4 of the TOEIC test.

▶ Listening Links

▶ Related Words

▶ Paraphrasing

Listening Comprehension Test

This Listening Comprehension Test covers Parts 1, 2, 3, and 4 of the TOEIC® test. Allow 45 minutes to complete this test. Mark all your answers on the separate Listening Comprehension Test Answer Sheet provided on page 317.

Part 1

85 Directions

For each question, you will hear four statements about a photograph. Listen and select the one statement: (A), (B), (C), or (D), that best describes the picture. Then mark your answer on the Answer Sheet. You will hear the statements only once.

EXAMPLE

(A) ●

The best description of the picture is statement (B), "A man's giving a presentation to a small group of people." You should mark answer choice (B) on your Answer Sheet.

1.

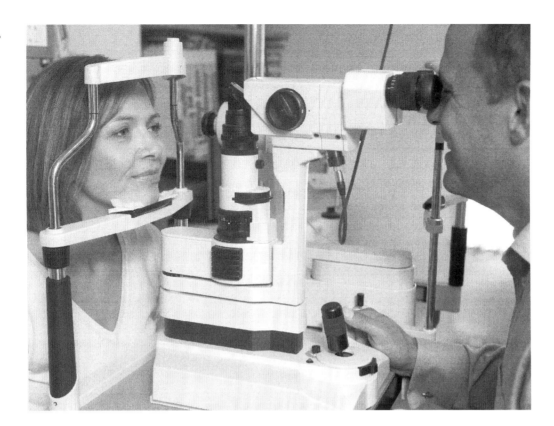

2.

GO ON TO THE NEXT PAGE

3.

4.

5.

6.

GO ON TO THE NEXT PAGE ➤

Part 2

Directions

Listen to these questions and statements. After each question or statement, you will hear three responses. Select the most appropriate response: (A), (B), or (C). Then mark your answer on the Answer Sheet. You will hear each question or statement, and the responses, only once.

EXAMPLE

You hear: Would you mind helping me finish this report?

You then hear: (A) That's very kind of you.

                    (B) I thought you would.

                    (C) No, not at all.

The best response to the question "Would you mind helping me finish this report?" is answer choice (C), "No, not at all." You should mark answer choice (C) on your Answer Sheet.

---

7. Mark your answer on the Answer Sheet.

8. Mark your answer on the Answer Sheet.

9. Mark your answer on the Answer Sheet.

10. Mark your answer on the Answer Sheet.

11. Mark your answer on the Answer Sheet.

12. Mark your answer on the Answer Sheet.

13. Mark your answer on the Answer Sheet.

14. Mark your answer on the Answer Sheet.

15. Mark your answer on the Answer Sheet.

16. Mark your answer on the Answer Sheet.

17. Mark your answer on the Answer Sheet.

18. Mark your answer on the Answer Sheet.

19. Mark your answer on the Answer Sheet.

20. Mark your answer on the Answer Sheet.

21. Mark your answer on the Answer Sheet.

22. Mark your answer on the Answer Sheet.

23. Mark your answer on the Answer Sheet.

24. Mark your answer on the Answer Sheet.

25. Mark your answer on the Answer Sheet.

26. Mark your answer on the Answer Sheet.

27. Mark your answer on the Answer Sheet.

28. Mark your answer on the Answer Sheet.

29. Mark your answer on the Answer Sheet.

30. Mark your answer on the Answer Sheet.

31. Mark your answer on the Answer Sheet.

Part 3

Directions

You will hear thirteen conversations. For each conversation, read the three questions and the four answer choices that follow each question. Select the most appropriate answer: (A), (B), (C), or (D). Then mark your answer on the Answer Sheet. You will hear each conversation only once.

32. Who is the woman talking to?
    (A) A police officer
    (B) A garage mechanic
    (C) A recovery truck driver
    (D) A firefighter

33. Why is the woman concerned?
    (A) She may be late for an appointment.
    (B) She cannot find her credit card.
    (C) She is feeling uncomfortably hot.
    (D) She has lost a rental agreement.

34. What will the man do next?
    (A) Call a taxi
    (B) Carry out a repair
    (C) Order spare parts
    (D) Take the car away

35. What is the woman's job?
    (A) Accounting clerk
    (B) Store manager
    (C) Sales agent
    (D) Cashier

36. What offer is the man interested in?
    (A) Free delivery
    (B) A monthly discount
    (C) Buy one, get one free
    (D) A complimentary gift

37. What will the man probably purchase in addition to the router?
    (A) Stationery
    (B) Software
    (C) Furniture
    (D) Ink supplies

38. What are the man and woman discussing?
    (A) Shorts
    (B) Sandals
    (C) Glasses
    (D) Earrings

39. What does the man want to do?
    (A) Return a purchase
    (B) Get medical help
    (C) Exchange some goods
    (D) Make a complaint

40. Why is the woman unable to agree to the man's request?
    (A) The man failed a credit check.
    (B) The manager would not approve.
    (C) The goods are not in mint condition.
    (D) The rate of exchange is very poor.

41. Who most likely are the speakers?
    (A) Corporate lawyers
    (B) Police detectives
    (C) Telemarketers
    (D) Investment bankers

42. What does the man say about the past two months?
    (A) His work has been going well.
    (B) The weather has been fine.
    (C) The workload has kept increasing.
    (D) He has fallen behind schedule.

43. What is the man concerned about?
    (A) A delayed payment
    (B) His coworker's behavior
    (C) The lack of support
    (D) Communication problems

GO ON TO THE NEXT PAGE

44. What is the woman's occupation?
   (A) Personal assistant
   (B) Property developer
   (C) Real estate agent
   (D) Interior designer

45. What does the man ask the woman to do?
   (A) Send directions
   (B) Meet at 2:00 P.M.
   (C) Make an apology
   (D) E-mail an associate

46. What does the man mean when he says, "I have a meeting that finishes around two across town"?
   (A) He is busy all of the morning.
   (B) He may be late for the appointment.
   (C) He might need to reschedule.
   (D) He would rather meet in a different location.

47. What are the speakers most likely discussing?
   (A) A research experiment
   (B) An oral exam
   (C) A written test
   (D) An opinion poll

48. Why was the man surprised?
   (A) The figures were inaccurate.
   (B) The result was inconclusive.
   (C) It took longer than expected.
   (D) Not many people turned up.

49. How does the man probably feel?
   (A) Unconvinced
   (B) Disillusioned
   (C) Offended
   (D) Stoical

50. Where does this conversation take place?
   (A) At a garden center
   (B) At a tourist office
   (C) At a theme park
   (D) At a wildlife sanctuary

51. What does the woman advise the man to do?
   (A) Return the next day
   (B) Allow more time
   (C) Explore the island
   (D) See a show

52. What will the man probably do next?
   (A) Buy some tickets
   (B) Visit Waverley Gardens
   (C) Ask for directions
   (D) Speak to his family

53. What is the woman doing?
   (A) Arranging a delivery
   (B) Signing for a package
   (C) Filling out a questionnaire
   (D) Accepting an award

54. What does the woman infer about the item?
   (A) It is large.
   (B) It is heavy.
   (C) It is unwanted.
   (D) It is late.

55. What does the man say he tried to do earlier?
   (A) Print out a report
   (B) Contact the woman
   (C) Check the exact time
   (D) Get further details

56. What is indicated about the company?
- (A) It was founded a year ago.
- (B) It needs more capital.
- (C) It is an export business.
- (D) It has many investors.

57. Who most likely is Gavin Helmsley?
- (A) A shareholder
- (B) A tax official
- (C) An accountant
- (D) A board member

58. What will happen on Friday?
- (A) A press conference will be held.
- (B) Funds will be transferred.
- (C) An expansion will be announced.
- (D) A financial report will be submitted.

---

59. What are the speakers mainly discussing?
- (A) A redesigned catalog
- (B) The launch of a website
- (C) A range of new products
- (D) A photography exhibition

60. Why does the woman say, "You can say that again"?
- (A) To ask for repetition
- (B) To show enthusiasm
- (C) To grant permission
- (D) To express agreement

61. According to the man, what should the woman do?
- (A) Ask for more money
- (B) Proceed as planned
- (C) Send an estimate
- (D) Question the bill

Bus number	Destination	Arriving in ...
17	Harford Park	5 mins
219	Blackhorse Lane	8 mins
33	Lime Marshes	10 mins
85	St. Martin's Center	20 mins

62. What will the man do later this evening?
- (A) Prepare a presentation
- (B) Watch television
- (C) Heat up a pizza
- (D) Attend a meeting

63. Look at the graphic. Which bus will the man take?
- (A) 17
- (B) 219
- (C) 33
- (D) 85

64. What will the woman do tomorrow?
- (A) Visit a family member
- (B) Attend a funeral
- (C) Give a presentation
- (D) Go to the hospital

GO ON TO THE NEXT PAGE

65. What does the woman imply?
- (A) They have plenty of time.
- (B) They avoided a speeding fine.
- (C) They are in good health.
- (D) They are about to arrive.

66. Look at the graphic. Which show are they going to see?
- (A) Evening in Manhattan
- (B) Musical Extravaganza
- (C) Two Times Two
- (D) Mystery of Marston Moor

67. What will the man most likely do next?
- (A) Prepare a snack
- (B) Book a babysitter
- (C) Check some details
- (D) Use his cell phone

Show	Start time
Evening in Manhattan	7:15 P.M.
Musical Extravaganza	7:30 P.M.
Two Times Two	7:45 P.M.
Mystery of Marston Moor	8:00 P.M.

68. Look at the graphic. Which country is represented by Line 4?
- (A) Germany
- (B) Spain
- (C) Denmark
- (D) Sweden

69. What does the woman suggest?
- (A) Seeking out new markets
- (B) Going on a fact-finding trip
- (C) Appointing a new distributor
- (D) Monitoring the climate

70. What does the man decide to do?
- (A) Compile some new data
- (B) Explore possible options
- (C) Take legal action
- (D) Consult a coworker

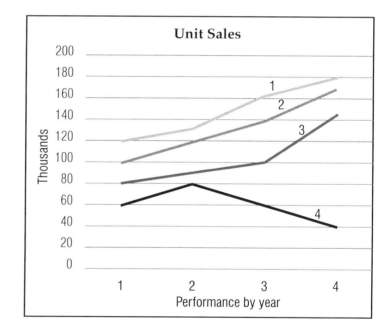

Part 4

Directions

You will hear ten short talks given by a single speaker. For each short talk, read the three questions and the four answer choices that follow each question. Select the most appropriate answer: (A), (B), (C), or (D). Then mark your answer on the Answer Sheet. You will hear each short talk only once.

71. Who is this talk intended for?
- (A) Fitness enthusiasts
- (B) Senior citizens
- (C) Personal trainers
- (D) Gym members

72. What is the main purpose of the talk?
- (A) To protest the economic downturn
- (B) To discuss healthcare options
- (C) To promote an exercise gadget
- (D) To introduce a special guest

73. What will listeners do next?
- (A) Listen to a lecture
- (B) Do some exercises
- (C) Take a short break
- (D) Leave immediately

74. What is most likely the speaker's occupation?
- (A) Portrait artist
- (B) Delivery driver
- (C) Personal assistant
- (D) Interior decorator

75. Why is the speaker calling?
- (A) To report a problem
- (B) To cancel an order
- (C) To request a brochure
- (D) To arrange a meeting

76. What does the speaker ask Mrs. Shibata to do?
- (A) Speak to a store assistant
- (B) Postpone an appointment
- (C) Get in touch urgently
- (D) Reschedule for Monday

77. Where is the talk taking place?
- (A) In a school
- (B) In a courtroom
- (C) In a cafeteria
- (D) In a TV studio

78. What have listeners just heard?
- (A) A sociology lecture
- (B) A political debate
- (C) An election result
- (D) A strategy seminar

79. What does the speaker mean when he says, "I certainly don't intend to be partisan"?
- (A) He does not support discrimination.
- (B) He would rather the situation was more balanced.
- (C) He is apologizing for being prejudiced.
- (D) He wants to appear impartial.

80. What is being advertised?
- (A) A skin care product
- (B) A medicated shampoo
- (C) A brand of work gloves
- (D) A health gadget

81. Who would be interested in this advertisement?
- (A) Welding technicians
- (B) Compliance managers
- (C) Software engineers
- (D) Sustainability consultants

82. How are listeners asked to respond?
- (A) Online
- (B) By phone
- (C) In person
- (D) By fax

GO ON TO THE NEXT PAGE ➤

83. What kind of organization has been reached?

(A) A government tax office

(B) A financial advice center

(C) An import and export agency

(D) A corporate finance department

84. What should callers who want to change their registration details do?

(A) Continue to hold

(B) Press 1

(C) Go to the website

(D) Call back later

85. What can be inferred from the message?

(A) Many customers are waiting to be assessed.

(B) Some demands for payment have been issued incorrectly.

(C) The website is experiencing technical problems.

(D) Almost all payments are made via the Internet.

86. What does the speaker say about the Alberta Enterprise Award?

(A) Past winners have gone on to be very successful.

(B) The standard this year is higher than ever.

(C) It has been very difficult to choose a winner.

(D) The competition is open to all Alberta residents.

87. According to the speaker, what is the most important factor needed for success?

(A) Talent

(B) Luck

(C) Energy

(D) Determination

88. What is Ms. Hargreaves' occupation?

(A) Pottery artist

(B) Playwright

(C) Illustrator

(D) Graphic designer

89. Who is the speaker addressing?

(A) Conference delegates

(B) A group of tourists

(C) Health inspectors

(D) High school students

90. What is the talk mainly about?

(A) Cancer risks

(B) Health issues

(C) Sun safety

(D) Summer fashions

91. What are listeners asked to do?

(A) Wear more formal clothing

(B) Stay indoors as much as possible

(C) Drink plenty of liquids

(D) Decide on their itinerary

92. Who is Ms. O'Hara?

(A) A professional dancer

(B) A student of the arts

(C) A competition winner

(D) A cultural reporter

93. Why does the speaker say, "What about that, folks"?

(A) He is requesting clarification.

(B) He is unsure how the listeners feel.

(C) He wants to ask for opinions.

(D) He is emphasizing an achievement.

94. When will the program most likely end?

(A) At 10:30 A.M.

(B) In five minutes

(C) In half an hour

(D) At midday

OFFICE SUPPLIES DIRECT
Delivery Note

Ship to:
UV Automotive Inc.
Lambeth Business Park
San Francisco
CA91422

Quantity	Item code	Description
6 boxes	PP-0022	Pacific Paper multipurpose copy paper
6 boxes	PP-1450	Pacific Paper colored paper
6 boxes	PP-750	Pacific Paper heavy coated paper
3 cartridges	AB-0025	AllBrite printer toner

Thank you for your business!

Evaluation Form

Lecture title ....

Date of lecture..

Lecture given by ....

Answer the following questions in as much detail as you wish.

1. Was the topic covered effectively? ....

2. Were the explanations clear and helpful? ....

3. Were the assignments relevant to the topic? ....

4. How useful were the handouts/course materials?........................

5. Was the use of visual aids effective?................................

6. What was the best part of the lecture?................................

7. What areas could be improved?................................

8. Any other comments?................................

Thank you!

---

95. Who is this telephone message intended for?
- (A) A customer services agent
- (B) A marketing director
- (C) An employee of Pacific Paper
- (D) A UV Automotive administrator

96. Look at the graphic. Which item was incorrectly delivered?
- (A) Multipurpose copy paper
- (B) Colored paper
- (C) Heavy coated paper
- (D) Printer toner

97. What will the speaker do next?
- (A) Correct the stationery order
- (B) Contact the delivery company
- (C) Look for an alternative supplier
- (D) Send an e-mail to a colleague

98. Why are the answers on the form important to the speaker?
- (A) He can learn more details about his students.
- (B) His senior manager wants the information.
- (C) They help him when he is planning future lectures.
- (D) They are useful for designing assessment tasks.

99. Look at the graphic. Which question are students asked NOT to answer?
- (A) Question 3
- (B) Question 4
- (C) Question 5
- (D) Question 7

100. What should the students do with the forms?
- (A) Return them directly to the speaker
- (B) Give them to a member of staff
- (C) Leave them on the table in the room
- (D) Hand them in to the administration office

This is the end of the Listening Comprehension Test.

READING

Guide to the Reading Test

The second section of the TOEIC® test is Reading. In this section, the test focuses on how well you read and understand written English. There are three parts in this section.

Part 5: Incomplete Sentences   30 questions   *10 min*
Part 6: Text Completion   16 questions   *10 min*
Part 7: Reading Comprehension   54 questions   *55 min*

You will have 75 minutes to complete this section of the TOEIC test.

Directions are given for each part. You need to mark your answers on the separate Answer Sheet provided.

Part 5 and Part 6 focus mainly on your knowledge and use of grammar and vocabulary. Part 5 requires you to choose the correct word or phrase to complete each sentence you read. In Part 6, you have to complete each short text you read by selecting the correct missing words. You also need to identify which of four sentences best fits the context, so this question tests your comprehension. In Part 7, you are tested on your ability to understand the texts you read. There are up to ten single passages, two double passages, and finally three triple passages. You need to answer a number of comprehension questions on each passage. Together, these three parts comprise the Reading section of the test.

> ### QUICK CHECK
>
> How many parts are there in the Reading section of the TOEIC test?
> How many questions are there?
> How much time do you have to complete the Reading section?
> Where do you mark your answers?
> Which part focuses mainly on your reading comprehension ability?

1 MIN

Guide to this section of *Pass the TOEIC Test*

The Reading section of *Pass the TOEIC Test* covers Parts 5, 6, and 7 of the TOEIC test. First, you study important *Grammar* and *Vocabulary*. This is because Part 5 and Part 6 share the same grammar and vocabulary testing points. Focusing on this language first allows for more complete preparation, and more authentic practice. Each part begins with an *Overview*, which gives an example and explains the main challenges you will face. In *Steps to Success* you practice special strategies for taking each part of the test, before *Strategy Review and Tips* summarizes key guidance and gives useful advice. Finally, you put everything into practice in a *Review Test*. You then continue to Part 7, which is presented as an individual section.

GRAMMAR

This section reviews the grammar you need to improve your score on Part 5 and Part 6 of the TOEIC® test.

Study this *Grammar* section carefully and use it as a handy reference. It is a detailed summary of the main grammatical and structural points commonly featured in the TOEIC® test. Take the Mini Test to help identify your strengths and weaknesses. Notice what problems you have, and focus on the areas you need to improve.

Modals and Semi-Modals

Modal verbs (*can*, *might*, *should*, *must*, etc.) express ideas such as possibility, obligation, and advice. Several modal verbs have more than one meaning. However, they never change their form, and are followed by the infinitive without *to* (*We could leave early*) when referring to the present, or *have* + past participle when referring to the past (*We could have left early*). They cannot be followed by *to*, the gerund (*-ing* form), a past participle, or another modal verb. Semi-modals (*had better, ought to, have to, be able to*, etc.) are similar to modal verbs as they are all modal in meaning, but they behave differently. For example, some semi-modals can change form to agree with the subject (*have to—has to*), or indicate tense (*was able to*).

Ability

Sam **could not** drive until he was 26.	For general ability, use *can/cannot*, or *could/could not* in the past.
I **was able to** finish the report in an hour.	For specific events, use *be able to* (meaning *manage to*).

Willingness

They **will not** reduce the price any further. Our delivery truck **would not** start this morning	For refusal, use *will not*, or *would not* for the past. Also use *will/would* (*not*) for inanimate objects.

Possibility/Probability

Temperatures **can** rise as high as 50 degrees.	For general or theoretical possibility, use *can*.
The meeting **may/might/could** last all day. We **may/might/could well** be here until 6 P.M. Tim **may/might/could have missed** his flight.	For specific or future possibility, use *may/might/could*. Add *well* to increase the likelihood. Add *have* + past participle to refer to the past.
You **could have hurt** yourself with those shears.	Use *could have* + past participle for something that was possible, but didn't actually happen.
The office **should** be closed by now.	For more certain possibilities, use *should*.

Permission

Can I leave early this evening? **Could/May/Might** I ask you a question?	For permission, use *can*. To be more polite, use *could*, *may*, or *might*.

Prohibition

You **cannot** bring food or drink into the auditorium. Visitors to the library **must not** make any noise. Women **could not** join this golf club until 2010.	For prohibition in the present, use *cannot* (*can't*). Also use *must not* to indicate prohibition. For prohibition in the past, use *could not* (*couldn't*).

Requests

Can you give me a hand packing these catalogs? **Could/Will/Would** you wait for me at the main entrance, please?	For requests, use *can*. For more polite requests, use *could, will*, or *would*.

Deductions

You **must** be relieved that the exam is over.

She **cannot** be here yet because her car is not outside.

Daniel **must have bought** a new car.

They **cannot have repaired** the printer because the paper still jams.

It's 7:00 P.M., so the performance **will** be starting.

They **will have finished** the meeting by now.

For logical deductions, use *must*.

Use *cannot* to express a negative deduction.

Add *have* + past participle to refer to the past.

Use *cannot* or *could not* + *have* + past participle for negative deductions in the past.

For very certain deductions in the present or future, use *will/will not*.

Use *will have* + past participle to refer to a completed action in the future.

Advice/Recommendations

We **should** think about expanding the business.

You **had better** check that the alarm is on before you leave.

Someone **should have told** me the meeting was canceled.

You **should not have forgotten** your passport!

You **ought not to have spoken** so bluntly.

You really **must** go and see the new Bond movie.

For general advice or recommendations, use *should* or *ought to*.

Use *had better* (*not*) for strong advice.

Use *should have* + past participle to refer to something that was a good idea, but didn't happen.

Use *should not have* + past participle to refer to something that was a bad idea, but happened.

The negative of *ought to* is *ought not to*. This is rare, especially in spoken English.

For strong personal recommendations, use *must*.

Obligation/Necessity

All candidates **have to** pass a series of rigorous tests.

I **must** do some shopping on my way home.

We **had to** evacuate the building because the fire alarm went off.

These plastic bottles **should** be in the blue recycling bin by the door.

Administration staff **do not have to** work on weekends.

You **needn't** unpack those bags just yet.

Tina **needn't have worried** as she passed all her exams.

For strong external obligation (from someone else), use *have to* (or *need to*).

For strong personal obligation (from ourselves), use *must*.

In this context, the past of *must* is *had to*.

For weak obligation, use *should* (or *be supposed to*).

To show there is no obligation, use *do not have to*.

Also use *needn't* (meaning *do not need to*) to show there is no obligation.

Use *needn't have* + past participle for something that happened but wasn't necessary (compared to *didn't need to* where the action may or may not have happened).

Verb Forms and Tenses

Study the chart below to familiarize yourself with the main verb forms and their functions.

Present simple

Our ice-cream sales **drop** in the winter months.	for facts and situations that are always true
We **hold** training sessions on Friday afternoons.	for regular events
Most employees here **don't belong** to a union.	for generalizations
I **play** tennis twice a week at a local sports center.	for habits

➤ Look for time markers such as adverbs of frequency (*always, usually, often, sometimes, hardly ever, rarely, seldom, never*), *every day/month/year, once/twice a day/week, on Sundays/Mondays, in the afternoons*, and *on the weekends*.

Past simple

We **launched** the product last month.	for completed actions in the past
Jim **walked** into the office, **sat** down, and **started** work.	for consecutive actions in the past
I **worked** in investment banking for ten years.	for situations that existed for a period of time in the past
In my previous job, I **walked** to work every day.	for habits or repeated actions in the past

➤ Look for time markers such as *yesterday, last night/week/month/year, on Saturday, in July, in 2012, for* (+ period of time), duration + *ago, then, after, before*, and *previously*.

Present perfect simple

Mr. Ono **has visited** every branch in our company.	for general experience
How long **have** you **worked** here?	for situations that began in the past and are still in progress
We can't complete the project as the manager **has left**.	for recent actions with present consequences
The C.E.O. of Lanark International **has resigned**!	for newsworthy events
I **have bought** a new wireless printer.	for events that happened very recently

➤ Look for time markers such as *recently, lately, so far, until now, since* (+ point in time), and *for* (+ period of time).

Past perfect simple

Before we could sell our stocks, the price **had collapsed**.	for one action that happened before another action in the past
By 11:00 A.M. most guests **had checked out** of the hotel.	for events that happened before a particular time in the past

➤ Look for time markers such as *by 7:30 A.M./Monday/2018*, and *by the time/before* (+ past simple).

Continuous Verb Forms

Continuous verb forms are used for actions that take place over a period of time, where the duration of the action is important. They are also used to indicate a temporary situation, or to give an idea of incompletion.

Present continuous

Mike **is giving** a presentation in Room 4.	for activities that have begun and are still in progress
Are you **watching** that new soap opera on TV?	for activities happening at about this time
We **are renting** these premises while our offices are being refurbished.	for temporary events and activities

➤ Look for time markers such as *right away*, *still*, *right now*, *now*, *at the moment*, *currently*, *today*, and *this morning/evening*.

Past continuous

Who **were** you **speaking** to when we arrived?	for situations or activities that were in progress before a point in the past
It **was raining** all weekend, so I stayed home.	for longer past actions
At 6:00 P.M., we **were** still **trying** to install the system update.	for actions happening around a particular time in the past
Our company **was expanding** year by year.	to indicate change or development in the past
We **were relaxing** by the pool when the thunderstorm broke.	to suggest incompleteness (due to interruption) in the past
My previous boss **was** always **forgetting** my name.	Used with *always* (or *continually*, *constantly*, etc.) to indicate a repeated past action or behavior (often annoying).
I **was wondering** if you could help me with this report.	for polite or tentative requests

Present perfect continuous

How long **have** you **been waiting** to see a doctor?	for actions that began in the past and are still happening now
Sue's arms ache because she **has been lifting** heavy boxes.	for recently completed actions that have results in the present

Past perfect continuous

I **had been standing** in line for nearly an hour before I got a seat.	for longer past situations or activities that were in progress before something else in the past
During the lecture Jill **hadn't been concentrating**, so she failed the test.	to show cause and effect

Stative Verbs

When verbs describe states, they are called "stative" verbs. These verbs are generally only used in the simple form, not the continuous.

Your offer of free shipping in return for prompt payment **seems** very fair.

How **do** you **know** which of these levers to pull?

I **did not realize** that internet connection speeds could vary so much.

Stative verbs include:

➤ verbs describing thoughts and opinions (*consider, doubt, expect, feel, imagine, know, realize, think*)

I **expect** you will be impressed by the quality and the low prices.

➤ verbs related to perception and the senses (*appear, hear, look, notice, resemble, see, seem, smell*)

The supervisor **appeared** confused by the latest shift system.

➤ verbs related to possession (*belong to, consist of, constitute, contain, own, possess*)

Dinner **consisted of** a sandwich and soft drink.

➤ verbs associated with emotions and attitudes (*appreciate, hate, like, love, prefer, regret*)

We **appreciate** the time and care you have taken to draw up this proposal.

➤ verbs to do with unchangeable states (*fit, measure, weigh*)

How much **does** this pallet of goods **weigh**?

States vs. Actions

The same verb can sometimes be used to describe both a state and an action. These verbs can be used differently or change meaning in their simple and continuous forms.

States	
	I **expect** you are tired. (imagine)
	I **see** what you mean. (understand)
	When **do** you **think** you will be home? (suppose)
	This shirt **doesn't fit** me anymore. (It's the wrong size.)
	Your suitcase **weighs** 23 kilograms. (measurement)
Actions	
	I **am expecting** Jim to arrive at any moment. (waiting for)
	We **are seeing** Liz for lunch later. (meeting)
	They**'re thinking** about canceling their trip. (considering)
	The engineer **is fitting** a new safety valve. (installing)
	We **are weighing** the benefits against the risks. (evaluating)

Note: Some verbs that describe physical feelings (*feel, ache, hurt*) can be used in the simple or continuous form with no change of meaning.

● I *feel/am feeling* tired.

● My back *hurts/is hurting*.

● My feet *ache/are aching*.

Time and Tense

Verbs in the present *tense* or the past *tense* do not always relate to present *time* or past *time*.

Present simple (for past time)

President **wins** second term in office	for printed headlines
In the movie, Ms. Dobson **plays** an ageing heiress intent on revenge.	for descriptions (reviews, stories, jokes, etc.)

Present simple (for actions happening now)

Edwards **runs** forward… **shoots**… and **scores**!	for dramatic effect when commentating on sports action
I **declare** this conference formally open.	for official or ceremonial occasions

Present simple (for future time)

What time **does** your train **leave**?	for scheduled future events
Let's stay in the hotel until it **stops** raining.	after time conjunctions (*as soon as*, *before*, *once*, *until*, *when*, *while*, etc.)
Next year's overtime payments **are to be** based on gross salary.	with *be* + infinitive for officially scheduled future events

Present continuous (for future time)

Mrs. Wilson **is meeting** a client at 2:30 P.M.	for future arrangements

➤ Look for time markers such as *in ten minutes*, *tomorrow*, and *next weekend*.

The Future

There are various ways to express the future in English. The present simple can refer to scheduled future events (*We meet every week*), and the present continuous can refer to arrangements (*We're meeting at ten o'clock tomorrow*). Here are the other main ways to express the future in English.

Future simple (*will* + infinitive)

Some people are at the door. **I'll go** and let them in.	for decisions made at the moment of speaking (always contracted)
You **will have** a great time at the awards ceremony.	for things we predict will happen in the future
The next seminar **will start** at three o'clock.	for facts about the future
I **will not agree** to sell the land for such a low price.	to express refusal (often contracted as *won't*)
I **will help** you to find a new job, if you like.	to indicate willingness (in requests, offers, invitations, etc.)

be going to + infinitive

We **are going to ask** the bank for another loan.	for intentions or plans
Judging by the exit polls, this election **is going to be** very close.	to make predictions based on evidence

Future continuous

While you are away on vacation, we **will be working** hard.	for actions in progress at a time in the future
I'll be reviewing these test results later, so please do not call me.	to refer to future actions that are already arranged
Will you **be coming** to our annual conference this year?	to politely ask about future plans
John is away this week, so he **won't be needing** his parking space.	to make predictions about the future

➤ Look for time markers such as *after*, *before*, *in a week's time*, *later*, *next month*, *this time*, *when*, and *while*.

Future perfect simple

They **will have finished** the extension by August.	for actions that will be completed before a point in the future
Surely Gavin **won't have signed** the contract without telling us?	to speculate about a past situation

➤ Look for time markers such as *by the time*, *as of next week/month*, and *on Friday/weekends*.

Future perfect continuous

As of next month, I **will have been living** here for 20 years.	to refer to the duration of an action in progress at a future time
I expect the dog **will have been barking** the entire time we were out.	to speculate about a past situation

Phrases that refer to the future

We are **on the point of** agreeing on a major deal. The government is **about to** announce a new austerity plan.	For actions that will take place very soon, use *on the point of* + *-ing*, *on the verge of* + *-ing*, or *about to* + infinitive.
Our first meeting is **due to** take place on June 30.	For planned future events, use *due to* + infinitive or *set to* + infinitive.
The boss is **bound to** find out we were late again.	For future events we think are certain (though we may be wrong), use *bound to* + infinitive.

The Passive

The passive is formed by the verb *be* + past participle. Study the chart below to familiarize yourself with the various forms of the passive.

Present simple	This desk **is made** of solid mahogany.
Past simple	A heavy storm **was forecast** for that evening.
Present perfect simple	Your application for a work permit **has been approved**.
Past perfect simple	Before the accident, steps **had been taken** to improve safety.
Present continuous	Witnesses **are being sought** following a jewelry heist in central Paris.
Past continuous	The goods **were being loaded** onto trucks when we arrived.
Future simple	A revised quotation **will be sent** immediately.
Future perfect simple	We **will have been married** for ten years this April.

Note: Other forms (e.g., present perfect continuous and past perfect continuous) are not common in the passive.

Modal verbs (*should*, *might*, *could*, etc.) are also used in the passive.

- The fire at the chemical factory **could be seen** for miles around.
- These invoices **should have been sent** last week.

The passive is generally used when the object of an action (the person or thing affected by it) is more important than the agent (the person or thing doing it). Study these examples of the passive. Notice how the passive is used.

Uses

All new recruits **are required** to complete a 12-week training program.	for factual descriptions of processes or procedures
New subscribers **will be eligible** to receive a free luxury pen.	when the agent is not important or not known
Dr. Parks **was arrested** at his home late last night.	when the agent is obvious
During the trials, participants **were monitored** for signs of psychological stress.	for more formal contexts or academic writing
You **were asked** to complete this form three weeks ago.	to make statements less personal
It is thought that a rise in inflation rates is imminent.	when making general reports (*It can be seen that/It is said that*, etc.)

Sometimes it is important to state *who* is/was responsible. To include the agent in a passive sentence, add the preposition *by* after the verb.

- This painting **was done by** Picasso during his Blue Period.
- All the safety switches **should be serviced by** a qualified electrician.

Intransitive verbs (i.e., verbs that do not take an object) cannot be used in the passive.

- My cell phone **has disappeared**. (not *My cell phone ~~has been disappeared~~*.)

Causative verbs

Use *have* and *get* to show how one person causes another to carry out an action.

The director **had** an accountant **check** all the figures.	Use *have* (someone) *do* (something) to indicate authority.
Do you **get** them **to agree** to a discount?	Use *get* (someone) *to do* (something) to suggest persuasion.

need -ing vs. *have (something) done*

The office **needs painting**. Our desks **need to be replaced**. We decided to **have** our office **refurbished**.	Use *need + -ing* or *need to be* + past participle for things that it is necessary to do. Use *have* (something) *done* for things that other people do for us.

Conditionals

Conditional clauses usually contain "if" and can be divided between *real* conditionals that relate to true actions or situations, and *unreal* conditionals for imaginary or unlikely events and situations.

Real conditionals

If you **heat** water to 100 degrees, it **boils**. If you **order** online you **get** a discount.	Use the zero conditional (usually *if* + present + present) for facts and things that are certain to happen.
The engine **starts** when you **press** this button. If sales **do not improve**, the company **will go** bankrupt. We **won't receive** a bonus if we **miss** these targets. If nobody **serves** us soon, I'm **going to complain** to the manager.	The conjunction *when* can be used instead of *if*. Use the first conditional (usually *if* + present + future) for possible present and future events and their likely consequences. The structure *going to* can be used to express intention.

Real conditionals may use the present simple, present continuous, or present perfect tense.

- If you **have not achieved** the grades, you **will not be enrolled** in the program.
- If you **are not coming** to the gala dinner tonight, please **tell** me now.

It is sometimes possible to use more than one tense with no change in meaning.

- The roof **leaks** when it **rains/is raining**.
- We **will return/are returning** the goods if they **are** faulty.
- **I will meet** you at six o'clock if I **finish/have finished** this report by then.

For offers, advice, and instructions, the imperative can be used.

- **Park** over by the main entrance if there is a space.
- If you need to get in touch, **do not hesitate** to contact me.

The second conditional (usually *if* + past + *would* + infinitive) is used for less likely present and future events. Compare these two sentences:

If they **offer** me the job, I **will move** to Florida.	I think it is likely I will get the job. (first conditional)
If they **offered** me the job, I **would move** to Florida.	I am less confident I will get the job. (second conditional)

Unreal conditionals

What policies **would** you **change** if you **controlled** the company?	Use the second conditional for imaginary or hypothetical situations.
If I **did not live** so close to my office, I **would not be able** to walk to work.	
If our founder **were** alive today, she **would be** thrilled at the progress we have made.	Use the second conditional for situations or events that cannot possibly happen.
What **would** you **do** if you **were** in my position?	Use the second conditional to ask for or give advice.
If I **were** you, I **would ask** for a raise.	
If we **had arrived** on time, **we would not have missed** the start of the movie.	Use the third conditional (usually *if* + past perfect + *would have* + past participle) to express impossibility in the past.
They **would have reserved** a table for us if we **had asked** them.	

Unreal conditionals can use a variety of tenses to indicate past, present, or future time.

- Perhaps if you **had rehearsed** your presentation, you **would not feel** so nervous now.
- If you **are not coming** to the gala dinner tonight, please **tell** me.
- I **would not have agreed** to the deal if I **did not think** it was fair.

In unreal conditionals, use *could*/*might* (*have*) in place of *would* (*have*) to show possibility.

- We **could not have upgraded** our computers if we **had not received** a grant.
- If you **spoke** French, you **might have been sent** to the trade fair in Paris.

Use *if... were* + infinitive for future situations that are less likely or more hypothetical (but not with stative verbs such as *know*).

- **If** the company **were to relocate** to Boston, what **would** you **think**?

Use *if it were not for* or *were it not for* + noun phrase to show how one situation depends on another.

- **If it were not for** the rain, our vacation would be perfect.
- **Were it not for** Sue's hard work, we might have lost the contract.

Use *if it had not been for* or *had it not been for* + noun phrase to show how one situation depends on another in the past.

- **If it had not been for** your support, I could not have achieved so much.
- I would not be here today **had it not been for** the paramedics who saved my life.

I wish I **earned** more money. If only Daniel **were** here to give us some advice. I wish Jen **hadn't taken** all the brochures. I wish you **would** hurry up.	Use *I wish* + past simple to express regrets about the present. Use *I wish* + past perfect for regret about past actions. Use *I wish* + *would* to express irritation.

These time clauses can sometimes replace *if*.

In case anyone **calls**, please **take** a message. The outdoor concert will not go ahead **unless** the weather improves.	Use *in case* when there is a possibility something will happen. Use *unless* to mean *except if* or *if... not*.

These conjunctions can introduce various conditional clauses.

Even though the chairman disagreed, the motion was passed. We should insure the cargo, **even if** it is expensive. I will stay on as manager, **as long as** I get a pay raise.	Use *even though* (meaning *although*) to emphasize a contrast. Use *even if* to show that a situation should not change irrespective of other factors. Use *as long as* or *provided that* to express a condition.

Infinitives and *-ing* Forms

Infinitives and the *-ing* form are found in many sentences, in both the affirmative and the negative. The infinitive may be used with or without *to*.

Infinitives with *to*

After most adjectives

It is **impossible to predict** the outcome of the election. Why was it so **difficult to book** tickets online? Nobody was **surprised to hear** Fiona had resigned.	*able, afraid, bound, difficult, disappointed, due, easy, essential, fortunate, glad, good, great, happy, hard, impossible, interesting, kind, liable, likely, lucky, nice, pleased, possible, relieved, shocked, sorry, surprised*

After certain verbs

They have not **agreed to waive** the transfer fees. How did you **manage to convince** them to award a pay increase? The economic situation does not **appear to be** getting worse.	*afford, agree, aim, appear, arrange, ask, attempt, choose, claim, consent, dare, decide, decline, demand, deserve, expect, fail, forget, happen, hesitate, hope, hurry, intend, learn, manage, mean, need, neglect, offer, plan, prepare, pretend, promise, refuse, remember, seem, struggle, swear, tend, threaten, try, volunteer, wait, want, wish*

After certain verbs that are followed by an object

Our accountants **advised us to declare** bankruptcy. Who **encouraged you to apply** for a scholarship?	*advise, allow, appoint, cause, challenge, compel, convince, direct, enable, encourage, entitle, forbid, force, help, hire, instruct, invite, motivate, oblige, order, permit, persuade, press, recommend, remind, request, require, teach, tell, tempt, train, urge, warn*

Note: Some verbs may be followed by the infinitive or by an object + infinitive: *ask, beg, expect, hate, help, like, love, need, prefer, want, wish*.

- We **expect to make** a healthy profit from this venture.
- I **expect you to arrive** in plenty of time for the rehearsal.

After *enough* and *too*

There were not **enough people** to achieve a quorum. It was **too cold** to stay at the beach for long.	*enough = sufficient* *too = an excess*

After certain nouns

This assignment will give you the **opportunity to prove** yourself. There is no **need to repaint** the boardroom ceiling. It's **time to change** the batteries in this smoke detector.	*attempt, decision, idea, need, opportunity, plan, refusal, time*

To express purpose in noun phrases

I called this meeting **to discuss** our marketing strategy. **To process** these last-minute orders, we need more staff.	here *to = in order to*

Infinitives without *to*

After *let, make,* and *would rather/sooner*

Please do not **make me repeat** myself. Could you possibly **let us leave** early tonight? I **would rather work** here than anywhere else.	Both *let* and *make* need an object, but *would rather/sooner* do not need an object.

After some modals and semi-modals

They **could report** the matter to the authorities. With professional tradesmen, you **needn't worry** about the quality of workmanship.	*can't, could, had better, may, might, must, needn't, shall, should, will, would*

-ing Forms

When the *-ing* form is used as a noun, it is called a gerund. When it is used as a verb, it is called a participle.

(gerund)	**Swimming** is my favorite sport.
(present participle)	I saw several people **swimming** in the hotel pool.
(participle adjective)	Simon works as a part-time **swimming** instructor.

After many adjectives followed by a preposition

Would you be **interested in having** dinner tonight?

This virus is **capable of destroying** our entire computer system.

accustomed to, afraid of, angry at, ashamed of, capable of, content with, delighted at, excited about, good at, famous for, fond of, interested in, proud of, responsible for, sorry about, surprised at, tired of

After certain verbs

Did you **practice making** your speech?

I doubt we can **avoid raising** our prices again this year.

admit, avoid, can't help, can't stand, consider, contemplate, delay, deny, detest, discuss, dislike, don't mind, dread, enjoy, envisage, finish, give up, go on, hate, imagine, involve, keep, mention, mind, miss, postpone, practice, recall, resent, risk, suggest, start, stop

After certain verbs followed by a preposition

We shall **start by reviewing** last month's sales figures.

The new C.E.O is **focusing on restructuring** the company.

I have been **thinking about going** to the convention in Peru.

e.g., *begin/close/finish + by*

e.g., *depend/insist/rely + on*

e.g., *complain/talk/wonder/worry + about*

After some verbs followed by an object

I **spotted Gary sleeping** at his desk yesterday.

catch, discover, find, leave, spot

After some verbs followed by an object + preposition

The director **blames me for losing** the sale.

I would like to **congratulate you on passing** your final exams.

accuse (of), blame (for), condemn (for), congratulate (on), criticize (for), deter (from), discourage (from), forgive (for), keep (on), prevent (from), prohibit (from), punish (for), stop (from), suspect (of), thank (for)

After certain prepositions

What do you want to do **after graduating** from college?

Before coming here, where did you work?

after, before, by, despite, for, on, since, without

After verbs followed by *to* where *to* is a preposition

Hanbro Inc. **have admitted to fixing** their prices.

Shelby quickly **adapted to working** freelance.

adapt, adjust, admit, confess, look forward, object, own up, resort

After possessive adjectives

Does **my sitting** here cause you a problem?
Someone should say something about **Beryl's smoking**.

After certain nouns

Did you have any **trouble parking**?
Doctors say there is still **hope of finding** a donor.

difficulty (in), hope of, thought of, trouble

After *busy* and *worth*

The income is so low it is hardly **worth renting** our spare office.
We have been **busy interviewing** prospective candidates.

Infinitive or *-ing*

Sometimes, both the infinitive and the *-ing* form can be used.

After *attempt, begin, cease, continue, intend, propose, start*

When are you going to **start looking** for a job?
When are you going to **start to look** for a job?

There is no difference in meaning.

Note: After a verb in the continuous form, the infinitive is generally used.

- I am **beginning to understand**.

After *can't bear, can't stand, like, love, hate, prefer*

I **like to sing**.
I **like singing**.

There is no significant difference in meaning.

Notes: The *-ing* form is perhaps more general, while the infinitive is used for more specific events or occasions. The infinitive is more common in American English.

Only the infinitive can be used after *would + like/love/hate/prefer*.

- **I would love to come** to the summer fête.

After *hear, notice, observe, overhear, see, watch*

Everyone heard the referee **blow** his whistle.
Everyone heard the referee **blowing** his whistle.

for completed actions
for actions in progress

Note: The bare infinitive and *-ing* may be used, with a slight difference in meaning.

After *forget, remember, stop*

I **remembered to buy** more toner.
I **remembered buying** more toner.

I remembered, and then the action happened.
The action happened, and then I remembered.

Note: There is a significant difference, depending on which action happened first.

After *try*

I **tried to learn** origami, but it was too difficult.
Have you **tried going** to evening classes?

Use the infinitive to refer to the goal itself.
Use the gerund to refer to a method for achieving a goal.

Note: There is sometimes a difference in meaning after *try*.

Quantifiers and Pronouns

Quantifiers are used to express number and quantity. Countable nouns are nouns that can be counted (objects, people, etc.), and can be singular or plural. Uncountable nouns (materials, ideas, etc.) cannot be counted, and can only be used in the singular.

With countable nouns

There were **not many** people at the planning meeting.	*many = a lot of/lots of*
Is taking **too many** vitamins bad for your health?	*too many* is negative (here = *more than necessary*)
Shall we draw up **a few** proposals for the committee?	*a few = some*
Since the last power outage, we have encountered **few** problems.	*few = not many*
Reports indicate that **several** passersby were injured in the explosion.	*several = more than a few*
With **fewer** trucks, we will not be able to deliver all our goods.	*fewer = a smaller amount* (comparative of *few*)

With uncountable nouns

Luckily, there was **not much** traffic on the way to the stadium.	*much = a lot of/lots of/a great deal of*
I cannot take a vacation as I have **too much** work to do.	*too much* is negative (here = *more than comfortable*)
Would you like **a little** help with those bags?	*a little = some*
Simon has **very little** chance of being promoted.	*very little = hardly any*
There is **less** space in this room than I thought.	*less = not as much* (comparative of *little*)

With singular countable nouns

We should look at the strengths of **each** candidate.	Use *each* to refer to things separately.
At the gala dinner, **every** guest was given a present.	Use *every* to refer to things all together, as a group.

With plural countable nouns

This merger is in the interests of **both** companies.	Use *both* to refer to two things.

With countable and uncountable nouns

I have **some** questions I would like to ask.	Use *some* for positive sentences.
Could I have **some** chicken, please?	Use *some* for requests or invitations.
Is there **some** coffee left in that pot?	Use *some* when we expect a positive answer.
Were **any** passengers injured in the crash?	Use *any* for questions and negative sentences.
We don't have **any** time to waste.	
These drugs have **hardly any** side effects.	*hardly any = very few*
Any approved garage can carry out the repairs.	*any = it does not matter which*
There are **no** toner cartridges left.	*no = not any*
We cannot enroll **more** students in this program.	*more = a larger number*
Without **more** evidence, we cannot prosecute.	*more = a larger amount*

Don't **most** companies hire based on qualifications? **Most** research into cancer focuses on cures, not prevention.	*most = the majority of*
We only have **enough** supplies to last one week. Will we have **enough** time to visit the science museum? The concert was so crowded there was **hardly enough** space to stand up.	*enough = sufficient* *hardly enough = barely/only just sufficient*
All workers undergo rigorous security clearance tests. **All** cargo should be stowed according to the order of discharge. **All** I need is a cup of tea and something to eat.	*all = the total number/amount of* *all = the only thing*

Notes

Could **any of** these ads possibly cause offense? It was decided that **neither of** the proposals would work.	Most quantifiers (except *no* and *every*) can be used with *of* + *the/these/her*, etc., + noun.
We have **far too many** graduates who cannot find work. There is **way too much** salt in this soup!	Add *far* or *way* to intensify *too much/many*.
They had **so many** complaints that the product was withdrawn. Liam does not have **as much** experience as the other applicants. If you make **too many** mistakes, you will be dismissed.	Use *many/much* for negative sentences and questions. They can also be used in positive statements, after *so*, *as*, and *too*.

Common uncountable nouns: *advice, applause, assistance, baggage, cash, clothing, cutlery, employment, equipment, evidence, fun, furniture, garbage, harm, health, housework, housing, information, jewelry, leisure, litter, luck, luggage, machinery, money, music, news, parking, pay, pollution, publicity, research, safety, scenery, shopping, sightseeing, transportation, weather, work*

Certain nouns can be either countable (when thinking of individual units) or uncountable (when thinking of type): e.g., *cake, chicken, coffee, fruit, paint, success.*

Sometimes, nouns change their meaning when used countably and uncountably: e.g., *business, competition, glass, iron, paper, property, room, sight, space, speech, time, work.*

- It is a small apartment so there is not much **room**.
- There are only three **rooms** in the apartment.

Indefinite pronouns for people and things	
As **no one** voted in favor, the motion was rejected unanimously. Is there **anywhere** we can sit down for five minutes?	*any, every, some* + *body/one/thing/where* *no* + *body/one/thing/where*

Indefinite pronouns as subjects	
Everyone is here now, so we can begin. **Something** has to be done to improve our safety record.	Use the singular verb form.

Relative Clauses

Relative clauses give more information about people, places, or things mentioned in the main clause. There are two basic types of relative clauses: *defining* relative clauses (where the information is essential for the sentence to make sense), and *non-defining* relative clauses (where the information is extra).

Defining relative clauses	
Dr. Lee is the surgeon **who/that** will be operating.	Use *who/that* for people.
We did not get the discount **which/that** we were hoping for.	Use *which*, and more commonly *that*, for things.
The office **where** I work is on the tenth floor.	Use *where* for places.

For people, use *whose* to indicate the possessive.

- The assistant **whose** name you never remember is called Fiona.

For places, *where* can be replaced by *which* + preposition.

- The factory **where** we went was in Idaho.
- The factory **which** we went **to** was in Idaho.

The relative pronoun can be omitted if it is the object of the relative clause.

- The car (**which/that**) you sent to pick up Professor Yang was late.

The relative pronoun cannot be omitted if it is the subject of the relative clause.

- The presenter **who/that** was late was Professor Yang.
- The apartment **where** I am staying is very small.

Non-defining relative clauses	
Frank Vinny, **who** I told you about, is a first-class athlete.	These clauses give extra, nonessential information.
My car, **which** is only a year old, broke down yesterday.	There is always a comma before the pronoun.

Use *who*, *which*, or *where*, but not *that*, in non-defining relative clauses.

- Mr. Baker, **who** completed his internship last month, has been offered a job.
- The hospital, **which** had a good reputation, has been closed indefinitely.
- Histon College, **where** I studied for three years, is in California.

It is not possible to omit the pronoun in non-defining relative clauses, even when it is the object.

- The Freetown music festival, **which** we go to every year, will take place next month.
- I work in Paris, **where** our company set up its main office last year.

Which can be added to refer to a complete preceding clause.

- Tickets for the concert sold out within a hour, **which** surprised many people.

What (meaning *the things that*) is used when there is no antecedent.

- **What** surprised many people is that tickets for the concert sold out within an hour.

Participles

The present participle (*-ing*) and the past participle (*-ed*) can be used in a variety of ways.

As adjectives

Plenary speeches tend to be very **motivating**.	The present participle has an active meaning.
Delegates felt highly **motivated** after hearing the speech.	The past participle has a passive meaning.

As adverbs

Most staff stay at their desks **working** during the lunch break.

The storage closet had been left open, **crammed** with papers.

To identify a noun

The manager **interviewing** the candidates was from HR.	= *who was interviewing*
The program **launched** last year has been a success.	= *that was launched*

As adverbial clauses to give additional information

Tim came into the room **carrying** a large display board.	for actions taking place at the same time as the main clause
Completing his research, Nigel left the library.	for actions taking place just before the main clause

Note: Use the perfect participle (*having* + past participle) to emphasize the action being completed before the main clause.

- **Having looked** through the report, the director slowly shook his head.

To show a causal relationship between two actions

Realizing there was not much time left, we decided to hurry.	Use *-ing* clauses to describe reasons and results.
Not thinking it would rain, we did not bring an umbrella.	Use *not* before the participle to make the negative.

Articles

Articles come before nouns or at the start of a noun phrase, and help to specify what the noun refers to.

The indefinite article (*a/an*)

We watched **a movie** on TV last night.	for a single person or thing
Julie wants to study to be **an archaeologist**.	for professions
An apartment is usually smaller than **a house**.	for generalizations
Do you have **a pen** I can borrow?	when it does not matter which one
This novel is **a thriller** set in the 1930s.	for classifications
The rent is $750 **a month**.	for numbers and measurements (meaning *per*)

The definite article (*the*)

Who told you **the shipment** had already been sent?	for particular people or things (singular or plural)
Please close **the door** on your way out.	when it is clear what we mean
The company has chartered a yacht in **the Mediterranean**.	for oceans, seas, and rivers
Can you tell me where **the train station** is, please?	to refer to certain public places (*airport, bus station*, etc.)
We stayed at **the Plaza Hotel**, near **the Science Museum**.	for stores, hotels, museums, etc.
The president is **the man** sitting on the far right.	before nouns where the person or thing is identified
How many miles is **the earth** from **the sun**?	when there is only one of something
The train is becoming cheaper these days.	with a singular noun to describe a class of things
What cultural influences did **the Italians** bring?	for groups of people or nationalities
Sue was brought up in **the Netherlands**.	for plural countries
We went to **the West Indies** on vacation last year.	for islands, mountain ranges (*the Rockies*), and regions (*the Far East*)

Zero article

Cell phones must be switched off before you enter.	for people or things in general
Loyalty is a quality we admire in this company.	for generalizations using abstract nouns
Did you major in **physics**?	for school subjects
Dr. Pieterson worked in **Asia** for ten years.	for continents
Lake Tanganyika in Africa is over 600 kilometers long.	for lakes, towns, cities, and most countries

Notes

The cell phones sold in that store are overpriced. **The loyalty** of our staff is the key to our success.	The definite article **the** is used when referring to something specific, or that has been previously referred to.
Ted is in **the hospital**.	In American English, use *in the hospital* rather than *in hospital*. Some common phrases that use zero article include *in bed, at college, on duty, at home, on location, in prison, on stage, on tour, on vacation,* and *at work*.
Would you like **a coffee**? Use **the coffee** in this packet. I do not drink **coffee**.	Some nouns can be countable, or uncountable (or use zero article) with a change in meaning.

Subject-Verb Agreement

Every verb must "agree" with its subject. This means that if the subject is singular, a singular verb must be used, and if the subject is plural, then a plural verb must be used—even when separated.

Singular subjects	
Every delegate **needs** to have a badge.	for *every*
Each person here **is** from a different company.	for *each*
Whoever **finishes** the race first will win a prize.	for *whoever/whatever,* etc.
Neither of the candidates **is** suitable.	for *either/neither (of…)*
If anyone **has** a problem, just let me know.	for *anyone, everywhere,* etc.
Twenty miles **is** the most I have ever run.	for distances
Is 28 days the standard cooling-off period?	for lengths of time
Fifty thousand dollars **is** a lot of money.	for money and prices
Four kilograms **is** not too overweight, is it?	for weights
Three times nine **is** twenty-seven.	for calculations

Plural subjects	
A couple of viable solutions **were** presented to us.	for *a couple of, a group of, a lot of, a number of,* etc.
The French **take** great pride in their culinary expertise.	for groups or classes of people
All our new drilling machines **run** on biofuel.	after *all*
Few **believe** that the economic situation will improve.	after *few*
The directors and the president **were** in agreement.	or *and/both… and*

Notes:

Some subjects may take the singular or plural, depending on what they refer to (*a lot of, all, any, more, most, none, some,* etc.).

- None of the music **was** to my taste.
- Unfortunately, none of the assistants **were** able to help me.

Variations occur when speaking in general or referring to a group.

- A number of mistakes **are** made on each shift.
- However, the number of mistakes **is** decreasing.

For sentences with *or/nor*, and *not only… but also*, the verb matches the subject that is closest to it.

- Neither the union leaders nor the managing director **wants** to take legal action.
- Neither the managing director nor the union leaders **want** to take legal action.

MINI TEST Grammar

Choose the most appropriate answer: (A), (B), (C), or (D), to complete each sentence.

1. Does anyone know who the black leather briefcase that has been left by the front entrance _____ to?
   (A) is belonging
   (B) belong
   (C) belonging
   (D) belongs

2. Because there have been _____ problems with the design of the chassis, the launch of our new XR2 diesel buses has been delayed a further three months.
   (A) less
   (B) a few
   (C) any
   (D) little

3. If you would like to make a formal complaint about the treatment you have received, please contact Mr. Ito, who _____ take up the matter on your behalf.
   (A) is to
   (B) will
   (C) has
   (D) would

4. Demolition of the old factory will begin on schedule next month, _____ permission has been granted by the local authorities.
   (A) even though
   (B) unless
   (C) as long as
   (D) except for

5. The C.E.O. of Helsbring Group has asked _____ to show him around the city while he is visiting this week.
   (A) our
   (B) we
   (C) us
   (D) ours

6. Several delegates missed the last shuttle bus from the hotel to the conference site, but at least they _____ get a taxi without difficulty.
   (A) had to
   (B) needed to
   (C) were able to
   (D) would

7. Why have there been _____ many complaints to the head office this year from our customers in Europe?
   (A) too
   (B) so
   (C) far
   (D) very

8. May I ask if Mr. Wilson _____ the use of a car while he is staying with us?
   (A) will be needing
   (B) is needing
   (C) will have needed
   (D) is bound to need

9. Ever since reports of the mine closure leaked to the press, we _____ protests from the workforce regarding the possibility of compulsory layoffs.
   (A) expect
   (B) are expecting
   (C) have been expecting
   (D) will expect

10. The seminar on Entrepreneurship and Innovation, _____ is to be given by Prof. Michelle Brent, will be held in Training Room C at 4:30 P.M. tomorrow afternoon.
    (A) that
    (B) where
    (C) who
    (D) which

---

1. Ⓐ Ⓑ Ⓒ Ⓓ   4. Ⓐ Ⓑ Ⓒ Ⓓ   7. Ⓐ Ⓑ Ⓒ Ⓓ   10. Ⓐ Ⓑ Ⓒ Ⓓ
2. Ⓐ Ⓑ Ⓒ Ⓓ   5. Ⓐ Ⓑ Ⓒ Ⓓ   8. Ⓐ Ⓑ Ⓒ Ⓓ
3. Ⓐ Ⓑ Ⓒ Ⓓ   6. Ⓐ Ⓑ Ⓒ Ⓓ   9. Ⓐ Ⓑ Ⓒ Ⓓ

11. Since we could not get the librarian
    .... the fine, we had to pay $16 for
    the overdue books.
    (A) to waive
    (B) waiving
    (C) waive
    (D) waives

12. The bright red files are all marked highly
    confidential, which means anyone without
    authority .... look inside them.
    (A) has not managed to
    (B) does not need to
    (C) should not have to
    (D) is not supposed to

13. The problem appears to be that whenever
    the control bar to the upper handle is
    depressed, the recoil spring attached to
    the flywheel ....
    (A) is unwinding
    (B) unwinds
    (C) unwound
    (D) to unwind

14. Trisha Robbins, speaking on behalf of all
    investors, reaffirmed that she .... the
    directors would agree to issue shares on
    the stock exchange.
    (A) wants
    (B) wishes
    (C) would like
    (D) likes

15. If it had not been possible to restore power
    within 24 hours, do you know what level
    of compensation the energy company
    .... liable to pay out?
    (A) is to be
    (B) was being
    (C) has been
    (D) would have been

16. At the press conference, the chairman
    announced that the company planned
    .... its telecommunications network
    subsidiary.
    (A) selling
    (B) having sold
    (C) to sell
    (D) sale

17. Have you .... drawn up a proper
    business plan, after all these years?
    (A) ever
    (B) never
    (C) still
    (D) yet

18. The marble floor in the rear stairwell has
    just been polished, so please ask guests to
    take care when exiting .... they slip.
    (A) if
    (B) when
    (C) unless
    (D) in case

19. The annual summer vacation could not
    have come at a better time, as the entire
    production team .... hard all year
    without a break.
    (A) had been working
    (B) has worked
    (C) were working
    (D) are working

20. Although there were a number of
    witnesses to the robbery, ... were
    willing to come forward and testify in court.
    (A) not any
    (B) nobody
    (C) no one
    (D) none

11. (A) (B) (C) (D)   14. (A) (B) (C) (D)   17. (A) (B) (C) (D)   20. (A) (B) (C) (D)
12. (A) (B) (C) (D)   15. (A) (B) (C) (D)   18. (A) (B) (C) (D)
13. (A) (B) (C) (D)   16. (A) (B) (C) (D)   19. (A) (B) (C) (D)

21. Before the staff meeting finishes, our sales director will take the opportunity .... the business plan for the coming year.
    (A) summarize
    (B) summarizing
    (C) to summarize
    (D) having summarized

22. The product we are most optimistic about for this season is Red Deer, which is a new vitamin health drink, rich in .... vitamins and antioxidants.
    (A) every
    (B) both
    (C) each
    (D) any

23. Just as for most limited companies, at the end of the financial year Heekin and Associates will be required to have its accounts .... by an independent chartered accountant.
    (A) audited
    (B) auditing
    (C) audit
    (D) audits

24. The safety inspector insisted that .... operators of handheld chainsaws at the timber plant be given protective clothing and footwear.
    (A) every
    (B) all
    (C) each
    (D) either

25. A table has been booked for 12:30 P.M. at Leonardo's, the restaurant .... I told you about last week.
    (A) what
    (B) where
    (C) which
    (D) whose

26. In the end we decided to wire the money to the client directly from our bank, as the rate offered by the foreign exchange broker was .... disadvantageous.
    (A) a lot
    (B) as much
    (C) so many
    (D) even more

27. Ms. Takahashi's flight has been canceled due to thick fog at Osaka Airport, so she .... here for dinner later tonight.
    (A) will not be
    (B) has not been
    (C) is not being
    (D) was not to be

28. The board recommends that a thorough study of the market for reconditioned ventilation units be undertaken in order to confirm that $3,500 .... a fair price for each unit.
    (A) are
    (B) is
    (C) be
    (D) has

29. None of the progress we have made on this project would have been possible .... it not for the tremendous hard work and determination of all the staff.
    (A) were
    (B) had
    (C) is
    (D) has

30. Quite apart from the fact that it has a positive impact on workforce performance, employers have a legal responsibility to look after .... of all their workers.
    (A) health
    (B) a health
    (C) healthiness
    (D) the health

21. Ⓐ Ⓑ Ⓒ Ⓓ 24. Ⓐ Ⓑ Ⓒ Ⓓ 27. Ⓐ Ⓑ Ⓒ Ⓓ 30. Ⓐ Ⓑ Ⓒ Ⓓ
22. Ⓐ Ⓑ Ⓒ Ⓓ 25. Ⓐ Ⓑ Ⓒ Ⓓ 28. Ⓐ Ⓑ Ⓒ Ⓓ
23. Ⓐ Ⓑ Ⓒ Ⓓ 26. Ⓐ Ⓑ Ⓒ Ⓓ 29. Ⓐ Ⓑ Ⓒ Ⓓ

31. Any applicants who .... a reply from the selection committee within two weeks may assume that their application has been unsuccessful.

(A) are not receiving
(B) will not receive
(C) have not received
(D) would not receive

32. .... as it was to see so many doctors at the convention, it was disappointing that several renowned experts in the field of neurology were unable to attend.

(A) Gratified
(B) Gratifying
(C) Gratify
(D) Gratifies

33. Using viral marketing, we were able to promote the company effectively and increase brand awareness among a wider audience than would otherwise .... possible.

(A) to be
(B) had to be
(C) have been
(D) been

34. The attached standard letter template .... to be used as the basis for all official outgoing correspondence until further notice.

(A) shall
(B) will
(C) is
(D) does

35. The consul assured local residents caught up in the conflict that all possible measures to protect their safety ....

(A) were being taken
(B) have been taking
(C) are taken
(D) had taken

36. After he was sued for malpractice, there was a general consensus among the other partners at the practice that it was time for Dr. Pearson .... his job.

(A) quitting
(B) quit
(C) quits
(D) to quit

37. Many of the junior faculty members at the university have been complaining that they are expected to work .... harder than those in senior positions.

(A) as
(B) more
(C) far
(D) so

38. This production manages to bring the modern-day parallels with medieval France to life, while sticking to the original text .... faithfully that it never seems to miss a beat.

(A) such
(B) ever
(C) still
(D) so

39. Ms. Cho said that .... she has worked with in her time here, especially in the HR department, has been hard-working and conscientious.

(A) whoever
(B) everyone
(C) anybody
(D) someone

40. The free-standing BX23 dishwasher .... on your company's website is exactly what we have been looking for.

(A) featured
(B) feature
(C) featuring
(D) to feature

31.	Ⓐ	Ⓑ	Ⓒ	Ⓓ	**34.**	Ⓐ	Ⓑ	Ⓒ	Ⓓ	**37.**	Ⓐ	Ⓑ	Ⓒ	Ⓓ	**40.**	Ⓐ	Ⓑ	Ⓒ	Ⓓ
32.	Ⓐ	Ⓑ	Ⓒ	Ⓓ	**35.**	Ⓐ	Ⓑ	Ⓒ	Ⓓ	**38.**	Ⓐ	Ⓑ	Ⓒ	Ⓓ					
33.	Ⓐ	Ⓑ	Ⓒ	Ⓓ	**36.**	Ⓐ	Ⓑ	Ⓒ	Ⓓ	**39.**	Ⓐ	Ⓑ	Ⓒ	Ⓓ	Score .... /40				

VOCABULARY

This section reviews the vocabulary you need to improve your score on Part 5 and Part 6 of the TOEIC® test.

Study this *Vocabulary* section carefully and use it as a handy reference. It is a detailed summary of the main lexical areas commonly featured in the TOEIC® test. Take the Mini Test to help identify your strengths and weaknesses. Notice what problems you have, and focus on the areas you need to improve.

Word Forms

In Parts 5 and 6 of the TOEIC test, you are often required to select the correct part of speech in order to complete a sentence. The form of a word varies according to the suffixes and prefixes used. Recognizing the form of verbs, nouns, adjectives, and adverbs is an important skill.

Prefixes

Prefixes are added to the beginning of a word in order to change the meaning, while usually keeping the same part of speech.

Verb prefixes

Prefix	Meaning/Use	Examples
co-	together	coexist, cooperate, coordinate
de-	do the opposite of	deregulate, deselect, devalue
dis-	gives the opposite meaning	disagree, disallow, disappear, discontinue, dislike, dissolve
en-	make	encourage, enforce, enlighten, enlist, enliven
fore-	earlier, before	foreclose, foresee, forewarn
inter-	between	interact, intermingle, interrupt, intervene
mis-	badly, or wrongly	misappropriate, misbehave, misinform, misjudge, mislead, misplace, mistake, misunderstand
out-	exceed	outbid, outdo, outperform
over-	too much	overflow, overpay, overreact, oversleep, overwork
pre-	before	predate, predict, prejudge, preview
re-	again	reappear, rearrange, reassess, rebuild, re-evaluate, refinance, restructure, retype, revise, revisit, rewrite
sub-	below	subcontract, subdivide, submerge
trans-	across, through	transform, translate, transplant
un-	gives the opposite meaning	undo, undress, unfasten, unlock
under-	not enough	underfund, undersell, undervalue

Noun prefixes

Prefix	Meaning/Use	Examples
anti-	against	antibiotic, anticlimax, antidote, antithesis
auto-	referring to one	autobiography, autograph, autonomy
co-	joint	co-founder, co-pilot, co-signatory, coworker
counter-	against	counter-intelligence, counterpart, counter-revolution
dis-	the opposite of	discomfort, dislike, dissatisfaction, distaste, distraction
ex-	former	ex-chair, ex-president, ex-wife
hyper-	extreme	hyperactivity, hypermarket, hypertension

in-	the opposite of	incompatibility, incompetence, ineptitude, insomnia
inter-	between	interaction, interruption, intervention
mal-	not good	malfunction, malnutrition, malpractice
mis-	bad	misconduct, misfortune, mismanagement
neo-	new	neologism, neonatal
post-	after	postgraduate, post-mortem, postscript
pro-	before	prologue, pronoun
re-	again	reaction, readjustment, reassessment, replay, revision
semi-	half	semicircle, semicolon
sub-	below	sub-zero, subdivision, submarine
sur-	over	surcharge, surfeit, surtax
under-	too little	under-development
vice-	deputy	vice-captain, vice-chairman, vice president

Adjective prefixes

Prefix	Meaning/Use	Examples
anti-	against	antisocial, anti-war
bi-	two	biannual, bifocal, bilateral, bilingual
dis-	against	dishonest, disgraceful, disloyal, dissatisfied, dissimilar
hyper-	excessive	hypercritical, hypersensitive
il-	not (before *l*)	illegal, illegible, illiterate, illogical
im-	not (before *m* or *p*)	immature, impatient, imperfect, impolite, impossible, improbable
in-	not	inadequate, inattentive, incoherent, incompatible, inconvenient, inefficient, inhumane, invisible
ir-	not (before *r*)	irrational, irregular, irrelevant, irreplaceable, irresponsible, irreversible
multi-	having many	multicultural, multifunctional, multilingual, multimedia, multinational, multi-purpose
non-	not	nonexistent, nonfiction, non-refundable, nonsensical
pro-	in favor of	pro-government
semi-	half or in part	semicircular, semiconscious, semi-final, semi-skilled, semi-retired
un-	not	unappealing, unfit, unfortunate, unhygienic, unjust, unpopular, unwilling
under-	too little	undercooked, underemployed, underpaid

Suffixes

Suffixes are added to the end of a word, and usually change the form of the word (e.g., from a noun to an adjective).

Verb suffixes		
Suffix	**Meaning/Use**	**Examples**
-ate	become	accelerate, activate, aggravate, captivate, collaborate, commiserate, demonstrate, devastate, differentiate, duplicate, elevate, eradicate, fabricate, fascinate, incorporate, initiate, insulate, isolate, liberate, liquidate, mitigate, originate, reciprocate, regulate, segregate
-en	make or become added to make verbs from adjectives and nouns	awaken, broaden, darken, deepen, fasten, flatten, frighten, lengthen, lighten, liven, moisten, ripen, sharpen, shorten, strengthen, sweeten, weaken, widen
-ify/-efy	make or become added to make verbs from adjectives and nouns	amplify, beautify, certify, clarify, classify, electrify, exemplify, falsify, fortify, intensify, justify, magnify, modify, notify, petrify, purify, quantify, rarefy, ratify, simplify, solidify, specify, stupefy, testify, terrify, unify, verify
-ize	become or make	acclimatize, apologize, authorize, capitalize, centralize, characterize, computerize, criticize, emphasize, energize, generalize, hospitalize, immunize, industrialize, legalize, modernize, monopolize, neutralize, normalize, organize, pressurize, prioritize, sanitize, scrutinize, specialize, stabilize, sterilize, symbolize, sympathize, synchronize, theorize, utilize, vandalize, visualize

Noun suffixes		
Suffix	**Meaning/Use**	**Examples**
-acy	state or quality of	accuracy, conspiracy, delicacy, diplomacy, illiteracy, intricacy, legacy, literacy, obstinacy, privacy
-age	state, act, or collection of	baggage, breakage, forage, package, salvage, storage, wastage
-al	act or process of added to some verbs to make nouns	arrival, denial, dismissal, proposal, refusal
-ance	state or condition of	abundance, acceptance, allowance, appearance, arrogance, assistance, attendance, clearance, defiance, elegance, endurance, extravagance, fragrance, ignorance, instance, maintenance, relevance, reluctance, resistance, significance, tolerance, vengeance
-ancy	state or quality of	expectancy, hesitancy, militancy, occupancy, redundancy, vacancy

-ant	person or agent	assistant, consultant, informant
-dom	state or quality of, or position	freedom, kingdom, wisdom
-ence	action, state, or quality of	absence, competence, dependence, eminence, impudence, incoherence, insistence, interference, obedience, occurrence, persistence, preference, sequence
-ency	state or quality of	currency, efficiency, emergency, expediency, frequency, leniency, urgency
-er	someone who	advertiser, astronomer, buyer, carrier, explorer, interpreter, retailer, ruler, teacher, trainer, worker
-ery	relating to, quality of, or place where	bravery, bribery, discovery, misery, nursery, recovery, refinery, robbery, stationery
-hood	state or quality of added to make abstract nouns from nouns	adulthood, childhood, livelihood, motherhood, neighborhood
-ice	condition or quality of	justice, malice
-ion	relating to	discussion, election, emission
-ism	belief or manner of	altruism, feminism, heroism
-ist	someone who	economist, journalist, pianist, psychologist, realist, soloist, typist, violinist
-ity	condition or quality of	ability, authenticity, capacity, civility, clarity, curiosity, equality, flexibility, publicity, responsibility, similarity, vanity, veracity
-ment	state, process, or result of added to make nouns from verbs	amendment, employment, enjoyment, entertainment, excitement, procurement, punishment, refreshment
-ness	condition or state of added to make abstract nouns from adjectives	consciousness, darkness, goodness, kindness, stubbornness, weakness
-or	someone who	director, governor, instigator, operator, supervisor, survivor
-ship	quality of, or position	citizenship, fellowship, friendship, internship, kinship, leadership, relationship
-sion	state of	admission, concussion, expansion, inclusion
-sy	state or quality of	controversy, courtesy, fantasy, heresy, jealousy
-tion	state or act of added to make nouns from verbs	administration, admiration, alteration, celebration, communication, demonstration, deviation, inspiration, justification, pollution, separation, transition

Adjective suffixes

Suffix	Meaning/Use	Examples
-able	can be done added to make adjectives from verbs	avoidable, countable, drinkable, expandable, fashionable, payable, portable, presentable, reliable, replaceable, suitable, washable
-al	relating to added to make adjectives from verbs or nouns	accidental, annual, beneficial, brutal, central, commercial, economical, emotional, financial, gradual, industrial, influential, legal, manual, musical, neutral, optional, political, provincial, regional, universal
-ary	relating to, or quality of	auxiliary, cautionary, complimentary, contrary, customary, honorary, legendary, momentary, ordinary, primary, revolutionary, secondary, stationary, temporary
-ate	quality of added to make adjectives from verbs or nouns	adequate, commensurate, compassionate, considerate, disparate, fortunate, legitimate, moderate, obstinate
-en	made of, or state or quality of	ashen, frozen, wooden
-ent	relating to, or quality of added to make adjectives from verbs	confident, dependent, different, eloquent, equivalent, excellent, latent, urgent
-ful	full of added to make adjectives from nouns or verbs	beautiful, delightful, dutiful, hopeful, peaceful, resourceful, shameful, skillful, thoughtful
-ible	can be done	accessible, edible, flexible, legible, permissible, sensible, visible
-ic	the nature of added to make adjectives from nouns	athletic, heroic, historic, metallic, mythic, poetic, scenic, scientific, symbolic
-ical	the nature of added to make adjectives from nouns	alphabetical, economical, logical, musical, practical, statistical
-ing	quality of	amazing, amusing, confusing, entertaining, interesting, relaxing, surprising, vexing
-ish	origin, nature	childish, foolish, selfish, sluggish
-ive	causing, quality of added to make adjectives from verbs	active, attractive, conclusive, creative, destructive, effective, extensive, imaginative, impressive, persuasive, repetitive, selective
-less	without added to make adjectives from nouns or verbs	careless, endless, homeless, hopeless, mindless, painless, thoughtless, useless, worthless
-ly	quality of	costly, friendly, orderly
-ory	relating to	advisory, contradictory, directory, preparatory

-ous	quality of added to make adjectives from nouns	advantageous, anxious, contagious, continuous, courageous, courteous, dangerous, envious, famous, furious, invidious, jealous, ludicrous, mysterious, nauseous, nervous, nutritious, ominous, perilous, poisonous, spacious, victorious
-worthy	quality of added to make adjectives from nouns	creditworthy, newsworthy, praiseworthy, roadworthy, trustworthy
-y	having, like added to make adjectives from nouns	bumpy, chilly, filthy, foggy, gaudy, greedy, juicy, lucky, miserly, pithy, pricey, risky, shiny, shoddy, sleazy, sturdy, witty

Notes:

The ending -ish can be added to adjectives (and also ages or times) to make them less precise (e.g., *red – reddish*). A hyphen is required in some cases.

- We have arranged to meet around nine-**ish** tomorrow morning.

Most adjectives are gradable, meaning they can be used in the comparative form and after adverbs like *fairly, very*, and *extremely* to indicate a greater or lesser degree (e.g., *fairly expensive, very persuasive, extremely fortunate*).

However, some adjectives cannot be graded in this way, usually because they already reflect a maximum degree (e.g., *impossible, amazing, massive*). We cannot say ~~fairly~~ impossible, ~~very~~ amazing, or ~~extremely~~ massive. If we want to intensify non-gradable adjectives, we often use *really*.

- The concert we went to last night was **really** amazing.

Adverb suffixes

Suffix	Meaning/Use	Examples
-ally	manner or degree added to make adverbs from adjectives	annually, enthusiastically
-ly	in the manner of	busily, clearly, daily, eagerly, faintly, fortunately, monthly, neatly, ordinarily, partially, precisely, relatively, slightly, weekly
-ward	in the direction of	backward, downward, forward, northward, upward
-wide	throughout an area	countrywide, nationwide, statewide, worldwide
-wise	in the manner of, pertaining to	clockwise, health-wise, lengthwise

Notes:

Some adverbs are irregular.

- You will have to act **fast** and try **hard** to if you are to do **well** in the selection test.

Adverbs of degree (e.g., *absolutely, completely, totally*) are used to indicate amount, and are usually only used with gradable adjectives.

The adverb *quite* can have two distinct meanings:

| (fairly) | We were *quite* pleased with the result. |
| (completely) | You are *quite* right. |

Words that Look Alike

Some questions on Parts 5 and 6 of the TOEIC test require you to choose between words that look similar, although their meanings are different. Words might look similar if they share the same prefix, suffix, or root, or because they have similar spelling. Study these examples. Use your dictionary to check the meaning of any words you do not know.

Same prefix

disapprove, disassemble, disassociate, disavow
irrational, irregular, irrelevant, irreverent
miscalculate, miscarry, misconceive, misconstrue
monogram, monologue, monopoly, monotony
overlap, overlie, overload, overlook
posterior, posterity, postscript, posture
realignment, realism, realization, reallocation
subject, submit, subside, subsist

Same suffix

abolishment, accomplishment, admonishment, astonishment
abstain, pertain, refrain, restrain
actual, factual, habitual, residual
ascribe, inscribe, prescribe, transcribe
calcification, calibration, certification, classification
indelible, inedible, ineligible, infallible
renegotiate, repatriate, repudiate, retaliate
scandalize, serialize, socialize, specialize

Same root

ascertain, certain, certainly, certify
conclusive, included, reclusive, secluded
credential, creditable, creditor, incredible
dissatisfaction, faction, factor, manufacture
enumerate, innumerable, numerate, numerous
hospice, hospital, hospitality, inhospitable
immortality, mortal, mortician, mortification
injection, interjection, projectile, trajectory

Same beginning and end

acceleration, accentuation, acclimatization, accreditation
amiably, ardently, astutely, avidly
concurrence, consequence, convalescence, convergence
exclamation, expectation, explanation, exploration
incalculable, inconsiderable, inconsolable, incontestable
productive, progressive, prospective, provocative
referral, refusal, removal, renewal
transferred, transfixed, transformed, transmitted

Similar spelling

accent, ascent, ascertain, assent
calcify, certify, clarify, classify
capital, clavicle, clerical, clinical
esteem, extinct, extract, extreme
immunity, impunity, impurity, mutiny
inveterate, venerate, veteran, veterinarian
refuge, refugee, refuse, refute
thorough, though, through, trough

Words with Similar Meanings

Words with similar meanings are called *synonyms*. On Parts 5 and 6 of the TOEIC test, you sometimes have to choose between various synonyms in order to complete a sentence. Which word best fits a sentence can depend on its exact meaning, and the structure of the sentence. Study this example. The four words in bold are similar in meaning, but they cannot be used interchangeably.

As a writer, Lebussier first came to **prominence** in the 1990s.
Dr. Fredericks has an excellent **reputation** in the field of chemical engineering.
Teachers in some countries enjoy a higher social **status** than elsewhere.
The vice president is a man of **distinction** and charisma, slated for the very top.

Use a dictionary to review the use and meaning of these groups of words.

abandon, disregard, neglect, overlook
abide, endure, tolerate, undergo
abolish, demolish, destroy, devastate
absolve, excuse, exonerate, vindicate
abstinence, control, moderation, restraint
abundant, ample, comprehensive, inclusive
accept, acquire, obtain, receive
acclaim, admiration, commendation, praise
accompany, escort, guide, usher
accounts, data, files, records
accuse, blame, charge, indict
ache, pain, soreness, twinge
achieve, execute, perform, realize
acknowledge, admit, compromise, concede
adhesion, commitment, compulsion, devotion
adroit, deft, dexterous, nimble
advance, credit, loan, mortgage
allege, assert, claim, stress
allege, claim, contend, imply
alike, comparable, equivalent, identical
alteration, discrepancy, divergence, variation
amount, capacity, extent, quantity
analyze, detect, observe, scrutinize
ancient, antique, archaic, dated
appreciation, approval, authorization,
   endorsement
apprentice, novice, subordinate, trainee
apt, liable, likely, prone
aptitude, capacity, competence, proficiency
arise, augment, boost, ensue
arrears, debit, debt, overdraft
assert, command, decree, proclaim
assess, deem, estimate, gauge
assist, expedite, facilitate, support
associate, implicate, insinuate, involve
assumption, hypothesis, premise, theory
auspicious, beneficial, favorable, propitious
ban, forbid, prohibit, veto
barrier, drawback, hitch, obstruction
betray, deceive, delude, mislead
bias, chauvinism, injustice, prejudice
bill, fee, rate, tab
bizarre, distinctive, remarkable, unique
blemish, deficiency, flaw, imperfection
booming, fertile, lush, thriving
breakthrough, creation, discovery, invention
bystander, eyewitness, observer, spectator
cargo, consignment, freight, load

cargo, goods, provisions, supplies
categorize, label, orchestrate, systematize
celebrity, genius, legend, prodigy
charming, picturesque, quaint, scenic
check, frustrate, prevent, thwart
coach, instructor, lecturer, tutor
coercion, domination, repression, supremacy
collaboration, cooperation, partnership, teamwork
collective, common, mutual, reciprocal
commotion, muddle, tumult, upheaval
confrontation, hostility, opposition, resistance
conscientious, precise, rigorous, scrupulous
conservation, maintenance, preservation,
   retention
constancy, integrity, reliability, veracity
constraint, obligation, prerequisite, requirement
convivial, cordial, genial, hospitable
correct, remedy, renovate, repair
cost, price, value, worth
coverage, exposure, leak, revelation
custom, habit, routine, tradition
decline, desist, forsake, relinquish
delay, interrupt, linger, suspend
deliberate, memorize, muse, reminisce
delicate, faint, familiar, intimate
depreciate, diminish, minimize, weaken
deserve, justify, merit, warrant
development, enhancement, enrichment,
   supplement
diligence, perseverance, preparedness,
   watchfulness
directive, ordinance, regulation, statute
discard, dispose, eradicate, reject
discharge, exonerate, forgive, vindicate
distinctive, eccentric, idiosyncratic, weird
diversity, mixture, selection, variety
dormant, quiescent, quiet, sluggish
elucidate, exemplify, expound, illustrate
encourage, promote, soar, sustain
equitable, fair, impartial, just
erratic, inconsistent, patchy, unreliable
ethical, just, moral, proper
evolution, headway, progression, sequence
exchangeable, negotiable, redeemable,
   transferable
excursion, expedition, journey, voyage
exemplar, hypothesis, paradigm, premise
expedient, functional, pragmatic, serviceable

fault, guilt, liability, responsibility		infuse, permeate, pervade, saturate
formula, method, scheme, stratagem		irremediable, irreparable, irretrievable, irreversible
hazard, peril, risk, vulnerability		lawful, legal, legitimate, official
hinder, inhibit, repress, stifle		lean, meager, slight, slim
impulse, inkling, instinct, suspicion		logical, rational, reasonable, sensible
indignant, resentful, vengeful, vindictive		prevalent, ubiquitous, universal, widespread

Prepositions

Sometimes on Parts 5 and 6 of the TOEIC test, you have to complete a sentence by choosing between various prepositions. To select the correct preposition, you need to look at the nouns, adjectives/participles, and verbs before and after the blank.

Prepositions of time		
at	times	at 7:30 A.M.
	times of day	at breakfast/lunchtime/midday at night
	holidays	at New Year's/Thanksgiving
	present time	at the moment/present
in	parts of the day	in the morning/afternoon/evening(s)
	seasons	in spring/summer/fall/winter
	months, years	in May in 2013
	decades, centuries	in the '90s/the 1950s in the twenty-first century
	time in the future (meaning *within*)	in two hours/three weeks in a moment
on	dates	on the 12th/October 30
	days	on Monday on Sunday afternoon

Note: The word *time* can be used in a variety of ways, with different prepositions.

Please try to be **on time** for the meeting.	punctual (not late)
Will you arrive **in time** for lunch?	before
At times I wonder why I took this job.	sometimes
The security light must be left on **all the time**.	continuously
Our rivals undercut our prices **time after time**.	repeatedly
Please wait here **for the time being**.	for the moment
The server needs to be rebooted **from time to time**.	periodically/at intervals
It's **high time** we updated our catalog.	should have happened already

Prepositions of place		
at	addresses	at 7234 East Avenue
	buildings	at the train station/post office
	particular points	at the bus stop/main entrance
	places	at college/home/the office/work
	specific locations	at the bottom/end/top
in	countries/states	in Australia/New South Wales
	cities	in Detroit
	buildings/places (meaning *inside*)	in the hotel/a taxi
	rooms	in the kitchen/bathroom/bedroom
	containers	in the storage closet/bottom drawer
	seas/oceans, etc.	in the Pacific
	continents	in Asia/Europe
on	streets	on Main Street
	floors of a building	on the twelfth floor
	coasts	on the West Coast
	certain locations	on the corner/a bus

Note: Other uses of *at*/*in*/*on* include:

at first/last/least/most/once/short notice

in danger/debt/difficulty/general/line/part/particular/private/public/the middle of/trouble/writing

on business/foot/purpose/sale/schedule/television/vacation

Be careful of:

at the end (conclusion) vs. **in the end** (finally)

in the way (obstructing) vs. **on the way** (traveling to)

Commonly confused prepositions

➤ *after*/*afterward*

After the meal, the director gave a speech.	preposition used before a noun
We had a meal, and the director gave a speech **afterward**.	adverb, usually at the end

Note: This rule also applies to *before*/*beforehand*.

➤ *beside*/*besides*

Who was the woman sitting **beside** Carl?	next to
Besides Karen, who else was at the meeting?	in addition to/apart from

➤ *between*/*among*

Let's keep this **between** you **and** me.	referring to two
Morale **among** the workforce has never been higher.	referring to three or more

➤ *between… and*/*from… to*

Staff are recruited **between** October **and** November.	after one time and before another
The performance review looked at sales **from** 2012 **to** 2013.	giving a range

➤ *by*

Please try to be here **by** midday.	before a certain point
The ladder is over there **by** the window.	= *beside/next to*
Will they be shipping the goods **by** sea or **by** air?	to indicate means of transportation

Note: Other uses of *by* include:

by accident/chance/check/credit card/day/e-mail/far/hand/letter/mistake/surprise

➤ *during*/*while*

Feel free to ask me more questions **during** the break.	within a period of time
Everyone felt nervous **while** the inspectors were at the plant.	conjunction, meaning *throughout the time that something is happening*

➤ *for*/*since*

Mr. Tims has been waiting **for** half an hour.	a period of time
Diane has been our accountant **since** 2010.	a point of time

Note: *for* is also used to indicate purpose:

- Julia has gone to the stockroom **for** some more toner.

Note: Other uses of *for* include:

for free/good/rent/sale

➤ *like*/*alike*

The Grand, **like** the Plaza, is a very large hotel.	= *similar to*
The movie is suitable for children and adults **alike**.	adverb, meaning *equally*

➤ *until*

I am afraid you cannot check in **until** 3:00 P.M.	up to a certain point

---

Verb + preposition

account for	believe in	consent to	dream about/of
accuse of	belong to	consist of	dress in
adjust to	benefit from	consult with	elaborate on
admit to	care about/for	contribute to	emerge from
advise against	cater to	cooperate with	engage in
afford to	chat to/with	cope with	escape from
agree on/to/with	check for/to	count on	fight against/for/with
apologize for/to	choose between	deal with	focus on
appear to	claim to	decide against/on/to	forget about
apply for	collide with	dedicate to	hear about/from/of
approve of	comment on	depend on	hide from
argue about/with	compare to/with	despair of	hope for
arrange for	compete for/with	develop into	insist on
arrive at/in	complain about/to	differ from	insure against
beg for	concentrate on	disapprove of	interfere in/with
begin by/with	confess to	divide among/between	invest in

joke about	provide for	separate from	turn to
know about/of	quarrel about/with	shout at	volunteer for/to
learn from	react to	specialize in	vote for
long for	recover from	stand for	wait for/on
look forward to	refer to	stare at	wish for
object to	rely on	stem from	withdraw from
operate on	resign from	subscribe to	wonder at
participate in	respond to	succeed in	work on
pay for	result in	suffer from	worry about
persist in	retire from	swear to	
plan on	search for	talk about/to/with	
prepare for	see to	think about/of	

Verb + preposition + infinitive

beg to	happen to	neglect to	refuse to
begin to	hesitate to	object to	struggle to
care to	hide from	offer to	tend to
choose to	hope to	plan to	threaten to
deserve to	learn from/to	prepare to	wait to
expect to	manage to	pretend to	wish to
fail to	mean to	promise to	

Noun + preposition

access to	dealings with	information about	reason for
admiration for	decrease in	intention of	reduction in
advantage of	delay in	interest in	relationship with
agreement with	demand for	involvement in	reliance on
alternative to	desire for	knowledge of	reputation for
appointment with	development in/of	lack of	responsibility for
approach to	difficulty in/with	link with	result of
association with	disadvantage of	meeting with	rise in
attack on	drop in	need for	room for
attitude to	effect of/on	negotiations with	satisfaction with
awareness of	example of	notice of	solution to
belief in	exception of/to	opinion about/of	source of
cause of	excuse for	participation in	supply of
change in	experience in/with	pleasure in	sympathy for
characteristic of	expert at/in/on	possibility of	taste of/for
combination of	explanation for	preference for	tax on
comparison between	hope for	price of	threat of/to
connection between	idea for	probability of	trouble with
contact with	impact on	problem with	truth about
contract with	improvement in	process of	understanding of
contribution to (toward)	increase in	protection from	use for/of
cure for	indication of	quality of	variety of
danger of	influence on	reaction to	victim of

accustomed to	confused about/by	good at	responsible for/to
acquainted with	conscious of	identical to	rich in
afraid of	content with	ignorant of	safe from
amazed at/by	delighted at	impressed by/with	satisfied with
angry about/at/with	dependent on	inferior to	shocked by
annoyed about/by/with	different from	insistent on	short of
anxious about	disappointed by/in/with	inspired by	sick of
ashamed of	eager for	interested in	similar to
astonished at/by	eligible for	involved in	sorry about/for
attached to	enthusiastic about	made of	suitable for
aware of	essential for/to	necessary for	superior to
based on	excited about/by	optimistic about	sure about/of
bored with	expert at	perfect for	surprised at/by
capable of	familiar with	pleased with	terrible at
careless about	famous for	preferable to	tired of
certain of	free from/of	proficient in	typical of
close to	frightened by/to	proud of	unfamiliar with
compatible with	frustrated at	ready for	useless at
concerned about/by/for	full of	related to	worried about

according to	as regards	for the sake of	in connection with
ahead of	by means of	in accordance with	in consideration of
along with	compared to/with	in addition to	in contrast to/with
apart from	contrary to	in case of	in favor of
as a consequence of	due to	in charge of	in place of
as a result of	except for	in comparison to/with	in spite of

Commonly Confused Words

Study the differences between these words that are easy to confuse.

accept	to receive or agree (to do)	**except**	not including
adjacent	next to	**adjoining**	sharing a boundary with
adverse	unfavorable	**averse**	opposed to/unwilling
advice	recommendation (noun)	**advise**	to recommend (verb)
affect	to change (verb)	**effect**	result (noun) or to bring about (verb)
aid	to give help	**aide**	assistant
aisle	passageway between seats	**isle**	island
all together	all in one place/at one time	**altogether**	completely
allude	to suggest/refer indirectly to	**elude**	to escape/evade

ally	supporter	**alley**	path/lane
ambiguous	unclear/with more than one meaning	**ambivalent**	having mixed feelings/ undecided
amicable	friendly/harmonious (for things)	**amiable**	likeable (for people)
appraise	to evaluate	**apprise**	to explain/inform/notify
appreciable	noticeable	**appreciative**	grateful
assent	agreement	**ascent**	movement upward
assign	to allocate/dispense	**consign**	to condemn/transfer
biannual	twice a year	**biennial**	every two years
bravado	daring/overconfidence	**bravery**	courage
canvas	thick cotton cloth	**canvass**	to poll/campaign
censure	to criticize/disapprove of	**censor**	to edit/disallow
childish	immature	**childlike**	innocent
chord	musical notes	**cord**	length of string/rope
classic	typical/important	**classical**	relating to ancient Greece or Rome
clench	to hold tightly	**clinch**	to secure a business deal
climactic	relating to peak of excitement	**climatic**	relating to weather
complacent	self-satisfied/smug	**complaisant**	willing to please
complement	to add to/match	**compliment**	to praise/admire
compose	to create/arrange	**comprise**	to consist of/include
comprehensive	wide-ranging/inclusive	**comprehensible**	intelligible
confidant	close friend	**confident**	sure/certain
conscience	sense of right and wrong	**conscious**	aware of
contemptible	shameful/disgraceful	**contemptuous**	scornful/condescending
continual	repeated/chronic	**continuous**	nonstop/incessant
councilor	member of a council/ committee	**counselor**	someone who gives advice/ guidance
credible	believable/convincing	**creditable**	admirable/worthy of praise
currant	dried grape	**current**	modern/contemporary
defective	faulty/flawed	**deficient**	inadequate/lacking in some degree
deferential	respectful/reverent	**differential**	degree of difference
definite	precise/exact	**definitive**	ultimate/authoritative
defuse	to soothe/calm	**diffuse**	to disperse/scatter
demur	to object/take exception to	**demure**	quiet/modest
dependent	needing support	**dependable**	reliable

deprecate	to denounce/disapprove of	**depreciate**	to decrease in value
desert	arid area/wasteland	**dessert**	sweet course of a meal
desperate	frantic	**disparate**	unrelated
device	gadget/appliance	**devise**	to invent/plan
discreet	confidential/diplomatic	**discrete**	distinct/separate
disinterested	fair-minded/impartial	**uninterested**	indifferent/not interested
dispel	to get rid of unpleasant feelings	**expel**	to force to leave
dual	double/having two parts	**duel**	fight/contest
effectual	effective	**efficient**	effective without wasting time/effort/money
elicit	to extract or draw out (a response)	**illicit**	unlawful
emigrate	to leave one's home country to live in another	**immigrate**	to move into a country to live there
eminent	renowned/distinguished	**imminent**	about to happen
ensure	to make certain	**assure**	to promise/guarantee
envelop	to surround/enclose	**envelope**	paper cover for a letter
excess	a larger amount than is needed	**access**	to gain entry
exempt	excused from	**except**	not including
exhort	to encourage/spur on	**extort**	to extract through intimidation
faint	pale/dim	**feint**	trick/pretense
fallacious	erroneous	**fallible**	likely to fail
farther	more (distance)	**further**	to a greater degree
fictional	imagined	**fictitious**	untrue/fabricated
flaunt	to show off	**flout**	to disobey or defy
foreword	preface/introduction	**forward**	onward
formally	officially	**formerly**	previously
fortunate	lucky	**fortuitous**	by chance (in a way that is convenient or lucky)
frantic	excessively agitated or worried	**frenetic**	very fast and with a lot of energy
idle	inactive	**idyll**	perfect place
illusion	false impression/fantasy	**allusion**	reference
illusive	misleading/false	**elusive**	indefinable/mysterious
immoral	morally wrong	**amoral**	unconcerned with morality
implicit	inherent/implied	**explicit**	clear/unequivocal
imply	to suggest/entail	**infer**	to deduce/surmise

incredible	hard to believe/astonishing	**incredulous**	disbelieving/skeptical
ingenious	very clever/inventive	**ingenuous**	simple/sincere
insidious	gradually causing harm	**invidious**	unfair and so likely to offend
invent	to create/design something that did not exist before	**discover**	to determine the existence of
later	afterward	**latter**	last/concluding
lay	to put down/arrange	**lie**	to recline
lightening	making lighter	**lightning**	flash of light during a storm
loose	baggy/moveable	**lose**	to misplace/be defeated
malevolent	wishing harm to others	**malignant**	dangerous to health
militate	to exert a strong influence	**mitigate**	to alleviate/diminish
obtrusive	conspicuous	**intrusive**	invasive (upon privacy)
official	authorized/certified	**officious**	self-important/intrusive
pallet	platform for storing goods	**palette**	artist's board for mixing paints
pedal	lever/handle	**peddle**	to sell/advocate
perpetrate	to commit/carry out (a crime)	**perpetuate**	to continue/prolong
persecute	to harass/mistreat/cause to suffer	**prosecute**	to put on trial
personal	private/delicate	**personnel**	workers/staff
pleas	appeals/requests	**please**	used when being polite
practice	preparation/training	**practice**	to perform/observe
prescribe	to recommend/stipulate	**proscribe**	to ban/disallow
presumption	belief based on evidence	**assumption**	supposition (no evidence)
principal	major/foremost	**principle**	code/belief
regrettable	unfortunate/deserving regret	**regretful**	apologetic/feeling regret
respectfully	politely/with respect	**respectively**	in a certain order
review	survey	**revue**	show (with songs, dancing, humor)
select	exclusive	**selective**	choosy
sensible	prudent/reasonable	**sensitive**	aware/easily upset
simple	not complicated	**simplistic**	naive/crude/overly simple
site	location/position	**cite**	to quote from
skeptic	cynic	**septic**	infected
specially	for a particular purpose	**especially**	particularly
stationary	motionless/inactive	**stationery**	paper, pens, etc.
subsequently	happening after a time	**consequently**	as a result of
summary	synopsis/brief account	**summery**	relating to summer

sympathy	acknowledging another person's suffering and giving support	**empathy**	understanding firsthand what someone else is experiencing
tasteful	refined/stylish	**tasty**	full of flavor
temerity	audacity/recklessness	**timidity**	lack of courage or self-confidence
tortuous	convoluted/complicated	**torturous**	painful/hurtful
ultimately	at the end of a process or activity	**eventually**	after a long time (often delayed)
vain	conceited/futile	**worthless**	having no value

Words with Multiple Meanings

Many words in English have more than one meaning. The meaning used can depend on the part of speech, as well as the context. For example:

file

Were you able to open the PDF **file** I sent?   (noun – electronic document)
Keep all your expenses in this blue **file**.   (noun – container)
Do you have your employee medical **file**?   (noun – collection of papers/records)
You can smooth the rough edges with this **file**.   (noun – tool)

Please **file** this report under "Confidential."   (verb – to store)
You need to **file** your tax return before the 31st.   (verb – to submit)
Mourners started to **file** past the president's coffin.   (verb – to walk in a line)
Tina wants to **file** a suit for wrongful dismissal.   (verb – to initiate legal proceedings)

Check the various meanings of these words in your dictionary.

act	coach	funny	point	sign
appear	cobble	grave	popular	sink
bank	crane	gross	prune	solution
bill	critic	ground	raise	spare
body	current	hamper	refrain	square
bow	custom	harbor	release	support
buckle	doctor	hatch	reservation	tie
cabinet	draft	just	responsible	top
calculate	drag	last	riot	trip
cave	duty	lie	row	try
central	engaged	match	safe	unfair
certain	exact	mean	sanction	unique
change	fairly	means	season	vision
channel	fine	method	seat	wave
cheap	fix	place	see	yard
clear	foil	plane	sentence	

Collocations

Collocations are words that "go together." It is useful to know as many collocations as possible.

Verb + noun collocations	
abandon	an attempt/hope/a policy/all pretense/ship
apply for	a grant/a loan/permission/a rebate
assume	authority/command/leadership/power/responsibility
attend	a conference/a function
broach	a (delicate) subject
cause	alarm/concern/damage/problems/trouble
cease	operations/production/publication/trading
chair	a committee/a meeting
close	a deal/the gap/ranks/a sale
combat	crime/fraud/inflation/a threat/unemployment
conclude	an agreement/a contract/a deal/a treaty
conduct	an interview/a review/a survey
deserve	credit/praise/recognition/respect
discontinue	a line/a product
dismiss	an allegation/a claim/an offer/a suggestion
divulge	information
draw	attention to/a conclusion
exercise	caution/restraint
express	concern/frustration/a view
fight	a battle/corruption/crime/discrimination/prejudice
file	for bankruptcy/for divorce
fuel	criticism/fears/rumors/speculation/suspicion
gain	acceptance/an advantage/confidence/entry/popularity/speed/recognition
gauge	reaction
grow	impatient/restless/tired
hold	a conference/an election/an inquiry/a meeting/a rally/a referendum
honor	a contract/an obligation
inflict	damage/a defeat/misery
interpret	data/findings/results
issue	an apology/an injunction/a statement/an ultimatum/a warning
join	a club/forces/a union
launch	a campaign/an initiative/an investigation/a product

lead	a discussion
lift	a ban/a curfew/an embargo/sanctions
limit	the amount/capacity/growth/the scope
meet	expectations/needs/wishes
negotiate	a deal/a settlement/terms/a treaty
overcome	adversity/obstacles/problems/resistance
pay	a compliment/dearly for/dividends/a fine/interest/your respects to/tribute to
pose	a challenge/dilemma/risk/threat
postpone	an engagement/a meeting/a trip
propose	an idea/a plan/reform/a solution
pursue	an ambition/a career/a goal/an objective/a policy
reach	an agreement/a compromise/a conclusion/a decision/a limit/a verdict
register	a complaint/concern/displeasure/an objection/a protest
secure	payment/permission/a seat
settle	an argument/a debt/your differences/a disagreement/a dispute
suffer	a defeat/a loss/a setback
supplement	your income
support	an argument/a claim/a contention/a hypothesis
suspend	judgment/services
tackle	a challenge/a crisis/a problem/a question/a task
undermine	authority/confidence/credibility/legitimacy/morale
voice	concern/doubts/misgivings
withstand	pressure

abolish/cut/evade/impose/levy	a tax
accept/confront/deny/face up to	(the) reality
accomplish/attain/pursue/set	a goal
achieve/assert/establish	dominance
achieve/declare/gain/maintain/win	independence
acquire/earn/establish/gain	a reputation
acquire/gain/obtain/possess	a qualification
address/attend/chair/convene/hold	a meeting
address/attend/hold/host	a conference
adopt/develop/devise/formulate/implement	a strategy
adopt/develop/devise/pioneer	a method

Verb + noun	
affect/enhance/improve/maintain	quality
alleviate/combat/ease/generate/relieve	stress
alleviate/compound/exacerbate	a problem
allow/block/gain/grant/limit/restrict	access
amend/approve/draft/oppose	a bill
analyze/collate/interpret/release	(the) results
apply/ease/enforce/impose/lift	sanctions
appreciate/exaggerate/grasp/highlight	the significance (of)
assume/exert/relinquish/seize	control
attract/avoid/generate/shun	publicity
attract/mobilize/pledge/rally	support
avoid/initiate/maintain/resume	contact
award/break/fulfill/honor/renew/win	a contract
bend/break/flout/relax/stick to	the rules
boost/depress/lower/raise/slash	the price
combat/control/monitor/tackle	pollution
come to/finalize	an arrangement
command/deserve/lose/show	respect
conclude/ratify/secure/sign	an agreement
conduct/fight/lead/mount/spearhead	a campaign
confirm/deny/dismiss/refute/release	a report
consider/grant/ignore/refuse/repeat	a request
cross/establish/overstep	a boundary
encounter/experience/face	difficulties
encourage/maintain/inhibit/stimulate/stunt	growth
enhance/guarantee/maintain/promote	safety
establish/extend/regain/take	a lead
establish/follow/form/reveal	a pattern
lodge/outline/raise/voice	an objection

Adjective + noun collocations	
annual	insurance/leave/return/turnover
brief	encounter/glimpse/moment/period/visit
careful	analysis/consideration/timing
commercial	bank/mortgage/property

convivial	atmosphere
corporate	culture/identity/image/strategy/structure
designer	label
desperate	attempt/bid/effort
detailed	account/analysis/investigation/study
direct	intervention/involvement
dreadful	mistake
due	care/consideration/notice/respect
economic	crisis/downturn/growth/policy/reform/slowdown
effective	deterrent/means/protection/treatment
emergency	meeting/service
false	allegation/assumption/hope/impression/premise
firm	belief/conviction
general	conclusion/consensus/principle/rule
groundless	accusations/charges/claims/fears/suspicions
growing	awareness/concern/discontent/tension/unrest
hard	bargain
heavy	fine/losses/rain/snow/traffic
high	cost/expectations/hopes/proportion/quality/speed/standard
joint	agreement/control/declaration/venture
key	element/factor/feature/figure/role
major	breakthrough/concern/factor/influence/setback/upheaval
mass	exodus/market/movement/protest
mutual	benefit/respect/trust
noticeable	change/difference/drop/improvement
outstanding	achievement/result
overwhelming	desire/majority/need/sense/temptation
particular	attention/concern/emphasis/relevance
plausible	argument/explanation/scenario/theory
popular	belief/misconception/myth/view
positive	attitude/feedback/reinforcement/response
practical	advice/purpose/solution
rapid	change/decline/deterioration/expansion
realistic	alternative/expectation/prospect/target
reliable	indication/measure/predictor

rising	trend/unemployment
severe	difficulty/hardship/setbacks/shortage
sheer	luxury
sound	advice/decision/judgment/principle
thick	fog
tough	assignment/call/decision/fight
undue	burden/delay/hardship/influence/pressure/strain
vague	hint/idea/impression/memory/recollection/suspicion
whirlwind	visit

abiding/false/indelible/misleading/overall	impression
abject/heartfelt/humble/sincere	apology
absolute/dogged/grim/sheer	determination
accurate/bleak/confused/gloomy/vivid	picture
accurate/detailed/general/vivid	description
active/enthusiastic/unanimous/widespread	support
added/adequate/effective	protection
adequate/proper/reasonable/sensible	precaution(s)
adverse/devastating/negative/profound	impact
adverse/gut/initial/instinctive/knee-jerk	reaction
adverse/outspoken/severe/unjust	criticism
alphabetical/chronological/numerical/random	sequence
alternative/clean/renewable	energy
alternative/complementary/herbal	medicine
alternative/likely/nightmare/worst-case	scenario
alternative/literal/plausible/subjective	interpretation
ambitious/innovative/special	project
ample/clear/conclusive/irrefutable/tangible	proof
ample/historic/tremendous/unique	opportunity
anecdotal/compelling/empirical/vital	evidence
annoying/bad/unfortunate	habit
antisocial/disruptive/threatening/unacceptable	behavior
apparent/complete/distinct/sheer	lack
arduous/formidable/onerous/thankless/unenviable	task
astonishing/bewildering/enormous/infinite	variety

atrocious/foul/mild/unsettled	weather
bad/fatal/minor/serious/tragic	accident
bare/broad/rough/vague	outline
basic/essential/legal/statutory	requirement
beneficial/detrimental/knock-on/profound	effect
bewildering/colorful/dazzling/vast	array
binding/broken/empty/rash	promise
bitter/fierce/harsh/scathing/unprovoked	attack
blatant/downright/outright/transparent	lie
blind/pure/sheer/total	panic
breathtaking/panoramic/spectacular/stunning	view
brief/conflicting/eyewitness/vivid	account
broad/popular/universal/wide	appeal
calculated/potential/unacceptable	risk
careful/close/detailed/intense/rigorous	scrutiny
careful/detailed/due	consideration
casual/close/detailed	observation
central/main/overriding	concern
clear/encouraging/ominous/telltale/visible	sign
closing/final/formative/preliminary	stage
combined/cumulative/final/grand/overall/running	total
common/everyday/isolated/rare	occurrence
compelling/legitimate/primary/valid	reason
competitive/hostile/stable/working	environment
comprehensive/extensive/major/wide-ranging	review
concerted/decisive/prompt/remedial/urgent	action
concerted/determined/strenuous/team/valiant	effort
conservative/realistic/rough	estimate
considerable/genuine/healthy/mutual	respect
constructive/helpful/practical/sensible	suggestion
contentious/controversial/pressing/thorny	issue
controversial/momentous/strategic/unanimous	decision
costly/deliberate/disastrous/grave	mistake
critical/crucial/precise	moment
crucial/decisive/key/major	factor

crucial/focal/key/main	point
crucial/immense/strategic/utmost	importance
cultural/educational/ethnic/privileged	background
current/existing/proposed	legislation
daunting/formidable/major	challenge
dead-end/menial/skilled/well-paid	job
dire/disastrous/serious/unforeseen	consequences
disastrous/inauspicious/promising/rocky	start
distinctive/key/special/striking	feature
domestic/hazardous/industrial/toxic	waste
dramatic/marked/massive/substantial	increase
dramatic/sharp/spectacular/substantial	rise
drastic/harsh/repressive/severe	measure
educated/informed/inspired/rough	guess
essential/key/principal/vital	component
exceptional/extenuating/unforeseen	circumstances
excruciating/intense/searing/stabbing	pain
expert/impartial/legal/professional	advice
extensive/global/international	network
extensive/irreparable/permanent/untold	damage
faint/false/forlorn/vain	hope
far-reaching/fundamental/radical/sweeping	reform
fierce/healthy	competition
final/random/stringent/thorough	check
formal/urgent/written	request
fundamental/insoluble/intractable	problem
glaring/inadvertent/surprising	omission
great/outstanding/useful/valuable	contribution
harsh/salutary/valuable	lesson
horrific/minor/severe/slight	injury
ideal/practical/satisfactory/workable	solution
inevitable/logical/obvious/tentative	conclusion
irresistible/overwhelming/powerful/strong/sudden	urge
rapid/steady/uninterrupted	growth

Noun + noun collocations

advertising	campaign
bank	account/balance/charges/statement
brand	awareness/loyalty
business	opportunity/partner/plan/trip
cash	injection
chain	store
company	policy
consumer	confidence
credit	crunch/history
customer	satisfaction/service
human	resources
interest	rates
job	satisfaction
market	forces/leader/share
material	goods/possessions/rewards/wealth
product	range
profit	margin
quality	control
sales	figures/representative
target	audience/market
takeover	bid

Verb + adverb collocations

agree	completely/reluctantly/unanimously/unreservedly
approve	thoroughly/wholeheartedly
argue	forcefully/passionately/persuasively/strongly
beat	comfortably/convincingly/soundly
borrow	heavily
change	dramatically/drastically/fundamentally/rapidly/significantly
choose	carefully/sensibly/well
climb	dramatically/rapidly/sharply/steadily/steeply
differ	markedly/substantially
fail	abysmally/completely/miserably/narrowly
fall	dramatically/rapidly/sharply/steadily/steeply
fight	desperately/doggedly/hard/tenaciously

improve	dramatically/greatly/markedly/vastly
listen	attentively/carefully/closely/hard/intently
object	bitterly/formally/strenuously/vehemently
obtain	dishonestly/fraudulently/illegally/unlawfully
promote	actively/heavily/strongly/vigorously
react	adversely/angrily/unfavorably/violently
recommend	heartily/thoroughly/unreservedly/wholeheartedly
reduce	dramatically/drastically/gradually/substantially
reject	categorically/decisively/outright
remember	distinctly/rightly/vaguely
rise	dramatically/rapidly/sharply/steadily/steeply
search	diligently/frantically/painstakingly/systematically
treat	badly/equally/harshly/leniently/unfairly
wait	anxiously/eagerly/expectantly/impatiently/quietly
watch	avidly/helplessly/idly/incredulously/intently
weaken	considerably/fatally/seriously/severely
win	comfortably/convincingly/easily/narrowly
work	closely (with/toward)/steadily

Adverb + adjective collocations	
absolutely	appalled/astonished/convinced/delighted/essential/furious
badly	needed/worded
bitterly	fought/opposed
commercially	successful/viable
completely	different/natural/satisfied/separate/unacceptable
critically	ill
deeply	committed/divided/hurt/moved/offensive
entirely	blameless/fair/unaware
extremely	hard/interested/simple/successful
fully	aware/informed/recovered
greatly	appreciated/influenced
heavily	committed/involved
highly	competitive/controversial/educated/irregular/paid/recommended/unlikely
immensely	proud/rich
increasingly	common/concerned/popular
patently	false/obvious

relatively	modest/unknown
seriously	affected/damaged/hurt/injured/worried/wounded
spectacularly	successful
thoroughly	ashamed/enjoyable/miserable/unpleasant
utterly	absurd/devastated/impossible/ridiculous/useless
well	matched/suited

Common verb collocations

➤ break
a habit, the ice, the law, a leg, the news, a promise, a record, the rules

➤ catch
a bus, a cab, a chill, a cold, fire, the flu, sight of, someone's eye

➤ do
the accounts, your best, business, the chores, damage, exercises, harm, someone a favor, a job, overtime, research

➤ get
angry, a bonus, into debt, experience in, the hang of, home, the impression, a job, lost, the message, permission, to the point, a promotion, a raise, ready, started, into trouble

➤ give
advice, feedback, the impression, your opinion, a performance, priority to, a speech

➤ go
abroad, astray, bankrupt, into business, out of business, dark, freelance, online, into partnership, into production, on vacation

➤ have
an accident, an argument, a chat, difficulty, a feeling, fun, an idea, a meal, a meeting, an operation, a problem, a rest, a shock, a snack, sympathy, time

➤ keep
an appointment, calm, control, a journal, a promise, quiet, a record, a secret, a suggestion, in touch, your word

➤ make
an announcement, an apology, an appointment, an attempt, changes, a contribution, a deal, a difference, an effort, a fuss, a good impression, a guess, a living, a loss, a mess, a mistake, money, a noise, some photocopies, a point of, a profit, progress, room, a sale, a speech, a suggestion, time for, trouble

➤ pay
attention, the bill, cash, a compliment, with a credit card, a fine, interest, the price, your respects

➤ save
electricity, energy, face, money, someone a seat, space, your strength, time

➤ take
action, a break, the bus, a chance, a dislike to, an exam, inspiration from, a look, measures, a nap, notes, notice of, responsibility for, a rest, a seat, a shower, a size 12, a taxi, someone's temperature, a vacation

Connecting Ideas

Conjunctions and connecting adverbs are used to link ideas within sentences and paragraphs. Study these examples to understand their meaning and use.

contrast

although/though/even though/while + subject + verb

The CX20 is not our best-selling model, **although/though** it is popular.	*though* can also go at the end of a sentence
Even though we have fulfilled more orders, our pre-tax profit has gone down.	*even though* is stronger than *although/though*
While they agreed with our position, they refused to issue a refund.	*while* is used at the start of a sentence

Note: Compare *even though* and *even if*:

- Let's replace the copy machine, **even though** it's expensive. [It is expensive to replace.]
- Let's replace the copy machine, **even if** it's expensive. [It may or may not be expensive to replace.]

in spite of/despite (the fact that)

In spite of the disappointing results, the company expanded operations.	+ noun phrase
Darren chaired the meeting, **despite** feeling under the weather.	+ verb *-ing*
We arrived at the concert early, **despite the fact that** the traffic was bad.	+ *the fact that* + subject + verb

whereas/yet

Sasha started last month, **whereas** Tim has worked here for years.	can start or come in the middle of a sentence
There was plenty to eat, **yet** nobody was hungry.	cannot start a sentence

however/even so

The new offices are close to the station. **However**, the rent is very high.	Notice how *even so* introduces a surprising contrast.
The new offices are close to the station. **Even so**, the rent is low.	

nevertheless/on the other hand

The Grand is an expensive hotel. **Nevertheless**, it is usually fully booked.	= *even so*
We could fly to New York. **On the other hand**, it's cheaper to drive.	to express an opposing view

Note: These words and phrases can also be used to connect sentences indicating a contrast: *after all, all the same, anyway, by/in contrast, in any case, instead of, on the contrary.*

reason/result/purpose

Dr. Philips was appointed **because of** her experience in biomechanics.	+ noun
As/Because/Since the shipment was over 100 kilos, we had to pay a fine.	+ subject + verb
Owing to/Due to the delay in shipping your order, we are offering a 10 percent discount.	= *on account of* (+ noun)
Please wear this name badge **so that** everyone knows who you are.	to indicate purpose
One of the servers was overheating, **so** we shut it down.	= *as a result/consequence*
The merger was a success, **in that** no jobs were lost.	adds detail to give a reason

Note: These words and phrases can also be used to connect sentences indicating reason or result: *as a result, consequently, hence, seeing as/seeing that, therefore, thus*.

addition

Apart from/Besides the HR director, nobody was in favor of the proposal.	Note that *besides* can mean *apart from* and *in addition to*.
In addition to/As well as/Besides the HR director, the C.E.O. also supported the proposal.	
The trial was a failure, and **furthermore/what is more/moreover** it was very expensive.	= *in addition*; can be used interchangeably
Both the upper **and** lower floors of the warehouse were destroyed in the fire.	*both... and*
They did not offer a discount, **nor** did we ask for one.	after a negative statement, to add extra information
The conference center was **not only** well appointed, **but also** a very good value.	used for emphasis
Unemployment leads to poverty, and **similarly**, high employment creates wealth.	= *likewise*

Note: These words and phrases can also be used to connect sentences by adding information: *after all, too*.

Note the inversion after *not only* when beginning a sentence.

- The presentation was **not only** long, **but also** very boring.
- **Not only** was the presentation long, **but also** it was very boring.

condition

Do you know **if/whether** the motion will be approved?	Use *whether* or *if* for indirect *Yes/No* questions.
Ben cannot decide **whether** to retire early.	Use only *whether* before an infinitive.
The issue is **whether or not** we should take legal action.	= *whether we should or we shouldn't*
You can look around the library **providing/provided that** you are quiet.	= *on condition that/as long as*
We cannot send payment **unless** we receive an invoice first.	= *except if* or *if... not*

Where did Deborah live **before** she moved to Seattle?	+ subject + verb
Please vacate your room **before** checking out of the hotel.	+ -ing (or having + past participle)
Fiona has been with us for six months. **Previously**, she worked at ARC Pharma.	= before that
Mr. Sykes was **formerly** a partner at Anton Associates.	= previously (formal)
As/While the goods were being unloaded, a pallet broke.	happening at the same time
The movie started **just as** we got to our seats.	to emphasize the exact moment
Safety regulations changed a lot **during** the last decade.	= within a period of time
Throughout his time as managing director, Mr. Timpson never took a day off.	= from the beginning to the end
Following/After the ceremony, there was a banquet.	+ noun
Please call me **as soon as** Ms. Bennet gets in.	= immediately after (+ subject + verb)
You are free to leave **once/when** you have completed the test.	= after (+ subject + verb)

Phrasal Verbs

A phrasal verb is a verb followed by one or more prepositions or adverbs that change its meaning. Sometimes the meaning is clear (e.g., Please **pick up** those papers). However, most phrasal verbs have an idiomatic usage, which means it is not usually possible to guess the meaning. Study these examples of common phrasal verbs.

Many two-part phrasal verbs cannot be separated. The object must come after the final preposition or particle.

Two-part phrasal verbs – inseparable	
Shareholders decided to **call for** the C.E.O.'s resignation.	require/demand
Todd did not **come across** very well in the interview.	give an impression
Analysts agree that the government must **deal with** inflation.	handle
There was no internet so we had to **do without** all week.	forgo/manage without
If you do not work hard, you will **end up** failing the test.	finish by/have the result of
Could you **go through** these figures before next Monday?	check
Why would Dr. Williamson suddenly **hang up** like that?	end a phone call
Please **hold on** while the documents are printed.	wait
If costs **keep on** rising, we will have to increase prices.	continue
In case of fire, the ship will **make for** the nearest port.	move in the direction of
What do you **make of** the Jameson report?	have an opinion of/think about

It was a surprise to **run into** another board member.	meet by chance
Let's quickly **run through** our presentation for tomorrow.	practice
More supporters are expected to **show up** at the rally.	attend/arrive
Somebody needs to **speak out** against corruption.	protest
This firm does not **stand for** bullying in the workplace.	tolerate
The study focused on people who **take after** their parents.	resemble/behave like
The anesthetic will start to **wear off** in about an hour.	diminish

Some two-part phrasal verbs can, but do not always have to, be separated by the object.

Two-part phrasal verbs – separable

Radical reforms are needed to **bring about** real change. / How can we **bring** this **about**?	cause to happen
We should be able to **bring** the board **around** to our view.	persuade
When will they **bring out** the new 5G cell phone?	launch
Why not **bring** this matter **up** at the next staff meeting?	raise
It took several years to **build** this company **up**.	increase/develop
Officials decided to **call off** the game due to poor visibility.	cancel
Be sure to **carry** these instructions **out** to the letter.	fulfill
Are we going to **draw up** any contingency plans?	prepare/develop
Our driver will **drop** your order **off** tomorrow.	deliver
Please **fill out** this questionnaire before you leave.	complete
Did investigators ever **find out** the cause of the accident?	discover
All healthcare workers are advised to **give up** smoking.	stop (a habit)
Bad weather might **hold** construction **up** for a week.	delay
Could we **leave** the break clause **out** of the contract?	omit
The team promised not to **let down** their supporters.	disappoint
The sooner we **pay** this mortgage **off**, the better.	end (a debt)
When are they coming to **pick up** these packages?	collect
Do not press that button or you will **set off** the alarm.	activate
Dr. Ng will **set out** plans for restructuring the college.	explain
Some clubs intend to **set up** a rival tournament.	establish
These new brochures really help **show off** our products.	display proudly
Our aim is to **sort** the matter **out** as soon as possible.	find a solution
If only we could **take back** what we said.	retract
AVK Inc. announced plans to **take on** 3,000 new staff.	employ
When did Justine **take** golf **up**?	start (a hobby)

The supervisor came to **tell** us **off** for wasting time.	reprimand
Why did DT Inc. **turn** the offer of a merger **down**?	reject
Do not forget to **turn** all the office lights **off** at night.	switch off/stop using
Engineers are doing their best to **work out** a solution.	find

➤ When the object is a pronoun, this must come between the verb and the particle.

Turn the radio on. / Turn on the radio. / Turn **it** on.

➤ The same phrasal verb can change meaning depending on whether it is separated or not.

What caused the diesel generator to **break down**?	stop working
Please **break** these costs **down** into monthly estimates.	separate into parts
We hope everything will **turn out** well.	end
This factory can **turn** 300 cars **out** a month.	produce
Let's hope the delegation does not **turn up** late.	arrive
Could you **turn** the TV **up** a little, please?	increase the volume/heat

➤ A few transitive phrasal verbs *must* be separated by the object.

Please **get** this message **through** as quickly as possible.	convey
Please **keep** your safety goggles **on** during the experiment.	continue to wear

➤ Exactly the same phrasal verb can have more than one meaning.

How long did the meeting **go on** for?	last
Please ignore the noise outside and **go on** working.	continue
As the months **go on**, you should feel more settled.	pass (time)
Why don't you **go on** without me?	go ahead
You need to **go on** a higher dose of medication.	start to take
Sorry to interrupt. Please **go on**.	resume talking
There is very little data here for us to **go on**.	base an opinion on
We heard the generator **go on** in the basement.	start to work

Three-part phrasal verbs usually consist of a verb + adverb + preposition. They are mostly inseparable.

Three-part phrasal verbs	
It would not be a good idea to **back out of** the deal now.	withdraw from
What can we do to **catch up with** the competition?	reach the same level as
Who else has **come down with** the flu this week?	become ill with a disease
The former coach will **come in for** some harsh criticism.	encounter/suffer
We expected to **come up against** stronger opposition.	be confronted by
Can anyone **come up with** a way to reduce energy costs?	think of
This year we must try to **cut back on** our legal costs.	reduce
These reforms should **do away with** outdated regulations.	abolish/remove
Scandal caused Mr. Cho to **drop out of** the mayoral race.	leave (a program)
Will the C.E.O **go back on** her decision to close the plant?	retract/change your mind
The company will **go out of** business as of next month.	cease (trading/producing)

Do you think we should **go through with** the takeover?	carry out (a plan)
The Reds will **go up against** the Giants in the final.	compete with
Production is barely able to **keep up with** demand.	proceed at the same rate as
Did the gala dinner **live up to** everybody's expectations?	reach (expectations)
How can we **make up for** the inconvenience caused?	compensate for
The accountant says we will **run out of** money soon.	use all of something
Exploited workers need to **stand up for** their rights.	defend/support
We have been asked to **take care of** all the key accounts.	look after
How could Timothy **walk out on** the family business?	desert/leave

➤ The vast majority of three-part phrasal verbs are inseparable, but in a few cases the object comes immediately after the verb.

- They cannot **do** you **out of** your pension, can they?   unfairly prevent someone from having
- Can I **let** you **in on** a secret?   reveal a secret to someone

Other examples include *help on with, put down as, put up to, take up on,* and *talk out of*.

Several verbs can be used with multiple prepositions or adverbs, and consequently have many different meanings. Look at these examples for the verbs *get*, *look*, and *put*. Use your dictionary to find more phrasal examples for these and other verbs.

Phrasal verbs with several meanings	
get	
get across	convey/communicate
get along (with)	have a good relationship (with)
get around	spread/avoid (something difficult)
get (a)round to	find time for
get at	criticize/try to say/find
get away with	avoid punishment for
get back at	take revenge on
get by	cope/manage
get down	become depressed
get down to	give serious attention to
get on with	continue
get out of	avoid responsibility for/be excused from
get over	recover from
get rid of	be free from (something unwanted)
get through	accomplish
get through to	contact

look

look after	oversee; take care of
look down on	feel superior to
look for	search
look forward to	eagerly anticipate
look into	investigate
look out	be careful
look out for	be alert to/take care of
look over	examine
look through	peruse
look up	find (in a dictionary)
look up to	respect

put

put back	replace
put by	save
put in	submit
put off	distract/postpone
put out	extinguish
put up	raise
put up with	tolerate

Choose the most appropriate answer: (A), (B), (C), or (D), to complete each sentence.

1. A survey by the real estate research firm Gommersall Group has raised concerns over the increasingly high .... rate in the US retail property market.
   (A) vacancy
   (B) vacate
   (C) vacant
   (D) vacuous

2. In recent months, several unfortunate and wholly avoidable outbreaks of salmonella and other food-borne illnesses have served to .... public concerns over food safety.
   (A) tighten
   (B) enlighten
   (C) heighten
   (D) straighten

3. While the screenplay is excellent, the premise on which the plot hinges is so inherently .... as to almost insult the intelligence of the audience.
   (A) implacable
   (B) impregnable
   (C) imponderable
   (D) implausible

4. Critics have called into question the .... of a $10 billion high-speed rail project that, if approved, would connect key cities across southwest Florida.
   (A) legal
   (B) legality
   (C) legalize
   (D) legally

5. After his selection was announced, Doug McCarten told waiting reporters that he was .... proud to be representing his country in the 100-meter relay race in Seoul.
   (A) immensely
   (B) greatly
   (C) patently
   (D) absolutely

6. Inspectors at the metal processing plant commented that the outdated personal protective equipment given to workers offered .... protection against noise exposure.
   (A) inconclusive
   (B) intractable
   (C) inadequate
   (D) incoherent

7. Mr. Marshall sold the barn with the .... of raising money for new farm machinery.
   (A) intent
   (B) intended
   (C) intends
   (D) intention

8. In a touching closing speech, Dr. Jenson paid .... to his former colleague and longtime friend Professor Cheng.
   (A) compliment
   (B) tribute
   (C) praise
   (D) honor

1. (A) (B) (C) (D)   4. (A) (B) (C) (D)   7. (A) (B) (C) (D)
2. (A) (B) (C) (D)   5. (A) (B) (C) (D)   8. (A) (B) (C) (D)
3. (A) (B) (C) (D)   6. (A) (B) (C) (D)

9. Senator Wilson possesses a strong moral compass that compels her to voice her concerns over government policies rather than toe the party line, which is an .... trait in a politician.
(A) admiration
(B) admirably
(C) admirable
(D) admiring

10. Nominations for the next chair of the Federal Reserve System will take place .... the present incumbent, Sam Sheppard, announces the date of his departure.
(A) during
(B) following
(C) while
(D) once

11. A customer-driven approach, together with a management ethos of responsible leadership, is essential in the .... of successful outsourcing partnerships.
(A) facilitation
(B) limitation
(C) mitigation
(D) excitation

12. According to the chief accountant, there is no way to .... paying withholding tax on dividends from foreign stocks and other funds, although it can be offset against profits.
(A) get away with
(B) get through
(C) get out of
(D) get back at

13. The printed instruction manual that came with the new fax machine is barely 5 pages long, ... the online e-manual is over 120 pages.
(A) owing to
(B) unless
(C) in that
(D) whereas

14. Gonzales followed his first-round victory with a truly .... second round of 67 to ensure he goes into the final day of the tournament with a three-stroke lead.
(A) memorable
(B) memorably
(C) memorial
(D) memorized

15. Ms. Evans complained to the Press Commission that the remarks she had made at the charity ball had been .... and taken out of context.
(A) miscalculated
(B) misconceived
(C) misconstrued
(D) miscarried

16. Mrs. Fabre was offered the role of vice president at Partec Industries on account of her extensive experience in the fashion business, and because shareholders value her .... business judgment.
(A) sheer
(B) vast
(C) tough
(D) sound

9. (A) (B) (C) (D)   12. (A) (B) (C) (D)   15. (A) (B) (C) (D)
10. (A) (B) (C) (D)   13. (A) (B) (C) (D)   16. (A) (B) (C) (D)
11. (A) (B) (C) (D)   14. (A) (B) (C) (D)

17. Due to the popularity of the summer music festival, tickets are limited to two per person and reserving early is ....
(A) advise
(B) advisable
(C) advisably
(D) advisability

18. The judge dismissed all charges against the defendant, Mr. Brice, and issued instructions that he be released immediately without a .... on his character.
(A) flaw
(B) deficiency
(C) blemish
(D) spot

19. As for gratuities, it is the role of the restaurant manager to ensure an .... distribution among all front-of-house and kitchen staff.
(A) equal
(B) equally
(C) equality
(D) equaled

20. In readiness for her retirement, for many years Helen has been putting .... a small amount of money from her salary each month.
(A) up
(B) by
(C) out
(D) off

21. Customers wishing to arrange collection of commercial or industrial waste may do so .... they have completed form AT23 and received the necessary environmental consent.
(A) while
(B) so that
(C) whether
(D) as long as

22. Of the many factors .... to bacterial growth, the most significant include warmth, moisture, temperature, and light.
(A) favorable
(B) favored
(C) favorite
(D) favorably

23. Thanks to his brusque manner and quarrelsome nature, within two months Toby had managed to .... almost all of his coworkers.
(A) estrange
(B) alienate
(C) isolate
(D) segregate

24. All visitors to Portsdown Refinery must sign in at the Visitor Center and be sure to listen .... to the safety demonstration briefing before entering the facility.
(A) steadily
(B) thoroughly
(C) closely
(D) completely

17. Ⓐ Ⓑ Ⓒ Ⓓ **20.** Ⓐ Ⓑ Ⓒ Ⓓ **23.** Ⓐ Ⓑ Ⓒ Ⓓ
18. Ⓐ Ⓑ Ⓒ Ⓓ **21.** Ⓐ Ⓑ Ⓒ Ⓓ **24.** Ⓐ Ⓑ Ⓒ Ⓓ
19. Ⓐ Ⓑ Ⓒ Ⓓ **22.** Ⓐ Ⓑ Ⓒ Ⓓ

25. .... launch vehicles are intended to be used just once, yet are still the preferred launch system for space cargo because of their lower cost and the reduced risk of mission failure.
(A) Expend
(B) Expended
(C) Expendably
(D) Expendable

26. The race to see who can take the number-one spot on the music charts has never been closer, with .... competition among the three top bands.
(A) severe
(B) annual
(C) exciting
(D) fierce

27. After the collapse of bailout talks, senior executives at Hartley Steel came to the .... conclusion that the shipyard would have to close.
(A) inestimable
(B) inescapable
(C) ineligible
(D) ineffectual

28. Gear Unlimited announced plans to .... forces with AXI Life to host a series of sports training camps for teenagers across Kentucky.
(A) link
(B) join
(C) fuse
(D) unite

29. Reports that legendary coach Ricardo Girelli had left the Tigers to join arch-rivals the Bears were initially met with widespread .... by thousands of the club's fans.
(A) disbelief
(B) disbelieve
(C) disbelieving
(D) disbelieved

30. Three years on from the now-infamous jewelry heist at The Museum of Ancient Antiquities, only a .... of the priceless jade figurines that were stolen have been recovered.
(A) faction
(B) function
(C) fraction
(D) friction

31. In order to contain the growing humanitarian crisis developing in the region, the decision was made to partially lift sanctions and allow a .... of imports of medical equipment.
(A) presumption
(B) consumption
(C) resumption
(D) compunction

32. Producer Dan Frederick's .... against all odds, combined with his sheer grit and determination, have resulted in the creation of a cinematic masterpiece.
(A) perseveres
(B) persevere
(C) persevered
(D) perseverance

25. Ⓐ Ⓑ Ⓒ Ⓓ   **28.** Ⓐ Ⓑ Ⓒ Ⓓ   **31.** Ⓐ Ⓑ Ⓒ Ⓓ
26. Ⓐ Ⓑ Ⓒ Ⓓ   **29.** Ⓐ Ⓑ Ⓒ Ⓓ   **32.** Ⓐ Ⓑ Ⓒ Ⓓ
27. Ⓐ Ⓑ Ⓒ Ⓓ   **30.** Ⓐ Ⓑ Ⓒ Ⓓ

33. Surveillance cameras have been installed in and around the proposed construction site in several .... locations, in order to help identify intruders and prevent further acts of vandalism.
(A) inconspicuous
(B) inconsistent
(C) inconsiderable
(D) inconsequential

34. Allegations of misconduct on the part of three senior executives at Arenco Motor Corporation's Shanghai plant were today .... as "unfounded" and "totally groundless" by the company chairman.
(A) dismissed
(B) refused
(C) abandoned
(D) flouted

35. Members of the Curriculum Committee at Denton Community College are meeting to discuss what .... subjects should be introduced into the curriculum for undergraduate students.
(A) compulsion
(B) compelled
(C) compulsory
(D) compulsorily

36. A hospital spokesperson declined to comment .... allegations of negligence on the part of anesthesiologists going back several years.
(A) for
(B) on
(C) at
(D) over

37. Senior management at the mining firm described the walkout by workers, unhappy over a reduced pay deal and new flextime working conditions, as completely ....
(A) indefatigable
(B) indefinable
(C) indefensible
(D) indescribable

38. The success of this year's employee training program is in no small measure due to the .... and knowledgeable workshop leaders.
(A) enthusiasm
(B) enthusiastic
(C) enthused
(D) enthusiastically

39. The results of the nationwide survey on attitudes to climate change showed a clear preference .... strong and immediate action to mitigate the dangers.
(A) in
(B) that
(C) for
(D) over

40. The claim that the recent dramatic rise in drug prices is purely due to increasing research and development costs faced by the pharmaceutical industry is simply not ....
(A) credulous
(B) creditable
(C) credited
(D) credible

33. Ⓐ Ⓑ Ⓒ Ⓓ 36. Ⓐ Ⓑ Ⓒ Ⓓ 39. Ⓐ Ⓑ Ⓒ Ⓓ
34. Ⓐ Ⓑ Ⓒ Ⓓ 37. Ⓐ Ⓑ Ⓒ Ⓓ 40. Ⓐ Ⓑ Ⓒ Ⓓ
35. Ⓐ Ⓑ Ⓒ Ⓓ 38. Ⓐ Ⓑ Ⓒ Ⓓ   Score .... /40

PART 5 INCOMPLETE SENTENCES

This part of the TOEIC® test consists of 30 sentences, each with a missing word or phrase. There are four answer choices for each item, and you must choose the answer that best completes each sentence.

The purpose is to test your knowledge of grammar and vocabulary. You need to demonstrate your understanding of a wide variety of grammatical structures, and show that you are familiar with their correct usage. You also need to show that you have a broad range of vocabulary, and understand not only the meaning of the target words, but how these words change their form, and the ways in which they are used. Topics cover common business and social themes, as well as more specialized contexts. An extensive vocabulary is therefore essential if you are to achieve a very high score on the test.

The language used throughout this section of the test is reflective of the formal, written English that is common in the workplace.

QUICK CHECK

How many questions are in this part of the TOEIC test?

What are the language areas that are being tested?

How many answers choices are there for each question?

What kind of language does this part of the test focus on?

What is the biggest single factor behind boosting your score?

1 MIN

You may find it useful to review the Grammar and Vocabulary sections before you start.

OVERVIEW

Challenges

In Part 5, you need to work fast to complete all 30 sentences as quickly as possible. You have to read each sentence, understand the general context, and identify what feature of grammar or vocabulary is being tested. Here are some factors to be aware of on this part of the test.

 Timing

Time is your biggest enemy. With so many questions to get through, it can be easy to become bogged down, especially when you come up against language you are not familiar with. Nevertheless, you must work quickly, maintain momentum, and move forward smoothly and efficiently question by question.

 Variety

Each sentence is unique, with its own context and language focus. What is being tested differs from question to question, and it is vital not to let this constant change slow you down. You need to rapidly assimilate the different scenarios and home in on the target language.

 Sentence length

Sentences can vary considerably in length, from as few as 10 words to as many as 25, and sometimes even more. The longer the sentence, the more language you need to process, and the more time it takes to read. Most sentences tend to be long, around 20 words or more.

 Range

There is no limit to the scope of language covered, so the range of grammatical and lexical testing points you may face is enormous. The more difficult sentences include complex grammatical structures and sometimes highly specialized vocabulary that you may not be familiar with.

▶ **Answer choices**

Some answer choices may all look alike, or share similar meanings that you need to consider carefully. Others may present you with different forms of the same word, or require you to choose between parts of speech, prepositions, conjunctions, pronouns, etc. You may also need to choose between various tenses, forms, and functions. It is easy to become confused when faced with such an array of multifaceted answer choices.

STEPS TO SUCCESS

This section presents an effective, step-by-step approach to use when answering questions on Part 5 of the TOEIC® test.

The steps shown here are designed to help you achieve the highest possible score when you take the test. By following these steps, you should be able to maximize your score on this part of the test.

1 ▶ Read the sentence and look at the answer choices. *If you are sure of the answer, mark your answer immediately and move on to the next question*. If you are not sure of the answer, proceed to Step 2.

2 ▶ Read the answer choices again. Then look at the words before and after the blank space in the sentence. Ask yourself whether the language focus is grammar or vocabulary, and try to identify exactly what is being tested.

3 ▶ Eliminate any answer choices you are sure are incorrect. If you can't decide between two or more options, read the clause containing the blank space silently to yourself with each answer choice in place. Which one "sounds" right?

4 ▶ Mark your answer.

TIMING ▶ Maintaining a brisk pace is essential on this part of the test. Keep a watch in front of you and check the time regularly. You should aim to spend an average of 15 seconds on each question, so that you spend a maximum of 7.5 minutes on this part of the test.

PRACTICE ▶ As timing is the most important skill to master on this part of the test, for each of the three Practice sections that follow you will have a time limit of 2.5 minutes to answer the ten questions. Before you begin, review the steps explained above. Be sure to follow these steps when completing the Practice exercises.

2.5 MIN

1. Cleveland County's public hospital, stricken by massive .... shortfalls, has announced plans to cut costs by $12 million within the next fiscal year.
   (A) fund
   (B) funds
   (C) funding
   (D) funded

2. TX Routemaster, San Fernando Valley's main provider of intercity bus transportation, is .... recruiting for coach operators.
   (A) currently
   (B) coherently
   (C) collectively
   (D) customarily

3. Troy Nielsen is one of six athletes being considered for the national synchronized diving team .... this weekend's trials in Washington.
   (A) among
   (B) during
   (C) through
   (D) into

4. .... recently moved to a new, purpose-built warehouse, Hudson Stationery Inc. is delighted to guarantee next-day delivery on almost all in-stock items.
   (A) Having
   (B) After
   (C) Because
   (D) Unless

5. Online sites .... as SavingPlus showcase the very best coupons and deals that cannot be found in stores.
   (A) like
   (B) such
   (C) just
   (D) so

6. .... of the workers at the quarry knew they were being dismissed until they received an e-mail Tuesday morning.
   (A) Some
   (B) All
   (C) Most
   (D) None

7. The business model adopted by DynoTorp two years ago has not proved to be a success, ... the results are interpreted.
   (A) nevertheless
   (B) even
   (C) although
   (D) however

8. Forrester's two-part adaptation of Wolf's masterpiece has been widely praised for its .... and historical accuracy.
   (A) realist
   (B) realistic
   (C) realistically
   (D) realism

9. Angel investors may wish to serve as advisors to the start-ups they engage with, depending on .... work experience and investing style.
   (A) they
   (B) their
   (C) them
   (D) theirs

10. To unlock a world of digital entertainment, simply .... your satellite receiver to any broadband router using an Ethernet cable or wireless network adapter.
    (A) assign
    (B) transmit
    (C) connect
    (D) relate

1. Ⓐ Ⓑ Ⓒ Ⓓ 4. Ⓐ Ⓑ Ⓒ Ⓓ 7. Ⓐ Ⓑ Ⓒ Ⓓ 10. Ⓐ Ⓑ Ⓒ Ⓓ
2. Ⓐ Ⓑ Ⓒ Ⓓ 5. Ⓐ Ⓑ Ⓒ Ⓓ 8. Ⓐ Ⓑ Ⓒ Ⓓ
3. Ⓐ Ⓑ Ⓒ Ⓓ 6. Ⓐ Ⓑ Ⓒ Ⓓ 9. Ⓐ Ⓑ Ⓒ Ⓓ   Score .... /10

1. With a wide variety of merchandise on display, the Freetown Handicraft Festival makes .... a perfect one-stop shop for all hand-made items.
   (A) up
   (B) for
   (C) out
   (D) over

2. Nearly three-quarters of survey respondents indicated that they would not mind .... increased taxes in order to fund the government's ambitious healthcare reforms.
   (A) pay
   (B) to pay
   (C) paying
   (D) paid

3. .... to popular belief, Christopher Columbus did not discover the continent of North America, but a series of islands in what are today known as the Bahamas.
   (A) Contradictory
   (B) Converse
   (C) Conflicting
   (D) Contrary

4. It took our library customers a while to get .... to the new catalog search function.
   (A) uses
   (B) use
   (C) used
   (D) using

5. Under the food assistance program, items such as pet foods and paper products are .... for federal food stamps.
   (A) ineligible
   (B) indelible
   (C) inedible
   (D) infallible

6. This comprehensive study clearly indicates that the mandatory use of bicycle helmets would help reduce the incidence and severity of head and brain ....
   (A) injuries
   (B) damages
   (C) wounds
   (D) impairments

7. Please tell us if there is anything we .... have done to improve your stay.
   (A) would
   (B) ought
   (C) must
   (D) could

8. Climate scientists are beginning to ask whether the international consensus for action on global warming is on the verge of .... and needs to be revisited.
   (A) collapsed
   (B) collapses
   (C) collapse
   (D) collapsible

9. An analysis of buying style variables concluded that there was no .... difference between the two consumer groups.
   (A) appreciated
   (B) appreciable
   (C) appreciative
   (D) appreciation

10. Regardless of the number of hours they work per week, all employees are entitled to receive a written contract of employment .... two months of starting work.
    (A) by
    (B) within
    (C) before
    (D) until

1. Ⓐ Ⓑ Ⓒ Ⓓ 4. Ⓐ Ⓑ Ⓒ Ⓓ 7. Ⓐ Ⓑ Ⓒ Ⓓ 10. Ⓐ Ⓑ Ⓒ Ⓓ
2. Ⓐ Ⓑ Ⓒ Ⓓ 5. Ⓐ Ⓑ Ⓒ Ⓓ 8. Ⓐ Ⓑ Ⓒ Ⓓ
3. Ⓐ Ⓑ Ⓒ Ⓓ 6. Ⓐ Ⓑ Ⓒ Ⓓ 9. Ⓐ Ⓑ Ⓒ Ⓓ Score .... /10

Practice 3 2.5 MIN

1. New ways of tackling income inequality have
   .... if we are to prevent the gap between
   the world's rich and poor from becoming
   ever wider.
   (A) to find
   (B) been found
   (C) to be found
   (D) being found

2. It was only after testing the new ....
   recognition software for five months that law
   enforcement officials announced that the
   beta version was a success.
   (A) face
   (B) faces
   (C) facet
   (D) facial

3. Under the circumstances, the union leaders
   agreed there was no other course of action
   .... to call a general strike.
   (A) except
   (B) apart
   (C) besides
   (D) despite

4. These stone ramparts and the ruins of the
   main gate are all .... remain of the castle
   following a fire in 1523.
   (A) which
   (B) what
   (C) that
   (D) where

5. The news that Spartans coach Bill Dwyer
   was to be replaced came as no surprise after
   the team's tenth .... defeat last Saturday.
   (A) consecutive
   (B) consecrated
   (C) consequent
   (D) consensual

6. Next week's in-house training workshop will
   focus on the essential sales skill of how to
   .... a deal effectively.
   (A) take
   (B) join
   (C) close
   (D) form

7. This initiative is intended to crack down on
   tax avoidance schemes, yet its success
   has .... placed in doubt due to fierce
   resistance by multinational corporations.
   (A) had
   (B) to
   (C) not
   (D) been

8. Investors appear to be turning away from
   gold, hedge funds, and long-term bonds in
   .... of high fees and lackluster results.
   (A) favor
   (B) consequence
   (C) terms
   (D) spite

9. A period of .... rainfall over much of
   central Europe since Friday has led to
   widespread flooding in several states.
   (A) rigorous
   (B) strenuous
   (C) forceful
   (D) intense

10. The industrial park off Interstate 89 is
    the brainchild of TransCom, a nonprofit,
    .... funded organization set up to
    support the local business community.
    (A) private
    (B) privately
    (C) privatized
    (D) privatization

1. Ⓐ Ⓑ Ⓒ Ⓓ 4. Ⓐ Ⓑ Ⓒ Ⓓ 7. Ⓐ Ⓑ Ⓒ Ⓓ 10. Ⓐ Ⓑ Ⓒ Ⓓ

2. Ⓐ Ⓑ Ⓒ Ⓓ 5. Ⓐ Ⓑ Ⓒ Ⓓ 8. Ⓐ Ⓑ Ⓒ Ⓓ

3. Ⓐ Ⓑ Ⓒ Ⓓ 6. Ⓐ Ⓑ Ⓒ Ⓓ 9. Ⓐ Ⓑ Ⓒ Ⓓ Score .... /10

Strategy Review and Tips

Remember, in the test…

Work fast! You should aim to read each sentence quickly, but carefully.

When you come to a blank, quickly look through the four answer choices, and then finish reading the sentence.

Consider the answer choices. If you know the correct answer, mark your answer right away and go on to the next question.

If you are not sure of the answer, decide if the focus is grammar or vocabulary. Look at the words before and after the blank to help you. Then look more closely and ask yourself what exactly is being tested.

Read the sentence again and eliminate any answers that you are sure are wrong.

If you are still not sure which answer to choose, don't waste time. Decide quickly and move on to the next item.

TIPS *Here is some advice that people taking the TOEIC test have found useful for this part. Choose the tips you like, and try to use them.*

"I know some people leave the tricky questions and go back later, but I don't. I go through this part once and once only. It is much better to answer the questions straight away than waste time going back."
Da-Xia Liang

"Narrow the options down by eliminating as many answer choices as you can; then always guess answer choice (C) if it is still available. If (C) isn't available, choose (B)."
Jean Marchal

"Keep looking at your watch. It is easy to spend a little too long on the problematic ones, and before you know it you will be way behind time. Be strict, and do your best not to fall behind."
Jo Kwon

"Always go with your instinct. Never start to doubt yourself, because once you start to change your mind you begin to doubt everything!"
Yuka Kato

Review Test

Directions: Read each sentence. You will notice that there is a word or phrase missing. Study the four answer choices and select the one answer: (A), (B), (C), or (D), that best completes the sentence. Then mark your answer.

1. Regulators have called for swift action against any lobbyists found to have exerted .... influence on the awarding of government contracts.
   (A) alternative
   (B) unequal
   (C) gratuitous
   (D) undue

2. Apprentices benefit by gaining real-world experience, and are required to use .... skills and talents in order to progress to recognized qualifications.
   (A) diverse
   (B) diversity
   (C) diversify
   (D) diversely

3. According to the test engineer, either a problem with the internal wiring or electrical interference might have .... the generator to fail.
   (A) causes
   (B) caused
   (C) causing
   (D) cause

4. Senior executives at AggreMax Corp. continue to release upbeat assessments of the company's performance, ... the data clearly suggests otherwise.
   (A) despite
   (B) even though
   (C) however
   (D) notwithstanding

5. Thanks to some enterprising initiatives put forward by the shop floor, employee .... has decreased significantly over recent months.
   (A) morale
   (B) relations
   (C) absenteeism
   (D) access

6. Australia is .... becoming a global hub and conduit for cybercrime, as online criminals increasingly shift their focus toward Asia.
   (A) soon
   (B) ever
   (C) yet
   (D) fast

1. Ⓐ Ⓑ Ⓒ Ⓓ   3. Ⓐ Ⓑ Ⓒ Ⓓ   5. Ⓐ Ⓑ Ⓒ Ⓓ
2. Ⓐ Ⓑ Ⓒ Ⓓ   4. Ⓐ Ⓑ Ⓒ Ⓓ   6. Ⓐ Ⓑ Ⓒ Ⓓ

7. A spokesperson told reporters that authorities were concentrating their search for survivors of the crash .... an area around Lightning Ridge.
   (A) on
   (B) at
   (C) about
   (D) into

8. An accomplished equestrian, Tina Morgan participates in show jumping competitions and dressage events .... she is able.
   (A) whatever
   (B) whichever
   (C) whenever
   (D) whoever

9. .... reduced production costs, shipbuilding firm Fairfax Seaway is hopeful it can increase profitability and win more orders for its LNG carriers.
   (A) With
   (B) In
   (C) By
   (D) For

10. Huxol Construction .... recently secured an expressway construction project in the Middle East worth $275 million.
    (A) did
    (B) is
    (C) was
    (D) has

11. By the time the last episode of the TV drama series *Lakeview Valley* .... aired, ratings were at an all-time low and viewership in an irreversible decline.
    (A) was
    (B) will be
    (C) had
    (D) were

12. Novice investors must make sure they are .... informed of the risks, and the associated costs, involved in trading on the equities market.
    (A) exclusively
    (B) fully
    (C) openly
    (D) quite

13. After a lengthy and .... search for a credible candidate, Judy Harrelson has finally been put forward as the city's next chief financial officer.
    (A) surreptitious
    (B) unabashed
    (C) painstaking
    (D) repentant

7. Ⓐ Ⓑ Ⓒ Ⓓ   10. Ⓐ Ⓑ Ⓒ Ⓓ   13. Ⓐ Ⓑ Ⓒ Ⓓ
8. Ⓐ Ⓑ Ⓒ Ⓓ   11. Ⓐ Ⓑ Ⓒ Ⓓ
9. Ⓐ Ⓑ Ⓒ Ⓓ   12. Ⓐ Ⓑ Ⓒ Ⓓ

14. EU think tank InTrax has revealed that one-fifth of workers no longer think they will be able to .... to retire, but expect to work indefinitely.
(A) accept
(B) afford
(C) allow
(D) admit

15. Mackenzie Industrial, a major player in the global construction ...., won a bid from the Vietnamese government to build a coal-powered electricity plant.
(A) region
(B) zone
(C) sector
(D) district

16. Software developer KeyNet has .... their GlobalOffice app free for Android and iOS users, with an extra 5 gigs of storage for three years.
(A) announced
(B) granted
(C) promised
(D) made

17. What makes Procter such an enthralling player to watch is the .... of his excellent attacking skills and superb mental toughness.
(A) combination
(B) transformation
(C) amalgamation
(D) orientation

18. Mike Branson, who is overseeing the launch of KTV's digital video service, does not anticipate any problems .... from the closure of the firm's e-commerce division.
(A) arise
(B) arisen
(C) arises
(D) arising

19. .... the amount of time it has taken to develop the online management system, the fact there are so many bugs is extremely disappointing.
(A) Whereas
(B) Considering
(C) Though
(D) Allowing

20. Use the links in the panel on the right of the console .... access guidance on how to operate the system in standard and overdrive modes.
(A) so
(B) for
(C) to
(D) in

14. (A) (B) (C) (D) 17. (A) (B) (C) (D) 20. (A) (B) (C) (D)
15. (A) (B) (C) (D) 18. (A) (B) (C) (D)
16. (A) (B) (C) (D) 19. (A) (B) (C) (D)

21. The basic _____ behind the movie, that a bunch of arch-villains and gangsters might join forces with law enforcement, seems utterly implausible.
   (A) premise
   (B) foundation
   (C) theory
   (D) inference

22. Parties on _____ side of the political spectrum are accusing each other of ineptitude and financial timidity in tackling the state's budget deficit.
   (A) the
   (B) both
   (C) either
   (D) any

23. There is no doubt that it has been tough _____ for the Jaguars so far this season, chalking up just two wins in their first six games.
   (A) going
   (B) conditions
   (C) progress
   (D) making

24. Nobody in the company imagined that the outcome would have _____ any different had the buyout plan succeeded.
   (A) been
   (B) to be
   (C) be
   (D) being

25. The issue of customers' not being suitable for the financial products they were being sold was raised in the commission's report, _____ was published last month.
   (A) what
   (B) when
   (C) that
   (D) which

26. This easy-to-use graphic presentation tool enables sales agents to store and retrieve complex data with the aim _____ creating customized spreadsheets for clients.
   (A) is
   (B) of
   (C) for
   (D) to

27. To increase the _____ of the rocket, it was necessary to elongate the body, increase the area of the fins, and add weight to the nose cone.
   (A) stabilization
   (B) stabilizing
   (C) stability
   (D) stabilizer

28. Turnpike Clothing's grip on the apparel industry _____ loosened as production costs rise and leading brands look for new suppliers elsewhere.
   (A) had been
   (B) is being
   (C) has to
   (D) was

21. Ⓐ Ⓑ Ⓒ Ⓓ 24. Ⓐ Ⓑ Ⓒ Ⓓ 27. Ⓐ Ⓑ Ⓒ Ⓓ
22. Ⓐ Ⓑ Ⓒ Ⓓ 25. Ⓐ Ⓑ Ⓒ Ⓓ 28. Ⓐ Ⓑ Ⓒ Ⓓ
23. Ⓐ Ⓑ Ⓒ Ⓓ 26. Ⓐ Ⓑ Ⓒ Ⓓ

29. This postgraduate diploma is intended for those that have .... been excluded from full participation in higher education.

(A) earlier

(B) before

(C) former

(D) hitherto

30. The idea that universes similar in nature to our own may exist presents an .... reality that can inspire and absorb in equal measure.

(A) alteration

(B) alternated

(C) alternate

(D) alternant

29. Ⓐ Ⓑ Ⓒ Ⓓ **30.** Ⓐ Ⓑ Ⓒ Ⓓ   Score .... /30

EXTRA PRACTICE ONLINE

Go to **www.pass-the-toeic-test.com** for more grammar and vocabulary exercises to help improve your score on Part 5 of the TOEIC test.

PART 6 TEXT COMPLETION

This part of the TOEIC® test consists of four short texts. Each text has four blanks – these are spaces where a word, phrase or a sentence is missing. There are four answer choices for each blank and you must choose the answer that best completes the sentence. The texts are short, and cover a variety of business correspondence such as notices, articles, e-mails, letters, advertisements, and announcements. The language is typical of that used in formal, written English.

In the same way as for Part 5, the main purpose is to test your knowledge of grammar and vocabulary. You need to show you have a thorough command of grammar, and that you have an extensive vocabulary.

The only difference between Part 5 and Part 6 is that here you are faced with a text, rather than single sentences. For the most part, all the information you need to choose the correct answer can be found in the sentence containing the blank. Occasionally, however, you will need to understand the wider context, and this requires you to look in the sentences that come before or after the blank.

One question for each text asks you to identify a missing sentence. This question aims to test your reading comprehension. You may need to read the text more carefully to get a general idea of the purpose and context.

> ## QUICK CHECK
>
> How many questions are in this part of the TOEIC test?
> What are the language areas that are being tested?
> How many answer choices are there for each question?
> In what way is Part 6 different from Part 5?

1 MIN

You may find it useful to review the Grammar and Vocabulary sections before you start.

OVERVIEW

EXAMPLE

LONDON, 27 September—The tension in the air is almost palpable, as with just two weeks remaining before the winners of this year's Nobel Prizes ....**1**........ , the eyes of the world start to focus on the Stockholm Concert Hall in Sweden once more. Ever since 1901, when they were established, the Nobel Prizes have been awarded annually to the best and brightest of the world's cultural and scientific intelligentsia. Nominations are invited each year by the Nobel Committees, ...**2**........ then choose from the worthy scientists, scholars, and statesmen based on the nominees' contributions and achievements. ....**3**........ . As Nobel laureates, they each receive a medal, a cash award well in excess of $1 million, and the distinction of being admitted into one of the world's most elite societies—as ....**4**........ of the uniquely designed and highly decorated Nobel Diploma.

---

1. (A) have been announced
   (B) will have been announced
   (C) **are announced**
   (D) were announced

> The present simple passive completes this time clause using the conjunction *before* to reference the future.

2. (A) and
   (B) **who**
   (C) they
   (D) to

> This relative pronoun relates to the members of the Nobel Committees, and correctly matches the syntax and grammar of the sentence.

3. (A) **Five fortunate winners are selected.**
   (B) The world's media is always informed.
   (C) The prize originates in Norway.
   (D) Election to the committee lasts 6 years.

> This sentence fits best as it introduces the subject *winners*, which is referenced in the following sentence *they each receive*.

4 (A) affiliates
   (B) patrons
   (C) members
   (D) **holders**

> The plural noun *holders (of)* relates to the award *Nobel Diploma*, and is the only noun that can complete this lengthy noun phrase.

Challenges

In Part 6, you need to read each text quickly, understand the general context, and then complete the text by choosing the correct missing words/phrases or sentence for each blank. You need to do this as quickly as you can. As in Part 5, you should try to identify what feature of grammar or vocabulary is being tested, but for missing sentence items you also need an understanding of the context and purpose of the text. After marking your answer, you need to move straight on to the next question. Here are some factors to be aware of on this part of the test.

▶ Timing

When faced with a text, it can be tempting to read it carefully in order to digest its content before moving on to complete the sentences. You must resist this urge. There is simply not enough time available to do this. All you need to do is identify the missing information. Quickly skim the text and then focus *immediately* on completing each sentence. If you spend too long on this section, you will not have enough time for Part 7, which holds far more marks and where the texts require much closer attention.

▶ Text length

Some texts are longer than others. This is deliberate, as longer texts take longer to read. This is a trap for weaker test-takers who may feel they have to read every word before they can complete the sentences. Do not waste time reading every word.

▶ Reference

Occasionally you will not be able to identify the correct answer without looking elsewhere in the text. This is especially common when conjunctions, time markers, and tenses are being tested. In such cases, you will need to read information that comes before or after the sentence with the blank. This can take more time, but do not be fooled into thinking you need to read every word in every text as a result.

▶ Missing sentences

One item in every text will be a missing sentence. Rather than focus on grammar or vocabulary function, this item tests your reading comprehension.

▶ Range

As in Part 5, you may be tested on any aspect of your grammatical and lexical knowledge. Some texts will include complex grammatical structures or obscure words and expressions that you may not know.

STEPS TO SUCCESS

This section presents an effective, step-by-step approach to use when answering questions on Part 6 of the TOEIC® test.

The steps shown here are designed to help you achieve the highest possible score when you take the test. By following these steps, you should be able to maximize your score on this part of the test.

1 ▶ Quickly identify the type of text (letter, advertisement, e-mail, etc.) and then skim the text to get a general idea of its content. Do *not* look at the answer choices.

2 ▶ Go straight to the first sentence with a blank. Read the sentence and study the answer choices. *If you are sure of the answer, mark your answer immediately and move on to the next question*. If you are not sure of the answer, proceed to Step 3.

3 ▶ Read the sentence again and identify exactly what is being tested.

- For a grammar/vocabulary question, ask yourself what kind of word or phrase you need to complete the sentence (a modal verb, noun, etc.). Study the words that come before and after the blank space. If you can't decide, ask yourself which option "sounds" right.

- For a missing sentence, consider the purpose of the text. Examine how each of the four possible sentences connects with the sentences that come before and after in the text. If necessary, quickly read the text again to help you better understand the context and purpose.

4 ▶ Study the answer choices once again and eliminate any you are sure are incorrect. Mark your answer. Then repeat steps 2 through 4 for the remaining questions.

TIMING It is vital you do not slow down and waste time by reading these texts unnecessarily. Keep a watch in front of you and check the time regularly. You should aim to spend a maximum of 8 minutes on this part of the test.

PRACTICE For each of the three Practice sections that follow you will have a time limit of 2 minutes to preview the text and answer the four questions. Before you begin, review the steps explained above. Be sure to follow these steps when completing the Practice exercises.

Whatever journey you are planning to take, whether it be the trip of a lifetime or just a relaxing few days away, ensuring quick and safe access to your money is no longer a headache. Most ....**1**........ opt for a mixture of cash and debit or credit cards, but remember to always get some local currency *before* you leave, so you can get the best exchange rates. ....**2**........ deciding how you will carry your travel money and cards, go for an inconspicuous wallet which you can keep in a secure pocket on your body. It is preferable to keep some notes and coins separate for routine expenses on the go. Of course, before ....**3**........ off you should make sure your debit and credit cards are not about to expire, as getting replacements when abroad can be tricky and time-consuming. Finally, be sure you note your card details and keep the phone numbers of the card issuers handy. ....**4**........

1. (A) lodgers
     (B) visitors
     (C) travelers
     (D) passengers

2. (A) When
     (B) After
     (C) Whereas
     (D) Even

3. (A) getting
     (B) making
     (C) leaving
     (D) setting

4. (A) This will be useful in an emergency.
     (B) Thank you for following these rules.
     (C) Not all card issuers are easy to contact.
     (D) Enjoy your time abroad and don't worry unnecessarily!

1. Ⓐ Ⓑ Ⓒ Ⓓ   **2.** Ⓐ Ⓑ Ⓒ Ⓓ   **3.** Ⓐ Ⓑ Ⓒ Ⓓ   **4.** Ⓐ Ⓑ Ⓒ Ⓓ

Practice 2

2 MIN

To:	coramcdonald@officedepository.com
From:	dougrichards@benwest.com
Sent:	March 12
Subject:	Invoice 43875-AS

Dear Cora,

.............**1**............. When we placed an order in January for your Valiant-Pro thermal laminator, which you kindly expedited at the time, on the invoice it read, "We are pleased to offer you a further 10 percent discount on your next purchase. Simply use coupon code NTYA873 when placing your next order." I just tried to use this code and it was rejected. I e-mailed your customer service department, only to be told that the code ....**2**............. . However, there is nothing on the invoice that suggests there is a time limit on its use.

So far, we have been very satisfied with the range of products and competitive pricing from The Office Depository, but this issue has given us ....**3**............. to reconsider. If a code has an expiration date, it should be clearly stated on the invoice. I am sure you can appreciate that ....**4**............. I known, I would have placed my order earlier. As you were so helpful before, could I please ask you to look into this and get back to me?

Doug Richards
Office Manager, Ext. 143

---

1. (A) I have a problem with your customer services.
   (B) I would like to thank you for your assistance.
   (C) Please find following an answer to your query.
   (D) Could you please clarify your coupon code policy?

2. (A) would expire
   (B) had expired
   (C) will expire
   (D) is expiring

3. (A) authority
   (B) decision
   (C) chance
   (D) cause

4. (A) if
   (B) were
   (C) had
   (D) should

---

1. Ⓐ Ⓑ Ⓒ Ⓓ **2.** Ⓐ Ⓑ Ⓒ Ⓓ **3.** Ⓐ Ⓑ Ⓒ Ⓓ **4.** Ⓐ Ⓑ Ⓒ Ⓓ

2 MIN

Dear Dr. Lefebvre:

It was a pleasure to make your acquaintance at last week's International Medical Trade Fair in Dubai. I very much enjoyed our discussion, and ....1........ with you wholeheartedly about the importance of translational research in accelerating the discovery of new treatments.

As I mentioned, the main focus of our work here at the Heart and Vascular Institute is arrhythmia, cardiomyopathy, and preventative cardiology research. The project I outlined to you focuses on ....2........ heart disease, and as this is your area of specialization we would be most honored if you would agree to participate as a partner in our genetic testing program. Please find enclosed our proposal, entitled "Gene Therapy Approaches for Hypertrophic Cardiomyopathy," and an addendum which ....3........ out the planned interactive collaboration.

This project aims to establish proof-of-principle for a novel gene therapy for HCM, using cutting-edge techniques and methods at the forefront of cellular and molecular biology. ....4........

Sincerely,

Raymond Zhou

Dr. Raymond Zhou
Medical Executive Director of Research

1. (A) agree
   (B) agreed
   (C) have agreed
   (D) was agreeing

2. (A) inherit
   (B) inheritance
   (C) inherited
   (D) inheritor

3. (A) proves
   (B) spells
   (C) makes
   (D) puts

4. (A) I will conduct further genetic tests in due course.
   (B) Good luck with the research paper presentation.
   (C) We look forward to welcoming you on board.
   (D) Thank you for your help, which has been invaluable.

1. Ⓐ Ⓑ Ⓒ Ⓓ 2. Ⓐ Ⓑ Ⓒ Ⓓ 3. Ⓐ Ⓑ Ⓒ Ⓓ 4. Ⓐ Ⓑ Ⓒ Ⓓ

Strategy Review and Tips

Strategy Review Reading Test – Part 6

Remember, in the test...

Quickly preview each text, but do not read every word. You just need to identify the type of text and get a general idea of the purpose and context.

Go straight to the first sentence with a blank. Read the sentence, mark your answer if you can, and move on to the next question.

If you are not sure of the answer, look at the words before and after the blank and try to identify exactly what is being tested; grammar, vocabulary, or (for a missing sentence) reading comprehension.

Do not forget that you may need to look at the previous and following sentences to help you identify the correct answer. This is especially true when you need to identify a missing sentence.

If you are still not sure which answer to choose, don't waste time. Decide quickly and move on to the next item.

 TIPS *Here is some advice that people taking the TOEIC test have found useful for this part. Choose the tips you like, and try to use them.*

"I try to answer each question as I read the text. When I get to the end, I have usually answered two or three. This saves time."
Mike Nguyen

"For grammar or vocabulary items, I read the word before and the word after the blank with all four answer choices in place. I find I can often eliminate at least one or two answer choices by doing that."
Saburo Kobayashi

"To help me choose the correct missing sentence, I always read the text again and ask myself what the purpose is."
Claude Leblanc

"I really push myself to get through this part as quickly as possible. To me, it is nothing more than an obstacle in the way of getting to Part 7. It's only there to slow you up, so don't waste time!"
Michelle Thomas

Review Test

Directions: Read each text. You will notice that there are four blanks. These are places where a word, phrase, or sentence is missing. For each blank, study the four answer choices and select the one answer: (A), (B), (C), or (D), that best completes the sentence. Then mark your answer.

Question 1–4 refer to the following advertisement.

Stella*Go*—Digital Publishing at its Best

Excelling in solutions that enhance growth

StellaGo Software is a leading provider of digital publishing solutions to the global publishing industry. We play an integral role in supporting publishers with a suite of products and platforms designed to render content across multiple channels.

_____**1**_____ There's *GoManager*, a dynamic, cloud-based production workflow management system, and *GoAnalytics*, an analytics tool designed for publishers, administrators, and educators. For those wanting a state-of-the-art engine to turn content into multimedia-rich e-books, there is *GoSuite*, while if you want an intuitive collaborative digital publishing platform then *GoCreate* is for you. _____**2**_____ , we can help you sell your content, too, with *GoStore*, our cloud-based store for selling digital products.

With a particular emphasis on mobile development, StellaGo is ready and waiting to help you develop next-generation digital learning products. We have over ten years' experience _____**3**_____ extensively with global publishers and distributors. Let us help you to create cross-channel content monetization opportunities. Contact us today for full details of our products and services at stellagosoft@gmail.com. We promise to get back _____**4**_____ a competitive quote within 24 hours of your request. StellaGo – the complete solution to all your digital publishing needs.

---

1. (A) Some platforms are more popular than others.
   (B) We have many cutting-edge solutions to choose from.
   (C) Digital publishing has changed a lot over time.
   (D) Competition is fierce throughout the digital industry.

2. (A) For instance
   (B) On the other hand
   (C) Nevertheless
   (D) Furthermore

3. (A) work
   (B) worked
   (C) working
   (D) to work

4. (A) to
   (B) with
   (C) about
   (D) into

---

1. (A) (B) (C) (D)   2. (A) (B) (C) (D)   3. (A) (B) (C) (D)   4. (A) (B) (C) (D)

Vacation Entitlement

Attention all staff

This is a gentle reminder that there are now only three months remaining of the current vacation year. Please note that any accrued entitlement that remains unused will only _____5_____ over to the new vacation year in exceptional circumstances. Therefore, we would encourage members of staff to review their leave entitlement and make arrangements to use any remaining days as appropriate.

Remember that your three personal days and bonus diversity day, _____6_____ being in addition to your vacation allowance, cannot be saved up. Karen has kindly sent out updated reports to heads of department today, which also detail unscheduled absences (sick days, doctor appointments, etc.), _____7_____ please check with your line manager how many days you have left.

If you have any questions, please do not hesitate to contact me directly. _____8_____

Lorraine Dingley
HR and Training Manager

5. (A) be carried
   (B) have carried
   (C) to carry
   (D) be carrying

6. (A) are
   (B) even
   (C) while
   (D) because

7. (A) can
   (B) then
   (C) and
   (D) so

8. (A) My door is always open.
   (B) Actions speak louder than words.
   (C) Thank you for your support.
   (D) Everyone needs a vacation.

5. (A) (B) (C) (D) 6. (A) (B) (C) (D) 7. (A) (B) (C) (D) 8. (A) (B) (C) (D)

Nigel Baines
35 Oak Tree Drive
Manchester MR2 6BP

November 21

Dear Mr. Baines:

I am delighted to be sending you a copy of our new magazine, *Global Family.* This first issue is crammed with news of all the great projects that TransWorld Aid is _____**9**_____ in around the world, thanks to the generous support of people like you. Please take a moment to read about the ways in which your support is helping to transform the lives of children and communities in over 30 developing countries.

We are working hard to improve the lives of over 70,000 people affected by poverty through a holistic approach to sustainability and self-help. None of the work we do _____**10**_____ be possible without your support. I hope you enjoy finding out more about the work we do. Please pass this magazine on to family members, friends, and colleagues when you are finished with it. I am sure they would like to hear the news also, and possibly even contribute to our efforts. _____**11**_____

Together, we are making a _____**12**_____ .

Elizabeth Hawking
Elizabeth Hawking
Chief Executive, TransWorld Aid

9. (A) engrossed
   (B) engulfed
   (C) engaged
   (D) engrained

10. (A) might
    (B) would
    (C) should
    (D) must

11. (A) The cost of publishing the magazine is not inconsiderable.
    (B) We rely entirely on charitable donations to fund our work.
    (C) Thank you for the generous increase in your donation.
    (D) We aim to help those who cannot help themselves.

12. (A) difference
    (B) complaint
    (C) will
    (D) claim

9. (A) (B) (C) (D)   10. (A) (B) (C) (D)   11. (A) (B) (C) (D)   12. (A) (B) (C) (D)

Question 13–16 refer to the following memo.

To: All Staff
From: Thomas Castelli
Date: September 24
Subject: New starter

I am pleased to announce that we have recruited a new Overnight Kitchen and Public Area Cleaner for the Parker Center.

Jakub Brozec joins us with five years' experience in a similar _____**13**_____ working nights at the Grand Harbor Hotel in Charlestown. He will be responsible for all overnight deep-cleaning and heavy work duties, as well as routine _____**14**_____ of restaurant kitchen equipment, washing and polishing the marble floors, vacuuming carpets, emptying trash, cleaning public restrooms, wiping down tables, etc.

_____**15**_____ . He will be completing two weeks of days for training purposes, and then all being well he will be ready to start night shifts by the end of the month. Some of you may _____**16**_____ . Jakub when he completed a trial shift last week, but if not, please extend a warm welcome when you see him.

13. (A) task
    (B) role
    (C) work
    (D) duty

14. (A) cleanliness
    (B) cleaner
    (C) cleanly
    (D) cleaning

15. (A) No further appointments will be made.
    (B) We pride ourselves on our friendly reputation.
    (C) This work is very important to us all.
    (D) Jakub will start on Tuesday, October 10.

16. (A) meet
    (B) have met
    (C) met
    (D) meeting

13. Ⓐ Ⓑ Ⓒ Ⓓ   14. Ⓐ Ⓑ Ⓒ Ⓓ   15. Ⓐ Ⓑ Ⓒ Ⓓ   16. Ⓐ Ⓑ Ⓒ Ⓓ
Score _____/16

EXTRA PRACTICE ONLINE

Go to **www.pass-the-toeic-test.com** for more grammar and vocabulary exercises to help improve your score on Part 6 of the TOEIC test.

This part of the TOEIC® test consists of a series of short passages. The passages are followed by between two and five questions, each with four answer choices. You must choose the best answer for each question.

The purpose is to test your reading comprehension. You need to show you can understand a wide range of texts of varying length, covering different text types, such as e-mails, memos, letters, faxes, notices, advertisements, and articles. Before each passage, there is an introductory statement that specifies the type of passage you will read.

Questions will test your understanding of the main ideas as well as specific details, and will sometimes require you to make inferences. You will also need to show you can make connections between up to three texts. Some questions test your understanding of words and phrases in context. Occasionally for single passages you also need to choose where to insert a missing sentence. Topics cover common work-related and social themes, as well as more specialized contexts. The language is typical of that used in formal, written business correspondence and everyday work activities.

There are usually ten single passages, with between two and four questions each. This first section has a total of 29 questions. There are then two double reading passages, and three triple reading passages. These multiple passage items each have 5 questions.

> ### QUICK CHECK
>
> How many questions are in this part of the TOEIC test?
> What kinds of skills are being tested?
> How many double reading passages are there?
> How many questions are there for each multiple reading passage?
> What kinds of passages are covered in this part?
>
>
> **1 MIN**

EXAMPLE 1 - a single passage

Summer Festival Line-Up

The line-up for this year's festival has now been confirmed. Taking place on two days, and across three venues, the festival will host the following outstanding array of distinguished professionals and internationally eminent individuals, all leaders in their field. We welcome renowned dramatists Dorothy Lennox and Leonard Batley; playwright Chris Fellows; historians Dale Carpenter and Will Rastrew; politician Mary Shard; this year's Stanforth Prize-winner R. S. Peppard; Sports Personality of the Year Samantha Howard; memoirist Susan Coe; film critic Jasper Pertwee; and chroniclers of the 1930s Depression era Nancy Clifford and Anne Gwyer. Plus, the prominent activist Alison Vickers will be exploring the resurgence of feminism, and biographer Jim Crumpsall will be helping us all to feel on first-name terms with rowing legend and five-time Olympic Gold medal-winner Tony Brice. Don't miss our special pre-festival event, which gives you the chance to rub shoulders with all these well-known figures, and many more. The full program will be launched on our website, summerfestival.com, on Friday, June 3. The Grand Theater box office opens on Friday, June 10. Adult $12; Child $9; 30% member discount.

Priority booking

Priority online booking opens Monday, June 6. If you are not already a Friend, then you still have time to join before regular booking opens. For more information on how to join, visit our website.

1. What is the purpose of this announcement?
   - (A) **To promote an upcoming literary event**
   - (B) To announce the participants in a competition
   - (C) To advertise the opening of a theatrical production
   - (D) To publicize a new online service for members

> The notice is advertising an upcoming *festival*. We can infer from *dramatists, playwright, memoirist, chroniclers*, and *biographer* that there is a literary theme.

2. From what date can Friends of the Festival buy their tickets?
   - (A) May 27
   - (B) June 3
   - (C) **June 6**
   - (D) June 10

> The final paragraph indicates that Friends are eligible for *priority online booking*, which opens *Monday, June 6*.

3. What is NOT mentioned in the announcement?
   - (A) The venue where the event takes place
   - (B) The ticket price for non-members
   - (C) The duration of the festival
   - (D) **The time the event starts**

> We can assume the venue is the *Grand Theater* (A), the prices of tickets for non-members (B) are given, and at the start we read the festival lasts *two days* (C). Only the time the festival starts (D) is not mentioned.

EXAMPLE 2 – a single passage with a missing sentence

To: <m.carter@simmonscollege.com>
From: <p.romano@astralsolutions.co.us>
Subject: Meeting follow-up
Date: April 23

Dear Ms. Carter

Thank you for sparing the time to show me around Simmons College yesterday. It was wonderful to meet you and your colleagues. ---[1]--- I was most impressed by the campus and the facilities you have on-site, and now have a better understanding of your requirements.

---[2]--- Could I first check that you want us to cover all twelve of the laser printers and the five copiers throughout the Administration Division, as well as the eight copiers and three printers in the Teaching Department? ---[3]--- Also, all our annual plans include travel, labor and parts cost (excluding consumable items), but please note that the Anytime Plan does not entitle you to a loan machine should an on-site repair not be possible. Our Return to Base Plan does cover this, of course, but at a 10 percent premium. Which would you like me to quote for?

Please note that payment is required in full at the beginning of the term. ---[4]--- I can confirm we are happy to offer a free health check for all insured devices at the start of your contract.

Looking forward to your response.

Best regards

Pasquale Romano, Head of Operations

1. What is the main purpose of the e-mail?
   (A) To recommend a service
   (B) To request a meeting
   (C) **To confirm some details**
   (D) To advertise a product

Before he can quote, Mr. Romano needs to confirm how many machines cover is required for, and what service plan Ms. Carter prefers.

2. What is indicated about Astral Solutions?
   (A) It provides training for administrative staff.
   (B) It manufactures printers and copiers.
   (C) It sells travel insurance to businesses.
   (D) **It repairs and maintains office equipment.**

Mr. Romano is preparing a quote to *cover* (i.e., *insure*) printers and copiers. The plans he refers to offer labor and parts, so we can infer his company repairs this equipment.

3. In which position marked [1], [2], [3], and [4] does the following sentence best belong?
   "I will get a detailed proposal to you shortly."
   (A) [1]
   (B) **[2]**
   (C) [3]
   (D) [4]

This sentence fits best here as the following sentence, beginning *Could I first check...* , directly relates to it. He can't send a proposal until he knows the exact requirements.

EXAMPLE 3 – a double passage

✦ Matheson Domestic Services ✦

100 Cedar Street, Monterey, CA 93942

✦ Five-time winner of California's Domestic Staffing Agency of the Year Award ✦
Owned and managed by the Lamb family since 1922 ✦ Discretion assured

September 4

Ms. L. Morgan
45 Lorca Lane
Carmel, CA 93924

Dear Ms. Morgan:

It was a pleasure to talk with you this morning, and thank you for choosing Matheson Domestic Services. Let me confirm the details of our conversation as follows:

You are looking for a highly skilled, reliable kitchen supervisor for a full-time position at Sunny Bay View Residential Care Home. The position is temporary, starting as soon as possible and running to January 1 of next year. The successful candidate should have experience designing and preparing varied and nutritionally balanced menus for elderly people. Ideally, this person will also have previously worked in a residential nursing home. Some of your residents have specific cultural and dietary needs that need to be accommodated.

We have a number of potential candidates in our books, but there is one individual who I am confident will fit the bill to a T. She is both a qualified dietician and a trained cook. You can expect to hear from her within the next week. Please arrange an interview directly, and assuming you feel she is suitable, agree between yourselves on a mutually convenient start date. If you have any questions or concerns, please do not hesitate to contact me personally.

Thank you for giving Matheson Domestic Services the opportunity to assist with your staffing needs once again. We value your patronage, and are always pleased to be of service.

Sincerely yours,

Josephine Lamb

Josephine Lamb
Manager, Matheson Domestic Services

September 7

Ms. L. Morgan
45 Lorca Lane
Carmel, CA 93924

Dear Ms. Morgan:

Ms. Lamb of Matheson Domestic Services has contacted me regarding the kitchen supervisor position you have available over the coming months.

I have been in the food preparation industry for over 20 years, working in all kinds of schools, hospitals, and community centers. I am well used to devising menus, including for elderly people. In fact, from 2009 to 2012 I worked at Blue Valley Cultural Day Center as Food and Beverage Manager, where I prepared a lunch for about 80 senior citizens daily, featuring many ethnic dishes, and also supervised the delivery of meals to people at home. I am enclosing a sample of the typical five-week menu cycle we operated. I am an American Culinary Federation-accredited Certified Culinary Administrator, and have always prided myself on making sure there is a good choice of nutritious and tasty food at every mealtime.

I visited the Sunny Bay View website, and it certainly looks like an ideal place for someone with my expertise. I have my own car and only live a few miles away, so I will not need accommodation. I am not working at present as my contract at Nielsen Social Club ended just last week. I could therefore start at your earliest convenience, but of course need to talk with you about working hours, conditions, etc., first.

I look forward to hearing from you and meeting with you soon.

Kind regards,

Gina Park

Gina Park

1. Who is Ms. Morgan?
   (A) **An established client of Matheson Domestic Services**
   (B) A long-standing employee at Sunny Bay View
   (C) The owner and manager of a nursing home
   (D) An experienced cook and kitchen supervisor

> In her letter, Ms. Lamb, the manager of Matheson Domestic Services, refers to assisting with Ms. Morgan's staffing needs *once again*, so she must be an established client of the company. (B) and (C) cannot be inferred. (D) relates to the job position Ms. Morgan is seeking to fill.

2. Why did Ms. Lamb write to Ms. Morgan?
   (A) To inquire about a vacancy
   (B) **To summarize her requirements**
   (C) To respond to an inquiry
   (D) To request more information

> Ms. Lamb wrote to *confirm the details* of the earlier *conversation* they had had about the vacancy at Sunny Bay View. She is not inquiring about the vacancy (A), and she has all the information she needs (D). Ms. Morgan did not make an inquiry (C), but rather she asked Ms. Lamb to source a suitable person to fill the vacancy.

3. What is suggested about Gina Park?
   (A) **She is not Ms. Lamb's first choice for the job.**
   (B) She was dismissed from her previous position.
   (C) She has visited Sunny Bay View in the past.
   (D) She may not be willing to work full-time.

> Ms. Lamb recommends a candidate who is *a qualified dietician and a trained cook*. Gina Park does not mention these points in her letter, saying only that she worked as a *Food and Beverage Manager* and is a *Certified Culinary Administrator*. (B) and (D) cannot be inferred. Ms. Park did not visit Sunny Bay View (C), only the Sunny Bay View *website*.

4. In the second letter, the word "accredited" in paragraph 2, line 5, is closest in meaning to
   (A) specialized
   (B) professional
   (C) experienced
   (D) **qualified**

> Here, *accredited* means *qualified* or *authorized*.

5. Why might Ms. Park NOT be suitable for the position?
   (A) She is unable to fill the vacancy when needed.
   (B) She lacks the necessary expertise and qualifications.
   (C) **She has not worked in a residential care home before.**
   (D) She is not available for the entire period of the contract.

> Ms. Park says she has worked in *all kinds of schools, hospitals, and community centers*, but she does not mention a residential care home.

EXAMPLE 4 – a triple passage

Computer Learning Center
Course Schedule Winter – Spring

All classes are from 7:30 P.M. – 9:30 P.M.

Monday	Genealogy 1: Online family history research
Tuesday	Statistical Computing
Wednesday	Modeling for Business Analysis
Thursday	ITIL Foundation Certificate
Friday	App Development

To: Charlotte Briggs
From: Robina Michelson
Re: Our movie date next week

Hi Charlotte

I'm sorry, but I can't make it next week to see that Canadian movie you were raving about. The Training Manager here, Karen, has signed me up for a computer course, and it starts that evening. It's bound to be a waste of time and I'd much rather see the movie, but I have to keep in her good books. I just looked at the program – the Italian movie looks fun. If you're free then, maybe we can go to that?

Sorry for the last-minute change in plans.
Hope to see you next week.
Robina

FAIRFAX COUNTY
International Film Festival Week

Monday 6	Sands of Eternity	This Oscar-nominated Iranian movie examines the conflict between generations in a small town.
Tuesday 7	Mission to Jupiter	A German-Polish collaboration following in the tradition of Hollywood sci-fi movies.
Wednesday 8	My Name Is Elspeth	A sympathetic treatment of deafness and disability in Ottawa by the award-winning Canadian Director Jacques Corrigan.
Thursday 9	Once Upon a Time in Siberia	This Russian movie scored a near-record 98.5% approval rating on the Rate This Movie site, and had audiences all over Europe rolling in the aisles.
Friday 10	Fortune Never Returns	This poignant award-winning Indian movie broke all box-office records when it was first shown last year.
Saturday 11	Don't Forget the Kids	There's a laugh a minute in this hilarious Italian comedy set in a holiday resort on the Adriatic.

1. Which course is Robina due to attend?
   - (A) Statistical Computing
   - (B) **Modeling for Business Analysis**
   - (C) ITIL Foundation Certificate
   - (D) App Development

   > Robina apologizes in her e-mail that she can't see that Canadian movie. From the movie program, we can see this must be *My Name is Elspeth*, showing on Wednesday. The class schedule indicates *Modeling for Business Analysis* is scheduled for Wednesdays.

2. What is probably true about Robina?
   - (A) She gets on well with her manager.
   - (B) Her computer skills are below average.
   - (C) **She is not looking forward to the course.**
   - (D) She watches many international movies.

   > Robina writes that she would *much rather see the movie* and fears the course will be *a waste of time*. (A), (B), and (D) cannot be inferred.

3. Which day does Robina suggest meeting?
   - (A) Wednesday
   - (B) Thursday
   - (C) Friday
   - (D) **Saturday**

   > Robina suggests the *Italian movie*, which is on *Saturday 11*.

4. Which movie is a comedy?
   - (A) Sands of Eternity
   - (B) Mission to Jupiter
   - (C) **Once Upon a Time in Siberia**
   - (D) Fortune Never Returns

   > The movie program says audiences watching *Once Upon a Time in Siberia* were *rolling in the aisles* (i.e., *laughing a lot*).

5. In the e-mail, the phrase "raving about" in paragraph 1, line 1, is closest in meaning to
   - (A) **praising**
   - (B) reviewing
   - (C) slandering
   - (D) fabricating

   > The verb *to rave about* means to speak very enthusiastically about something, or praise it.

Challenges

In Part 7, you have to quickly look through each text to find answers to the comprehension questions that accompany it. You need to keep focused, and work efficiently as you progress from one text to the next. Here are some factors to be aware of on this part of the test.

▶ Timing

When faced with a text, it can be tempting to read it carefully in order to understand it fully before moving on to answer the questions. You must resist this urge. There is simply not enough time available to read every word, and you do not need to understand the entire text in order to answer the comprehension questions. All you need to do is locate the information you need to find. This is especially true of double and triple passage items. You must focus *solely* on finding the answers to the questions. If you spend too long reading the texts unnecessarily, you will run out of time on this section, and your score on the test will suffer. Do not think of the texts as "passages" to read, but see them as "containers" of key information.

▶ Text length

Some texts are much longer than others. Longer texts have more information for you to sift through, so it might take you longer to answer the questions. Typically, longer texts also have more questions. Nevertheless, the amount of time you spend on each text should be related to the number of questions, not the length of the text.

▶ Text type

Text genre usually varies from one passage to the next, and you need to quickly assimilate each genre. Remember that the type of text can affect where you need to look to find the information you need. For example, key details may be hidden in the subject field of an e-mail or memo, in the heading of an article, or below the signature in a letter.

▶ Content

Depending on the type of text and the style of written English, the sentence structure and syntax can be convoluted and this might cause confusion. Also, the more difficult passages tend to focus on niche contexts and subject matter, which can include terminology and jargon you might not be familiar with.

▶ Reference

Some questions require you to connect information or ideas across a single text, or across two or three texts in the case of double and triple passages. This can sometimes be tricky and time-consuming.

▶ Question type

The questions you are faced with vary considerably. Some questions focus on the meaning of a single word, or are straightforward comprehension questions that request specific information. These types of questions can be answered fairly quickly. However, other questions ask you to identify information that is NOT contained in the text, meaning you need to find three items of information in order to determine what is missing. Questions that ask about the purpose of a text, or require you to make inferences, can also be challenging. Where the information you need is not directly stated, you have to think more carefully before marking your answer. For questions that test your ability to identify the meaning of a word or phrase in context you may need to think about the wider context. Also, for single passages, occasionally you need to decide *where* to insert a sentence into a text.

IMPROVE YOUR PERFORMANCE

In this section you will practice ways to improve your score on Part 7 of the TOEIC® test.

These are the exercises you will cover:

Question Types — dealing with questions about the purpose, topic, and audience; detail questions; inference questions; NOT questions; vocabulary questions; meaning in context questions; missing sentence questions

Key Skills — understanding previewing, skimming, and scanning

Text Types — quickly reading various text types in order to locate the information you need

Multiple passages — reading two or three related passages and referencing information in both texts

As you work through *Improve Your Performance*, try to identify any weaknesses you have, and focus on the areas you need to improve.

Question Types

Purpose Questions

In Part 7 of the TOEIC test, you are often required to identify the purpose behind a text. The purpose is not always stated directly, so you may need to consider carefully and weigh several factors in order to determine the correct answer. Look for questions such as:

Why was the letter written?
What is the purpose of the notice?

- As you read, ask yourself: *Why* was this text written?
- You do not need to read every word in a text in order to understand the purpose.

Topic Questions

Questions that ask about the topic are also common. Again, this may not always be stated directly, so you need to be prepared to link several points across a text in order to correctly identify the topic. Look for questions such as:

What is the article mainly about?
What is the subject of the press release?
What product is being reviewed?

- As you read, ask yourself: *What* is this text about?
- You do not need to read every word in a text in order to understand the topic.

Audience Questions

Sometimes you need to identify the target audience (i.e., who the text was written for). This is rarely stated in the text, so it means you have to think "behind" the text and notice clues to help you identify who it is intended to be read by. Look for questions such as:

Who is this e-mail intended for?
Who would be most interested in this information?

- As you read, ask yourself: *Who* is this text for?
- You do not need to read every word in a text in order to identify the audience.

Detail Questions

Questions in Part 7 that test your ability to identify and understand important details may focus on any number of specific details. Look for questions such as:

On what day will the factory tour take place?
When is the assignment scheduled to finish?
Who issued the invitation?
What most likely is Mrs. Shipley's job?
In what department does Ms. Kim work?

- Make sure you know exactly what information you need to find before you go to the text.
- Focus only on finding the information you need to answer the question.

Inference Questions

Questions in Part 7 routinely test your ability to understand things that are not directly stated. These questions require you to think more carefully, and draw conclusions based on what you read. Look for questions such as:

What is suggested about Mr. Parker?
What does the article imply about the GTX Model 50?
What is indicated in the letter?
What is probably true about OneTelGlobal Corporation?

 • Quickly work through the answer choices, eliminating statements that are incorrect.
• Do not read all the answer choices if you do not need to. When you have verified the correct answer, move on to the next question.

NOT Questions

Some questions ask you to identify information that is NOT in the passage. These questions take more time. Rather than simply find one correct answer, you must identify three incorrect answer choices before you can mark your answer. Look for questions such as:

What is NOT suggested about Arts Magazine?
What is NOT offered as part of the executive package?

 • Work through the answer choices to find the three statements that are correct.
• Do not waste time looking if you cannot quickly find the information you need. That might be the correct answer choice!

Vocabulary Questions

Some questions test your knowledge of specific words. If you are not sure of the meaning of the word, you need to try to guess the meaning from the context. Look for questions such as:

The word "protagonist" in paragraph 1, line 3, is closest in meaning to...

 • Carefully read the sentence in the text that contains the target word, and identify the meaning of any key words and ideas that it relates to.
• Consider the sentence as a whole, and work through the answer choices to choose the one that makes the most sense.

Meaning in context Questions

For a few questions, you need to choose the correct meaning of a word or phrase based on the context. These questions are usually in single texts and often relate to online chat or text message chains. They test your knowledge of colloquial and idiomatic English. Look for questions such as:

At 10:41 P.M., what does Fiona mean when she writes "Just my luck!"?

- The target word or phrase is often a reaction to what has just been written. Study carefully the few lines that come immediately *before*, and consider how these may impact the response.
- Some words or phrases have multiple meanings. You need to think about the wider context to identify the correct meaning being used in the target item.

Missing sentence Questions

Some texts have a sentence that has been extracted and you need to identify where to insert it. These questions are always in single texts and aim to test your understanding of the content and structure of the text. Look for questions such as:

In which position marked [1], [2], [3], and [4] does the following sentence best belong?
"Please continue to keep us posted of developments as they arise."

- Consider the purpose of the sentence. Is it changing topic, asking for information, making a recommendation or giving clarification? Study the organization of the text and ask yourself where this sentence might best be placed.
- There are four possible places where the sentence could go. It is usually possible to eliminate one or two simply by looking at the syntax and structure of what comes before and after.

Key Skills

Previewing

In Part 7, it is important that you start by previewing the text. This means you should read the opening statement that describes the text type, and very quickly take note of the length and layout of the text. You should then check how many questions there are that relate to the text, and read each question. Do not read the answer choices yet. Just read each question so you have a general idea of what information you need to find.

Skimming

Skimming a text means quickly reading through to get a general idea of its content. You must read quickly. Do not worry about words you do not understand, and do not stop reading until you get to the end of the text. Notice any headings. As you read, think about how the text is organized and what it is about. When you finish skimming the text, you should have a good idea of its content, and how it is structured.

Scanning

Scanning a text means looking through the text quickly to find specific information you need. The fundamental point about scanning is that you must know what information you are looking for *before* you look in the text. Read the question, then read the answer choices, and be sure you know what information you need to find. Only then should you go back to the text. Do not start reading from the beginning. Decide which section might contain the information you need, and go straight there. Do not read every word. Read quickly until you find the right area, and only then slow down and read more carefully. Refer back to the question and the answer choices as you focus your search. As soon as you have the information you need, stop reading.

The next section presents a variety of texts and question types. Remember the advice and the skills covered here as you work your way through the section. Try to complete each text in the time suggested.

Text Types

MINI TEST E-mails

Read this e-mail and choose the most appropriate answer: (A), (B), (C), or (D), for each question.

E-Mail Message	
To:	customerrelations@energyplus.com
From:	Tony Garcia <tgarcia@inworlddesign.com
Date:	Nov 16
Subject:	URG: Boiler issues

On November 12 I called your service center to report that the EP3000 boiler at our offices was functioning erratically. The thermostat fails to detect when the temperature has dropped below the 21°C threshold, and the heating does not come back on until many hours have passed. A repair was scheduled for the next morning, but when the engineer arrived the system had reset itself overnight, and came on without problems. However, he left before the 21°C threshold had been reached, and so could not witness or determine the cause of the fault. He simply put the lockout down to dry joints in the PCB, which he replaced.

Since then, the same fault has recurred on no fewer than three occasions. I have repeatedly called the Repair Hotline listed on your website, only to be kept waiting in an automated queue for as long as 40 minutes before hanging up in frustration. The last week has been very cold, and now union officials are threatening a walk-out unless the issue is resolved soon.

Today I received an invoice for $785.64 for work carried out during the engineer's visit. Apparently, the coverage offered by your WorkCare 300 policy does not include PCB repairs. As the problem has not been resolved, I hope you can understand my reluctance to authorize payment.

All this has caused a great deal of trouble, stress, and wasted time over many phone calls. Could you please reply at once with a specific plan to resolve these matters?

Best regards,
Tony Garcia, Office Manager

---

1. Why did Mr. Garcia send the e-mail?
- (A) To schedule an emergency repair
- (B) To complain about poor service
- (C) To explain why he will not pay a bill
- (D) To report a faulty heating appliance

2. What is suggested about the EP3000 boiler?
- (A) Its insurance is no longer valid.
- (B) It has recently been repaired.
- (C) It has a history of PCB failures.
- (D) It must be turned off overnight.

3. The word "erratically" in paragraph 1, line 2, is closest in meaning to
- (A) involuntarily
- (B) precipitously
- (C) unpredictably
- (D) inadequately

4. What does Mr. Garcia NOT refer to in the e-mail?
- (A) The possibility of a strike action
- (B) The shortcomings of the Repair Hotline
- (C) The continued bad weather forecast
- (D) The inconvenience he has suffered

---

1. Ⓐ Ⓑ Ⓒ Ⓓ   **2.** Ⓐ Ⓑ Ⓒ Ⓓ   **3.** Ⓐ Ⓑ Ⓒ Ⓓ   **4.** Ⓐ Ⓑ Ⓒ Ⓓ

Score ..../4

4 MIN

Read this memo and choose the most appropriate answer: (A), (B), (C), or (D), for each question.

To: Events Team
From: Caroline Walford, Planning Manager
Date: Friday, June 6
Subject: Update

MEMO

With training going on tomorrow morning I thought it best to get this update out to you now to help you plan for next week.

The Krieger Institute of Manufacturing program is now in week 2, and Sue Bale tells me the group have settled in well and are extremely happy with their bedrooms and the facilities. ---[1]--- Also, Commerce International Bank returns this coming weekend with their third group, and others on-site include Streit Communications, Aardvark Assessment, Enterprise Partnership, and beginning next Friday the return of Ballard EXPO for their Annual Summer School, which runs through July. It goes without saying that it is essential to get them all off to a good start. ---[2]--- Lots to keep us on our toes!

Staffing-wise, as many of you will know, Lorraine O'Donnell finishes her work placement tomorrow and is then off on a well-deserved break. I am sure that you will agree that she has been a tremendous asset to the Events team. With this in mind, I am very pleased to say that as Lorraine returns to college she will be staying on with us one day a week, transferring her support to the Reception team in order to gain more diverse experience, and also to continue the successful buddying between the Events and Reception teams. ---[3]--- We wish her the best of luck as she makes the transition both back to college and to the new role.

Yuki Iwata joins the team on Tuesday, as Overseas Program Event Planner, and as she begins her induction I know you will welcome and support her as she builds her knowledge in this new role. Her linguistic skills will certainly be valuable to us as we grow our business in Japan and China. ---[4]---

---

1. Where do the recipients of the memo most likely work?
   (A) At a residential convention center
   (B) At a higher educational academy
   (C) At an international research institute
   (D) At a public relations agency

2. What is indicated about Yuki Iwata?
   (A) She will be employed on a full-time basis.
   (B) She has previous experience in her role.
   (C) She is Lorraine O'Donnell's replacement.
   (D) She can speak several languages.

3. In which position marked [1], [2], [3], and [4] does the following sentence best belong?
   "As they are new clients, let's all keep up the good work."
   (A) [1]
   (B) [2]
   (C) [3]
   (D) [4]

4. According to the memo, what will occur next week?
   (A) A staff member will retire.
   (B) An award will be presented.
   (C) An important client will arrive.
   (D) A major expansion will take place.

---

1. (A) (B) (C) (D)   2. (A) (B) (C) (D)   3. (A) (B) (C) (D)   4. (A) (B) (C) (D)

Score ..../4

Read this letter and choose the most appropriate answer: (A), (B), (C), or (D), for each question.

Brunswick Hydration Services
for all your water hydration needs

September 3

Mr. T. Clarkson
Haslingfield Analytics
Fairview Industrial Estate
Alberta T1U 6SR

Dear Mr. Clarkson:

As you will note from our new letterhead, we have recently changed the name of our company from Speedy Water Delivery Co. to Brunswick Hydration Services. This is in line with the continued development of the company as we diversify our water filtration services and expand throughout southeastern Georgia. Rest assured there has been no change in management, and our promise to deliver unrivaled customer service and value for your money remains as strong as ever.

In addition to supplying and maintaining our range of free-standing EasyFlo water coolers to your company, we are now pleased to offer DualFlo dispensers, enabling your workers to also enjoy tea, coffee, and hot chocolate. Thanks to our patented cutoff valve there is no risk of accidental burns should the lever be inadvertently pressed. We are also excited to also offer a new, high-quality water purification system, ideal for commercial applications. Easy to install and use, the ExcelProOne is a reliable, complete reverse osmosis drinking water purification and delivery system. It contains everything you need to purify and deliver water throughout your premises, providing pure, great-tasting drinking water at every service point.

Please note that it has been our policy to supply two-, three-, and five-gallon bottles to all our customers. However, from October 1 we will only be supplying the five-gallon bottles, and our minimum order limit will be raised to three bottles at a time.

Please see the enclosed brochures for more information on our new products. A member of our client services team will contact you shortly to discuss your needs, and give details of a special, limited-time offer.

Sincerely,

Mildred Haffenstein

Mildred Haffenstein
Client Services

1. What is the main purpose of the letter?
   (A) To announce an expansion
   (B) To promote new products
   (C) To attract more customers
   (D) To explain company policy

2. What CANNOT be inferred about the DualFlo dispenser?
   (A) It uses heated water.
   (B) It is safe to use.
   (C) It is easy to install.
   (D) It uses five-gallon bottles.

3. How many brochures were most likely enclosed with the letter?
   (A) One
   (B) Two
   (C) Three
   (D) Four

4. What is indicated in the letter?
   (A) The ExcelProOne is for business use.
   (B) Speedy Water Delivery Co. was insolvent.
   (C) Mr. Clarkson works in telemarketing.
   (D) The special offer is for existing customers only.

1. Ⓐ Ⓑ Ⓒ Ⓓ   2. Ⓐ Ⓑ Ⓒ Ⓓ   3. Ⓐ Ⓑ Ⓒ Ⓓ   4. Ⓐ Ⓑ Ⓒ Ⓓ

Score ..../4

4 MIN

Read this fax and choose the most appropriate answer: (A), (B), (C), or (D), for each question.

FAX Transmittal Sheet   **<<<HTC Shipping >>>**
OUTBOUND Service
Sender: **Julia Ronson**   Contact person: **Matthew Delaney**
Tel no: **0834 – 984612**   E-mail: **jronson@garstonassociates.com**

Note: You only need to fill out one of these lines if you are either delivering to HTC or we are collecting from you. You choose the date.
Goods being delivered to HTC by [Date] ....
Goods to be collected by HTC on [Date] **July 21**   Time: **9:00 A.M. to 5:30 P.M.**

Collection from: **Garston Associates, 17 Connaught Way, Bloomsbury, London WC1E 8DR**
We will have **5** pieces @approx. **110** weight (kg)
If pallet dims .... by .... by ....
Commodity/Description of goods: **brochures (x1), sample books (x3), banners (x1)**

To be delivered to: **Stuttgart Book Fair, Stuttgart Aum Main, Germany**
Special instructions: **Leave at Stand number X843 in Hall 5. Stand contact will be Mark Stanton. +7513-823912 (cell). Must arrive on July 23 (day before start of exhibition).**
Authorized by: **Sharon Kennedy, Publishing Services Manager**

Return service from: **Stuttgart Book Fair, Stuttgart Aum Main, Germany**
Goods to be collected by HTC on [Date] **July 28**   Time: **3:00 P.M.** From: **Hall 5, Stand X843**
To be delivered to: **Garston Associates (as above)**
We will have **4** pieces @approx. **90** weight (kg)
If pallet dims .... by .... by ....
Commodity/Description of goods: **sample books (x3), banners (x1)**

Method of Payment   HTC account no: **3274GA**
                         Credit card no .... 3 digits on back ....
                         Type of card .... Expiry date ....

Please complete this form and return by fax to: +44 (0)1763 772 843   For assistance, contact: Peter Foxton +44 (0)1763 772 342

---

1. What is the purpose of this fax?
  (A) To confirm a delivery
  (B) To arrange transportation
  (C) To request an extension
  (D) To schedule a meeting

2. What is suggested about Mark Stanton?
  (A) He is an HTC Shipping employee.
  (B) He works with Matthew Delaney.
  (C) He is organizing the exhibition.
  (D) He will be in Germany in July.

3. What is indicated in the fax?
  (A) The Stuttgart Book Fair lasts seven days.
  (B) The shipment needs to be sent urgently.
  (C) Ms. Kennedy and Ms. Ronson are coworkers.
  (D) Garston Associates has used HTC Shipping before.

4. Which of these statements is probably true?
  (A) Mr. Foxton is a director at HTC Shipping.
  (B) Garston Associates is a printing firm.
  (C) The brochures weigh 20 kilograms.
  (D) It will not be possible to deliver the goods.

1. (A) (B) (C) (D)   **2.** (A) (B) (C) (D)   **3.** (A) (B) (C) (D)   **4.** (A) (B) (C) (D)

Score ..../4

Read this notice and choose the most appropriate answer: (A), (B), (C), or (D), for each question.

FRAUD PREVENTION

In recent weeks we have had reports of numerous fraudulent e-mails sent to staff asking for personal and company account information. This is known as phishing. Although these e-mails may look convincing, criminals are trying to lure you into divulging your details so they can access accounts and money or even steal your identity. Hyperlinks or attached files within phishing e-mails can also infect your computer with malicious software (malware). We have suffered three serious infections within the last month due to phishing scams, affecting both the KX accounting system and the Cluster system. In order to contain this situation, can all staff please be sure to follow the guidance below.

Always verify e-mails are genuine:

- **Check the e-mail address.** It should be the same as, not just similar to, the address you usually receive e-mails from.

- **Check the subject line.** Treat as suspicious anything along the lines of "There is a secure message waiting for you," "Security Alert," "System Upgrade," and so on.

- **Check the message title.** If it reads "Dear Customer" or if it isn't personalized at all, then you should be wary.

- **Check the language.** Look for casual or informal words, poor spelling, and grammatical mistakes.

Stay safe:

- **Never** click on hyperlinks, buttons, or attachments within unexpected e-mails.

- **Never** respond to prompts such as "Verify your password" or "Update your security details."

- **Never** be lured into entering confidential details at fake websites.

If in doubt, do not respond to suspicious e-mails. Contact the Computing Department at Ext. 527 and ask for advice.

---

1. For whom is this notice most likely intended?
   - (A) Bank employees
   - (B) The general public
   - (C) Company personnel
   - (D) Computing experts

2. What is NOT mentioned as a way to avoid phishing scams?
   - (A) Seeking help from experts
   - (B) Confirming e-mails are authentic
   - (C) Keeping security programs up-to-date
   - (D) Staying away from bogus websites

3. The word "divulging" in paragraph 1, line 3, is closest in meaning to
   - (A) confirming
   - (B) revealing
   - (C) updating
   - (D) changing

4. According to the notice, what is often missing in fraudulent e-mails?
   - (A) The name of the recipient
   - (B) The address it was sent from
   - (C) The date of the message
   - (D) The identity of the sender

1. Ⓐ Ⓑ Ⓒ Ⓓ   2. Ⓐ Ⓑ Ⓒ Ⓓ   3. Ⓐ Ⓑ Ⓒ Ⓓ   4. Ⓐ Ⓑ Ⓒ Ⓓ

Score ..../4

Read this advertisement and choose the most appropriate answer: (A), (B), (C), or (D), for each question.

DETOX RETREAT IN GOA

Come to sumptuous Belle View Harbor in Goa for a total body rebalance, designed especially to soothe away the stresses and strains of everyday life.

Let us combine ancient Ayurveda and holistic therapy techniques with modern medicine to create the perfect customized program for you. Our highly experienced dieticians, doctors, alternative therapists, neurolinguistic practitioners, and wellness consultants will help you rejuvenate and revitalize. Try our ten-day Detox program and you will emerge with radiant skin, a clear mind, and the means to attain physical and emotional balance.

Restore and invigorate your body, and cleanse your mind, at Belle View Harbor. We offer the ideal environment to alleviate your tense mind and weary soul. Join us on the path to complete health and well-being, and enjoy a new, more positive you. Our powerful coaching techniques, combined with yoga, meditation, and a holistic fitness program, will help you reach your goals.

Stay in one of our specially designed, aesthetically pleasing villas, and surround yourself in style and comfort as we balance your essential chakras…or just kick back and indulge your senses with a host of premium spa treatments.

Retreat package includes: 9 nights' luxury accommodation in your own private, superbly appointed villa. Welcome gift pack. 4 lifestyle coaching workshops. 1 luxury face treatment. 1 luxury body treatment. Daily classes in yoga, Pilates, targeted fitness, and meditation. 2 guided walks. Full-board healthy detox cuisine. Healthy snacks and mineral water, plus herbal teas. Airport transfers. Membership in the on-site spa (heated pool, sauna, and Jacuzzi) and gym.

E-mail: info@bvhgoa   www.belleviewharborgoa.com

---

1. Who would be most interested in this advertisement?
(A) Families with children
(B) Professional adults
(C) Older teenagers
(D) Senior citizens

2. What is implied in the advertisement?
(A) Therapists come from around the world.
(B) Participants are mostly from overseas.
(C) The amenities at the venue may change.
(D) The cost of the program is fixed.

3. The word "indulge" in paragraph 4, line 2, is closest in meaning to
(A) pamper
(B) unwind
(C) inspire
(D) explore

4. What is NOT included in the retreat package?
(A) All meals
(B) Spa treatments
(C) A laundry service
(D) Refreshments

---

1. Ⓐ Ⓑ Ⓒ Ⓓ   **2.** Ⓐ Ⓑ Ⓒ Ⓓ   **3.** Ⓐ Ⓑ Ⓒ Ⓓ   **4.** Ⓐ Ⓑ Ⓒ Ⓓ

Score ..../4

MINI TEST Articles

Read this article and choose the most appropriate answer: (A), (B), (C), or (D), for each question.

Is it still important to *dress smart?*

These days, it seems almost every company is doing away with dress codes. Wearing casual clothes instead of a formal business suit is becoming the ubiquitous norm for office workers, as "dress-down Friday" works its way inexorably across the rest of the week. One EU-wide survey by WorkData Inc. found that more than half of employers said they allow casual dress throughout the week. ---[1]--- Well, this phenomenon has been put down to the rise of Californian-based Internet and technology companies in the 1990s, led by high-profile gurus promulgating the view that casual dress helps creative thinking. So prevailing has this conviction become that it is not uncommon to see executives even at the most senior levels wearing jeans and t-shirts. Is it really true that what you wear at work doesn't matter anymore? ---[2]---

Well, no. What we wear does still matter. That's the conclusion of leading business guru and etiquette expert Dr. Lisa Hawkes. "What we wear at work sounds like a fairly simple matter, but how we dress has an impact not just on how we feel and present ourselves to others, but on the overall culture and atmosphere of the workplace." Dr. Hawkes adds that when the wrong decisions are made, staff morale and motivation can be severely affected. The over-zealous enforcement of strict dress codes may cause some employees to feel robbed of their individuality and creativity. Equally, an overly casual approach to workplace wardrobes, although creating an informal ambience, can lower standards and decrease productivity. "Dressing down per se does not guarantee a relaxed and forward-thinking environment," insists Dr. Hawkes. "A casual dress code can lead to a casual attitude toward work itself." ---[3]--- .

Interestingly, there is evidence of a backlash against the laid-back California approach, with some companies instituting "Formal Fridays," having employees wear suits at the end of the week. ---[4]--- Dr. Hawkes' own research revealed last month that over 80 percent of workers feel it is important to "dress to impress," and three-quarters found it easier to respect someone wearing a suit.

1. What is the article mainly about?
   - (A) The results of an international study
   - (B) Dr. Hawkes' recent research findings
   - (C) The trend toward less formal dress-code policies
   - (D) Attitudes to casual dress in the workplace

2. What is NOT stated as a possible effect of staff wearing casual clothes?
   - (A) It can reduce productivity.
   - (B) It can encourage originality.
   - (C) It can lower workers' self-esteem.
   - (D) It can create a relaxed atmosphere.

3. In which position marked [1], [2], [3], and [4] does the following sentence best belong?
   "But why is this the case?"
   - (A) [1]
   - (B) [2]
   - (C) [3]
   - (D) [4]

4. The word "inexorably" in paragraph 1, line 5, is closest in meaning to
   - (A) relentlessly
   - (B) deviously
   - (C) lethargically
   - (D) impatiently

1. (A) (B) (C) (D) 2. (A) (B) (C) (D) 3. (A) (B) (C) (D) 4. (A) (B) (C) (D)

Score ..../4

Read this online chat discussion and choose the most appropriate answer: (A), (B), (C), or (D), for each question.

Kathy Lim [2:19 P.M.]
Thanks for hooking up at short notice, guys. So, Wilkinson's has finally gone under. My question is, how much stock do we have and what do we do with it? Ann?

> **Ann Croft** [2:20 P.M.]
> We have 50 Excel Shower packs, 35 Imagine Towel Rails, 300 boxes of Alba Beige 600x200 tiles and a dozen Lux mirror cabinets… all boxed up at the factory and ready to go. I canceled this morning as soon as I heard the news.
>
> **Chloe Nickels** [2:20 P.M.]
> At our end we have orders for 40 Vola mixer taps and 10 Prestige vanity units, but they're still to be processed.
>
> **Yoko Sakai** [2:21 P.M.]
> I already reached out to some of our other customers, and offered a 15% discount on any items from Ann's list.

Kathy Lim [2:21 P.M.]
Good thinking, Yoko. Any response yet?

> **Yoko Sakai** [2:21 P.M.]
> Mackay's are getting back to me later. Maybe one or two others.
>
> **Bill Parsons** [2:22 P.M.]
> Do we need to offload them so soon? We can hold this stock for up to a month, I'd say, at Orchard Park. There is space.
>
> **Ann Croft** [2:22 P.M.]
> That's good to know, Bill.

Kathy Lim [2:23 P.M.]
OK, so, Chloe, just scrap those orders, and let's say whatever of Ann's stock Yoko can't shift by Friday we send over to Bill on Monday.

SEND

---

1. At 2:19 P.M., what does Ms. Lim mean when she writes, "Wilkinson's has finally gone under"?
(A) A colleague is missing.
(B) A client has ceased trading.
(C) A staff member has quit.
(D) A customer has fallen ill.

2. For what type of company does Ms. Lim most likely work?
(A) A building supplies firm
(B) A construction company
(C) A package delivery service
(D) A bathroom manufacturer

3. According to the discussion, what will happen to any unsold Lux mirror cabinets?
(A) They will be stored at Orchard Park.
(B) Mackay's will agree to take them.
(C) Ms. Sakai will discount the price.
(D) Ms. Croft will cancel the order.

4. What is indicated about Mr. Parsons?
(A) He has been at the company a long time.
(B) He is Ms. Croft's assistant supervisor.
(C) He disagrees with Ms. Lim's decision.
(D) He works at Orchard Park facility.

---

1. Ⓐ Ⓑ Ⓒ Ⓓ **2.** Ⓐ Ⓑ Ⓒ Ⓓ **3.** Ⓐ Ⓑ Ⓒ Ⓓ **4.** Ⓐ Ⓑ Ⓒ Ⓓ

Score ..../4

4 MIN

Read this text message chain and choose the most appropriate answer: (A), (B), (C), or (D), for each question.

Sue Chalmers   10:28 A.M.

Hi Phil. I'm running late – traffic's terrible! I won't be back for my 11 A.M. so can you please apologize for me to Dr. O'Brien from STF when he arrives. Ask him to wait in the conference room.

Phil Om   10:29 A.M.

Sure thing. Where are you?

Sue Chalmers   10:30 A.M.

Still in Brooklyn. Not even at the bridge yet.

Phil Om   10:30 A.M.

No way! It'll be at least 45 minutes from there. I'll get him a coffee, and one of the donuts left over from Shelly's birthday yesterday, if I can find one.

Sue Chalmers   10:32 A.M.

You'll be lucky! They were amazing…

Phil Om   10:32 A.M.

Tell me about it. I ate three ☺

Sue Chalmers   10:33 A.M.

Anyway, thanks for keeping him happy until I get there. C U later.

---

1. What is suggested about Ms. Chalmers?

(A) She forgot a coworker's birthday.

(B) She meets Dr. O'Brien regularly.

(C) She has postponed her travel plans.

(D) She is late for an appointment.

2. Why is Ms. Chalmers texting Mr. Om?

(A) To report an accident

(B) To place an order

(C) To make an apology

(D) To ask for assistance

3. At 10:32 A.M., what does Ms. Chalmers mean when she writes, "You'll be lucky!"?

(A) She doubts there will be any donuts left.

(B) She hopes Mr. Om will have good fortune.

(C) She does not expect to be at the meeting.

(D) She wishes Dr. O'Brien can be found.

4. What is the earliest time Ms. Chalmers might arrive at her office?

(A) 10:45 A.M.

(B) 11:00 A.M.

(C) 11:15 A.M.

(D) 11:30 A.M.

---

1. Ⓐ Ⓑ Ⓒ Ⓓ   **2.** Ⓐ Ⓑ Ⓒ Ⓓ   **3.** Ⓐ Ⓑ Ⓒ Ⓓ   **4.** Ⓐ Ⓑ Ⓒ Ⓓ

Score ..../4

5 MIN

Read this information and e-mail, and choose the most appropriate answer: (A), (B), (C), or (D), for each question.

Harrisford University Science Festival
Hands-on activities   Workshops   Events for all ages
<u>Saturday, July 9</u>

Unraveling genome secrets
An excellent chance to hear two of the Folan Institute's leading researchers, Dr. Neil Tims and Dr. Mandy Wu, explain how we can learn more about the genetic basis of human disease using the latest sequencing technology.

Talk, Pre-book, Ages 14+   10:00 A.M.–11:00 A.M.

Cosmology in crisis
Did you know the recent discovery of dark energy means that the universe is expanding and accelerating toward an infinite future? Learn from astronomer Professor Hugo Benoit about the latest theories that suggest we are part of a larger "multiverse" and find out what, if any, the solutions might be to the paradox of ever-expanding universes.

Talk, Pre-book, Ages 16+   11:15 A.M.–12:45 P.M.

Science and social media
From Facebook to Flickr, podcasts to vodcasts, Twitter to Tumblr, and WordPress to wikis, with her vast experience of the field as a web producer working in science communication, Dr. Nancy Long is the perfect person to explain how science is being promoted through the latest social media channels. Bring your smartphone/web-enabled device and join the action.

Workshop, Pre-book, Ages 8+   2:00 P.M.–3:00 P.M.

Good vibrations
Explore the relationship between music, science, and math in this intriguing and lively interactive family show with live demonstrations. Dr. Helen Dunwoody will explain how and why different instruments make different sounds. Learn about Pythagoras' musical discoveries, and take part in experiments in an educational music show that includes performances from a local chamber orchestra.

Workshop, Hands-on, Drop-in, All ages   3:30 P.M.–5:00 P.M.

Talks in the morning program will be held at the Folan Institute. Those taking placing in the afternoon will be in the Centennial Hall. Pre book tel:555-8923, e-mail info@harrisuniscday.com, or visit www.harrisunitickets.com, adults $20, reduced rate for under 18s/students $14, unsold tickets available at the door for cash

To:	Chris Smith <cssmith@harrisuni.com>
From:	Helen Dunwoody <htdunwoody@harrisuni.com>
Date:	July 4
Subject:	Science Festival

Dear Chris,

Sorry for the late notice, but until your e-mail this morning I had completely forgotten about the Science Festival. I have some bad news, I'm afraid. The research project I told you about last month was given the go-ahead yesterday by the Council, and I now have funding for my neurobiology study into childhood brain development. This is great news for me, of course, but the bad news is that I now need to go to the Early Education Research Center in Madison on Thursday to brief the team there before we start clinical research trials. I will be away for ten days. This unfortunately overlaps with this year's Science Festival. I was due to help out next Saturday, and I really am so sorry not to be able to take part, especially as it's the launch.

I know the details have already been announced, and I don't want to leave you in the lurch, so I have asked my research assistant Julie Brenner to stand in for me, and she has agreed. I have given Julie all my notes and a thorough briefing on what is planned. She will contact you tomorrow to discuss any changes she may want to make. Sorry again, but I am sure Julie will do a great job.

H

1. Why was the e-mail written?
   (A) To apologize for an oversight
   (B) To recommend someone for a position
   (C) To withdraw from a commitment
   (D) To report the progress of a project

2. What is indicated about the "Good vibrations" workshop?
   (A) It lasts longer than the other sessions.
   (B) Tickets must be booked in advance.
   (C) It is the only interactive event.
   (D) It includes a large group of people.

3. What is NOT suggested about the Science Festival?
   (A) It takes place on more than one day.
   (B) Some events are free of charge.
   (C) It covers a wide range of themes.
   (D) It is an annual event.

4. On which date will Dr. Dunwoody leave for Madison?
   (A) July 4
   (B) July 7
   (C) July 9
   (D) July 10

5. In the e-mail, the word "brief" in paragraph 1, line 5, is closest in meaning to
   (A) meet
   (B) prepare
   (C) assess
   (D) gather

1. Ⓐ Ⓑ Ⓒ Ⓓ 2. Ⓐ Ⓑ Ⓒ Ⓓ 3. Ⓐ Ⓑ Ⓒ Ⓓ
4. Ⓐ Ⓑ Ⓒ Ⓓ 5. Ⓐ Ⓑ Ⓒ Ⓓ   Score ..../5

7 MIN

Read this announcement, memo, and e-mail, and choose the most appropriate answer: (A), (B), (C), or (D) for each question.

Iconic Worldwide Albums presents:

The Crazy Crofters

(nationwide tour of this folk-rock supergroup)

With appearances by Special Guest Artists

National Festival Arena
Wednesday March 18, Thursday March 19,
Friday March 20, Saturday March 21
8:00 P.M.
Ticket prices: $50, $75, $100, $150, $200

From: marketing@rwtpromotions.net
To: All staff
Subject: Tickets to The Crazy Crofters concert

MEMO

Dear all,

We have been lucky enough to receive two complimentary tickets for the final The Crazy Crofters concert from one of our most valued suppliers. The concert is at the National Festival Arena, and the tickets are for the best seats in the house! The board has decided to pass on the tickets to a member of staff who will appreciate the music (we realize that the name The Crazy Crofters may not mean very much to younger members of staff – but some of us remember them!). If you and your guest would like to attend the concert, please let me know before the end of today. The CEO will then choose the lucky winner's name at random. Please do not apply for these tickets if you received a complimentary ticket for the Super Bowl last month – let someone else have the chance this time.

Gerry Lee
Deputy Manager, Marketing Department

E-Mail Message

From:	Donald.Martin@mymail.com
To:	fixtures@hatherbycountryclub.com
Subject:	March monthly golf tournament

Hi Carlos,

I'm writing to let you know I won't be able to play at this month's golf tournament. Sorry about that, and I hope it doesn't cause you any inconvenience. You know how I love to play in these competitions, but this month I'll be taking my wife into town to see The Crazy Crofters, her favorite band, in concert. I was lucky enough to receive two free tickets at work and, since it's our silver wedding anniversary this month, it seemed the perfect way to celebrate. I'll certainly be at the April tournament. No doubt I'll bump into you at the Club before then.
Best regards,
Donald Martin

---

1. How much are the two free tickets worth?
   (A) $100
   (B) $200
   (C) $300
   (D) $400

2. What is implied in Mr. Lee's e-mail?
   (A) The group was popular a long time ago.
   (B) Younger staff may not like folk-rock music.
   (C) Sporting events are as popular as concerts.
   (D) The Crazy Crofters are internationally famous.

3. Which evening will Mr. Martin attend the concert?
   (A) Wednesday
   (B) Thursday
   (C) Friday
   (D) Saturday

4. What is the main purpose of Mr. Martin's e-mail?
   (A) To give apologies for absence
   (B) To cancel a golf tournament
   (C) To tell Carlos about his anniversary
   (D) To schedule a meeting with Carlos

5. What is NOT indicated about Mr. Martin?
   (A) He entered into a prize drawing.
   (B) He has been married a long time.
   (C) He regularly plays golf.
   (D) He is a fan of The Crazy Crofters.

1. Ⓐ Ⓑ Ⓒ Ⓓ 2. Ⓐ Ⓑ Ⓒ Ⓓ 3. Ⓐ Ⓑ Ⓒ Ⓓ
4. Ⓐ Ⓑ Ⓒ Ⓓ 5. Ⓐ Ⓑ Ⓒ Ⓓ Score ..../5

STEPS TO SUCCESS

This section presents an effective, step-by-step approach to use when answering questions on Part 7 of the TOEIC® test.

The steps shown here are designed to help you achieve the highest possible score when you take the test. By following these steps, you should be able to maximize your score on this part of the test.

1 ▶ Read the opening statement that describes the type of text (e.g., Questions 165–168 refer to the following e-mail). Notice the length and layout of the text, and any prominent headings. Then read the questions. Do *not* look at the answer choices and do *not* read the text.

2 ▶ Read the text quickly to get a general idea. As you read, identify the main ideas in each paragraph or section, and think about the organization of the text (i.e., the topic of each paragraph or section). Do *not* worry about words you do not know, and do *not* stop reading until you get to the end of the text.

3 ▶ Read the first question and study the answer choices. The first question often asks about the main ideas. *If you are sure of the answer, mark your answer immediately and move on to the next question.* If you are not sure of the answer, make sure you know exactly what information you need to find, and return to the text. Locate the paragraph or section you think you need. Then slow down and read more carefully until you find the answer.

4 ▶ Refer again to the answer choices. Eliminate any answer choices you are sure are incorrect. Then mark your answer. Repeat steps 3–4 for the remaining questions.

TIMING It is vital you do not waste time by reading unnecessarily. Your goal is simply to answer the questions, not to read every word of every text. If you try to read each text in its entirety you will run out of time and your score will suffer. Focus only on finding the answers to the questions. There are lots of texts so keep a watch in front of you and check the time regularly. You should aim to spend between 1 and 2 minutes on each single passage. Allow more time for single texts with more questions. Try to spend no more than 5 minutes on each double passage, and 7 minutes on each triple passage.

PRACTICE For each of the three Practice sections that follow you will have a time limit of 16 minutes. Before you begin, review the steps explained above. Be sure to follow these steps when completing the Practice exercises.

Questions 1–3 refer to the following e-mail.

	E-Mail Message
To:	Undisclosed recipients
From:	j.travers@cattopeka.com
Subject:	Upcoming program
Date:	November 12

As a former attendee of a KIFC course, or someone who has previously expressed an interest in the work done at the KIFC, I thought I would contact you concerning our latest program of events. The Kansas Independent Film Consortium—the superb year-round film education organization operating here at the County Art Theater in Topeka—is dedicated to bringing you the very best indie and art-house movie entertainment, and this winter is no exception.

Here is a selection from our amazing range of upcoming events:

- Evening courses: Animation (starting Dec. 6), Scandinavian Crime Cinema (Dec. 14), and Early Film History (starting Jan. 3).
- Classic Cinema: an eclectic mix of restored classics brought to you in high-definition. Watch your favorite vintage movies digitally restored.
- Film Production Workshops including: Make A Movie Short and 60-second Film (Feb. 10).
- The 24-Hour Film Project: a timed filmmaking competition now in its tenth year. Each team is allocated a genre, a character, a prop, and a line of dialogue to use. Entrants have only 24 hours to write, shoot, and edit their films. Winning films will be screened around the state. Open to all Kansas residents.
- Movie Masterclass by experimental surrealist South Korean director and winner of this year's Golden Lion award Kim Jung-Min. Not to be missed. (Dec. 17).

The KIFC winter brochure is attached. If you would like a hard copy, just drop myself or my coworker Nancy Barker (n.barker@cattopeka.com) an e-mail with your contact details. Alternatively, go online where you can also find the screening schedule of all our live and encore opera and ballet performances, concerts, exhibitions, and other special events.

If you have any questions about the screenings and events, get in touch. We'd love to hear from you as we continue building up our member base around the region.

Jason Travers
Education Assistant

1. For whom is this e-mail most likely intended?
   (A) Film course participants
   (B) Competition entrants
   (C) Movie enthusiasts
   (D) Job seekers

2. Who is Nancy Barker?
   (A) A County Art Theater employee
   (B) A KIFC program coordinator
   (C) A theater production assistant
   (D) An educational outreach worker

3. What is indicated about the 24-Hour Film Project?
   (A) Entrants must pay a small fee.
   (B) Only KIFC members are eligible.
   (C) Winners receive a cash prize.
   (D) Entry to the competition is restricted.

1. Ⓐ Ⓑ Ⓒ Ⓓ
2. Ⓐ Ⓑ Ⓒ Ⓓ
3. Ⓐ Ⓑ Ⓒ Ⓓ

Questions 4–7 refer to the following memo.

MEMO

From: Stephàne Moreau

To: All Heads of Department

Date: July 23

Re: Staff focus group

With the recent change in role for James Cranston, the chair of our staff focus group for the last two years, the time has come to revisit and re-launch the process. The aim of the changes outlined below is to establish a small team with greater autonomy and decision-making responsibility to increase the ratio of ideas approved and the speed with which they are implemented.

The focus group serves to provide a forum for staff to discuss issues and proactively find ways to enhance their own working environment, as well as improve the customer journey, in addition of course to coming up with ideas to save money through efficient working practices without compromising quality.

From now on, the meetings will run quarterly and we are asking for each of the five departments to ideally send two representatives; a "team ambassador" to represent the department at each meeting for continuity, plus a changeable member of the team who will be able to bring new ideas and fresh perspectives, business levels permitting. The meetings will be chaired by Andrew Myers, who will be supported by Emily Wilson. There will be a confidential reporting system as before. The staff focus group meetings are an important part of our organizational communication. Andrew and Emily will take a fair and balanced approach to running these meetings, which will help to ensure a positive outcome.

Andrew and Emily will be meeting with James for a full handover in the next two weeks. Andrew will then arrange a date for the next meeting, giving ample notice to maximize attendance. Please do all you can to support Andrew and Emily as they step into these challenging but rewarding roles.

4. What does Mr. Moreau NOT mention in the memo?

(A) The benefits of the staff focus group

(B) How frequently the group currently meets

(C) Changes to the structure of the group

(D) Why the group is being re-launched

5. What is implied about James Cranston?

(A) He has been demoted within the company.

(B) He did not run the staff focus group effectively.

(C) He disagrees with some of the planned changes.

(D) He will no longer be part of the staff focus group.

6. What is indicated about the next staff focus group?

(A) It will take place the following month.

(B) At least seven employees will attend.

(C) Ms. Wilson will chair part of the meeting.

(D) Staff will receive a bonus for participating.

7. The word "autonomy" in paragraph 1, line 3, is closest in meaning to

(A) independence

(B) authority

(C) influence

(D) experience

4.	Ⓐ	Ⓑ	Ⓒ	Ⓓ
5.	Ⓐ	Ⓑ	Ⓒ	Ⓓ
6.	Ⓐ	Ⓑ	Ⓒ	Ⓓ
7.	Ⓐ	Ⓑ	Ⓒ	Ⓓ

Questions 8–12 refer to the following itinerary and letter.

Grayson *Tours* ➣
Specialists in European travel

Lisbon City Break

Enjoy three nights in Lisbon—the city of seven hills. Museums, palaces, parks, monuments, castles, sandy beaches… Lisbon has it all!

Day 1 ➣

On arrival at Lisbon Airport, you will be taken by coach to the centrally located three-star Beaufort Hotel. In the afternoon, your tour leader will show you some of the city's most famous sights, including the glorious monuments in the Belém district, along the Tagus River. See the Torre de Belém and the Jerónimos Monastery, two UNESCO World Heritage sites. Then take a leisurely stroll down picturesque lanes in Alfama, and marvel at the varied Baroque, Gothic, Romanesque, Manueline, and traditional Portuguese architecture of one of Europe's most historic and enchanting cities. In the evening, enjoy a three-course meal (excluding drinks) at the hotel's award-winning restaurant.

Day 2 ➣

Once a popular summer retreat for nobility and great artists, today Sintra attracts visitors eager to see its quaint streets, traditional houses, grand palaces, and magnificent gardens. A short 20-minute coach journey to this historical hilltop town will take you to the magical Pena Palace and the eighth-century Moorish fortress, where from the ramparts you can enjoy spectacular views over the surrounding hills. You will stop by at Cabo da Roca, the westernmost point of the European continent, en route back to the hotel. In the afternoon you will be free to explore.

Day 3 ➣

You will have the opportunity to relax on one of the sandy beaches, or try your hand at surfing, wind surfing, and kite surfing. Alternatively, take an optional half-day trip to the neighboring resort of Cascais (about ten minutes away) to saunter along the seafront promenade, and try freshly caught fish at one of the many small restaurants and traditional cafes.

Day 4 ➣

After breakfast, your coach will take you to Lisbon Airport for your return flight home.

➣ Price includes

Scheduled return flights from London Heathrow (regional departures available at a supplement)—three nights Bed-and-Breakfast accommodation (courtyard room) at the Beaufort Hotel—complimentary upgrade to a superior room (subject to availability) for Emerald members with 50 points or more—one three-course evening meal

---

Dear Sirs:

My husband and I recently took a trip to Lisbon with your tour company. Although we enjoyed ourselves immensely, there were one or two issues that marred the trip somewhat, not only for us but for others in the group, which I would like to bring to your attention. The hotel was in a rather shabby area of town, and the cost of drinks was scandalous. Our room was also very small (we had been told to expect a superior room) and did not have a sea view.

I would suggest you either lower your prices accordingly, by at least 20 percent, or review your choice of hotel.

Yours faithfully,

Mrs. K. Porter

8. What is the main purpose of the letter?
(A) To complain about poor value for money
(B) To request a partial refund of the tour cost
(C) To raise criticisms on behalf of other participants
(D) To recommend alternative accommodations

9. What is NOT included in the Lisbon City Break tour?
(A) A trip to an historic castle
(B) Dinner on the first evening
(C) A guided tour of the city
(D) A full-day excursion

10. What did Mrs. Porter most likely find satisfactory about the Beaufort Hotel?
(A) The prices
(B) The food
(C) The room
(D) The location

11. What is indicated about the Porters?
(A) They have traveled with Grayson Tours before.
(B) They ate lunch at a restaurant in Cascais.
(C) They had booked a room with a sea view.
(D) They paid extra to fly from a regional airport.

12. In the itinerary, the word "saunter" in paragraph 4, line 5, is closest in meaning to
(A) exercise
(B) parade
(C) wander
(D) relax

8.	Ⓐ	Ⓑ	Ⓒ	Ⓓ
9.	Ⓐ	Ⓑ	Ⓒ	Ⓓ
10.	Ⓐ	Ⓑ	Ⓒ	Ⓓ
11.	Ⓐ	Ⓑ	Ⓒ	Ⓓ
12.	Ⓐ	Ⓑ	Ⓒ	Ⓓ

Questions 13-17 refer to the following Web page, advertisement, and online discussion forum.

Q Optical Solutions Advisory Council

Are contact lenses right for me?

Millions of people across the world wear contact lenses. They are considered a safe and effective way to correct vision problems. There are different types of lenses, and one of them will definitely be suitable for you. Read the information below to help you make the right choice.

Hard lenses

Hard lenses are the oldest type of contact lenses. Decades ago, if you wanted to wear contact lenses these were your only choice. They are made of Plexiglass, a robust and long-lasting, though stiff and inflexible, acrylic plastic. Use of hard lenses has tapered off significantly over recent decades, as they are more uncomfortable to wear than other types and they impede the flow of oxygen to the eye. Hard lenses are still manufactured, however, as they can correct a wider range of vision problems than soft lenses.

Rigid gas permeable lenses

These were developed in the 1970s as a more comfortable alternative to hard lenses. Unlike hard lenses, they are porous and allow oxygen to reach the eye. They are small in size, usually covering about two thirds of the cornea. They are durable and easy to handle. These lenses can be worn for many more months than soft lenses and are therefore much cheaper. They take a couple of weeks of getting used to. They can often be prescribed for vision problems that soft contact lenses cannot help with.

Monthly disposable

These lenses are designed to be thrown away after a month's wear. They are very light, very pliable, being made from materials with a high water content. They must be cleaned and disinfected thoroughly each time they are removed from the eye and before they are worn again. They are comfortable to wear and practical, but they do not usually give the sharpness of vision afforded by rigid gas permeable lenses. They are not suitable for all vision problems.

Daily disposable

These lenses are discarded after each wearing. They are usually small in size, light, and very comfortable to wear. In fact, you may even forget that you are wearing lenses at all! Because of the very high water content, handling these lenses can sometimes be tricky. They are great for sports, traveling, and an active lifestyle. They are extremely convenient, but that convenience comes at a price!

Aquafine Contact Lenses

The latest technology ensures a high level of comfort. Breathable lens lets more oxygen through than other lenses and retains more moisture. Your eyes stay healthy and the lenses remain soft and flexible.

Aquafine contacts are ideal for people who have had difficulty with other lenses, have sensitive eyes, or require more comfort from their lenses. More economical than daily disposables.

Water percentage: 40%

Package details: 6 lenses per box

Damson_Jane [7:40 P.M.]

Hi guys. Can anybody here give me advice on contact lenses? I'm thinking of swapping my glasses for them. Do any of you wear lenses? What are your experiences with them? Any recommendations?

Big_Al [7:49 P.M.]

I tried them, but had to give them up. I work in a sawmill and the wood dust makes wearing contact lenses impossible, even when I'm wearing safety goggles.

Alice76 [9:13 P.M.]

I've been wearing the same type of lenses for 20 years, and have never had any problems. I've stayed with them as they're cheap and last a long time. I just have to be careful that I don't wear them for more than about 7 or 8 hours at a stretch, otherwise my eyes don't get enough oxygen.

JerryJ [9:20 P.M.]

If money was no object I'd recommend you for daily disposables. I've had them for years. They're by far the most comfortable and convenient.

Mighty_Mike [9:45 P.M.]

I'd never be able to play hockey or soccer without my contacts. I only wear them the couple of days I'm playing, so I don't find them an expensive option.

SunnySue [10:38 P.M.]

My teenage son got a serious infection after wearing soft lenses. The problem wasn't really the lenses; he didn't clean them regularly enough. You really do have to be meticulous about hygiene if you plan to wear lenses.

---

13. What sort of contact lenses are Aquafine?
    (A) Hard
    (B) Rigid gas permeable
    (C) Monthly disposable
    (D) Daily disposable

14. Which online discussion group member currently wears hard lenses?
    (A) Alice76
    (B) JerryJ
    (C) Might_Mike
    (D) SunnySue

15. According to the discussion, who should probably avoid wearing contact lenses?
    (A) Anyone wo suffers from allergies
    (B) People who have dry eyes
    (C) Children and young adults
    (D) Workers in dusty environments

16. What is indicated about daily disposable lenses?
    (A) Not everyone can afford them.
    (B) They can be easy to lose.
    (C) Keeping them clean is difficult.
    (D) They are more convenient than glasses.

17. In the online discussion, the word "meticulous" used by Sunny_Sue is closest in meaning to
    (A) experienced
    (B) knowledgeable
    (C) qualified
    (D) careful

13. (A) (B) (C) (D)
14. (A) (B) (C) (D)
15. (A) (B) (C) (D)
16. (A) (B) (C) (D)
17. (A) (B) (C) (D)

Score ..../17

16 MIN

Questions 1–3 refer to the following article.

Layoffs—a question of proportion and perspective

Sean Taylor, partner at management consultancy firm Weston Taylor

The recent spate of layoffs to hit the Bay Area has resulted in widespread shock, and reports throughout the local and national media of cataclysmic economic meltdown. I accept these events are newsworthy, and make for gripping news coverage, but I think we should all be asking ourselves: is it really so bad? ---[1]--- Indeed, turnover of staff is considered by many industry analysts to be a vital part of ensuring a healthy business. Companies need to regenerate and renew, bringing in new talent and fresh ideas. This cycle of renewal has marked the telecommunications, pharmaceutical, and automotive sectors for generations, so it amazes me why we are always so shocked when it happens.

Of course, it all depends on the type of people who are walking out the door. ---[2]--- If key staff and highly skilled workers are the ones to go, then it's time to worry. They are the people you want to hang on to. However, the departure of those who find themselves square pegs in round holes, and are miserable in their work as a consequence, should not be lamented. They are the deadwood that needs to be pruned. ---[3]--- Failure to tackle poor and underperforming workers will only hold a company back, stunting growth and leaving the door open for rivals to thrive.

Let's not forget that layoffs can be a positive experience not only for the companies seeking to shake things up, but also for those affected. ---[4]--- Sometimes, being forced to embrace change opens the door to something better. More than one person I know has spoken of their relief at being laid off. "It was what I needed" is something I have heard far more times than you might think. So, let's try to maintain a sense of perspective amidst all the hyperbole and anguished debate.

1. Why was this article written?
   (A) To challenge attitudes to job losses
   (B) To protest inaccurate media reports
   (C) To examine causes of company failure
   (D) To explain poor staff retention rates

2. In which position marked [1], [2], [3], and [4] does the following sentence best belong?
   "Layoffs are a normal part of business life?"
   (A) [1]
   (B) [2]
   (C) [3]
   (D) [4]

3. What is NOT suggested about workers who are unhappy in their jobs?
   (A) They should be confronted.
   (B) They are unproductive.
   (C) They need to be dismissed.
   (D) They are unsuited to their jobs.

1. Ⓐ Ⓑ Ⓒ Ⓓ 2. Ⓐ Ⓑ Ⓒ Ⓓ 3. Ⓐ Ⓑ Ⓒ Ⓓ

Questions 4–7 refer to the following advertisement.

⋆Fairline Fitness Center⋆

Ottawa's most innovative health club

At Fairline Fitness Center you will not only have 24/7 access to our state-of-the-art gym, priority booking for over one hundred classes, and use of the swimming pool, but you will also get your own fully qualified personal trainer to give ongoing support and motivation.

Fairline Fitness Center is the perfect venue to relax, get in shape, and have fun. We are a family-friendly, privately owned fitness center, where you can get away from the "look-at-me" scene common in many other gyms. Feel comfortable, make friends at our famous Juice Bar, and work your way to a more active lifestyle one step at a time.

Group exercise classes include: aerobics, body toning, interval training, kickboxing, Pilates, water aerobics, yoga, Zumba, step, and many more.

- Free 12-point health check (including blood pressure, BMI and cholesterol, and blood glucose levels)
- Free fitness assessment and workout with a certified trainer
- Specialist brand-name cardio, strength, and exercise equipment

- Sauna, steam bath, spa
- Tanning – Free session the day you join!
- Free on-site parking

★ ★ ★ ★ ★

Special offer! For a limited time, we're offering ***FREE*** membership for 30 days. Your trial pass will not convert automatically to a membership and no payment will be taken from your credit card without your authorization. Processing fee just $10. 30 days to help you get fit and feel great and to show you the value of joining Fairline Fitness Center.

★ ★ ★ ★ ★

Friends & Family Plan

Add up to five friends or family members to your plan for just $5 per person. Each person will receive the same access as regular members.

Come and try us. Drop by anytime, or call 555-0123 to speak to a member or our team. For more details of classes, times, and lots more, go to www.fairlinefitnesscenter.com. Full membership just $15 per month. No enrollment fees. No pushy salespeople!

4. What is the purpose of this advertisement?
   (A) To announce a grand opening
   (B) To introduce a new promotion
   (C) To advertise a special service
   (D) To reward regular members

5. How much would full membership cost a family of four every month?
   (A) $20
   (B) $25
   (C) $30
   (D) $60

6. What is indicated about the free trial offer?
   (A) A handling charge is payable.
   (B) Certain credit cards are not accepted.
   (C) Access to some facilities is not included.
   (D) It is only available for the next 30 days.

7. What are readers NOT asked to do?
   (A) Visit the center in person
   (B) Browse the website
   (C) Call for more information
   (D) Register in advance online

4. Ⓐ Ⓑ Ⓒ Ⓓ 5. Ⓐ Ⓑ Ⓒ Ⓓ 6. Ⓐ Ⓑ Ⓒ Ⓓ 7. Ⓐ Ⓑ Ⓒ Ⓓ

Questions 8–12 refer to the following letter and notice.

March 4

Joseph Nichols
Westgate Property Management
721 Sycamore Avenue
Dallas, TX 75007

Dear Mr. Nichols:

I am writing to express my concern over the new tenants that moved into Apt. 610 last month. As you know, this is immediately below my own apartment and since they arrived I have heard nothing but raucous behavior and loud music at all hours of the day and night. What's more, empty boxes and plastic bags have been left strewn all over the lobby, making access difficult, not to mention a hazard and a fire risk. To make matters worse, I noticed last weekend that they now have no fewer than three dilapidated trucks in the parking lot (occupying spaces allocated for visitors), two of which would appear not to be in use. A neighbor tells me one of the men's hobbies is restoring old trucks.

As you are responsible for this building, could I please ask you to deal with these problems as soon as possible, as all the commotion is making my life and that of the other residents here unbearable. I have been reluctant to raise these issues with them, not least because they have a large rottweiler, which is extremely intimidating.

Sincerely,

Fiona Delaney

Fiona Delaney (Apt. 710)

WARNING OF LEASE VIOLATION

Name of resident(s): _____ *Vernon and Maria Edwards* _____ Date: _____ *March 14* _____

Address: _____ *2381 Palm Drive, Apartment 610, Dallas, 75336* _____

The following Lease Violation(s) have been discovered and recorded in your tenant file:

☑ Littered patio/entry	☐ Working on vehicle	☑ Illegal parking
☑ Destruction of property	☑ Excessive noise	☐ Unauthorized modification of dwelling
☐ Unauthorized occupant	☐ Illegal activities	☐ Unauthorized pets
☐ Parked in a fire zone	☐ Foil on windows	☐ Inoperable parked vehicle
☐ Other		

You are in violation of your lease agreement and are hereby advised that failure to take action to correct the above-named problem(s) within _____ *14* _____ days from the date hereof will result in additional action as outlined in the apartment lease contract, which could result in termination of your occupancy. You have the right to respond to this notice within ten calendar days after the date of this notice.

Please note that you will be responsible for any repairs necessary to the leased premises as a result of the violation(s). If you have any questions, do not hesitate to contact the Manager. Thank you in advance for your cooperation.

Sincerely

_____ *Brenda Rawlinson* _____

☑ hand-delivered or ☐ mailed to ☑ resident or ☐ resident's apartment

For office use only: Corrective Measures Taken and When: _____

8. Who is Mr. Nichols?
- (A) The owner of Westgate Property Management
- (B) The manager of the apartments at 2381 Palm Drive
- (C) The landlord of the new tenants at Apt. 610
- (D) The proprietor of Ms. Delaney's apartment

9. What is NOT indicated about the new tenants?
- (A) They risk being evicted from their apartment.
- (B) They will be liable for the cost of any repairs.
- (C) At least one of them has met Ms. Rawlinson.
- (D) They have never spoken with Ms. Delaney.

10. By when should the tenants at Apt. 610 resolve the problems?
- (A) March 14
- (B) March 24
- (C) March 28
- (D) March 31

11. In the letter, the word "strewn" in paragraph 1, line 3, is closest in meaning to
- (A) distributed
- (B) scattered
- (C) isolated
- (D) draped

12. Which of these lease violations should also be marked on the notice?
- (A) Unauthorized pets
- (B) Inoperable parked vehicle
- (C) Unauthorized occupant
- (D) Working on vehicle

8.	Ⓐ	Ⓑ	Ⓒ	Ⓓ
9.	Ⓐ	Ⓑ	Ⓒ	Ⓓ
10.	Ⓐ	Ⓑ	Ⓒ	Ⓓ
11.	Ⓐ	Ⓑ	Ⓒ	Ⓓ
12.	Ⓐ	Ⓑ	Ⓒ	Ⓓ

Questions 13–17 refer to the following e-mail, online booking form, and schedule.

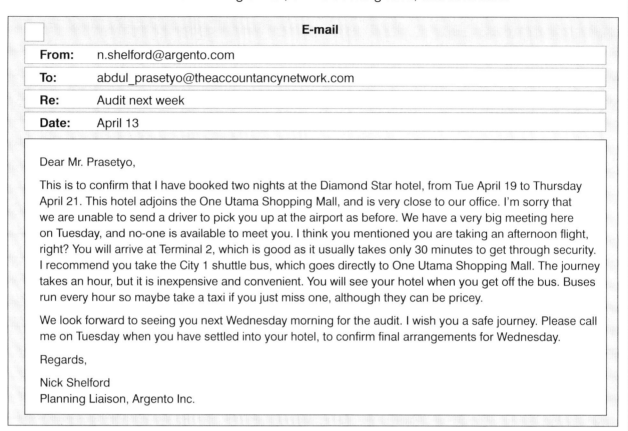

E-mail
From: n.shelford@argento.com
To: abdul_prasetyo@theaccountancynetwork.com
Re: Audit next week
Date: April 13

Dear Mr. Prasetyo,

This is to confirm that I have booked two nights at the Diamond Star hotel, from Tue April 19 to Thursday April 21. This hotel adjoins the One Utama Shopping Mall, and is very close to our office. I'm sorry that we are unable to send a driver to pick you up at the airport as before. We have a very big meeting here on Tuesday, and no-one is available to meet you. I think you mentioned you are taking an afternoon flight, right? You will arrive at Terminal 2, which is good as it usually takes only 30 minutes to get through security. I recommend you take the City 1 shuttle bus, which goes directly to One Utama Shopping Mall. The journey takes an hour, but it is inexpensive and convenient. You will see your hotel when you get off the bus. Buses run every hour so maybe take a taxi if you just miss one, although they can be pricey.

We look forward to seeing you next Wednesday morning for the audit. I wish you a safe journey. Please call me on Tuesday when you have settled into your hotel, to confirm final arrangements for Wednesday.

Regards,

Nick Shelford
Planning Liaison, Argento Inc.

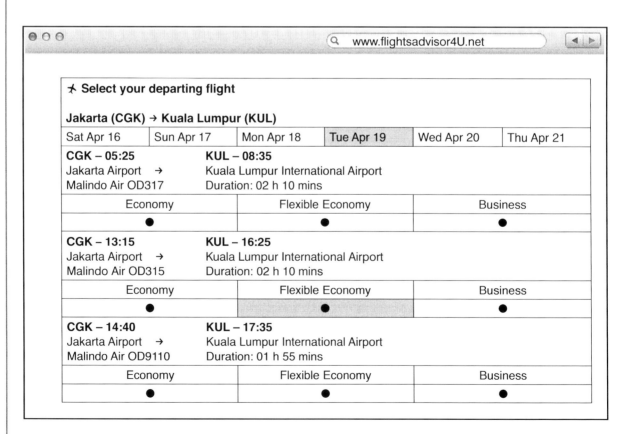

www.flightsadvisor4U.net

✈ Select your departing flight

Jakarta (CGK) → Kuala Lumpur (KUL)

Sat Apr 16	Sun Apr 17	Mon Apr 18	Tue Apr 19	Wed Apr 20	Thu Apr 21

CGK – 05:25		KUL – 08:35			
Jakarta Airport →		Kuala Lumpur International Airport			
Malindo Air OD317		Duration: 02 h 10 mins			

Economy	Flexible Economy	Business
●	●	●

CGK – 13:15		KUL – 16:25			
Jakarta Airport →		Kuala Lumpur International Airport			
Malindo Air OD315		Duration: 02 h 10 mins			

Economy	Flexible Economy	Business
●	●	●

CGK – 14:40		KUL – 17:35			
Jakarta Airport →		Kuala Lumpur International Airport			
Malindo Air OD9110		Duration: 01 h 55 mins			

Economy	Flexible Economy	Business
●	●	●

```
KUALA LUMPUR
INTERNATIONAL AIRPORT
City Shuttle Bus
Departure Times
CITY 1 SERVICE
One Utama Shopping Mall
```

Departs Bay 12	Arrives
4:30 A.M.	5:45 A.M.
and every 60m thereafter until	
12:30 A.M.	01:45 A.M.

Shuttles run between 4:30 A.M. and 12:30 A.M. every day. Tickets can be purchased at the Transportation Information Counter at Level G in the bus station area. There are no charges for luggage.

13. Why did Mr. Shelford send the e-mail?
(A) To confirm a hotel booking
(B) To check flight times
(C) To review travel plans
(D) To make an apology

14. What is suggested about Mr. Prasetyo?
(A) He works in financial insurance.
(B) He travels a lot for his work.
(C) His family live in Jakarta.
(D) He visited Argento previously.

15. What is indicated about Malindo Air?
(A) They have several flights to Kuala Lumpur.
(B) Some of their planes are older than others.
(C) Their business class seats are very popular.
(D) Jakarta is their base of operations.

16. Which shuttle bus will Mr. Prasetyo most likely take?
(A) 3:30 P.M.
(B) 4:30 P.M.
(C) 5:30 P.M.
(D) 6:30 P.M.

17. Which part of Mr. Prasetyo's trip does Mr. Shelford get wrong?
(A) The flight departure time
(B) The length of the bus ride
(C) The arrival terminal
(D) The date of the audit

13. Ⓐ Ⓑ Ⓒ Ⓓ
14. Ⓐ Ⓑ Ⓒ Ⓓ
15. Ⓐ Ⓑ Ⓒ Ⓓ
16. Ⓐ Ⓑ Ⓒ Ⓓ
17. Ⓐ Ⓑ Ⓒ Ⓓ

Score ..../17

Practice 3

Questions 1–3 refer to the following live chat discussion.

Alice from BuyRight   9:21 A.M.

Hey, I see you are looking at our Summer promotion. Anything I can help you with?

MikeB   9:23 A.M.

Hi. Yes, I want to get the Harvard desk lamp and have a coupon but it won't accept it.
Can you help?

Alice from BuyRight   9:27 A.M.

Absolutely! Please give me the item number and coupon details. I'll look into it for you.

MikeB   9:27 A.M.

Item is HDL32. My coupon is Summer10. It's a 10 percent discount, I think.
That's what the ad says in this month's Business Life magazine.

Alice from BuyRight   9:28 A.M.

Thank you. Please give me a moment.

Alice from BuyRight   9:30 A.M.

I have found the item. The reason you can't order is we are out of stock right now.
So sorry about that. I can contact the manufacturer to check delivery dates, if you like.

MikeB   9:31 A.M.

That's OK. I think I'll leave it.

Alice from BuyRight   9:31 A.M.

We have similar lamps if you're interested. Take a look at HJK7 and BD24.
They're both pretty cool!

MikeB   9:32 A.M.

Do I just type the number in the search box?

---

1. At 9:27 A.M., what does Alice mean when she writes, "Absolutely"?
   (A) She agrees completely with MikeB.
   (B) She is happy to provide assistance.
   (C) She is certain that MikeB is correct.
   (D) She has all the details she needs.

2. What is indicated about MikeB's coupon?
   (A) It is no longer valid.
   (B) He needs to use it quickly.
   (C) It only applies to certain items.
   (D) He received it recently.

3. What will MikeB most likely do next?
   (A) Make a purchase
   (B) End the discussion
   (C) Continue shopping
   (D) Leave his office

1. Ⓐ Ⓑ Ⓒ Ⓓ **2.** Ⓐ Ⓑ Ⓒ Ⓓ **3.** Ⓐ Ⓑ Ⓒ Ⓓ

Questions 4–7 refer to the following letter.

November 25

Ms. Denise Bertram
Huntingdon County Planning Dept.
Government Center
671 Euclid Street
Philadelphia, PA 19019

Re: PLANNING APPLICATION NO 1248-0741AE

Proposed erection of a 100-foot-tall wireless antenna on Carraway Road adjacent to Hope Farm, by TelCom Systems.

I am writing to you in connection with the above planning application, and wish to state that I am vehemently opposed to the proposed installation of a cell-phone antenna in this location. Our farm adjoins the land where the antenna is due to be placed. At such a height it will stand 40 feet above the highest tree nearby, meaning it will permanently scar the landscape in all directions. More importantly, not only will we be able to see it 24/7 for the rest of our lives, but as it will be less than half a mile from our house it will devalue our property considerably. I am also concerned about the possible impact on my family, having read several studies on the effects of long-term exposure to low-frequency microwave radiation from such antennas.

I appreciate that TelCom Systems wants to expand its network coverage across the county, and I have no issue with the other 20 or so towers they are due to erect elsewhere, but I would urge you to consider whether the ill-planned placement of this particular tower on Carraway Road should be given approval in light of the above points.

Sincerely,

Jo Newton

Joseph Newton

---

4. What is Ms. Bertram being asked to do?
   (A) Withdraw planning permission
   (B) Reject the application outright
   (C) Propose an alternative site
   (D) Suspend the case for further review

5. What is indicated about the cell-phone antenna?
   (A) It will be partially obscured.
   (B) It will be located on Hope Farm.
   (C) It will replace a smaller tower.
   (D) It will be a temporary structure.

6. What objection to the planned antenna installation is NOT mentioned?
   (A) The financial injury
   (B) The aesthetic impact
   (C) The risks to health
   (D) The environmental cost

7. The word "vehemently" in paragraph 1, line 2, is closest in meaning to
   (A) strongly
   (B) actively
   (C) openly
   (D) directly

4. Ⓐ Ⓑ Ⓒ Ⓓ　**5.** Ⓐ Ⓑ Ⓒ Ⓓ　**6.** Ⓐ Ⓑ Ⓒ Ⓓ　**7.** Ⓐ Ⓑ Ⓒ Ⓓ

Questions 8–12 refer to the following information and letter.

Terms & Conditions - General Conditions of Carriage (Passenger and Baggage)

Article 12: Refunds

We will refund any ticket or unused portion thereof, in accordance with the applicable fare rules as follows:

12.1   Unless otherwise stated, and providing that satisfactory proof of payment is presented, a refund shall only be made to the person who has paid for the ticket, irrespective of whosoever shall be named in the ticket.

12.2   Except in the case of a lost ticket, refunds will only be made on presentation to us of the original ticket.

12.3   In case of cancellation, or failure to operate according to schedule, failure to stop at your destination or Stopover, or where caused to miss a connecting flight for which you hold a reservation, the amount of the refund shall be equal to the fare paid. In cases where part of the ticket has been used, the refund shall be not less than the difference between the fare paid and the applicable fare for travel between the points for which the ticket has been used.

12.4   If you request a refund for reasons other than those mentioned in 12.3, the amount of the refund will be equal to the fare paid if no portion of the ticket has been used, less any reasonable service charges or cancellation fees.

12.5   If a ticket or portion thereof is lost, a refund will be made on payment of the applicable fee, provided that no portion of the ticket has been used.

12.6   We may refuse refund for applications made later than six months after the expiration date of the ticket.

12.7   No recompense shall be payable in any cases where passengers are considered to be at fault or responsible in any way for disruption and its consequent effects, or for flights booked on separate tickets, whether or not via an alternative carrier.

12.8   Subject to the foregoing provision, refunds will be made in the currency in which the fare was paid. Refunds due to tickets paid for with credit cards can only be credited to credit card accounts originally used for the ticket purchase. Please note that differences in conversion may result in the refundable amount to be credited to the credit card account of the card owner varying from the originally debited amount by the credit card company.

Sept. 20

Customer Services
OneJet Europe
Milan Malpensa Airport
Unit 65B
22010 Varese
Italy

Dear Sir/Madam:

On September 4 I was due to fly from Milan to Geneva on Flight OJ425, scheduled to leave at 3:00 P.M. However, the flight was repeatedly delayed, and finally took off over two hours late. This caused me to miss my connecting flight to Beijing with Pacific Airlines on flight PA151, which left Geneva on time at 6:15 P.M. I am enclosing the original return tickets for both flights for your records. You will see that the flight to Geneva cost €95, and the onward flight to Beijing cost €870.

When I finally arrived in Geneva I had to purchase a standby single ticket for €1330 from Air Oriental Airlines, which was the only airline with availability later that day. I was given a claim form (enclosed), and was told by your ground staff that I should contact your Customer Services department and you would reimburse the additional expense. As you will see from the photocopied receipts, my company paid for the ticket.

I would appreciate it if you could process payment as soon as possible.

Many thanks,

Ms. T. Andretti
Ms. T. Andretti

8. What is stated about refunds?

(A) Payment will be sent direct to ticket holders.

(B) Some deductions may be made before payment.

(C) There is no time limit on applying for a refund.

(D) The exact amount paid will be refunded.

9. How much compensation is OneJet liable to pay in this case?

(A) €95

(B) €460

(C) €870

(D) €1330

10. What is indicated about Ms. Andretti?

(A) Her company has a travel insurance policy.

(B) She has previously flown with Air Oriental Airlines.

(C) She does not have one of the original flight tickets.

(D) Her flight from Beijing was with Pacific Airlines.

11. In the letter, the word "records" in paragraph 1, line 4, is closest in meaning to

(A) minutes

(B) files

(C) archives

(D) proceedings

12. What does Ms. Andretti NOT include with her letter?

(A) Proof of payment

(B) Her flight tickets

(C) A claim form

(D) A booking reference

8. Ⓐ Ⓑ Ⓒ Ⓓ

9. Ⓐ Ⓑ Ⓒ Ⓓ

10. Ⓐ Ⓑ Ⓒ Ⓓ

11. Ⓐ Ⓑ Ⓒ Ⓓ

12. Ⓐ Ⓑ Ⓒ Ⓓ

Questions 13–17 refer to the following job advertisement, Web page, and e-mail.

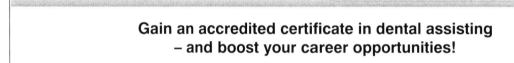

DENTAL ASSISTANT

Dental assistant required, preferably with a recognized qualification, for a friendly, busy practice offering a wide range of dental services, including children's dentistry and orthodontics. Under supervision, the successful applicant will:

- assist with the carrying out of general dental and radiographic procedures
- prepare and maintain dental equipment and supplies
- assist in the coordination of patient administration and record-keeping
- offer general support

Requirements:

- Certification preferred
- Administrative and basic computer skills
- Ability to work as part of a team in a clinical environment
- Knowledge of radiation safety procedures and protocols
- One year of experience preferred
- First aid knowledge

Please apply with résumé and two references to: office@westsidedentalclinic.net

---

www1.excelhealthtraining.org.

Gain an accredited certificate in dental assisting – and boost your career opportunities!

We offer four national certifications:

Certificate in Dental Assisting
Our entry-level qualification covers:
- Study skills
- Basic computing skills
- Dental terminology and anatomy
- Infection control
- Radiation safety
- Dental office administration

Qualified Dental Assistant
This state-certified qualification includes:
- Mouth anatomy and physiology
- Infection control
- Radiation safety
- First aid
- Dental equipment use and care
- Dental office management and administration
- Relevant computer software

Certificate in Preventive Dentistry
In this course you will cover:
- Mouth anatomy and physiology
- Infection control
- Radiation safety
- First aid
- Dental equipment use and care
- Dental pharmacology
- Topical fluoride application
- Dental cleaning, polishing and application of sealants
- Role of nutrition

Certificate in Orthodontic Dentistry Assisting
Our orthodontic course encompasses:
- Mouth anatomy and physiology
- Pediatric anatomy
- Infection control
- Radiation safety
- First aid
- Dental equipment use and care
- Introduction to appliances used in the mouth
- Introduction to oral surgical procedures

E-mail	
From:	Kiara.Jackson
To:	office@westsidedentalclinic.net
Date:	Aug 23
Subject:	Dental Assistant application

For the attention of the hiring manager

I would like to apply for the position of Dental Assistant advertised on the Medical Jobs for All Web site. I believe my experience and qualifications are a good match for the job. My résumé is attached to this e-mail.

I obtained my Qualified Dental Assistant certificate two years ago at Peninsula Park College, and since then I have been working full-time in a small dental practice in my locality. Last year I completed an evening course in Preventive Dentistry, and I am currently studying online for the Certificate in Orthodontic Dentistry Assisting. My current dental practice does not offer these specialties, and I am seeking a position where I can use these qualifications.

I have good interpersonal and communication skills and work well with others. I am sure I could make a significant contribution to your practice.

I look forward to hearing from you.
Sincerely,
Kiara Jackson

13. Which certificate is most relevant to this job application?
(A) Certificate in Dental Assisting
(B) Qualified Dental Assistant
(C) Certificate in Preventive Dentistry
(D) Certificate in Orthodontic Dentistry Assisting

14. What skill acquired by Kiara Jackson in her studies will NOT be needed in this job?
(A) Dental pharmacology
(B) First aid
(C) Radiation safety
(D) Administrative skills

15. In the job advertisement, the word "recognized" in paragraph 1, line 2, is closest in meaning to
(A) approved
(B) acclaimed
(C) advanced
(D) practical

16. What is indicated about Kiara Jackson?
(A) She is seeking a full-time position.
(B) She prefers to work near home.
(C) She is taking a distance-learning course.
(D) She has a Certificate in Orthodontic Dentistry Assisting.

17. What did Kiara Jackson omit to include with her letter of application?
(A) Her résumé
(B) References
(C) Copies of her certificates
(D) Her notice period

13. (A) (B) (C) (D)
14. (A) (B) (C) (D)
15. (A) (B) (C) (D)
16. (A) (B) (C) (D)
17. (A) (B) (C) (D)

Score ..../17

Strategy Review and Tips

Strategy Review Reading Test – Part 7

Remember, in the test…

Preview the passage(s) first, quickly noting the type of text, how long it is, and how many questions there are. Read *only* the questions.

Skim the passage to get a general idea. Read quickly, and keep going until you reach the end.

Answer the first question if you can. If not, be sure you know exactly what information you need to find *before* you look in the passage. Then scan the passage to quickly find the answer you are looking for.

Always cross-reference key details you find with the answer choices, eliminating any answers that you are sure are wrong.

Remember that for multiple readings you sometimes need to refer to two or even three passages to find the answer.

Do not spend too long on one question. Be aware of the time. If you are not sure of an answer, make a guess and move on.

TIPS *Here is some advice that people taking the TOEIC test have found useful for this part. Choose the tips you like, and try to use them.*

"In Part 5 and Part 6 you generally either know the answer or you don't, so spending time thinking about it doesn't really help. However, in Part 7 spending more time working out the answer really *does* help. That's why you need you get through Part 5 and Part 6 as quickly as possible."
Cecilia Hernandez

"I push through the single texts quickly so I have more time on the multiple passages. They are the ones with the most questions"
Gavin Schroeder

"Read the questions first, because as you are skimming the text you might be able to spot the answers—especially for any questions about main ideas."
Takeshi Saito

"If there is a NOT question, leave it until after you have done the other questions. By the time you get back to it you might know the answer."
Lien Nguyen

"I do Part 7 first, because if time is short, it is much easier to quickly rush through Part 5 and Part 6 and guess the answers than it is for Part 7."
Lukas Baptista

Review Test

Start time: ....

Finish time: ....

Directions: Read the texts. You will notice that each text is followed by several questions. For each question, decide which of the four answer choices: (A), (B), (C), or (D), best answers the question. Then mark your answer.

Questions 1–2 refer to the following news report.

The Talking Stops at **HandyTalk**

– Jan Kennedy, media correspondent

Many HandyTalk customers on MyPhoneNetwork will have had an unproductive day yesterday, unable to access e-mails or other data services on their cell phones. The outage hit users throughout Europe, although services in North America were not affected. The problem, which was traced to a router failure impacting mobile switching centers (MSCs) from southern Spain through to the Balkan states, has now been fixed. "Only those MSCs that have not yet been upgraded onto our new HSDPA system were down," insisted the mobile network operator's European head of operations, Erkan Ollson. Nevertheless, the timing of the incident is unfortunate given that HandyTalk is about to unveil its latest smartphone—the much-awaited GT20—on which the financial future of the company depends. That the fault was due to a MyPhoneNetwork service failure will be poor consolation for the hard-pressed smartphone manufacturer. Judging by the comments on social networking sites, customers are already blaming HandyTalk.

---

1. What is this report about?
   (A) A cellular service upgrade
   (B) A cell phone connectivity issue
   (C) A telecommunications dispute
   (D) A loss of data on handheld devices

2. What is indicated in the report?
   (A) MyPhoneNetwork is a European company.
   (B) Customers should expect further disruption.
   (C) The new HSDPA system is unreliable.
   (D) HandyTalks's future looks uncertain.

1. Ⓐ Ⓑ Ⓒ Ⓓ   2. Ⓐ Ⓑ Ⓒ Ⓓ

Matador Office Supplies

18 Gosford Avenue, Newcastle, NSW 2300

Purchase Order Number: 27954   Shipment Number: 15488

Purchase Order Date: February 13   Shipment Date: February 15

Bill to:	Ship to:
Livonia Exercise Equipment Livonia Place 1280 Moss Vale Avenue Sydney NSW 2000	TVP Warehousing and Stores Whitebushes Industrial Estate Wollongong NSW 2522

Shipping details: road transport via Fleet Distribution Services

Code	Description of Goods	Quantity/Units	Unit Price $	Total Price $
B976	Recycled printer paper	20 reams	4.00	80.00
B1432	Padded envelopes (large)	40 packs	2.50	100.00
D58	Laser printer toner cartridge	2	38.50	77.00

Items received in good order and condition

By (Name) .... Signature .... Date ....

3. What kind of document is this?

(A) An invoice

(B) A quotation

(C) A packing slip

(D) A purchase order

4. An employee of which company should sign this form?

(A) Matador Office Supplies

(B) Fleet Distribution Services

(C) Livonia Exercise Equipment

(D) TVP Warehousing and Stores

3. Ⓐ Ⓑ Ⓒ Ⓓ   **4.** Ⓐ Ⓑ Ⓒ Ⓓ

Questions 5–6 refer to the following text message chain.

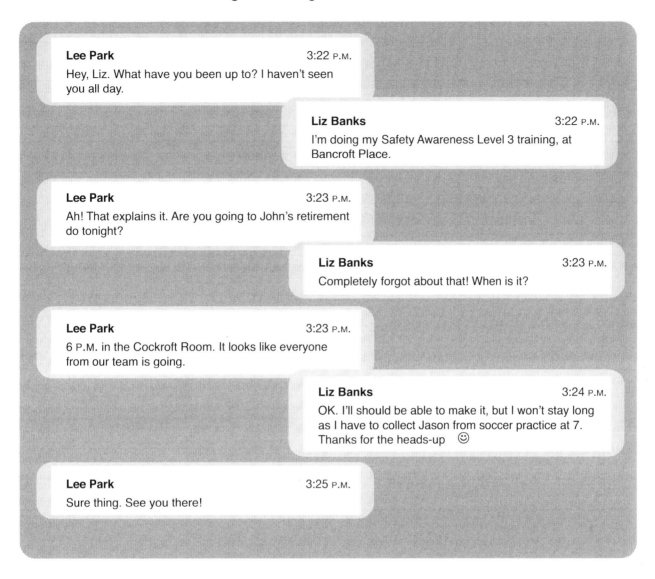

Lee Park   3:22 P.M.

Hey, Liz. What have you been up to? I haven't seen you all day.

Liz Banks   3:22 P.M.

I'm doing my Safety Awareness Level 3 training, at Bancroft Place.

Lee Park   3:23 P.M.

Ah! That explains it. Are you going to John's retirement do tonight?

Liz Banks   3:23 P.M.

Completely forgot about that! When is it?

Lee Park   3:23 P.M.

6 P.M. in the Cockroft Room. It looks like everyone from our team is going.

Liz Banks   3:24 P.M.

OK. I'll should be able to make it, but I won't stay long as I have to collect Jason from soccer practice at 7. Thanks for the heads-up ☺

Lee Park   3:25 P.M.

Sure thing. See you there!

5. At 3:25 P.M., what does Mr. Park mean when he writes, "Sure thing"?

(A) You're welcome.

(B) It's definite.

(C) All right.

(D) Yes, indeed.

6. What is implied about Ms. Banks and Mr. Park?

(A) They are married.

(B) They play sports.

(C) They have a son.

(D) They are coworkers.

5. Ⓐ Ⓑ Ⓒ Ⓓ   6. Ⓐ Ⓑ Ⓒ Ⓓ

121 Dunedin Avenue, Apt. 672
Vancouver, BC 58P 3A6
September 20

Mr. Ronaldo Lopez
Vancouver Home Solutions
608 Montgomery Road
Vancouver, BC 84Y 4VR

Dear Mr. Lopez:

Thank you for your letter of September 13. I have completed and signed the Rental Inspection Checklist you sent and am enclosing it with this letter.

As I have noted on the checklist, the electric kettle is faulty, and there is no toaster in the apartment. However, I have my own, so there is no need for new ones to be supplied. In addition, as you will see from the snapshot I e-mailed yesterday, knobs are missing on two of the kitchen drawers. This is not a major problem, but I would appreciate their replacement. More importantly, I have tested all the electrical equipment and the heating system, as requested, and noticed that the radiator in the main bedroom does not seem to be working. Since the temperature will no doubt drop very soon, I would appreciate your getting this fixed as soon as possible.

I feel unable to sign the section of the checklist that asks me to guarantee to check the smoke alarm each month. There is no way for me to reach the alarm, given that there is no stepladder in the apartment. Please can you look in the documentation to see whether one should be provided as a legal requirement of the tenancy?

Two letters arrived earlier this week for the previous tenant, so I am enclosing them with this letter. I trust you or one of your colleagues will be able to forward them on appropriately.

I will be in touch again next week when I will send you the first month's rental payment, due on October 1.

Sincerely,

Daisy Lee

Ms. Daisy Lee

7. Who most likely is Mr. Lopez?

(A) A homeowner

(B) A leaseholder

(C) A property agent

(D) A private landlord

8. What does Ms. Lee NOT refer to in her letter?

(A) Items of mail

(B) A photograph

(C) A bank check

(D) A signed form

9. What does Ms. Lee ask Mr. Lopez to do?

(A) Arrange for some repairs

(B) Supply her with a stepladder

(C) Replace some kitchen equipment

(D) Witness some legal documents

7. Ⓐ Ⓑ Ⓒ Ⓓ   8. Ⓐ Ⓑ Ⓒ Ⓓ   9. Ⓐ Ⓑ Ⓒ Ⓓ

Pre-shift Daily Checklist

This checklist must be completed by the operator at the start of each shift. Any unsafe features must be reported at once to your line manager, who will arrange repair by a qualified mechanic.

✓ Sufficient   ✗ Requires attention

	Mon	Tues	Wed	Thurs	Fri	Sat
Visual checks						
Ground/floor: free of obstacles						
Overhead guard: in place and in good condition						
Oil and fuel levels						
Radiator water level						
Tires: condition and pressure						
Fluid leaks: no damp spots on the ground						
Operational checks						
Engine sound: normal						
All gauges and instruments working						
Horn: loud						
Headlights; rear and warning lights						
Indicators: operational						
Steering: smooth, no binding						
Accelerator: working properly						
All brakes: effective						

Operator Number _____

10. Who most likely would be required to complete this chart?
    (A) A forklift driver
    (B) A lathe operator
    (C) A car mechanic
    (D) A storeroom clerk

11. What is it NOT necessary to check, according to the list?
    (A) Fluid levels
    (B) Foot pedals
    (C) Rear mirrors
    (D) Signaling devices

12. What should operators do if a fault giving cause for safety concerns is discovered?
    (A) Contact a qualified technician
    (B) Inform their immediate supervisor
    (C) Arrange for an urgent repair
    (D) Call the maintenance department

10. Ⓐ   Ⓑ   Ⓒ   Ⓓ   11. Ⓐ   Ⓑ   Ⓒ   Ⓓ   12. Ⓐ   Ⓑ   Ⓒ   Ⓓ

		MEMO
To:	All department heads and deputy heads	
From:	Loretta Day, Human Resources	
Date:	September 13	
Subject:	Visitors from Kiev	

We have had to make some changes to next week's schedule for the Ukrainian delegation. Please make a note if you are affected. ---[1]---

As you know, the delegation was due to arrive next Wednesday morning (the 19th), but due to the two-day work-to-rule by ground staff at the airport, which is scheduled to begin on Wednesday, they are now arriving on Tuesday afternoon. Unfortunately I will not be in the office on Tuesday, as I will be in Boston at the packaging trade fair.

I have arranged for a company minibus to pick the delegation up from the airport, take them briefly to their hotel to freshen up, and then bring them here. Is anyone free next Tuesday afternoon around midday to go with the minibus to welcome them, and help with their registration at the hotel? ---[2]---

Also, we need someone to keep them occupied once they get here for a couple of hours or so beginning about 3:00 P.M. If a few of you could take them out for dinner on Tuesday evening that would be most appreciated. I might be back in time to join you toward the end of the evening. ---[3]--- Please contact my assistant, James Muldrow, at x242 if you can assist with any of this.

The program for Wednesday will remain unchanged, but will have to start earlier, so the first session will be at 9:30 A.M. instead of at 11:30 A.M. Also, each session will now be half an hour longer than originally scheduled. ---[4]--- I'll confirm the final details in a memo to you all first thing on Monday.

Regards,

Loretta Day

HR Director, GTrax Inc.

---

13. In which position marked [1], [2], [3], and [4] does the following sentence best belong?
"It would be a huge help if so."
(A) [1]
(B) [2]
(C) [3]
(D) [4]

14. What will take place on Wednesday of next week?
(A) Staff will take part in a job action.
(B) A new airport will be opened.
(C) The Boston trade fair will end.
(D) A group will visit GTrax Inc.

15. What will Loretta Day do on September 17?
(A) Contact a buyer in the Ukraine
(B) Send out a final itinerary
(C) Organize client entertainment
(D) Attend a packaging exhibition

13. (A) (B) (C) (D) 14. (A) (B) (C) (D) 15. (A) (B) (C) (D)

Questions 16–18 refer to the following information.

Zoe Nielsen	[4:03 P.M.]
Hi guys. Re our crowdsourcing ideas campaign… As you know, this month HR is asking everyone to come up with innovative ways we can make savings across the company, from top to bottom. Please encourage members of your departments to chip in as many ideas as possible. How's it going so far?	
Paul Rankin	[4:03 P.M.]
Hey Zoe. Yes, I've been trying, but nothing yet. Sorry!	
Jess McPartlin	[4:04 P.M.]
Pretty slim pickings here too, I'm afraid.	
Reiko Ishii	[4:04 P.M.]
And here… What about having a prize for any ideas HR takes up?	
Beth Sayers	[4:05 P.M.]
What are you thinking of, Reiko? Cash, coupons…? [BTW, no response so far here either.]	
Zoe Nielsen	[4:05 P.M.]
How about a weekend break at Valley Ranch?	
Jess McPartlin	[4:05 P.M.]
Now you're talking!	
Paul Rankin	[4:06 P.M.]
Count me in! Their spa treatments are amazing.	
Zoe Nielsen	[4:06 P.M.]
The deadline is only 2 weeks away, so I'll send a memo to everyone telling them about this. Hopefully it will bring results.	
Beth Sayers	[4:07 P.M.]
It certainly won't hurt. Maybe add an e-mail address where they can send in ideas, rather than just use the Suggestions box in reception. It isn't that easy to find.	
Zoe Nielsen	[4:08 P.M.]
Good thinking, Beth. I'll get on it right away.	

16. At 4:07 P.M., what does Ms. Sayers mean when she writes, "It certainly won't hurt"?
    (A) Spa breaks are very relaxing.
    (B) The results should be negative.
    (C) The idea is a good one.
    (D) This is a painless option.

17. What is indicated about the discussion participants?
    (A) They are Heads of their department.
    (B) They work in different departments.
    (C) They have regular meetings together.
    (D) They all report to Human Resources.

18. What will Ms. Nielsen most likely do shortly?
    (A) Go to see Valley Ranch
    (B) Enter an online competition
    (C) Locate the Suggestions Box
    (D) Contact all the employees

16. (A) (B) (C) (D) **17.** (A) (B) (C) (D) **18.** (A) (B) (C) (D)

Clairmont Regional Medical Center

168 Hamilton Street • Conway, AR 72034

October 4

Dr. Robert Lubitsky
Little Rock Infirmary
100 Fern Avenue
Little Rock, AR 72260

Dear Dr. Lubitsky:

Re: Leonard Brogan

I have been treating Mr. Brogan for psoriasis for several years. Despite my having prescribed emollient creams and lotions and hydrocortisone 2.5% more recently, the condition has worsened. The patient's hands are rough and cracked, with bleeding sores. I would therefore like him to see a dermatologist, either you or one of your colleagues, ideally within the next month.

Copies of Mr. Brogan's medical records are enclosed. Apart from the psoriasis, he is in generally good health, with just a touch of arthritis in his hips, which is not at all debilitating. There is a history of diabetes in his family.

I have told Mr. Brogan to expect a call from you shortly. Once you have seen him and decided on treatment, could you please provide a written summary of your diagnosis and any prescribed medication or other recommended treatment for my records?

Sincerely,

Barbara Wagner

Barbara Wagner
Family Physician

---

19. What is the main purpose of this letter?
    (A) To commission a medical report
    (B) To provide a clinical diagnosis
    (C) To refer a patient for treatment
    (D) To prescribe a new medication

20. What health problem does Mr. Brogan principally suffer from?
    (A) A skin condition
    (B) A digestive disorder
    (C) Pain in the joints
    (D) Excessive bleeding

21. What will Dr. Lubitsky most likely do within the next few days?
    (A) Send a brief report to Dr. Wagner
    (B) Speak with Mr. Brogan directly
    (C) Call a specialist at the local hospital
    (D) Research Mr. Brogan's family history

19. Ⓐ Ⓑ Ⓒ Ⓓ **20.** Ⓐ Ⓑ Ⓒ Ⓓ **21.** Ⓐ Ⓑ Ⓒ Ⓓ

Water Control Symposium
◆Tackling 21st Century Challenges◆
Kennedy Convention Center, Miami, June 8

The fifth biennial Water Control Symposium is the largest and highest-profile event of its kind, bringing together key decision makers from government agencies, water supply organizations, technology suppliers, and equipment manufacturers from across the country. Offering an unrivaled platform for you to debate the important issues facing the water industry today, this symposium is a perfect opportunity for you to:

✦ Engage with the C.E.O.s of top WASCs and WOCs
✦ Discuss the main priorities of business and domestic water customers
✦ Learn about best practice in infrastructure asset management
✦ Share strategies for improving resilience and sustainability
✦ Find out how other companies are innovating their pricing policies
✦ Meet your peers from across the sector and influence policy change

Provisional Program

Session 1: Leakage Management   Despite heavy investment by government and utility companies, leakage remains a central issue. Last year's exceptionally cold winter and rapid thaw led to an unprecedented number of burst pipes. Through analysis of individual householders' and businesses' experiences, Pete McElroy of WasteField Systems will consider ways to manage and control leakage.

9:30–11:00 A.M.

Session 2: Investing in Infrastructure   Aging drinking-water pipes, sewers, and stormwater systems pose major problems. How can we finance the massive investment in water infrastructure needed? Eric Langhorn, C.E.O. of Continental Water, will explore the use of public-private partnerships in the renewal of water systems, citing the collaborative project between Continental Water and privately owned PowerBuild Technologies to design and construct Atlanta's newest water treatment works.

11:30 A.M.–1:00 P.M.

Session 3: Risk and Water Security   The water industry faces many threats with potentially catastrophic consequences, including natural disasters, emergencies, climate change, and criminal activity. A panel of experts from a range of backgrounds, including specialists from the disaster relief and ecological sectors, will offer suggestions on how to safeguard drinking water supplies.

2:00–3:30 P.M.

Session 4: Solutions to Water Shortages   The charity African Agriculture runs several successful rainwater-harvesting projects in farming communities in sub-Saharan Africa, combining traditional African agricultural practices, local know-how, and Western technology to irrigate crops. Outreach Officer Rachel McDonald will draw on two projects she has been instrumental in setting up, and will show the potential benefits of rainwater harvesting for high-tech companies looking for solutions to water shortages.

4:00–5:30 P.M.

Presentations and panel talks will be streamed in real time to enable wider participation. Video archives of all sessions will be made available after the symposium.

Registration opens March 1. For further news and the latest updates,
see our website, www.watercontrolsymposium.com

22. Who is this event primarily intended for?
- (A) Technology suppliers to the sanitation industry
- (B) Wastewater treatment plant engineers
- (C) Politicians and government energy advisors
- (D) Senior executives from water utility companies

23. What is suggested about Rachel McDonald?
- (A) She lives in sub-Saharan Africa.
- (B) She works for an aid organization.
- (C) She is a crop irrigation specialist.
- (D) She has a farming background.

24. What can be inferred about the symposium?
- (A) It takes place in June each year.
- (B) The program is not yet finalized.
- (C) The entire event is televised live.
- (D) It attracts delegates from abroad.

25. Which session will NOT include at least one case study?
- (A) Session 1
- (B) Session 2
- (C) Session 3
- (D) Session 4

22.	Ⓐ	Ⓑ	Ⓒ	Ⓓ
23.	Ⓐ	Ⓑ	Ⓒ	Ⓓ
24.	Ⓐ	Ⓑ	Ⓒ	Ⓓ
25.	Ⓐ	Ⓑ	Ⓒ	Ⓓ

Half Steam Ahead By Maxine Montgomery

The measures taken over recent months by the Federal Reserve to stimulate the economy appear to be starting to bear fruit—certainly in the Midwest. At least, that is the conclusion of a survey of business leaders released Monday.

"Home prices surged to a four-year high in Illinois last month, which reflects the increasing numbers of people prepared to take on loans," said Dr. Leona Sanchez, an economist at Omaha University, which oversaw the nine-state study. Keen to emphasize that this pattern is repeated across the region, Sanchez added that house construction has increased so much over the last quarter that some builders are complaining that they cannot find enough skilled workers to keep up with the demand for new homes. ---[1]--- She went on to dismiss the views of naysayers who attributed this surge in the housing market to a last-minute rush by home purchasers, eager to lock in favorable mortgage-rate deals before an expected rise in rates later this year. ---[2]--- In Michigan, the economy is gaining steam, with government figures showing unemployment has dropped by two percentage points in three months to 8 percent. Eight percent might still sound high to some, but just three years ago parts of Michigan had an unemployment rate of 12 percent. Ray Kenton, who runs a chain of fried-chicken restaurants across the state, has seen business at all 15 of his outlets rise so much that he is planning to open 3 new restaurants over the border in Ohio.

Sales of consumer goods and automobiles are also booming, as evidence suggests consumers feel confident enough to take out loans to fund their purchases. There is one problem, however—the goods being bought are not made in the U.S. ---[3]--- The strong dollar makes imports cheaper and thus more attractive to purchasers.

Even Dr. Sanchez admitted that American manufacturing companies are not reaping the same rewards as other sectors of the economy. ---[4]--- Indeed, this trade gap remains a worry for the Federal Reserve, which has also recently hinted at more inflation in the months ahead.

26. What is this article mostly about?
    (A) The positive effect of low mortgage interest rates
    (B) The state of the economy within an area of the US
    (C) The results of a study of economic recovery
    (D) The changing spending patterns of US consumers

27. What is NOT mentioned about the economic situation in Michigan?
    (A) The jobless rate is significantly lower than three years ago.
    (B) An increasing number of people are borrowing money.
    (C) The residential construction industry is experiencing a boom.
    (D) Manufacturing companies are starting to employ more workers.

28. In which position marked [1], [2], [3], and [4] does the following sentence best belong?
    "Other indicators back up Dr. Sanchez' findings."
    (A) [1]
    (B) [2]
    (C) [3]
    (D) [4]

29. According to the article, what is suggested about the U.S. economy?
    (A) More robust action should have been taken sooner.
    (B) Prices have been badly hit by overseas competition.
    (C) There are patchy signs of a recovery.
    (D) Agriculture has benefited to the detriment of industry.

26. (A) (B) (C) (D)
27. (A) (B) (C) (D)
28. (A) (B) (C) (D)
29. (A) (B) (C) (D)

E-mail

Date:	March 28
From:	Maria.Rivatoni@copebrown.com
To:	Sunetra.Patel@copebrown.com
Subject:	Wellington preparations

Hello Sunetra,

I am just checking in with you to see how the pre-trial preparations for the Wellington case are coming along. Have all the documents been collated and certified (where necessary)? Do we know the date of the pre-trial hearing yet, and can we find out which judge it will be?

Also, would you mind asking Ms. O'Donoghue whether she broached the idea of a settlement conference with the other side's counsel? As time is pressing, it would be good if we could reach a mutually acceptable resolution without having to go to a full trial.

My appointment at the hospital is for tomorrow, and I am expecting Dr. Davies to say the fracture has healed completely. All being well, they will remove the plaster cast there and then—in which case I will call you to confirm so you can notify all my key accounts that I will be back at my desk Monday.

Speak soon.
Maria

E-mail

Date:	March 29
From:	Sunetra.Patel@copebrown.com
To:	Maria.Rivatoni@copebrown.com
Subject:	RE: Wellington preparations

Dear Maria,

The court replied with a date of June 12. It will probably be Edward Humphreys. Ms. O'Donoghue is on vacation until Thursday, so I'll speak to her then to confirm. Her senior paralegal, Martin Jarvis, tells me he has finished gathering the last of the evidence and case papers. Anything that needed certifying has been signed and authorized, so as soon as he sends them over I will put all the documents on your desk for you to look at next week.

Everything else is in hand, so don't worry. Good luck at the hospital. We are all looking forward to seeing you back at work soon.

Warm regards,
Sunetra

30. Who is Ms. Patel?
- (A) An appeals specialist
- (B) A patent analyst
- (C) A legal secretary
- (D) A trial attorney

31. What can be inferred about Ms. Rivatoni?
- (A) She is suing for medical malpractice.
- (B) She is convalescing in the hospital.
- (C) She suffers from poor health.
- (D) She is recovering from an injury.

32. What information requested by Ms. Rivatoni is NOT provided in Ms. Patel's reply?
- (A) The date of the court hearing
- (B) If settlement talks will take place
- (C) Whether the documents are ready
- (D) The name of the presiding judge

33. In the first e-mail, the word "broached" in paragraph 2, line 1, is closest in meaning to
- (A) suggested
- (B) rejected
- (C) incited
- (D) approved

34. Who currently has the Wellington case papers?
- (A) Ms. O'Donoghue
- (B) Ms. Patel
- (C) Mr. Jarvis
- (D) Judge Humphreys

	(A)	(B)	(C)	(D)
30.	Ⓐ	Ⓑ	Ⓒ	Ⓓ
31.	Ⓐ	Ⓑ	Ⓒ	Ⓓ
32.	Ⓐ	Ⓑ	Ⓒ	Ⓓ
33.	Ⓐ	Ⓑ	Ⓒ	Ⓓ
34.	Ⓐ	Ⓑ	Ⓒ	Ⓓ

Pennsylvania Center for Innovators and Entrepreneurs
Young Entrepreneur of the Year Award

This award is designed to recognize a dynamic young business leader, whose innovative flair and accomplishments exemplify the passion and drive behind entrepreneurial businesses—whether socially oriented, family-owned, or private equity-backed—across the state of Pennsylvania. The award celebrates talent in the early stages of a business's development, and rewards a person whose entrepreneurial spirit has directly benefited the economy of the state.

Eligibility Criteria
Nominees must:
* have been running their business on a full-time basis, and been responsible for its day-to-day management, for at least two years

* be the owner or majority stockholder of the business
* be a permanent resident of Pennsylvania
* be between the ages of 18 and 35

The nominee's business should:
* have its head office in Pennsylvania
* be privately held
* be a sustainable business with the potential to scale and grow
* have a demonstrated track record of success since its launch

We regret that franchises and nonprofit organizations are *not* eligible for the award. Nominations must be submitted on the official form downloadable from our website, www.pcie.org, by May 31.

Pennsylvania Center for Innovators and Entrepreneurs
Young Entrepreneur of the Year Award

Nomination Form

Your name and address   Tyrone Greenberg, 788 Ross St., Harrisburg, PA 17111.

Are you related to the nominee?   No

Nominee's name   Matthew Bradley

Nominee's business name and address   Goldenridge Contracting, 1510 Atlas St., Harrisburg, PA 17113

Reason for nomination (max 150 words)

I am recommending my former apprentice, Matthew Bradley, as an excellent young entrepreneur and an inspiration to others. During his time at Miccoli Group he proved himself to be an exceptional trainee, excelling across all trades, especially bricklaying, carpentry, plastering, and interior systems (drywall). When he left two years ago, after completing his Advanced Diploma, he began working for his father. After just 12 months he started up his own building firm, specializing in home renovation. He is the sole proprietor, and to date has taken on five full-time and seven part-time employees to cope with his rapidly growing business. His company has become successful through word-of-mouth recommendation alone. I am now retired, but former coworkers tell me that Matthew finds time to drop in at Miccoli to mentor current apprentices, and has inspired many young people to go on and start their own businesses.

35. In which building trade sector does Goldenridge Contracting operate?
(A) New construction
(B) Residential remodeling
(C) Historic restoration
(D) Interior design

36. What is indicated about Tyrone Greenberg?
(A) He works in the construction industry.
(B) He is Matthew Bradley's partner.
(C) He was employed by Miccoli Group.
(D) He is a mentor to young people.

37. In the announcement, the word "flair" in paragraph 1, line 3, is closest in meaning to
(A) capacity
(B) talent
(C) taste
(D) tendency

38. What is NOT mentioned about Matthew Bradley?
(A) He employs several staff members.
(B) His company is expanding rapidly.
(C) He runs a successful family firm.
(D) He obtains most clients by referral.

39. Why will Matthew Bradley's nomination probably be rejected?
(A) He is above the upper age limit for entry.
(B) He has insufficient experience in his role.
(C) He is a minority shareholder in the business.
(D) His company is part of a larger franchise.

35. Ⓐ Ⓑ Ⓒ Ⓓ
36. Ⓐ Ⓑ Ⓒ Ⓓ
37. Ⓐ Ⓑ Ⓒ Ⓓ
38. Ⓐ Ⓑ Ⓒ Ⓓ
39. Ⓐ Ⓑ Ⓒ Ⓓ

Questions 40–44 refer to the following text message chain, e-mail, and Web page.

Mike Greggs   10:11 A.M.

Finally! Some good news. The new office site on Lexington Ave. is almost ready for us to move into… next month!

Paula Gates   10:11 A.M.

Fantastic ☺ It will make a huge difference, especially to us in HR.

Mike Greggs   10:12 A.M.

I need to get a microwave oven for the kitchen. The choices are mind-boggling! I never realized there were so many models!

Paula Gates   10:12 A.M.

Don't panic. We only need something simple. Get something with a low capacity, and not too many power levels.

Mike Greggs   10:13 A.M.

Yes. I think most people just heat up soup or a ready-made meal for lunch – nobody really cooks anything, do they?

Paula Gates   10:13 A.M.

No, but a defrost feature would be handy.

E-mail	
From:	Jay Gould
To:	Mike Greggs
Date:	September 12
Subject:	Microwave oven

Hi Mike,

Paula tells me you're looking for a microwave. My mother swears by hers (I checked the model; it's a Microsonic Gourmet XV). She raves about it, and I must admit, she produces some great meals using it. She's had it for 2 years and it's been very reliable. It seems to me that we need something that's trouble-free like that. It wasn't really that expensive, either. It's probably still available online, or maybe Gillingham's Electrical on Fourth Street will have one. I can go and check, if you want me to.

Best wishes,

Jay

Assistant Manager, Human Resources

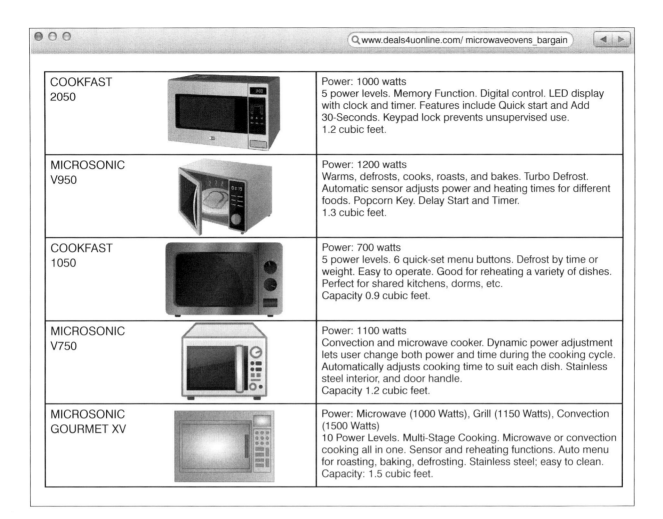

COOKFAST 2050		Power: 1000 watts 5 power levels. Memory Function. Digital control. LED display with clock and timer. Features include Quick start and Add 30-Seconds. Keypad lock prevents unsupervised use. 1.2 cubic feet.
MICROSONIC V950		Power: 1200 watts Warms, defrosts, cooks, roasts, and bakes. Turbo Defrost. Automatic sensor adjusts power and heating times for different foods. Popcorn Key. Delay Start and Timer. 1.3 cubic feet.
COOKFAST 1050		Power: 700 watts 5 power levels. 6 quick-set menu buttons. Defrost by time or weight. Easy to operate. Good for reheating a variety of dishes. Perfect for shared kitchens, dorms, etc. Capacity 0.9 cubic feet.
MICROSONIC V750		Power: 1100 watts Convection and microwave cooker. Dynamic power adjustment lets user change both power and time during the cooking cycle. Automatically adjusts cooking time to suit each dish. Stainless steel interior, and door handle. Capacity 1.2 cubic feet.
MICROSONIC GOURMET XV		Power: Microwave (1000 Watts), Grill (1150 Watts), Convection (1500 Watts) 10 Power Levels. Multi-Stage Cooking. Microwave or convection cooking all in one. Sensor and reheating functions. Auto menu for roasting, baking, defrosting. Stainless steel; easy to clean. Capacity: 1.5 cubic feet.

40. What can be inferred about Mr. Gould?

(A) He lives near Gillingham's Electrical.

(B) He often uses a microwave oven.

(C) He is Mr. Greggs' assistant.

(D) He works with Ms. Gates.

41. Which feature is NOT mentioned in any of the microwave ovens advertised on the Web page?

(A) An automatic sensor

(B) A wall mount

(C) A lockable control panel

(D) A memory capability

42. Why is the microwave oven suggested by Mr. Gould unsuitable?

(A) It is too sophisticated.

(B) It has no defrost feature.

(C) It is too large for the kitchen.

(D) The price is over-budget.

43. Which microwave oven is most suitable for the requirements of the office staff?

(A) Cookfast 2050

(B) Microsonic V950

(C) Cookfast 1050

(D) Microsonic V750

44. In the e-mail, the word "raves" in paragraph 1, line 2, is closest in meaning to

(A) cares

(B) quarrels

(C) enthuses

(D) worries

40. Ⓐ Ⓑ Ⓒ Ⓓ
41. Ⓐ Ⓑ Ⓒ Ⓓ
42. Ⓐ Ⓑ Ⓒ Ⓓ
43. Ⓐ Ⓑ Ⓒ Ⓓ
44. Ⓐ Ⓑ Ⓒ Ⓓ

Questions 45–49 refer to the following online booking form and e-mails.

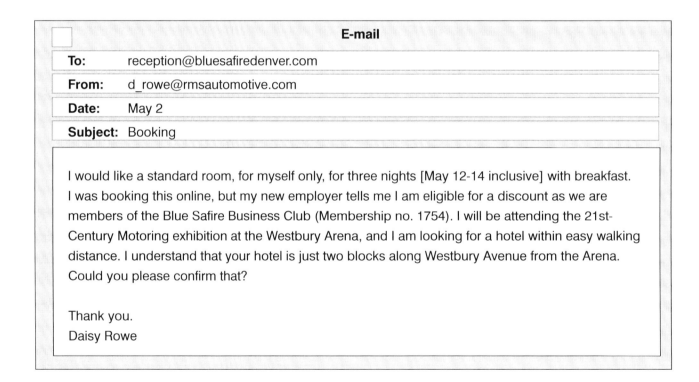

Blue Safire Hotel, Denver, Colorado					
Check in	Check out	Rooms	Adults	Children	UPDATE
May 12	**May 15**				
Superior Room 2 queen-sized beds		$180 per night		RESERVE	
Superior Room 1 king-sized bed		$180 per night		RESERVE	
Standard Room 2 queen-sized beds		$150 per night		RESERVE	
Standard Room 1 queen-sized bed		$120 per night		RESERVE	
Breakfast $15 extra. Pets allowed; Wi-Fi (at an additional charge); business center; restaurant; swimming pool					
NOTE: If your booking is at a discounted rate under our award-winning Blue Safire Business Club membership program, please call or e-mail our Reception Desk directly to make your booking. Please have the full details of your Blue Safire Business Club membership on hand.					

	E-mail
To:	reception@bluesafiredenver.com
From:	d_rowe@rmsautomotive.com
Date:	May 2
Subject:	Booking

I would like a standard room, for myself only, for three nights [May 12-14 inclusive] with breakfast. I was booking this online, but my new employer tells me I am eligible for a discount as we are members of the Blue Safire Business Club (Membership no. 1754). I will be attending the 21st-Century Motoring exhibition at the Westbury Arena, and I am looking for a hotel within easy walking distance. I understand that your hotel is just two blocks along Westbury Avenue from the Arena. Could you please confirm that?

Thank you.
Daisy Rowe

E-mail	
To:	d_rowe@rmsautomotive.com
From:	reception@bluesafiredenver.com
Date:	May 3
Subject:	Your booking query

Dear Ms. Rowe,

Thank you for your inquiry. We have a room available that meets your requirements. RMS Automotive is a long-standing and valued guest and member of our Blue Safire Business Club and we are pleased to offer you a discount of $20 per night on the advertised prices on our Web site. This rate includes breakfast. We are located close to the Westbury Arena, just one block further away than you thought. We have a full-service restaurant serving breakfast, lunch, and dinner, and there are several coffee bars in the hotel. In addition, there is a small swimming pool and sauna, which can be used for a nominal charge.

I will hold this booking for you until 6 P.M. tomorrow evening. If you would like to proceed with the reservation, please let me have your credit card details before then.

Sincerely,
Vince Legg
Reception Desk

---

45. What is suggested about RMS Automotive?
(A) It often sends employees to the Blue Safire Hotel.
(B) The company is exhibiting at the Westbury Arena.
(C) It is a founder member of a prominent Business Club.
(D) Its head offices are located in Denver, Colorado.

46. How far is the hotel from the Westbury Arena?
(A) 1 block
(B) 2 blocks
(C) 3 blocks
(D) 4 blocks

47. How much will Ms. Rowe pay in total for her stay?
(A) $285
(B) $300
(C) $360
(D) $405

48. What is indicated about Ms. Rowe?
(A) She has a disability and cannot walk far.
(B) She recently joined RMS Automotive.
(C) She seldom travels on business.
(D) She needs to use the Business Center.

49. What is Ms. Rowe asked to do?
(A) Book the room via the Web site.
(B) Pay for the booking that evening.
(C) Provide details of Club membership.
(D) Confirm the booking with reception.

45. Ⓐ Ⓑ Ⓒ Ⓓ
46. Ⓐ Ⓑ Ⓒ Ⓓ
47. Ⓐ Ⓑ Ⓒ Ⓓ
48. Ⓐ Ⓑ Ⓒ Ⓓ
49. Ⓐ Ⓑ Ⓒ Ⓓ

Questions 50–54 refer to the following program, Web page, and e-mail.

HOBART STARGAZERS SOCIETY

We meet twice a month, on the first and third Wednesdays, at 8:00 P.M. from March to November, when the evening skies are dark enough to enable us to do some serious stargazing (weather permitting). The first meeting of the month is a lecture evening held in St. Martin's Hall, Kingston Road, Hobart. Our second meeting is held outside in the darkness of Wellington Park.

Upcoming program of events		
March	Telescope Night – visit to the Astrophysics Department, University of Tasmania	
April	Mapping the Moon	Dr. J. Collier
May	Black Holes	Dr. R. Krantz
June	Astronomy in the 17th Century	Professor S. Patel
July	The Weirdest Galaxies in the Universe	Professor C. Lopez

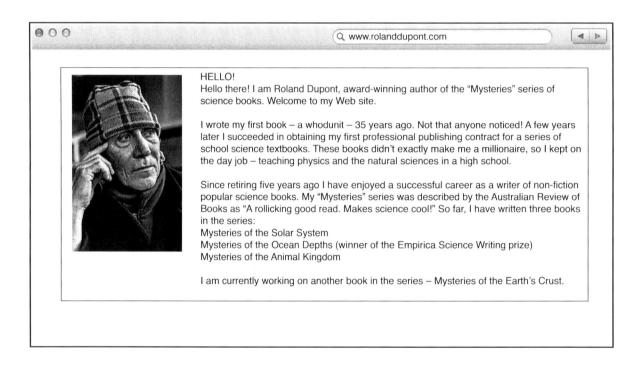

www.rolanddupont.com

HELLO!
Hello there! I am Roland Dupont, award-winning author of the "Mysteries" series of science books. Welcome to my Web site.

I wrote my first book – a whodunit – 35 years ago. Not that anyone noticed! A few years later I succeeded in obtaining my first professional publishing contract for a series of school science textbooks. These books didn't exactly make me a millionaire, so I kept on the day job – teaching physics and the natural sciences in a high school.

Since retiring five years ago I have enjoyed a successful career as a writer of non-fiction popular science books. My "Mysteries" series was described by the Australian Review of Books as "A rollicking good read. Makes science cool!" So far, I have written three books in the series:
Mysteries of the Solar System
Mysteries of the Ocean Depths (winner of the Empirica Science Writing prize)
Mysteries of the Animal Kingdom

I am currently working on another book in the series – Mysteries of the Earth's Crust.

E-mail

From:	secretary@hobartstargazers.com
To:	info@rolanddupont.com
Subject:	Invitation to speak

Dear Mr. Dupont,

Our Club, the Hobart Stargazers Society, is a group of friendly men and women – all amateurs – who are interested in astronomy and the cosmos. We meet twice a month most months, and for one of our monthly meetings we invite an outside speaker to talk to the group on a subject that interests them. I am writing to you because one of our speakers, who was due to speak on strange and unusual galaxies in the known universe, has had to pull out due to being granted research funding to study in the United States for three months. We would very much like you to come and speak to us in her place – I know that many of our members have read your book.

I note from your Web site that you are based in Hobart, so I hope you will be able to come and speak to us. We can only offer you a small honorarium, but I can guarantee an appreciative audience and a warm welcome.

I look forward to hearing from you.

Sincerely,
Jacob Mansell, Secretary

50. What can be inferred about the Hobart Stargazers Society?
(A) Its members are professional astronomers.
(B) It meets twenty times per year.
(C) It pays its speakers a small fee.
(D) Meetings take place regardless of weather.

51. In the e-mail, the phrase "pull out" in paragraph 1, line 4, is closest in meaning to
(A) abandon
(B) go away
(C) cancel
(D) retire

52. For which month is the invitation?
(A) April
(B) May
(C) June
(D) July

53. Which book does Mr. Mansell most likely want Roland Dupont to talk about?
(A) Mysteries of the Solar System
(B) Mysteries of the Ocean Depths
(C) Mysteries of the Animal Kingdom
(D) Mysteries of the Earth's Crust

54. What does Roland Dupont imply in his web page?
(A) He misses teaching at high school.
(B) His first book was not widely read.
(C) He is a keen astronomer.
(D) He prefers writing fiction.

50. Ⓐ Ⓑ Ⓒ Ⓓ   53. Ⓐ Ⓑ Ⓒ Ⓓ
51. Ⓐ Ⓑ Ⓒ Ⓓ   54. Ⓐ Ⓑ Ⓒ Ⓓ
52. Ⓐ Ⓑ Ⓒ Ⓓ

Score ..../54

EXTRA PRACTICE ONLINE

Go to **www.pass-the-toeic-test.com** for advice and useful exercises to help improve your score on Part 7 of the TOEIC test.

▶ Practice with NOT Questions
▶ Tips on Skimming and Scanning
▶ Further Comprehension Questions

Reading Test

This Reading Test covers Parts 5, 6, and 7 of the TOEIC® test. Allow 75 minutes to complete this test. Mark all your answers on the separate Reading Test Answer Sheet provided on page 317.

Part 5

Directions: Read each sentence. You will notice that there is a word or phrase missing. Study the four answer choices and select the one answer: (A), (B), (C), or (D), that best completes the sentence. Then mark your answer on the Answer Sheet.

101. Westbridge Valley University is committed to attracting a community of talented individuals .... of their financial circumstances or personal backgrounds.
(A) despite
(B) notwithstanding
(C) respectful
(D) regardless

102. Excess baggage charges are calculated on a one-way basis, are payable at the airport check-in counter, and cannot .... any circumstances be waived.
(A) at
(B) by
(C) for
(D) under

103. An e-mail was sent earlier this morning to all staff at Ushumu Electronics to tell them that the chairman, Mr. Ng, ... retiring at the end of the year.
(A) has
(B) will
(C) would be
(D) was going to

104. According to a Central Bank spokesperson, the major industrial economies cannot sustain significantly .... real rates of return at the present time.
(A) highly
(B) higher
(C) highest
(D) heighten

105. Bargain Gear Outfitters was just one of a number of major retail chains .... disappointing sales figures for the last financial quarter.
(A) report
(B) reports
(C) reported
(D) reporting

106. Most pundits agree that if Loretta Walford wants to run for the Senate next year, then she .... start organizing her election campaign soon.
(A) had better
(B) must have
(C) has had to
(D) should have

107. Alameira City Council yesterday bowed to local pressure and .... rejected the land developer's proposals to construct a five-acre sports complex around the historic port region of the city.
(A) soundly
(B) drastically
(C) extremely
(D) severely

108. After two weeks of discussions and with all avenues of negotiation ...., the union membership at Farley Components Inc. voted in favor of a strike.
(A) consumed
(B) exhausted
(C) drained
(D) depleted

109. While the ground floor of Dormalife's offices ...., the sales group shared the third-floor offices of the advertising department.
(A) will redecorate
(B) was being redecorated
(C) is being redecorated
(D) had been redecorating

110. .... completed, the new Maple Ridge development will provide 50 affordable apartments.
(A) Following
(B) After
(C) Once
(D) Until

111. New visa regulations recently announced by the government are clearly designed to reward .... who intend to contribute to the country's economic growth.
(A) they
(B) them
(C) these
(D) those

112. Turkey's increasing population and rapid urbanization makes the country .... for manufacturers of consumer goods.
(A) attract
(B) attractive
(C) attracted
(D) attracting

113. The supermarket chain MoreSave has .... up against community opposition to its proposal to build a new store next to the medieval castle in Trancheton.
(A) put
(B) set
(C) run
(D) got

114. According to recent statistics, motorcyclists are over eight times as .... to be injured in a traffic accident as car drivers.
(A) possible
(B) likely
(C) expected
(D) probably

115. Meteor showers happen when chunks of cosmic debris from asteroids and comets interact with the earth's atmosphere and create .... of light in the sky.
(A) streaks
(B) stakes
(C) strokes
(D) strikes

116. No matter .... careful people are when surfing the Internet or opening files, their computers can still be exposed to malicious viruses and malware.
(A) if
(B) who
(C) how
(D) that

117. Mr. Philips .... in the customer service department for over six months and hopes to be promoted to the role of assistant manager very shortly.
(A) works
(B) is working
(C) has been working
(D) had been working

118. The purchase of luxury goods is expected to decline by 5 percent this year as consumers .... down on luxury goods and nonessential items.
(A) cut
(B) fall
(C) reduce
(D) decrease

119. Dr. Hussein asked all patients to inform .... if they experienced any nausea or digestive problems while taking part in the medical trials.
(A) her
(B) herself
(C) his
(D) them

GO ON TO THE NEXT PAGE

120. Unemployment figures are _____ adjusted to take account of fluctuations across the months, such as when there are more job seekers at the end of the academic year.

(A) season
(B) seasonal
(C) seasonally
(D) seasonality

121. If Eduardo _____ me the advertisement for this job, which he came across by chance in the *Daily Announcer* newspaper, I would not be working here now.

(A) did not show
(B) would not show
(C) has not shown
(D) had not shown

122. In a survey published in this month's *Management Experience* journal, a majority of respondents said they valued _____ on the part of their bosses more than other qualities.

(A) deciding
(B) decision
(C) decisive
(D) decisiveness

123. The Ortolini Motor Company has designed a car _____ engine minimizes vibration and thus reduces noise to a minimum.

(A) that
(B) where
(C) which
(D) whose

124. Over 50 percent of the waste generated by our factories and industrial plants _____ used to produce aluminum and other materials.

(A) are
(B) has
(C) is
(D) will

125. Small businesses that are too _____ on one or two major clients risk going under themselves if a client's business founders.

(A) reliant
(B) relying
(C) rely
(D) reliable

126. ShawCal Holdings has not _____ the purchase price of the six brownfield sites it recently acquired from Banjada Securities.

(A) discerned
(B) discharged
(C) disclosed
(D) disclaimed

127. There were two security guards on duty at the time of the fire, but there is no evidence that _____ of them failed to perform their usual checks.

(A) either
(B) neither
(C) any
(D) two

128. The study concluded that if there _____ more bike lanes in the city, and better bike parking, then more local residents would cycle to work.

(A) are
(B) were
(C) would be
(D) had been

129. The identity of the defendants in the court case _____ kept secret because they were under 18, but their photographs appeared in a newspaper.

(A) would have
(B) should have been
(C) might be
(D) have had to

130. The date and venue for the first match in the Players Tour Championship Finals is _____ to be announced.

(A) already
(B) before
(C) but
(D) yet

Part 6

Directions: Read each text. You will notice that there are four blanks. These are places where a word, phrase or sentence is missing. For each blank, study the four answer choices and select the one answer: (A), (B), (C), or (D), that best completes the text. Then mark your answer on the Answer Sheet.

Questions 131–134 refer to the following letter.

4 Dunedin Way
Bunbury, WA 6065

June 16

Human Resources Manager
IntenSync Corporation
22 Mitchell Avenue
Perth, WA 6000

Dear Sir:

I am responding to your job posting for a deputy sales manager in yesterday's Bunbury Post. As you will see from my résumé, I have a _____131_____ background in technical sales, with over two years' experience at Murray Automotive Components in Kwinana. My position here involves visiting new and existing clients on a regular basis to promote, demonstrate, and sell the company's range of products. _____132_____, I have developed effective skills in contract negotiation and customer service, which I am sure will prove to be an asset to IntenSync.

I am fully computer-literate and have a clean driving record. In addition, I _____133_____ that my verbal and written communication skills are excellent.

I would welcome the opportunity to discuss with you the contribution I could make to IntenSync and look forward to your reply. _____134_____

Yours truly,

Simon Vargas

Simon Vargas

---

131. (A) rigorous
     (B) solid
     (C) categorical
     (D) determined

132. (A) Alternatively
     (B) Regardless
     (C) Consequently
     (D) Notwithstanding

133. (A) tell
     (B) am telling
     (C) told
     (D) am told

134. (A) Thank you for considering my application.
     (B) I wish you every success in the future.
     (C) It was a pleasure meeting you and your team.
     (D) All replies will be treated in the strictest confidence.

GO ON TO THE NEXT PAGE ➡

Proposed Tax Changes and Tepid Economy Explain Rise in Part-time Hiring

_____135_____ The downside is that almost three-quarters of these new employees are part-timers.

Faltering economic growth both at home and across the globe, as well as concern that the government's proposed tax reforms will drive up costs for small business owners, is behind employers' _____136_____ to hire permanent and full-time staff, according to employment analysts.

Employers justify the hiring of part-timers by pointing to the increased flexibility these staff offer. If the economy _____137_____, the part-timers can be offered full-time work. Critics say that the economy can only recover if consumers buy more goods and services, and low-paid part-timers, the majority of _____138_____ work in the lower-paid retail and food-service sectors, do not have the money to do that.

135. (A) Businesses are hiring more staff.
 (B) Our economy is finally improving.
 (C) Hiring practices are key to business success.
 (D) More employees are needed to boost growth.

136. (A) tendency
 (B) resolve
 (C) undertaking
 (D) reluctance

137. (A) recovers
 (B) recovered
 (C) will recover
 (D) would recover

138. (A) who
 (B) whom
 (C) whose
 (D) which

MEMORANDUM

To: All main office staff

From: Daniel Suarez

Date: July 9

Subject: Painting of the main entrance doors

As part of our ongoing renovation and refurbishment program, please be advised that contractors will be painting the wooden doors at the main entrance <u>next Tuesday, July 15</u>. ......**139**...... Notices erected inside and outside the building will advise staff to use the rear door by the kitchen.

Please do not arrange for clients or suppliers to visit on Tuesday the 15th. If you happen to have any visits ......**140**...... scheduled for this day, please consider moving them to another day, if at all feasible.

The corridor leading to the rear entrance is rather cramped and cluttered and as a result this does not give a ......**141**...... good impression of the company to outsiders.

Everything ......**142**...... to be back to normal on Wednesday, July 16.

Do not hesitate to contact me if you require more details.

139. (A) There should be no further disruption.
   (B) Please continue to use the entrance as normal.
   (C) This entrance will be closed on that day.
   (D) Thank you for your cooperation.

140. (A) already
   (B) just
   (C) still
   (D) yet

141. (A) distinctly
   (B) hardly
   (C) strictly
   (D) particularly

142. (A) is expected
   (B) expects
   (C) has expected
   (D) should expect

GO ON TO THE NEXT PAGE

Experienced Medical Biochemist

A leading Silicon Valley biotech company working primarily with government and NGOs has an exciting new opportunity for a medical biochemist. The successful applicant ....**143**........ at least 3 years of hands-on experience in a laboratory, preferably in a medical environment. You will be responsible for the examination and interpretation of medical samples and clinical data to help in the ....**144**........ and treatment of infectious diseases.

You will work in a small team that includes pathologists, biomedical scientists, and other healthcare specialists.

You will need excellent communication, organizational, and teamwork skills and will be expected to use your initiative. ....**145**........

E-mail your application and résumé to personnel@totalmeditech.com by June 14.

Please note that ....**146**........ the large volume of applications expected, only candidates who have been selected for an interview will be contacted.

143. (A) had
(B) is having
(C) has had
(D) will have had

144. (A) diagnose
(B) diagnoses
(C) diagnosis
(D) diagnostic

145. (A) There are good opportunities for promotion.
(B) We have read with interest your application.
(C) Biochemistry is a challenging field to work in.
(D) Your hard work and dedication is most appreciated.

146. (A) after
(B) due to
(C) regarding
(D) because

Part 7

Directions: Read the texts. You will notice that each text is followed by several questions. For each question, decide which of the four answer choices: (A), (B), (C), or (D), best answers the question. Then mark your answer on the Answer Sheet.

Questions 147–148 refer to the following advertisement.

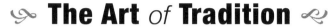

❧ The Art *of* Tradition ❧

250 Water Street, Boston, MA 02201

Turn your memories into masterpieces.

We are dedicated to the centuries-old craft of framing and provide the best service and craftsmanship you can find anywhere. Bring in your pictures, photos, mirrors, certificates, needlework, and sports jerseys, and see them transformed into works of art.

We also repair and retouch old photos.

We stock an extensive range of moldings and materials.

Our promise to you

We will come to your home or office for a consultation or to pick up and deliver goods (customers in the greater Boston area only). We ship worldwide.

All work guaranteed—if you're not happy, we'll put it right!
Phone: (617) 555-0120

147. Why might customers go to this store?
(A) To purchase a piece of artwork
(B) To have a document framed
(C) To get their photograph taken
(D) To buy decorative antique items

148. What does the store NOT claim to offer?
(A) Delivery to other countries
(B) Home and workplace visits
(C) An image restoration service
(D) A money-back guarantee

GO ON TO THE NEXT PAGE ➤

Questions 149–150 refer to the following live chat discussion.

Mandy from BuyRight   11:03 A.M.

Hello. Welcome to BuyRight Discount Online Store. How may I help you?

Guest   11:03 A.M.

Hi. I'm thinking of joining your SmartPass program. Can you confirm the first month is free?

Mandy from BuyRight   11:04 A.M.

Yes indeed. The free trial lasts a month and then you can choose to join or not. Most people do!

Guest   11:05 A.M.

Members get a 15% discount on everything they buy, is that right?

Mandy from BuyRight   11:07 A.M.

Yes, on all orders over $35. Below that you still need to pay postage. You also get a magazine once a month with special offers, competitions, etc. There are some really great deals! Would you like me to help you sign up?

Guest   11:08 A.M.

I'm still thinking about it. It's a little expensive.

Mandy from BuyRight   11:09 A.M.

I hear you. What about I offer you half price membership for the first six months? So, a free month and then $7.50 for the next 6 months. You'll need to sign up today though. Interested?!

149. At 11:09 A.M., what does Mandy mean when she writes, "I hear you"?

(A) I agree with you.
(B) I understand.
(C) I am listening.
(D) I can hear you.

150. What is indicated about the SmartPass program?

(A) Full membership costs $7.50 per month.
(B) Shipping is usually free of charge.
(C) Members may not always receive a discount.
(D) The pass can be used online and in stores.

Oregon Energy Supplies

Ms. M. Mendoza
9 NE Jessup Street
Portland, OR 97265

Customer Account No. BV/14/179215
Date of meter reading: February 15
Date payment due: March 5
Amount due: $224.07

Billing details
Previous balance (January 18): $285.75
Payment received (February 11): –$285.75
Overdue payment surcharge (February 7): $5.80
Balance as of February 15: $188.60
Current energy charges (February 15): $55.38

Total amount due: $249.78

Electricity used
Actual meter reading on February 15: 90875
Actual meter reading on January 18: 90463
Total electricity used: 412 kWh

Current energy charges breakdown
Distribution charges
Cost of metering and facilities: $10.60
Cost of delivery: $17.30 (412 kWh × $0.042/kWh)

Total distribution charge: $27.90

Energy supply charges
Generation and transmission charges: $26.37 (412 kWh × $0.064/kWh)
Sales tax: $1.11 ($26.37 × 4.2%)

Total current energy charges: $55.38

Year-by-year comparison of energy usage

Usage/day (kWh)		Charges/day		Average temperature/day	
This year	Last year	This year	Last year	This year	Last year
13.29	14.85	$1.79	$2.00	42°F	38°F

Next scheduled meter reading date: March 16

151. What information is NOT given on this document?
   (A) Total units of electricity used over the last month
   (B) Cumulative total units of electricity used
   (C) Cost incurred due to the installation of a new meter
   (D) Date when energy usage will be measured next month

152. What is indicated about Ms. Mendoza?
   (A) Her electricity consumption is higher than 12 months ago.
   (B) She qualifies for a discount because she lives alone.
   (C) Her energy account has recently been in arrears.
   (D) She uses less electricity than the average customer.

GO ON TO THE NEXT PAGE

Kitchenware queen can't stand the heat...

By Jack Miller

Amy McKinney, styled by the media as "the kitchenware queen," whose nostalgic range of crockery and kitchen accessories boosted sales fourfold during her time as Creative Director at Country Home and Style, has quit retail giant Cole & Corby after just two months.

Ms. McKinney had been appointed by Cole & Corby to invigorate the retailer's home and kitchenware division, amid rumors her remuneration package comprised a $400,000 salary, plus common stocks and stock options to sweeten the deal. ---[1]--- However, things apparently turned sour soon after her appointment. Sources say that Ms. McKinney erroneously believed she would have full control over the marketing and packaging of her designs. ---[2]--- She was also under the impression that Cole & Corby was planning to open six new stand-alone home and lifestyle stores to showcase her range, a plan that recently appointed C.E.O. Robert Ellison described as "never likely to take off."---[3]---

News of Ms. McKinney's departure comes just one week before Cole & Corby's annual general meeting, where Ellison will have to face an army of disgruntled private investors who have seen the value of their holdings drop by an average of 8 percent over the last three quarters. ---[4]--- Analysts expect the company to remain in the doldrums for at least the next quarter and are forecasting a 4 percent decline in underlying sales across all departments, with the exception of the food hall.

---

153. What is this news report mainly about?
(A) A dispute over directors' remuneration
(B) The resignation of a senior executive
(C) The appointment of a new C.E.O.
(D) A company's business performance

154. In which position marked [1], [2], [3], and [4] does the following sentence best belong?
"In fact this was not the case."
(A) [1]
(B) [2]
(C) [3]
(D) [4]

155. What is NOT true about the company Cole & Corby?
(A) It has scaled back plans for expansion.
(B) Sales have declined over the past nine months.
(C) A meeting with stockholders will take place shortly.
(D) It no longer sells edible goods.

E-mail	
From:	orders@preciousgiftsonline.net
To:	anita.gupta@globalmailservice.com
Date:	March 13
Subject:	Your order

Dear Customer,

Thank you for choosing Precious Gifts Online. We want to let you know that we have received your order and will be processing it shortly.

Your order number is W/01752. Please check the details below and inform us immediately by phone if any details are incorrect. Our customer service number is 905-555-0178.

Description: Precious Blessings—seasonal mixture of pink and white blooms
Delivery address: Liz and Sam Arnott, 68 Orchard Boulevard, Mississauga ON, L5L 2D5
Time of delivery: Thursday, March 14 (est. A.M.)

Your bouquet will be accompanied by the following message:

**Congratulations on the new arrival! I hope you won't get too many sleepless nights…
I can't wait to see all <u>three</u> of you soon. Love from Anita x**

All deliveries must be signed for. A text message will then be sent to the cell phone number you supplied when ordering.

We hope that you are satisfied with your purchase. Your opinion is important to us and will help us improve our service. Please leave a review on our website by clicking **here**.

Please do not attempt to reply to this message. We regret that this is an unmonitored address and replies to this e-mail cannot be responded to or read.

156. What did Ms. Gupta order?
(A) A selection of tea
(B) A floral arrangement
(C) A wall calendar
(D) A fruit basket

157. Why will Ms. Gupta be contacted again?
(A) To warn of any changes
(B) To update her details
(C) To confirm the delivery
(D) To ask for more feedback

158. What can be inferred about Liz Arnott?
(A) She has just returned from a trip.
(B) She suffers from insomnia.
(C) She will visit Ms. Gupta shortly.
(D) She has recently given birth.

GO ON TO THE NEXT PAGE ➡

Trinola Center

500 Mead Avenue   Oakland CA 94649

Tel: 555-0139   E-mail: info@trinola.org   www.trinola.org

July 15

Westcliff Electronics
1310 Tyler Street
Oakland, CA 94649

Dear Friends and Supporters:

We would like to express our profound and heartfelt gratitude for all your support over the past two years. Thanks to you, we have been able to provide after-school programs for hundreds of children from the deprived inner-city Trinola housing project. We offer these young residents a safe place to continue learning, play together, and take part in sports.

The Trinola Center was launched with the help of federal and state grants, but the popularity of our programs means that we have to also rely on personal and corporate donations to be able to continue our work.

We are currently short of functional computers for our technology and IT classes, which have proved very popular. I am therefore writing to ask if you have any old computers, laptops, printers, or other computer hardware that you could donate to us. Their age or condition does not matter, as we will rectify any faults. Transport is not a problem as our van can collect items directly from your home or place of work. Please call me at the above number if you can help.

We always like meeting our sponsors and supporters in person and we have open house between 5 P.M. and 7 P.M. on the last Monday of every month. We would love to see you there sometime, so why not stop by to see how your donations are making young people's lives better?

Sincerely,

Lydia Ortiz

Lydia Ortiz, Community Liaison Manager

159. What kind of organization does Ms. Ortiz work for?
(A) A community housing service
(B) A computer repair workshop
(C) A charitable organization
(D) A public high school

160. What is the main purpose of the letter?
(A) To appeal for money
(B) To seek a gift of goods
(C) To request information
(D) To issue an invitation

161. What can be inferred about Westcliff Electronics?
(A) It has already donated to the Trinola Center.
(B) It began doing business two years ago.
(C) It sells computer accessories.
(D) It is a successful local company.

Questions 162–163 refer to the following text message chain.

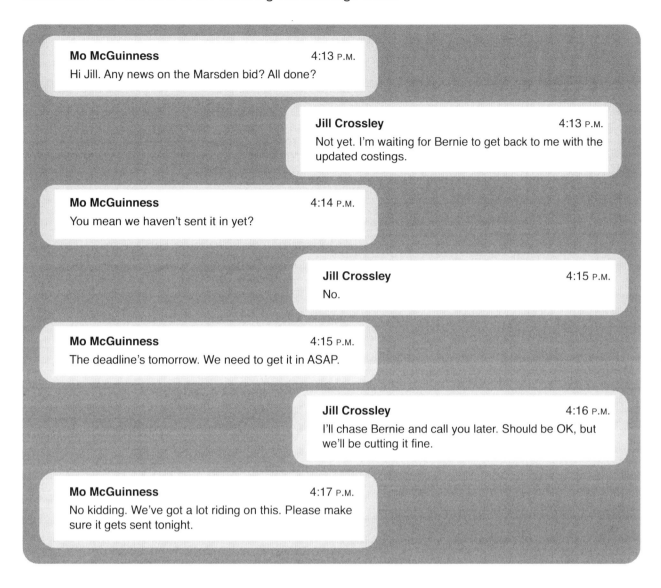

Mo McGuinness   4:13 P.M.
Hi Jill. Any news on the Marsden bid? All done?

Jill Crossley   4:13 P.M.
Not yet. I'm waiting for Bernie to get back to me with the updated costings.

Mo McGuinness   4:14 P.M.
You mean we haven't sent it in yet?

Jill Crossley   4:15 P.M.
No.

Mo McGuinness   4:15 P.M.
The deadline's tomorrow. We need to get it in ASAP.

Jill Crossley   4:16 P.M.
I'll chase Bernie and call you later. Should be OK, but we'll be cutting it fine.

Mo McGuinness   4:17 P.M.
No kidding. We've got a lot riding on this. Please make sure it gets sent tonight.

162. At 4:16 P.M., what does Ms. Crossley mean when she writes, "we'll be cutting it fine"?
(A) There will be nothing to lose.
(B) They will have just enough time.
(C) It will have to be cut very thinly.
(D) The deadline is too close.

163. What is implied about the Marsden bid?
(A) It has required a lot of resources.
(B) Some staff do not support it.
(C) It is important to the company.
(D) Costs have gone over budget.

GO ON TO THE NEXT PAGE

CLEVELAND GENERAL HOSPITAL
Visitation Guidelines

➤ All visitors must report to the Reception desk in the main lobby on arrival, where they will be issued with a visitor's sticker that must be visible at all times while on hospital premises. ---[1]---

➤ We welcome visitors to patients on the adult and maternity wards between 11 A.M. and 8 P.M. daily. Parents, legal guardians, and designated caretakers may visit the pediatric and neonatal wards, and the Intensive Care Unit, 24 hours a day, seven days a week, subject to prior agreement by the medical staff. Beds can be made available for these visitors.

➤ We regret that minors under 18 years of age will not be admitted to wards unless accompanied by a responsible adult, must be supervised at all times, and must leave if requested to do so by a nurse. ---[2]--- No child under 16 years of age may visit the Transplant or Intensive Care units. Parents of visiting children younger than 6 must complete a questionnaire to help us assess the child's risk of spreading infection. The staff at the Reception desk will give you the form and answer any questions you may have.

➤ Visitors to some areas of the hospital may be asked to wear special gowns, gloves, or masks and follow particular hand-washing procedures. ---[3]---

➤ A maximum of two guests may visit a patient at one time. Visitors may not consume food or drink at the bedside. Flowers and plants are not allowed on the Intensive Care and children's wards.

➤ The use of cell phones is prohibited in patient care areas. They may be used in the lobby, in public waiting rooms, and in the cafeteria. Photography is only permitted with the express consent of the patient, the patient's parent or guardian, or the hospital (for staff members). ---[4]---

---

164. In which position marked [1], [2], [3], and [4] does the following sentence best belong?
"Nurses will explain these procedures, if applicable."
(A) [1]
(B) [2]
(C) [3]
(D) [4]

165. What are all visitors to the hospital obliged to do?
(A) Wear protective clothing
(B) Wash their hands
(C) Fill in a questionnaire
(D) Display an ID badge

166. Who is NOT permitted to visit any hospital ward?
(A) Unaccompanied children
(B) Children under 6 years of age
(C) People not related to the patient
(D) Visitors with dirty hands

167. What are visitors allowed to do on children's wards?
(A) Make a phone call
(B) Eat their own food
(C) Take photographs
(D) Bring fresh flowers

Mandalatis Global Investment

Our best-selling funds

Mandalatis Premier All-Cap

Offering investors equity exposure to developed and emerging economies across the globe, this fund contains no domestic stocks and so is likely to be more volatile than a US fund. It should appeal to long-term investors who want to add an international dimension to an existing portfolio.

Minimum investment: $3,000

Mandalatis Federation Growth

Now in its eighteenth year, this popular fund invests in domestic stocks that managers feel are currently undervalued but that have the potential to grow substantially and return a healthy profit. Since this approach can be subject to significant short-term instability, investors should have a very long-term horizon. A useful diversification option in a portfolio too heavily biased toward foreign stocks.

Minimum investment: $3,000

Mandalatis Rapid Growth

This fund focuses on companies in emerging economies in Asia and Latin America that have high growth potential. The fund's managers employ an aggressive approach that seeks to take advantage of global economic expansion by investing in medium and small-sized companies undergoing rapid earnings growth. Investors should note that volatility is a feature of this fund.

Minimum investment: $3,000

Mandalatis 350 Index

The Mandalatis 350 Index fund tracks an index of medium-sized domestic companies. As a result, ongoing management costs are lower than for a managed fund. Investors should be aware that volatility for such companies tends to be greater than that of larger companies. This fund will suit passive investors who are seeking to add diversification to an existing portfolio.

Minimum investment: $10,000

Mandalatis Blue Chip 50

The Mandalatis Blue Chip 50 fund invests in a broad range of domestic blue-chip stocks to give diversification across a broad range of industry sectors. This fund is recommended for more cautious investors and for those close to retirement age who may value dividend income over capital growth.

Minimum investment: $10,000

168. Who is the intended audience for this information?
    (A) Individual investors
    (B) Company directors
    (C) Pension fund managers
    (D) Stock Exchange employees

169. Which fund provides the broadest geographical spread?
    (A) Mandalatis Premier All-Cap
    (B) Mandalatis Federation Growth
    (C) Mandalatis Rapid Growth
    (D) Mandalatis 350 Index

170. What is indicated about the Mandalatis 350 Index fund?
    (A) It is most suitable for short-term investments.
    (B) It is aimed primarily at inexperienced investors.
    (C) It has lower administrative charges than other funds.
    (D) It should appeal to those prepared to own high-risk stocks.

171. Who should probably NOT invest in the Mandalatis Federation Growth fund?
    (A) Savers wanting to avoid foreign companies
    (B) Young people investing for their retirement
    (C) Those wanting to realize profits in 3–4 years
    (D) Investors seeking significant capital growth

GO ON TO THE NEXT PAGE

Has time run out for WRISTWATCHES?

Once they were a common gift for graduations, birthdays, and other "rites of passage," but these days you could be forgiven for thinking that the once-ubiquitous wristwatch is being abandoned by American teens and young adults in growing numbers. Indeed, in a recent survey, 30 percent of 15- to 24-year-olds in the US said they had no need for a watch, preferring instead to check the time on their cell phone, tablet computer, MP3 player, or any number of other more versatile, multifunctional portable electronic devices. Is this, then, the end for the humble wristwatch?

While it is true that sales of wristwatches in North America and Europe have declined (by over 5 percent in the last three years), elsewhere we find a different story. In Asia and the Middle East sales are increasing steadily, and in South America, wristwatch sales are positively booming. What's more, a closer examination of the supposedly lackluster European and North American markets shows an interesting phenomenon. It is sales of cheaper, mass-produced watches that are on the decline. Mechanically complex and designer-label watches, which carry a much higher price tag, are bucking the trend with sales holding up well.

The fact is, an elegant, expensive timepiece epitomizes a successful career, status, wealth, and sophistication in a way no electronic device, however trendy, can quite manage. What's more, watch manufacturers are not resting on their laurels. They see a direct parallel between the wristwatch market today and the fountain pen market of the 1970s. Back then it was believed that the fountain pen would become obsolete thanks to the invention of the cheap ballpoint pen… yet, these days, sales of fountain pens are buoyant, with the traditional pen being valued by enthusiasts, collectors, and those favoring design, elegance, classical style, and luxury, who regard their pen as making a personal statement about themselves and their values.

It is this belief that underpins the current fight-back by forward-thinking watch manufacturers, who are now producing watches that are more fashionable, are better-designed, and do far more than simply tell time. Travelers can buy watches that show multiple time zones; watches aimed at joggers and other athletes measure speed, distance, and heart rate; sun worshippers can track UV radiation; and adventurers can have watches that give the temperature of the surrounding air or water or record altitude. Who knows what features watches might eventually have—streaming the latest news from the internet or downloading a street map, maybe? One thing is for sure: there's life in the humble wristwatch yet!

172. What is the main purpose of this article?
(A) To compare the wristwatch and fountain pen markets
(B) To promote sales of designer-label wristwatches
(C) To report on the status of the wristwatch market
(D) To review the various functions of wristwatches

173. According to the article, why do some people choose to buy a wristwatch these days?
(A) As a graduation gift
(B) As a birthday present
(C) As a status symbol
(D) As a cheap timepiece

174. What can be inferred from the article about the wristwatch market in North America?
(A) The majority of purchasers are wealthy people.
(B) Sales are declining among older generations.
(C) High-end watches are continuing to sell well.
(D) Almost all watches sold have digital displays.

175. The word "lackluster" in paragraph 2, line 8, is closest in meaning to
(A) advanced
(B) lamentable
(C) refined
(D) unimpressive

GO ON TO THE NEXT PAGE

The Reading Room
About us

| Home | Sign in | Help

Graham Burnett

Graham is the son of Sheila Burnett, who founded the agency over 30 years ago. He is our legal specialist and handles foreign and translation rights.

Zoe Charlton

Zoe is responsible for nonfiction, including travel, food and cookery, gardening, self-help, popular psychology, and spirituality. Before joining the Reading Room four years ago, Zoe had a distinguished career as publishing director at Hogan Howarth.

Michelle Grant

Michelle deals with authors of historical fiction and biography. As a successful published author herself, she knows exactly what publishers are looking for.

Luigi Russo

Luigi specializes in fiction titles and is credited with discovering Miranda McNeill. He's now looking for the next big blockbuster. He manages our sci-fi, horror, crime, romance, and contemporary fiction lists.

We do not handle children's literature, poetry, or screenplays.

Our authors include:

Simone Delors   James Garnett
Vanessa Long   Miranda McNeill
Lee Young

Submissions

Send in the first instance a preliminary letter, an outline (no more than 750 words), your résumé, and either the first three chapters (for fiction) or chapter headings, plus the introductory and one other chapter (for nonfiction). Include a stamped, self-addressed envelope. Our workload means that you should not expect to hear from us for at least three months.

---

75 Morello Crescent
Manchester M35 2ZY

May 17

The Reading Room
5 Churchill Square
London E5 6WS

Dear Sirs:

I read with interest details of your activities on your website and was impressed by the depth and range of your author list. I am looking for a reputable literary agent to take on a book I have written and consider worthy of publication. It is a novel set in tsarist Russia at the end of the nineteenth century and recounts events in the life of a wealthy landowner and his family. It is entitled *The Dukhanov Clan*.

I am a lecturer in Russian literature at The University of East Manchester and have a good knowledge of this period. My first novel, *Solace in the Steppe*, was published by a small local publishing house, the Cranford Press. I enclose a copy for your information.

As requested, I am sending you the first three chapters of my work, plus a brief synopsis. I also enclose my résumé, which lists the articles I have had published in academic journals. I can supply copies of these articles if you wish.

I very much look forward to hearing from you in due course.

Sincerely,

Oliver Rosberg

Oliver Rosberg

176. What is the purpose of Oliver Rosberg's letter?
(A) To seek representation
(B) To offer a service
(C) To make a compliment
(D) To request information

177. What can be inferred about The Reading Room?
(A) Its staff are all published authors.
(B) It welcomes inquiries sent by e-mail.
(C) It specializes in works of nonfiction.
(D) It has been in business for several decades.

178. Who is Miranda McNeill?
(A) A renowned publishing agent
(B) A client of The Reading Room
(C) A successful children's book author
(D) A character in a best-selling novel

179. To whom will Mr. Rosberg's letter most likely be passed?
(A) Graham Burnett
(B) Zoe Charlton
(C) Michelle Grant
(D) Luigi Russo

180. What does Mr. Rosberg send with his letter that is not specifically requested?
(A) A complete novel
(B) A journal article
(C) A book outline
(D) A career summary

GO ON TO THE NEXT PAGE

Trimmerdale Country Club

Southern California's most fashionable and luxurious country club, with spectacular ocean views, fine dining, and a full calendar of events to suit all tastes.

Amenities include an 18-hole golf course, 12 tennis courts, and a swimming pool. A luxurious clubhouse with award-winning restaurant. A Pro Shop managed by top professional golfer Ricky Fernandez.

- Social membership includes access to the pool, tennis courts, restaurant, and coffee bar.
- Out-of-town membership allows use of all facilities on no more than 30 days of the year for those who do not have a residence within 50 miles of the Country Club.
- Junior membership includes access to the golf course, tennis courts, and coffee bar.
- Dining membership allows the use of the clubhouse and its facilities only.
- Monthly payment plans are available for all membership types.

> **Membership Options**
>
> Single regular: $2,250
> Family regular: $4,000
> Out-of-town: $1,500 (per person)
> Junior (21 years or younger): $1,200
> Family social: $600
> Single social: $420
> Dining: $90 (per person)

Golf carts

Storage: We can store your golf cart in our cart shed for an annual fee, which includes fuel.

Rental: Hand and motorized carts are available for rent from the Pro Shop.

Private and group lessons are available for members. Ask at the Pro Shop. Membership coordinator: Erin Garcia (membership@trimmerdalecc.com)

1175 Crespo Street
La Jolla, CA 92037

May 20

Ms. Erin Garcia, Membership Coordinator
Trimmerdale Country Club
1 Balboa Avenue
Del Mar, CA 92014

Dear Ms. Garcia:

Thank you for showing me and my son around the Country Club last week. It certainly is a beautiful place, and we were very impressed not only by the warm welcome we received as newcomers, but also by the high standard of your facilities. We are both looking forward to hitting some balls across the fairway. I am only a mediocre player, but as I mentioned, Joel's handicap is much lower than mine, and as he has not yet turned 18, I have high hopes of his developing further.

Enclosed is a check to cover full membership for myself and Joel. I understand that you will issue us with membership cards and locker keys, after which we can begin using the facilities. I will be in New York on business for the next two weeks, so there is no hurry.

I forgot to mention when we spoke that I have my own motorized golf cart. Is it possible for you to keep this on your premises? Also, Joel will need some new clubs. Could you tell me the opening times of the Pro Shop and which brands are stocked?

I look forward to hearing from you and to starting to make use of the facilities at Trimmerdale Country Club.

Very truly yours,

Evan Montaigne

Evan Montaigne

181. Which category of member is allowed both to play golf and to swim?

(A) Out-of-town
(B) Junior
(C) Social
(D) Dining

182. What is the value of the check enclosed with Mr. Montaigne's letter?

(A) $3,000
(B) $3,450
(C) $4,000
(D) $4,500

183. Which of the following people's membership fees would be the lowest?

(A) A man wanting to eat in the restaurant after his weekly golf game
(B) A woman living 60 miles away who wants to play golf once a month
(C) A couple wanting to swim regularly and dine in the restaurant
(D) A 16-year-old high school student intending to take golf lessons every week

184. What does Mr. Montaigne ask about that is already explained in the advertisement?

(A) Brands of golf clubs
(B) Equipment storage
(C) Store hours
(D) Vehicle rental

185. What is indicated about Mr. Montaigne?

(A) He has more than one child.
(B) He is a proficient golfer.
(C) He is going away shortly.
(D) He is new to the area.

GO ON TO THE NEXT PAGE

Questions 186–190 refer to the following e-mail, letter, and schedule.

E-mail	
Date:	May 3
From:	Raymond Jarvis
To:	**Kayla Rodriguez, Jocelyn Martin, Dominic Ward, Marco Cannetti**
Subject:	Intern

Dear all,

Re Heidi Wagner's upcoming visit for work experience, I know we don't usually take interns but Heidi is the daughter of Erika Wagner, Managing Director of Rendell Building Systems. When Erika approached me with her request for her daughter to spend a week with us, I felt that we had an obligation. I know other clients of Rendell have agreed to host Heidi at other times during her college vacations and I do not want Prime Mover Construction to be seen as uncooperative, especially considering they are one of our largest suppliers and we have an important contract coming up for renegotiation later in the year.

Heidi will be here from Monday, May 16 to Friday, May 20. My assistant will take her around the building, and introduce her to everyone on her first morning. In the afternoon he will give her a general overview of the company and its activities. The following day I have arranged for Heidi to be taken on a site visit – she will spend the day at our new construction development near the river. I hope that's all right with you, Jocelyn, and your structural engineer colleagues. It would be good if one of you were there to welcome her and show her around. Thank you, Dominic, for agreeing to have her with you in the Logistics and Planning Department on the afternoon of Thursday, May 19. Kayla, could you find a couple of hours to talk with her about our community relationship program some time during the week? And Marco, please be on stand-by to talk to her about our health and safety policies at some point.

Thanks in advance to all of you for helping out on this. Let's hope the visit will have a positive outcome for future Rendell/ Prime Mover dealings.

Regards,

Raymond Jarvis

Chief Executive

May 5

Raymond Jarvis
C.E.O. Prime Mover Construction
8767 North Park Rd.
Tomball, TX 78723

Dear Mr. Jarvis:

Thank you for agreeing to allow me to spend a week in your offices later this month. As my mother probably told you, I am in my final year studying marketing and business administration at Ribblemore College. In the future I hope to follow a career in sustainable community development. I am particularly interested in the effects that the surrounding environment can have on people's mental and physical well-being, and during my work experience there I would appreciate being able to spend some time with your Occupational Health and Safety specialists, if at all possible.

I have gained a number of skills in previous vacation placements, and in my current role at Ribblemore on the Student Sustainable Leadership Council, and I will do my best to make a useful contribution to your company while I am with you.

Sincerely,

Heidi Wagner
Heidi Wagner

Employee: Kayla Rodriguez		Week: 16 May 16-20 May		
Monday 16	**Tuesday 17**	**Wednesday 18**	**Thursday 19**	**Friday 20**
morning	morning	morning	morning 10:00 A.M. Heads of department meeting (board room)	morning Full day seminar at Goldhouse University 10:30 A.M. – 11:45 A.M. My lecture
			12:30 P.M. Lunch with Vince Watson, City Council	
afternoon Visit to City Hall (to discuss Riverside project sewerage needs)	afternoon	afternoon afternoon off! (Leon's school show)	afternoon	afternoon 2:00 P.M. – 4:00 P.M. Member of panel discussion

186. What is true about Ms. Wagner?
(A) She is related to one of Prime Mover's directors.
(B) This is her first work experience assignment.
(C) She is worried about workers' health benefits.
(D) She serves as a member on a student committee.

187. Why did Mr. Jarvis agree to Mrs. Wagner's request?
(A) It may be in his company's financial interests.
(B) Mrs. Wagner is a close personal friend.
(C) He is impressed by Ms. Wagner's experience.
(D) His company has a large internship program.

188. Whom will Ms. Wagner probably be most interested in meeting?
(A) Kayla Rodriguez
(B) Jocelyn Martin
(C) Dominic Ward
(D) Marco Cannetti

189. In the e-mail, the word "obligation" in paragraph 1, Line 3, is closest in meaning to
(A) requirement
(B) agreement
(C) promise
(D) commitment

190. When will Ms. Rodriguez most likely meet Ms. Wagner?
(A) Monday A.M.
(B) Tuesday A.M.
(C) Wednesday A.M.
(D) Thursday P.M.

Valid only with photocard no.
ZVR788N

CLASS	TICKET TYPE	PRICE
STD	SEASON - 12MO	£2,400

Valid from
MAR 17

Number:
13789923

Between
PORTSMOUTH and SOUTHAMPTION

Valid
12 MONTHS

Route
ANY PERMITTED

NTK Associates - Employment Manual

Section 4   Annual season ticket loans

4.1   All salaried staff who have satisfactorily completed their six-month probationary period are eligible to apply for an annual interest-free season ticket loan, as long as their contract of employment is for a period that exceeds the expiration date of the ticket (i.e. a minimum of twelve months), and their net monthly salary is sufficient to cover the deduction of the loan.

4.2   Applications may be made for an interest-free loan (up to a maximum value of £8,000) to cover the cost of a 2nd-class annual season ticket between your home and the workplace. Loans are made in the form of a salary advance. The loan is then repaid via equal monthly deductions from your net salary over the course of the year.

Important information

4.2.1   The company will assess each application for a season ticket loan on an individual basis and may refuse the application.

4.2.2   Any loan issued will cover annual public transport costs only. It will not cover any costs associated with car use, including parking. Use of the loan for any other purpose could lead to disciplinary action.

4.2.3   If the season ticket is surrendered before the expiration date (for example, due to long-term sickness or maternity leave) the loan must be repaid in full within seven days.

4.2.4   Applicants for an annual season-ticket loan should supply proof of the cost of an annual season ticket to seasontickets@ntkassociates. co.uk.

34

E-mail	
From:	Carl.Roberts@ ntkassociates.co.uk.
To:	seasontickets@ ntkassociates.co.uk.
Date:	March 24
Subject:	Application for a season-ticket loan

I wish to apply for an interest-free season ticket loan to cover daily train travel between my hometown and the Southampton office. I bought and paid for an annual ticket myself last week (see photocopy attached). Before that, I was buying weekly tickets, but at £60 per week they were less economical than an annual season ticket. I am a salaried employee in the marketing department, having joined the company two months ago. I am committed to working for NTK Associates in the long term.

Thank you. I look forward to receiving the loan.

Carl Roberts
Assistant, Marketing Department

191. What is indicated about the company policy on season ticket loans?
(A) Loans are repaid in 12 instalments.
(B) Each loan is for train travel only.
(C) All staff are eligible for a loan.
(D) The loan is a taxable benefit.

192. What can be inferred about Mr. Roberts?
(A) He is a full-time employee.
(B) He cannot afford weekly tickets.
(C) He does not have a car.
(D) He lives in Portsmouth.

193. In the extract from a manual, the word "surrendered" in section 4.2.3, line 1, is closest in meaning to
(A) invalidated
(B) relinquished
(C) bequeathed
(D) forfeited

194. Why will NTK Associates probably refuse Mr. Roberts' application?
(A) He is not a salaried employee.
(B) His season ticket costs too much.
(C) He has not worked there long enough.
(D) His salary is too low to repay the loan.

195. If Mr. Robert's application for a loan were successful, how much would he repay each month?
(A) £60
(B) £200
(C) £240
(D) £260

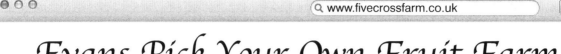

⬤⬤⬤ 🔍 www.fivecrossfarm.co.uk ◀ ▶

Evans Pick Your Own Fruit Farm

This month's opening times: 10:00 A.M. – 6:00 P.M. daily
No reservation required – just turn up!
A fun day out for all the family! Healthy too!

This month's crops include:

Blackberries	$2.75/lb
Strawberries	$2.25/lb
Tomatoes	$1.50/lb

Fruit weighed in the shop on departure.

Please remember that *Evans Pick Your Own Fruit Farm* is a working farm. That means it is often dusty or muddy. We recommend that you wear sensible shoes and appropriate clothing, and that you bring plenty of sunscreen with you. Be sure to keep a good distance away from our tractors and other farm machinery.

Please follow these other important rules:
1. Please watch your children at all times!
2. Please do not feed our farm animals.
3. Do NOT leave any gates open.

Thank you for your co-operation.

Fruit doesn't come any fresher than at Evans!

AllDays
Your friendly local supermarket
Our fresh picks of the week

Whole white mushrooms	79¢ per 8 oz
California peaches	$2.30 per 2lb
Bartlett pears	$2.49 per 3lb
Farmers' Choice apples	$2.25 per 3lb
Mangoes	65¢/each
Tomatoes	99¢/lb
Strawberries	$1.99 per lb

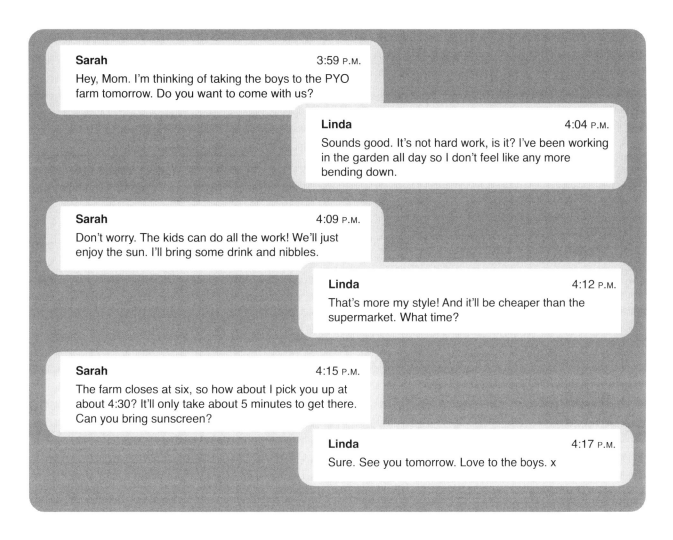

Sarah   3:59 P.M.

Hey, Mom. I'm thinking of taking the boys to the PYO farm tomorrow. Do you want to come with us?

Linda   4:04 P.M.

Sounds good. It's not hard work, is it? I've been working in the garden all day so I don't feel like any more bending down.

Sarah   4:09 P.M.

Don't worry. The kids can do all the work! We'll just enjoy the sun. I'll bring some drink and nibbles.

Linda   4:12 P.M.

That's more my style! And it'll be cheaper than the supermarket. What time?

Sarah   4:15 P.M.

The farm closes at six, so how about I pick you up at about 4:30? It'll only take about 5 minutes to get there. Can you bring sunscreen?

Linda   4:17 P.M.

Sure. See you tomorrow. Love to the boys. x

196. What is true about Evans farm?
- (A) It is advisable to book in advance.
- (B) Children must be supervised.
- (C) Suitable clothing is provided.
- (D) Some animals can be dangerous.

197. What will Linda most likely do at Evans farm?
- (A) Pick as much fruit as she can
- (B) Go shopping for clothes
- (C) Look after her grandchildren
- (D) Relax outside and sunbathe

198. Which fruit can be picked at the farm, but is unavailable at AllDays supermarket?
- (A) Blackberries
- (B) Strawberries
- (C) Apples
- (D) Peaches

199. What is suggested about Linda?
- (A) She lives near her daughter.
- (B) She dislikes working hard.
- (C) Her home is near Evans farm.
- (D) She really enjoys gardening.

200. What information does one of the women get wrong in her text message?
- (A) The farm's closing time
- (B) The location of AllDays
- (C) The price of produce
- (D) The likely weather

Appendices

Answer Sheets

Listening Comprehension Test

1. Ⓐ Ⓑ Ⓒ Ⓓ	26. Ⓐ Ⓑ Ⓒ	51. Ⓐ Ⓑ Ⓒ Ⓓ	76. Ⓐ Ⓑ Ⓒ Ⓓ
2. Ⓐ Ⓑ Ⓒ Ⓓ	27. Ⓐ Ⓑ Ⓒ	52. Ⓐ Ⓑ Ⓒ Ⓓ	77. Ⓐ Ⓑ Ⓒ Ⓓ
3. Ⓐ Ⓑ Ⓒ Ⓓ	28. Ⓐ Ⓑ Ⓒ	53. Ⓐ Ⓑ Ⓒ Ⓓ	78. Ⓐ Ⓑ Ⓒ Ⓓ
4. Ⓐ Ⓑ Ⓒ Ⓓ	29. Ⓐ Ⓑ Ⓒ	54. Ⓐ Ⓑ Ⓒ Ⓓ	79. Ⓐ Ⓑ Ⓒ Ⓓ
5. Ⓐ Ⓑ Ⓒ Ⓓ	30. Ⓐ Ⓑ Ⓒ	55. Ⓐ Ⓑ Ⓒ Ⓓ	80. Ⓐ Ⓑ Ⓒ Ⓓ
6. Ⓐ Ⓑ Ⓒ Ⓓ	31. Ⓐ Ⓑ Ⓒ	56. Ⓐ Ⓑ Ⓒ Ⓓ	81. Ⓐ Ⓑ Ⓒ Ⓓ
7. Ⓐ Ⓑ Ⓒ	32. Ⓐ Ⓑ Ⓒ Ⓓ	57. Ⓐ Ⓑ Ⓒ Ⓓ	82. Ⓐ Ⓑ Ⓒ Ⓓ
8. Ⓐ Ⓑ Ⓒ	33. Ⓐ Ⓑ Ⓒ Ⓓ	58. Ⓐ Ⓑ Ⓒ Ⓓ	83. Ⓐ Ⓑ Ⓒ Ⓓ
9. Ⓐ Ⓑ Ⓒ	34. Ⓐ Ⓑ Ⓒ Ⓓ	59. Ⓐ Ⓑ Ⓒ Ⓓ	84. Ⓐ Ⓑ Ⓒ Ⓓ
10. Ⓐ Ⓑ Ⓒ	35. Ⓐ Ⓑ Ⓒ Ⓓ	60. Ⓐ Ⓑ Ⓒ Ⓓ	85. Ⓐ Ⓑ Ⓒ Ⓓ
11. Ⓐ Ⓑ Ⓒ	36. Ⓐ Ⓑ Ⓒ Ⓓ	61. Ⓐ Ⓑ Ⓒ Ⓓ	86. Ⓐ Ⓑ Ⓒ Ⓓ
12. Ⓐ Ⓑ Ⓒ	37. Ⓐ Ⓑ Ⓒ Ⓓ	62. Ⓐ Ⓑ Ⓒ Ⓓ	87. Ⓐ Ⓑ Ⓒ Ⓓ
13. Ⓐ Ⓑ Ⓒ	38. Ⓐ Ⓑ Ⓒ Ⓓ	63. Ⓐ Ⓑ Ⓒ Ⓓ	88. Ⓐ Ⓑ Ⓒ Ⓓ
14. Ⓐ Ⓑ Ⓒ	39. Ⓐ Ⓑ Ⓒ Ⓓ	64. Ⓐ Ⓑ Ⓒ Ⓓ	89. Ⓐ Ⓑ Ⓒ Ⓓ
15. Ⓐ Ⓑ Ⓒ	40. Ⓐ Ⓑ Ⓒ Ⓓ	65. Ⓐ Ⓑ Ⓒ Ⓓ	90. Ⓐ Ⓑ Ⓒ Ⓓ
16. Ⓐ Ⓑ Ⓒ	41. Ⓐ Ⓑ Ⓒ Ⓓ	66. Ⓐ Ⓑ Ⓒ Ⓓ	91. Ⓐ Ⓑ Ⓒ Ⓓ
17. Ⓐ Ⓑ Ⓒ	42. Ⓐ Ⓑ Ⓒ Ⓓ	67. Ⓐ Ⓑ Ⓒ Ⓓ	92. Ⓐ Ⓑ Ⓒ Ⓓ
18. Ⓐ Ⓑ Ⓒ	43. Ⓐ Ⓑ Ⓒ Ⓓ	68. Ⓐ Ⓑ Ⓒ Ⓓ	93. Ⓐ Ⓑ Ⓒ Ⓓ
19. Ⓐ Ⓑ Ⓒ	44. Ⓐ Ⓑ Ⓒ Ⓓ	69. Ⓐ Ⓑ Ⓒ Ⓓ	94. Ⓐ Ⓑ Ⓒ Ⓓ
20. Ⓐ Ⓑ Ⓒ	45. Ⓐ Ⓑ Ⓒ Ⓓ	70. Ⓐ Ⓑ Ⓒ Ⓓ	95. Ⓐ Ⓑ Ⓒ Ⓓ
21. Ⓐ Ⓑ Ⓒ	46. Ⓐ Ⓑ Ⓒ Ⓓ	71. Ⓐ Ⓑ Ⓒ Ⓓ	96. Ⓐ Ⓑ Ⓒ Ⓓ
22. Ⓐ Ⓑ Ⓒ	47. Ⓐ Ⓑ Ⓒ Ⓓ	72. Ⓐ Ⓑ Ⓒ Ⓓ	97. Ⓐ Ⓑ Ⓒ Ⓓ
23. Ⓐ Ⓑ Ⓒ	48. Ⓐ Ⓑ Ⓒ Ⓓ	73. Ⓐ Ⓑ Ⓒ Ⓓ	98. Ⓐ Ⓑ Ⓒ Ⓓ
24. Ⓐ Ⓑ Ⓒ	49. Ⓐ Ⓑ Ⓒ Ⓓ	74. Ⓐ Ⓑ Ⓒ Ⓓ	99. Ⓐ Ⓑ Ⓒ Ⓓ
25. Ⓐ Ⓑ Ⓒ	50. Ⓐ Ⓑ Ⓒ Ⓓ	75. Ⓐ Ⓑ Ⓒ Ⓓ	100. Ⓐ Ⓑ Ⓒ Ⓓ

Reading Test

101. Ⓐ Ⓑ Ⓒ Ⓓ	126. Ⓐ Ⓑ Ⓒ Ⓓ	151. Ⓐ Ⓑ Ⓒ Ⓓ	176. Ⓐ Ⓑ Ⓒ Ⓓ
102. Ⓐ Ⓑ Ⓒ Ⓓ	127. Ⓐ Ⓑ Ⓒ Ⓓ	152. Ⓐ Ⓑ Ⓒ Ⓓ	177. Ⓐ Ⓑ Ⓒ Ⓓ
103. Ⓐ Ⓑ Ⓒ Ⓓ	128. Ⓐ Ⓑ Ⓒ Ⓓ	153. Ⓐ Ⓑ Ⓒ Ⓓ	178. Ⓐ Ⓑ Ⓒ Ⓓ
104. Ⓐ Ⓑ Ⓒ Ⓓ	129. Ⓐ Ⓑ Ⓒ Ⓓ	154. Ⓐ Ⓑ Ⓒ Ⓓ	179. Ⓐ Ⓑ Ⓒ Ⓓ
105. Ⓐ Ⓑ Ⓒ Ⓓ	130. Ⓐ Ⓑ Ⓒ Ⓓ	155. Ⓐ Ⓑ Ⓒ Ⓓ	180. Ⓐ Ⓑ Ⓒ Ⓓ
106. Ⓐ Ⓑ Ⓒ Ⓓ	131. Ⓐ Ⓑ Ⓒ Ⓓ	156. Ⓐ Ⓑ Ⓒ Ⓓ	181. Ⓐ Ⓑ Ⓒ Ⓓ
107. Ⓐ Ⓑ Ⓒ Ⓓ	132. Ⓐ Ⓑ Ⓒ Ⓓ	157. Ⓐ Ⓑ Ⓒ Ⓓ	182. Ⓐ Ⓑ Ⓒ Ⓓ
108. Ⓐ Ⓑ Ⓒ Ⓓ	133. Ⓐ Ⓑ Ⓒ Ⓓ	158. Ⓐ Ⓑ Ⓒ Ⓓ	183. Ⓐ Ⓑ Ⓒ Ⓓ
109. Ⓐ Ⓑ Ⓒ Ⓓ	134. Ⓐ Ⓑ Ⓒ Ⓓ	159. Ⓐ Ⓑ Ⓒ Ⓓ	184. Ⓐ Ⓑ Ⓒ Ⓓ
110. Ⓐ Ⓑ Ⓒ Ⓓ	135. Ⓐ Ⓑ Ⓒ Ⓓ	160. Ⓐ Ⓑ Ⓒ Ⓓ	185. Ⓐ Ⓑ Ⓒ Ⓓ
111. Ⓐ Ⓑ Ⓒ Ⓓ	136. Ⓐ Ⓑ Ⓒ Ⓓ	161. Ⓐ Ⓑ Ⓒ Ⓓ	186. Ⓐ Ⓑ Ⓒ Ⓓ
112. Ⓐ Ⓑ Ⓒ Ⓓ	137. Ⓐ Ⓑ Ⓒ Ⓓ	162. Ⓐ Ⓑ Ⓒ Ⓓ	187. Ⓐ Ⓑ Ⓒ Ⓓ
113. Ⓐ Ⓑ Ⓒ Ⓓ	138. Ⓐ Ⓑ Ⓒ Ⓓ	163. Ⓐ Ⓑ Ⓒ Ⓓ	188. Ⓐ Ⓑ Ⓒ Ⓓ
114. Ⓐ Ⓑ Ⓒ Ⓓ	139. Ⓐ Ⓑ Ⓒ Ⓓ	164. Ⓐ Ⓑ Ⓒ Ⓓ	189. Ⓐ Ⓑ Ⓒ Ⓓ
115. Ⓐ Ⓑ Ⓒ Ⓓ	140. Ⓐ Ⓑ Ⓒ Ⓓ	165. Ⓐ Ⓑ Ⓒ Ⓓ	190. Ⓐ Ⓑ Ⓒ Ⓓ
116. Ⓐ Ⓑ Ⓒ Ⓓ	141. Ⓐ Ⓑ Ⓒ Ⓓ	166. Ⓐ Ⓑ Ⓒ Ⓓ	191. Ⓐ Ⓑ Ⓒ Ⓓ
117. Ⓐ Ⓑ Ⓒ Ⓓ	142. Ⓐ Ⓑ Ⓒ Ⓓ	167. Ⓐ Ⓑ Ⓒ Ⓓ	192. Ⓐ Ⓑ Ⓒ Ⓓ
118. Ⓐ Ⓑ Ⓒ Ⓓ	143. Ⓐ Ⓑ Ⓒ Ⓓ	168. Ⓐ Ⓑ Ⓒ Ⓓ	193. Ⓐ Ⓑ Ⓒ Ⓓ
119. Ⓐ Ⓑ Ⓒ Ⓓ	144. Ⓐ Ⓑ Ⓒ Ⓓ	169. Ⓐ Ⓑ Ⓒ Ⓓ	194. Ⓐ Ⓑ Ⓒ Ⓓ
120. Ⓐ Ⓑ Ⓒ Ⓓ	145. Ⓐ Ⓑ Ⓒ Ⓓ	170. Ⓐ Ⓑ Ⓒ Ⓓ	195. Ⓐ Ⓑ Ⓒ Ⓓ
121. Ⓐ Ⓑ Ⓒ Ⓓ	146. Ⓐ Ⓑ Ⓒ Ⓓ	171. Ⓐ Ⓑ Ⓒ Ⓓ	196. Ⓐ Ⓑ Ⓒ Ⓓ
122. Ⓐ Ⓑ Ⓒ Ⓓ	147. Ⓐ Ⓑ Ⓒ Ⓓ	172. Ⓐ Ⓑ Ⓒ Ⓓ	197. Ⓐ Ⓑ Ⓒ Ⓓ
123. Ⓐ Ⓑ Ⓒ Ⓓ	148. Ⓐ Ⓑ Ⓒ Ⓓ	173. Ⓐ Ⓑ Ⓒ Ⓓ	198. Ⓐ Ⓑ Ⓒ Ⓓ
124. Ⓐ Ⓑ Ⓒ Ⓓ	149. Ⓐ Ⓑ Ⓒ Ⓓ	174. Ⓐ Ⓑ Ⓒ Ⓓ	199. Ⓐ Ⓑ Ⓒ Ⓓ
125. Ⓐ Ⓑ Ⓒ Ⓓ	150. Ⓐ Ⓑ Ⓒ Ⓓ	175. Ⓐ Ⓑ Ⓒ Ⓓ	200. Ⓐ Ⓑ Ⓒ Ⓓ

Practice Test 1

Listening Comprehension

1. Ⓐ Ⓑ Ⓒ Ⓓ
2. Ⓐ Ⓑ Ⓒ Ⓓ
3. Ⓐ Ⓑ Ⓒ Ⓓ
4. Ⓐ Ⓑ Ⓒ Ⓓ
5. Ⓐ Ⓑ Ⓒ Ⓓ
6. Ⓐ Ⓑ Ⓒ Ⓓ
7. Ⓐ Ⓑ Ⓒ
8. Ⓐ Ⓑ Ⓒ
9. Ⓐ Ⓑ Ⓒ
10. Ⓐ Ⓑ Ⓒ
11. Ⓐ Ⓑ Ⓒ
12. Ⓐ Ⓑ Ⓒ
13. Ⓐ Ⓑ Ⓒ
14. Ⓐ Ⓑ Ⓒ
15. Ⓐ Ⓑ Ⓒ
16. Ⓐ Ⓑ Ⓒ
17. Ⓐ Ⓑ Ⓒ
18. Ⓐ Ⓑ Ⓒ
19. Ⓐ Ⓑ Ⓒ
20. Ⓐ Ⓑ Ⓒ
21. Ⓐ Ⓑ Ⓒ
22. Ⓐ Ⓑ Ⓒ
23. Ⓐ Ⓑ Ⓒ
24. Ⓐ Ⓑ Ⓒ
25. Ⓐ Ⓑ Ⓒ

26. Ⓐ Ⓑ Ⓒ
27. Ⓐ Ⓑ Ⓒ
28. Ⓐ Ⓑ Ⓒ
29. Ⓐ Ⓑ Ⓒ
30. Ⓐ Ⓑ Ⓒ
31. Ⓐ Ⓑ Ⓒ
32. Ⓐ Ⓑ Ⓒ Ⓓ
33. Ⓐ Ⓑ Ⓒ Ⓓ
34. Ⓐ Ⓑ Ⓒ Ⓓ
35. Ⓐ Ⓑ Ⓒ Ⓓ
36. Ⓐ Ⓑ Ⓒ Ⓓ
37. Ⓐ Ⓑ Ⓒ Ⓓ
38. Ⓐ Ⓑ Ⓒ Ⓓ
39. Ⓐ Ⓑ Ⓒ Ⓓ
40. Ⓐ Ⓑ Ⓒ Ⓓ
41. Ⓐ Ⓑ Ⓒ Ⓓ
42. Ⓐ Ⓑ Ⓒ Ⓓ
43. Ⓐ Ⓑ Ⓒ Ⓓ
44. Ⓐ Ⓑ Ⓒ Ⓓ
45. Ⓐ Ⓑ Ⓒ Ⓓ
46. Ⓐ Ⓑ Ⓒ Ⓓ
47. Ⓐ Ⓑ Ⓒ Ⓓ
48. Ⓐ Ⓑ Ⓒ Ⓓ
49. Ⓐ Ⓑ Ⓒ Ⓓ
50. Ⓐ Ⓑ Ⓒ Ⓓ

51. Ⓐ Ⓑ Ⓒ Ⓓ
52. Ⓐ Ⓑ Ⓒ Ⓓ
53. Ⓐ Ⓑ Ⓒ Ⓓ
54. Ⓐ Ⓑ Ⓒ Ⓓ
55. Ⓐ Ⓑ Ⓒ Ⓓ
56. Ⓐ Ⓑ Ⓒ Ⓓ
57. Ⓐ Ⓑ Ⓒ Ⓓ
58. Ⓐ Ⓑ Ⓒ Ⓓ
59. Ⓐ Ⓑ Ⓒ Ⓓ
60. Ⓐ Ⓑ Ⓒ Ⓓ
61. Ⓐ Ⓑ Ⓒ Ⓓ
62. Ⓐ Ⓑ Ⓒ Ⓓ
63. Ⓐ Ⓑ Ⓒ Ⓓ
64. Ⓐ Ⓑ Ⓒ Ⓓ
65. Ⓐ Ⓑ Ⓒ Ⓓ
66. Ⓐ Ⓑ Ⓒ Ⓓ
67. Ⓐ Ⓑ Ⓒ Ⓓ
68. Ⓐ Ⓑ Ⓒ Ⓓ
69. Ⓐ Ⓑ Ⓒ Ⓓ
70. Ⓐ Ⓑ Ⓒ Ⓓ
71. Ⓐ Ⓑ Ⓒ Ⓓ
72. Ⓐ Ⓑ Ⓒ Ⓓ
73. Ⓐ Ⓑ Ⓒ Ⓓ
74. Ⓐ Ⓑ Ⓒ Ⓓ
75. Ⓐ Ⓑ Ⓒ Ⓓ

76. Ⓐ Ⓑ Ⓒ Ⓓ
77. Ⓐ Ⓑ Ⓒ Ⓓ
78. Ⓐ Ⓑ Ⓒ Ⓓ
79. Ⓐ Ⓑ Ⓒ Ⓓ
80. Ⓐ Ⓑ Ⓒ Ⓓ
81. Ⓐ Ⓑ Ⓒ Ⓓ
82. Ⓐ Ⓑ Ⓒ Ⓓ
83. Ⓐ Ⓑ Ⓒ Ⓓ
84. Ⓐ Ⓑ Ⓒ Ⓓ
85. Ⓐ Ⓑ Ⓒ Ⓓ
86. Ⓐ Ⓑ Ⓒ Ⓓ
87. Ⓐ Ⓑ Ⓒ Ⓓ
88. Ⓐ Ⓑ Ⓒ Ⓓ
89. Ⓐ Ⓑ Ⓒ Ⓓ
90. Ⓐ Ⓑ Ⓒ Ⓓ
91. Ⓐ Ⓑ Ⓒ Ⓓ
92. Ⓐ Ⓑ Ⓒ Ⓓ
93. Ⓐ Ⓑ Ⓒ Ⓓ
94. Ⓐ Ⓑ Ⓒ Ⓓ
95. Ⓐ Ⓑ Ⓒ Ⓓ
96. Ⓐ Ⓑ Ⓒ Ⓓ
97. Ⓐ Ⓑ Ⓒ Ⓓ
98. Ⓐ Ⓑ Ⓒ Ⓓ
99. Ⓐ Ⓑ Ⓒ Ⓓ
100. Ⓐ Ⓑ Ⓒ Ⓓ

Reading

101. Ⓐ Ⓑ Ⓒ Ⓓ
102. Ⓐ Ⓑ Ⓒ Ⓓ
103. Ⓐ Ⓑ Ⓒ Ⓓ
104. Ⓐ Ⓑ Ⓒ Ⓓ
105. Ⓐ Ⓑ Ⓒ Ⓓ
106. Ⓐ Ⓑ Ⓒ Ⓓ
107. Ⓐ Ⓑ Ⓒ Ⓓ
108. Ⓐ Ⓑ Ⓒ Ⓓ
109. Ⓐ Ⓑ Ⓒ Ⓓ
110. Ⓐ Ⓑ Ⓒ Ⓓ
111. Ⓐ Ⓑ Ⓒ Ⓓ
112. Ⓐ Ⓑ Ⓒ Ⓓ
113. Ⓐ Ⓑ Ⓒ Ⓓ
114. Ⓐ Ⓑ Ⓒ Ⓓ
115. Ⓐ Ⓑ Ⓒ Ⓓ
116. Ⓐ Ⓑ Ⓒ Ⓓ
117. Ⓐ Ⓑ Ⓒ Ⓓ
118. Ⓐ Ⓑ Ⓒ Ⓓ
119. Ⓐ Ⓑ Ⓒ Ⓓ
120. Ⓐ Ⓑ Ⓒ Ⓓ
121. Ⓐ Ⓑ Ⓒ Ⓓ
122. Ⓐ Ⓑ Ⓒ Ⓓ
123. Ⓐ Ⓑ Ⓒ Ⓓ
124. Ⓐ Ⓑ Ⓒ Ⓓ
125. Ⓐ Ⓑ Ⓒ Ⓓ

126. Ⓐ Ⓑ Ⓒ Ⓓ
127. Ⓐ Ⓑ Ⓒ Ⓓ
128. Ⓐ Ⓑ Ⓒ Ⓓ
129. Ⓐ Ⓑ Ⓒ Ⓓ
130. Ⓐ Ⓑ Ⓒ Ⓓ
131. Ⓐ Ⓑ Ⓒ Ⓓ
132. Ⓐ Ⓑ Ⓒ Ⓓ
133. Ⓐ Ⓑ Ⓒ Ⓓ
134. Ⓐ Ⓑ Ⓒ Ⓓ
135. Ⓐ Ⓑ Ⓒ Ⓓ
136. Ⓐ Ⓑ Ⓒ Ⓓ
137. Ⓐ Ⓑ Ⓒ Ⓓ
138. Ⓐ Ⓑ Ⓒ Ⓓ
139. Ⓐ Ⓑ Ⓒ Ⓓ
140. Ⓐ Ⓑ Ⓒ Ⓓ
141. Ⓐ Ⓑ Ⓒ Ⓓ
142. Ⓐ Ⓑ Ⓒ Ⓓ
143. Ⓐ Ⓑ Ⓒ Ⓓ
144. Ⓐ Ⓑ Ⓒ Ⓓ
145. Ⓐ Ⓑ Ⓒ Ⓓ
146. Ⓐ Ⓑ Ⓒ Ⓓ
147. Ⓐ Ⓑ Ⓒ Ⓓ
148. Ⓐ Ⓑ Ⓒ Ⓓ
149. Ⓐ Ⓑ Ⓒ Ⓓ
150. Ⓐ Ⓑ Ⓒ Ⓓ

151. Ⓐ Ⓑ Ⓒ Ⓓ
152. Ⓐ Ⓑ Ⓒ Ⓓ
153. Ⓐ Ⓑ Ⓒ Ⓓ
154. Ⓐ Ⓑ Ⓒ Ⓓ
155. Ⓐ Ⓑ Ⓒ Ⓓ
156. Ⓐ Ⓑ Ⓒ Ⓓ
157. Ⓐ Ⓑ Ⓒ Ⓓ
158. Ⓐ Ⓑ Ⓒ Ⓓ
159. Ⓐ Ⓑ Ⓒ Ⓓ
160. Ⓐ Ⓑ Ⓒ Ⓓ
161. Ⓐ Ⓑ Ⓒ Ⓓ
162. Ⓐ Ⓑ Ⓒ Ⓓ
163. Ⓐ Ⓑ Ⓒ Ⓓ
164. Ⓐ Ⓑ Ⓒ Ⓓ
165. Ⓐ Ⓑ Ⓒ Ⓓ
166. Ⓐ Ⓑ Ⓒ Ⓓ
167. Ⓐ Ⓑ Ⓒ Ⓓ
168. Ⓐ Ⓑ Ⓒ Ⓓ
169. Ⓐ Ⓑ Ⓒ Ⓓ
170. Ⓐ Ⓑ Ⓒ Ⓓ
171. Ⓐ Ⓑ Ⓒ Ⓓ
172. Ⓐ Ⓑ Ⓒ Ⓓ
173. Ⓐ Ⓑ Ⓒ Ⓓ
174. Ⓐ Ⓑ Ⓒ Ⓓ
175. Ⓐ Ⓑ Ⓒ Ⓓ

176. Ⓐ Ⓑ Ⓒ Ⓓ
177. Ⓐ Ⓑ Ⓒ Ⓓ
178. Ⓐ Ⓑ Ⓒ Ⓓ
179. Ⓐ Ⓑ Ⓒ Ⓓ
180. Ⓐ Ⓑ Ⓒ Ⓓ
181. Ⓐ Ⓑ Ⓒ Ⓓ
182. Ⓐ Ⓑ Ⓒ Ⓓ
183. Ⓐ Ⓑ Ⓒ Ⓓ
184. Ⓐ Ⓑ Ⓒ Ⓓ
185. Ⓐ Ⓑ Ⓒ Ⓓ
186. Ⓐ Ⓑ Ⓒ Ⓓ
187. Ⓐ Ⓑ Ⓒ Ⓓ
188. Ⓐ Ⓑ Ⓒ Ⓓ
189. Ⓐ Ⓑ Ⓒ Ⓓ
190. Ⓐ Ⓑ Ⓒ Ⓓ
191. Ⓐ Ⓑ Ⓒ Ⓓ
192. Ⓐ Ⓑ Ⓒ Ⓓ
193. Ⓐ Ⓑ Ⓒ Ⓓ
194. Ⓐ Ⓑ Ⓒ Ⓓ
195. Ⓐ Ⓑ Ⓒ Ⓓ
196. Ⓐ Ⓑ Ⓒ Ⓓ
197. Ⓐ Ⓑ Ⓒ Ⓓ
198. Ⓐ Ⓑ Ⓒ Ⓓ
199. Ⓐ Ⓑ Ⓒ Ⓓ
200. Ⓐ Ⓑ Ⓒ Ⓓ

Practice Test 2

Listening Comprehension

1. (A) (B) (C) (D)
2. (A) (B) (C) (D)
3. (A) (B) (C) (D)
4. (A) (B) (C) (D)
5. (A) (B) (C) (D)
6. (A) (B) (C) (D)
7. (A) (B) (C)
8. (A) (B) (C)
9. (A) (B) (C)
10. (A) (B) (C)
11. (A) (B) (C)
12. (A) (B) (C)
13. (A) (B) (C)
14. (A) (B) (C)
15. (A) (B) (C)
16. (A) (B) (C)
17. (A) (B) (C)
18. (A) (B) (C)
19. (A) (B) (C)
20. (A) (B) (C)
21. (A) (B) (C)
22. (A) (B) (C)
23. (A) (B) (C)
24. (A) (B) (C)
25. (A) (B) (C)

26. (A) (B) (C)
27. (A) (B) (C)
28. (A) (B) (C)
29. (A) (B) (C)
30. (A) (B) (C)
31. (A) (B) (C)
32. (A) (B) (C) (D)
33. (A) (B) (C) (D)
34. (A) (B) (C) (D)
35. (A) (B) (C) (D)
36. (A) (B) (C) (D)
37. (A) (B) (C) (D)
38. (A) (B) (C) (D)
39. (A) (B) (C) (D)
40. (A) (B) (C) (D)
41. (A) (B) (C) (D)
42. (A) (B) (C) (D)
43. (A) (B) (C) (D)
44. (A) (B) (C) (D)
45. (A) (B) (C) (D)
46. (A) (B) (C) (D)
47. (A) (B) (C) (D)
48. (A) (B) (C) (D)
49. (A) (B) (C) (D)
50. (A) (B) (C) (D)

51. (A) (B) (C) (D)
52. (A) (B) (C) (D)
53. (A) (B) (C) (D)
54. (A) (B) (C) (D)
55. (A) (B) (C) (D)
56. (A) (B) (C) (D)
57. (A) (B) (C) (D)
58. (A) (B) (C) (D)
59. (A) (B) (C) (D)
60. (A) (B) (C) (D)
61. (A) (B) (C) (D)
62. (A) (B) (C) (D)
63. (A) (B) (C) (D)
64. (A) (B) (C) (D)
65. (A) (B) (C) (D)
66. (A) (B) (C) (D)
67. (A) (B) (C) (D)
68. (A) (B) (C) (D)
69. (A) (B) (C) (D)
70. (A) (B) (C) (D)
71. (A) (B) (C) (D)
72. (A) (B) (C) (D)
73. (A) (B) (C) (D)
74. (A) (B) (C) (D)
75. (A) (B) (C) (D)

76. (A) (B) (C) (D)
77. (A) (B) (C) (D)
78. (A) (B) (C) (D)
79. (A) (B) (C) (D)
80. (A) (B) (C) (D)
81. (A) (B) (C) (D)
82. (A) (B) (C) (D)
83. (A) (B) (C) (D)
84. (A) (B) (C) (D)
85. (A) (B) (C) (D)
86. (A) (B) (C) (D)
87. (A) (B) (C) (D)
88. (A) (B) (C) (D)
89. (A) (B) (C) (D)
90. (A) (B) (C) (D)
91. (A) (B) (C) (D)
92. (A) (B) (C) (D)
93. (A) (B) (C) (D)
94. (A) (B) (C) (D)
95. (A) (B) (C) (D)
96. (A) (B) (C) (D)
97. (A) (B) (C) (D)
98. (A) (B) (C) (D)
99. (A) (B) (C) (D)
100. (A) (B) (C) (D)

Reading

101. (A) (B) (C) (D)
102. (A) (B) (C) (D)
103. (A) (B) (C) (D)
104. (A) (B) (C) (D)
105. (A) (B) (C) (D)
106. (A) (B) (C) (D)
107. (A) (B) (C) (D)
108. (A) (B) (C) (D)
109. (A) (B) (C) (D)
110. (A) (B) (C) (D)
111. (A) (B) (C) (D)
112. (A) (B) (C) (D)
113. (A) (B) (C) (D)
114. (A) (B) (C) (D)
115. (A) (B) (C) (D)
116. (A) (B) (C) (D)
117. (A) (B) (C) (D)
118. (A) (B) (C) (D)
119. (A) (B) (C) (D)
120. (A) (B) (C) (D)
121. (A) (B) (C) (D)
122. (A) (B) (C) (D)
123. (A) (B) (C) (D)
124. (A) (B) (C) (D)
125. (A) (B) (C) (D)

126. (A) (B) (C) (D)
127. (A) (B) (C) (D)
128. (A) (B) (C) (D)
129. (A) (B) (C) (D)
130. (A) (B) (C) (D)
131. (A) (B) (C) (D)
132. (A) (B) (C) (D)
133. (A) (B) (C) (D)
134. (A) (B) (C) (D)
135. (A) (B) (C) (D)
136. (A) (B) (C) (D)
137. (A) (B) (C) (D)
138. (A) (B) (C) (D)
139. (A) (B) (C) (D)
140. (A) (B) (C) (D)
141. (A) (B) (C) (D)
142. (A) (B) (C) (D)
143. (A) (B) (C) (D)
144. (A) (B) (C) (D)
145. (A) (B) (C) (D)
146. (A) (B) (C) (D)
147. (A) (B) (C) (D)
148. (A) (B) (C) (D)
149. (A) (B) (C) (D)
150. (A) (B) (C) (D)

151. (A) (B) (C) (D)
152. (A) (B) (C) (D)
153. (A) (B) (C) (D)
154. (A) (B) (C) (D)
155. (A) (B) (C) (D)
156. (A) (B) (C) (D)
157. (A) (B) (C) (D)
158. (A) (B) (C) (D)
159. (A) (B) (C) (D)
160. (A) (B) (C) (D)
161. (A) (B) (C) (D)
162. (A) (B) (C) (D)
163. (A) (B) (C) (D)
164. (A) (B) (C) (D)
165. (A) (B) (C) (D)
166. (A) (B) (C) (D)
167. (A) (B) (C) (D)
168. (A) (B) (C) (D)
169. (A) (B) (C) (D)
170. (A) (B) (C) (D)
171. (A) (B) (C) (D)
172. (A) (B) (C) (D)
173. (A) (B) (C) (D)
174. (A) (B) (C) (D)
175. (A) (B) (C) (D)

176. (A) (B) (C) (D)
177. (A) (B) (C) (D)
178. (A) (B) (C) (D)
179. (A) (B) (C) (D)
180. (A) (B) (C) (D)
181. (A) (B) (C) (D)
182. (A) (B) (C) (D)
183. (A) (B) (C) (D)
184. (A) (B) (C) (D)
185. (A) (B) (C) (D)
186. (A) (B) (C) (D)
187. (A) (B) (C) (D)
188. (A) (B) (C) (D)
189. (A) (B) (C) (D)
190. (A) (B) (C) (D)
191. (A) (B) (C) (D)
192. (A) (B) (C) (D)
193. (A) (B) (C) (D)
194. (A) (B) (C) (D)
195. (A) (B) (C) (D)
196. (A) (B) (C) (D)
197. (A) (B) (C) (D)
198. (A) (B) (C) (D)
199. (A) (B) (C) (D)
200. (A) (B) (C) (D)

Score Conversion Chart

Use this Score Conversion Chart to work out your probable TOEIC® score. This score can only provide a guide. It is intended to be a reasonable estimate of the score you may achieve on the TOEIC test.

Raw score [total number of correct answers]	Converted score [estimated TOEIC score]	
	Listening	Reading
0	5	5
1	5	5
2	5	5
3	5	5
4	5	5
5	5	5
6	10	5
7	15	5
8	20	5
9	25	5
10	30	5
11	35	5
12	40	5
13	45	5
14	50	10
15	55	10
16	60	15
17	65	20
18	70	25
19	75	35
20	80	40
21	85	45
22	90	50
23	95	55
24	100	60
25	105	65
26	110	70
27	115	75
28	120	80
29	125	85
30	135	90
31	140	95
32	145	105
33	150	110
34	155	115
35	165	120
36	170	130
37	175	135
38	180	140
39	185	145
40	190	150
41	200	160
42	205	165
43	210	170
44	215	175
45	220	180
46	230	185
47	235	190
48	245	195
49	250	200
50	255	210

Raw score [total number of correct answers]	Converted score [estimated TOEIC score]	
	Listening	Reading
51	260	215
52	265	220
53	275	225
54	280	230
55	285	235
56	295	245
57	300	250
58	305	255
59	310	260
60	315	265
61	320	275
62	325	280
63	330	285
64	340	295
65	345	300
66	350	305
67	355	310
68	360	315
69	375	320
70	380	325
71	385	335
72	390	340
73	395	350
74	400	355
75	405	365
76	410	370
77	420	375
78	425	385
79	430	390
80	435	395
81	440	400
82	445	405
83	455	410
84	460	415
85	465	420
86	470	425
87	475	430
88	480	435
89	485	445
90	485	450
91	490	460
92	490	465
93	490	470
94	495	475
95	495	480
96	495	485
97	495	490
98	495	495
99	495	495
100	495	495

Essential Vocabulary

In this section, you will find over 800 useful words and phrases that often appear in the TOEIC® test. Use this list as a self-study resource.

Occupations

actor, architect, artist, athlete, auto mechanic, baker, bank teller, baseball player, bookseller, box office clerk, cashier, car rental agent, carpenter, chef, cleaner, coach, computer programmer, conductor, consultant, cook, correspondent, curator, customs officer, dancer, decorator, dentist, driving instructor, electrician, engineer, factory worker, fashion designer, firefighter, flight attendant, florist, gardener, gas station attendant, graphic designer, hairstylist, handyman, health inspector, hotel manager, immigration officer, information officer, interior designer, jeweler, journalist, lawyer, librarian, lifeguard, manicurist, market researcher, mechanic, movie director, musician, news presenter, newspaper reporter, nurse, office clerk, optometrist, painter, parking attendant, personal assistant, pharmacist, pianist, pilot, plumber, police officer, politician, postal worker, printer, professor, psychologist, realtor, research analyst, sailor, sales representative, salesclerk, sculptor, security guard, singer, surgeon, tailor, technician, tourist information clerk, traffic officer, travel agent, veterinarian, waiter, waitress, website designer

Activities

apply for a promotion, attend a ceremony, board a ferry, book a trip abroad, call a press conference, catch a cab, chair a meeting, change a tire, check your e-mail, close a deal, do overtime, exercise in the gym, extend a warranty, finish a proposal, give a seminar, go for a job interview, go sightseeing, go to a lecture, have a picnic, inspect a factory, join a health club, leave a message, look for work, mail a package, make a purchase, open an account, participate in a conference call, perform a fire drill, place an order, prepare a bid, read a memo, relax on the beach, rent a car, replace a fuse, reserve a table, see a play, solve a problem, submit a proposal, take a break, take a course, take a nap, take the day off, transfer some money, walk on the beach, work on a report

Relationships

author-publisher, bank manager-client, cashier-shopper, coworkers, cruise passenger-steward, doctor-patient, employer-employee, flight attendant-passenger, gallery attendant-patron, lawyer-client, nurse-patient, pedestrian-motorist, police officer-prisoner, rail passenger-ticket inspector, salesperson-customer, student-teacher, tour guide-tourist

Locations

airport terminal, amusement park, apartment block, aquarium, art gallery, bakery, bank, beach, boathouse, bookstore, botanic gardens, bus stop, castle, classroom, clinic, computer store, concert hall, concourse, construction site, convention center, courtroom, dentist's office, doctor's office, dormitory, drugstore, embassy, factory, farm, fast-food restaurant, ferry slip, food court, football stadium, foundry, freeway, garage, gas station, golf course, grocery store, gymnasium, hair salon, hangar, hardware store, hospital, hostel, hypermarket, jewelry store, library, laundromat, lighthouse, mall, mansion, marina, market, mill, mine, motel, movie theater, nursery, nursing home, observatory, oil rig, opera house, palace, park, parking lot, police station, post office, power plant, prison, refinery, reservoir, resort, shed, skyscraper, sports center, stable, stadium, stationery store, storage silo, subway station, theater, train station, travel agency, warehouse, windmill, workshop, urgent care center, zoo

Feelings and Emotions

afraid, agitated, ambitious, amused, angry, annoyed, anxious, appreciative, ashamed, bored, calm, cheerful, composed, confident, confused, convinced, disappointed, disillusioned, distressed, doubtful, eager, ecstatic, elated, embarrassed, enthusiastic, envious, excited, exhausted, frustrated, greedy, irate, irritated, jealous, mad, miserable, nervous, offended, patient, pleased, protective, proud, relaxed, resentful, satisfied, shocked, sleepy, thankful, thrilled, timid, upset, weary, worried

Dining Out

appetizer, banquet, beverage, bill, boiled, broiled, buffet, check, dessert, diner, entrée, fried, grilled, junk food, main course, menu, order, organic, poached, portion, rare, reservation, server, service, side dish, specials, starter, steamed, tip, undercooked, well done, vegan, vegetarian

Sports and Entertainment

arena, audience, captain, concert, crowd, draw, entrance fee, exhibition, fan, gallery, matinee, museum, musician, opponent, orchestra, perform, recital, referee, rehearse, repertoire, review, score, seating, show, skipper, spectator, stadium, stage, symphony, theater, ticket office, trailer

Finance and Purchasing

approve a loan, assets, audit, balance, bill, bond, borrow, budget, calculate, capital, charge, checking account, commission, cost, credit, credit rating, currency, debt, deposit, discount, dividend, down payment, estimate, exchange rate, fee, forecast, funding, interest rate, investment, invoice, loan, mortgage, order, payroll, portfolio, profit, refund, sales, savings, statement, tax, teller, transaction, transfer, turnover, wages, withdraw

Health

ache, appointment, bandage, bruise, cavity, checkup, cholesterol, clinician, consultation, cough, dentist, diagnosis, examination, filling, graze, heal, hygienist, infection, injection, medical insurance, operation, pills, plaster, policy, prescription, surgery, treatment, waiting room, ward, virus

Travel and Transportation

aisle, amenities, baggage carousel, balcony, bay, board, boarding pass, brochure, cabin crew, cancellation, car rental, carriage, carrier, check-in, customs, delay, divert, excursion, ferry, gate, itinerary, jetlag, journey, layover, luggage, nonstop, one-way, package tour, passport, platform, reservation, resort, round-trip, scenery, schedule, seaside, seat belt, shuttle, sightseeing, souvenir, station, subway, suite, terminal, ticket, track, transfer, trip, vacation, vaccination, view, visa, voyage

Office and Business

assignment, cargo, catalog, conference, correspondence, deadline, filing cabinet, freight, marketing, memo, package, personal secretary, premises, promote, proprietor, raise, reception desk, schedule, shipping, stapler, stationery, storage closet, trade, voicemail

Contracts and Negotiations

agenda, ballot, bargain, bid, board meeting, chair, committee, labor relations, merger, negotiation, partnership, pension, policy, procedures, restructure, stockholder, strategy, takeover, unanimous, vote, warranty

Manufacturing and Technology

assembly line, blueprint, defective, design, electronics, engine, experiment, expertise, export, guidelines, hazardous, import, laboratory, machinery, merchandise, out of order, plant, quality control, raw materials, regulations, reliability, research, service, spare parts, specification, technology, tools, trade

Computing and I.T.

attachment, backup, bookmark, browser, chat room, cloud, components, crash, cursor, delete, desktop, download, e-mail, file, folder, flash drive, hard disk, hardware, homepage, install, keyboard, laptop, log on/out, memory, memory stick, monitor, mouse, notebook, online, photocopy, pop-up, scanner, search engine, software, spam, spreadsheet, tablet, upgrade, USB port, virus, website

News and Media

article, billboard, breaking news, broadcast, cable, circulation, correspondent, coverage, current affairs, editor, feature, journalist, media, network, newscast, on-air, press, report, satellite, studio

Shopping

cash register, chain store, coupon, display, exchange, franchise, image, label, market leader, outlet, price tag, promotion, range, receipt, refund, retail, return, sale, sample, special offer, stock

Advertising and Marketing

advertisement, agency, airtime, brand, campaign, classified, commercial, flyer, jingle, media, poster, promotion, slogan

Personnel

absence, application, benefits, candidate, dismiss, employ, entitlement, fire, hire, interview, job offer, lay off, misconduct, notice, post, position, promotion, qualified, quit, recruit, requirement, résumé, retire, salary, sick leave, sign, staff, terminate

Tips for Building your Vocabulary

- Write each word you don't know on a small card. Write the translation on the back. Carry these "flash cards" with you and test yourself regularly throughout the day.
- Make sentences using each word. Learning words in context is very effective.
- Choose the most useful words. Then use a dictionary to make a list of related words.

TOEIC Word List

Here is a comprehensive list of the most common words and phrases you will find in the TOEIC® test. Make sure you know their meaning, and are familiar with how they are used, and be sure to test yourself regularly. You can listen to the words and phrases using the accompanying audio tracks. You can also write the translation of each word in the space next to it. Cover the columns and test yourself!

89 A

ability
abroad
absolutely
accept
access
accessible
accident
accommodate
accommodation
accomplish
accomplishment
according
accordingly
accounting
accurate
achieve
acquire
act
actually
adapt
adapter
additional
adequate
adjust
adjustment
administration
admire
admit
admittance
advance
advanced
advantage
advantageous
advertise
advertisement
advice
advise
affect
afford
affordable
agency
agenda
agree

agreeable
agreement
agricultural
aid
aim
airline
aisle
alarm
allow
alternative
ambitious
amend
amount
amusing
analysis
analyze
announcement
annoying
annual
anticipate
anxious
apologize
appeal
appetizer
appliance
applicant
application
apply
appoint
appointment
appreciable
appreciate
appreciation
appreciative
apprentice
approach
appropriate
approve
approximate
arbitrate
area
argue
argument
arrange
arrangement

assemble
assess
assets
assign
assignment
assist
assistance
assume
attach
attachment
attend
attendance
attentively
attract
audience
audit
authority
authorize
availability
available
avoid
awareness
awkward

90 B

background
backpack
baggage claim
balance
bank
bankrupt
barcode
bargain
basic
behave
belongings
beneficial
benefit
beverage
bid
bill
binder
blanket
block
board

boarding pass
boardroom
boast
book
boost
bored
borrow
bother
bottom line
branch
brand
briefcase
briefing
broadcast
broaden
browser
brush
budget
bulletin

91 C

cabin crew
cafeteria
calculate
calculation
calculator
campaign
cancel
cancellation
candidacy
candidate
capacity
capital
career
careless
cash
cashier
cause
cautious
celebrate
celebration
cell phone
certificate
certification
chain

chain store
chair
chairman
chairperson
characteristic
characterize
charge
charity
cheap
check in
check out
chef
circumstances
claim
claimant
classification
classify
clerk
client
climate
closure
coach
code
collect
commence
commission
commit
committee
common
commonly
commute
commuter
company
comparable
compare
compatible
compensate
compensation
competent
competition
competitive
competitor
complain
complaint
complete
complex
complexity
compliment
complimentary
comply
comprehensive

compromise
compulsory
concede
concern
conclude
conclusion
concourse
condition
conduct
confirm
confirmation
confusion
connect
connection
consequence
consider
considerable
consignment
consist
consistent
consistently
constant
constantly
construction
consult
consultant
consume
consumer
contain
container
continual
continuation
continue
contribute
contribution
control
control panel
convenient
conveniently
convince
convincing
corporate
corporation
cost
counter
courier
cover letter
coverage
coworker
crash
credentials

credit
criteria
critical
criticize
crowd
crowded
crucial
cruise
currency
current
custom
customer
customs
cutting edge
cycle

92 D

daily
damage
deadline
deal
debit
debt
decision
decorate
decrease
dedicate
deduct
defect
defective
definite
definitely
degree
delay
delete
delight
delighted
deliver
delivery
demand
demanding
demonstrate
depart
department
departure
depend on
dependence
deposit
description
designate
desperate

dessert
destination
detail
detailed
detect
deterioration
determine
determined
develop
developer
development
device
diagnose
differential
director
disagree
disagreement
disappointing
disconnect
discount
discrepancy
discrimination
discuss
discussion
dish
dismiss
dismissive
display
disposable
dispose
dispute
disruption
distinctive
distinguish
distribute
distribution
dividend
document
donate
donation
double
download
downsize
downturn
downward
dramatic
drastic
drastically
draw
drawer
drive

drop
dull
duration
duty-free

93 E

earn
earnings
economical
economize
economy
effective
effectively
effectiveness
efficiency
efficient
efficiently
elderly
electrical
elevator
embark
emergency
emphasize
employ
employee
employer
employment
enable
enclose
encourage
endurance
endure
engineer
engineering
enhance
enroll
ensure
enterprise
enthusiastic
enthusiastically
entitlement
entrée
environment
environmental
equivalent
essential
estimate
evaluate
event
evidence
evolve
exact

examination
examine
excel
excellent
excursion
executive
exhibit
expand
expansion
expect
expectation
expenditure
expense
expensive
experience
experienced
experiment
exploration
explore
express
extend
extension
external

94 F

facilities
facility
factor
factory
fail
failure
fair
famed
fare
fault
faulty
favor
fax
feature
fee
feedback
field
figure
file
fill out
finance
financial
firm
fix
flexible
flight
flight attendant

fluctuate
fluctuation
focus
focused
fold
folder
force
forecast
foreign
forget
forgetful
form
forward
founded
frank
frankly
fuel
fulfill
function
functional
fundraising
furniture
further

95 G

gesture
goal
goods
gradually
grievance
grill
growth
guarantee
guidelines

96 H

haggle
handle
handy
harbor
harmful
hazardous
head office
headquarters
hesitate
hesitation
hide
highlight
highly
hike
hire
hold

homepage
host

97 I

identification
identify
imaginative
immediate
immediately
impact
impatient
implement
imply
impression
improper
improve
improvement
incentive
inclined
include
inclusion
income
inconvenience
increase
indicate
indication
individual
individually
inexperienced
infer
inflate
inflation
influence
influential
information
input
inquiry
install
installation
insurance
insure
intend
intention
intently
intern
internal
international
internship
interrupt
interview
invaluable
invent

invention
inventory
invest
investigate
investigation
investment
invite
invoice
isolate
issue
item
itemize
itinerary

98 J
jealous
jeopardize
jeopardy
jobless
join
joint
journal
journey
judge
justice
justification
justify

99 K
keen
keep
knock
know
knowledge
knowledgeable

100 L
label
labor
lack
landlord
laptop
launch
law
lay off
leak
lean
lease
leisure
lend
liability
license

licensing
lie
limited
limousine
list
livestock
loan
lobby
local
locate
log on
log out
loyal
luggage
luxurious
luxury

101 M
maintain
maintenance
major
manage
managerial
mandatory
manufacture
manufacturing
marketing
mechanic
medic
medical
medication
medicine
meeting
membership
memo
memorandum
mention
merchandise
mere
merge
merger
mileage
million
mishear
misleading
misrepresent
monitor
monument
mortgage
motivate
motivation

102 N
napkin
narrow
narrowing
neighborhood
network
nominate
nomination
notice
notify

103 O
objection
objective
obligation
oblige
obtain
obviously
occupation
occur
officer
official
onward
operate
operation
opinion
opportunity
optimistic
order
organization
organize
organized
original
outline
outlook
outstanding
overall
overdraft
overseas
overtime
overview
owe

104 P
package
package tour
parcel
parking lot
participant
particularly
passenger

patent
patented
patience
payment
perform
performance
permanent
permission
permit
personal
personalized
personnel
persuade
pessimistic
plant
platform
pleasant
plow
plug in
plumber
point
pointless
policy
polite
politician
politics
poll
pollute
popular
popularity
position
postpone
postponement
potential
power
practical
practically
predict
predictable
prefer
preference
premises
prepare
present
presentation
press
prevent
prevention
price
priceless
principal
principle

priority
private
probability
probably
probationary
process
profession
professional
profile
profit
profitability
profitable
progress
progressive
prohibit
project
promote
promotion
prompt
promptly
properly
property
protect
protection
publicity
publicize
purchase
purpose
pursue

105 Q

qualification
qualified
qualify
questionnaire
quotation
quote

106 R

raise
range
rare
rate
rational
raw materials
reach
realize
rearrange
reasonable
reasonably
receipt
receive

recent
reception
receptive
recipe
recognize
recommend
recommendation
recruit
recruitment
reduce
reduction
redundant
refrigerator
refund
refundable
refusal
refuse
regarding
regardless
regional
register
registration
regret
regular
regularly
regulate
rehearse
reject
relax
relaxation
release
relevant
remain
remarkable
remind
reminder
remittance
remove
remuneration
renovate
renovation
rent
repair
repayment
repetitive
replace
replacement
report
represent
representative
request
require

requirement
reschedule
rescue
resemble
reservation
reserve
resign
resist
resolve
respect
respectable
respectful
respond
responsibility
responsible
restore
restructure
résumé
retail
retire
retirement
review
revise
revised
right away
rival
roadside
roughly
route
runway

107 S

salary
sale
salvage
sample
satisfactory
satisfied
satisfy
save
scene
scenery
schedule
scrutinize
search engine
secluded
secretarial
secretary
select
selection
selective
seminar

senior
serious
service
several
shape
sharp
shift
shine
shipment
shipping
shortage
shuttle
sightseeing
significant
simplify
situation
slump
software
solar
spacious
spare part
spare time
specialize
specialty
specification
specify
spectator
stable
stadium
staff
stapler
stare
starter
stationery
steep
stock
strategic
strategy
streamline
strike
studio
submit
subscribe
subscription
subsidiary
suggest
suggestion
suit
suitability
suitable
supervise
supervision

supplier
supply
support
supporter
surrounding
suspicious
switchboard
systematic

108 T

takeover
target
tax
technical
technician
temporary
tenant
terminate
terrible
terrific
theoretical
theory
thorough
tidy
tip
tour
tourism
tourist

towel
tower
track
trade
tradition
traffic
training
transfer
transform
transformation
transit
transportation
tremendous
trend
trial
triumph
trust
turnover

109 U

unconditional
understand
unfavorable
unfortunately
uniform
unspoiled
unwrap
upcoming

update
upgrade
upset
upstairs
utility bill

110 V

vacancy
vacant
vacation
vaccination
valuables
varied
variety
various
vendor
venture
venue
virus
vital

111 W

wage
walkway
warehouse
warn
warning
warrant

warranty
wastage
waterproof
wealth
website
weight
welfare
wholesale
win
withdraw
withdrawal
workplace
workshop
worth
worthless
wrap

112 XYZ

X-ray

yearly
yield
youth

zero
zone

Understanding Accents and Spoken English

The Listening section of the TOEIC® test features speakers with American, British, Australian, and Canadian accents. The accents you will hear are all "standard," and although you do not need to identify the different accents, being familiar with them can help improve your listening comprehension score on the test. It is also useful if you understand various features of connected speech such as stress, linking, and intonation that native English-speakers use in everyday spoken discourse. This section of *Pass the TOEIC Test* gives you practice in listening to and understanding the different accents used in the test, and will help you recognize common features of connected speech.

Comparing Accents

Exercise A 113 Listen to the way these words are pronounced differently.

	American	British	Australian	Canadian
unique				
father				
quarrel				
regain				
sample				
bitter				
weather				
oranges				
vitamin				
controversy				

Exercise B 114 Listen to these sentences. Compare the pronunciation.

	American	British	Australian	Canadian
1. The house we rented wasn't far from my office.				
2. Do you know if Susan caught her flight earlier today?				
3. Could you water those plants at reception, please?				
4. The batteries in this portable radio need replacing.				
5. We're sorry to hear about the delay in production.				
6. You're not allowed to sit in the reserved seating area.				
7. Did you send the package by express mail as I asked?				
8. Farmers have been badly hit by the extreme weather.				
9. Who'd have thought the president would quit?				
10. Dan's knee injury took a long time to heal.				

American English 🇺🇸

Exercise A 🔘115 Listen to this conversation. Notice the speakers' pronunciation.

Woman: Could you tell me about your Life Drawing course, please? I've seen it in your brochure and it looks pretty interesting.

Man: Yes, of course. It runs every Thursday evening for ten weeks, starting next month, from seven till nine. It's for people of any ability, so don't worry if you're a beginner. You're lucky because there's still one place available.

Woman: Oh, I see. And what about the cost? I read something about fees and a charge for materials on top, but I'm a student so would I qualify for any support?

Man: Yes, if you're a full-time student then just bring in your student ID and the tuition fees are waived. I can give you the forms now, if you like.

Exercise B 🔘116 Listen and complete the sentences.

1. All the delegates are looking forward to _____the welcome ceremony_____ tomorrow night.

2. It should take us no more than half an hour to _____ from here.

3. Didn't you say you were going to _____, or shall I do it?

4. I could really use some help _____ before tomorrow's talk.

5. Mr. Cho e-mailed that he wants us to _____ .

6. Are you sure that _____ back to Seattle?

British English 🇬🇧

Exercise A 🔘117 Listen to this conversation. Notice the speakers' pronunciation.

Woman: Could you tell me about your Life Drawing course, please? I've seen it in your brochure and it looks pretty interesting.

Man: Yes, of course. It runs every Thursday evening for ten weeks, starting next month, from seven till nine. It's for people of any ability, so don't worry if you're a beginner. You're lucky because there's still one place available.

Woman: Oh, I see. And what about the cost? I read something about fees and a charge for materials on top, but I'm a student so would I qualify for any support?

Man: Yes, if you're a full-time student then just bring in your student ID and the tuition fees are waived. I can give you the forms now, if you like.

Exercise B 🔘118 Listen and complete the sentences.

1. I really think we need to review _____ before we go much further.

2. Has someone checked whether the new _____?

3. Ben will have to _____ before he can do our accounts.

4. The new law means that we all need to _____ .

5. Don't forget to _____ before you leave the office.

6. Can you tell me if you're taking any _____ at the moment?

Australian English 🇦🇺

Exercise A **119** Listen to this conversation. Notice the speakers' pronunciation.

Woman: Could you tell me about your Life Drawing course, please? I've seen it in your brochure and it looks pretty interesting.

Man: Yes, of course. It runs every Thursday evening for ten weeks, starting next month, from seven till nine. It's for people of any ability, so don't worry if you're a beginner. You're lucky because there's still one place available.

Woman: Oh, I see. And what about the cost? I read something about fees and a charge for materials on top, but I'm a student so would I qualify for any support?

Man: Yes, if you're a full-time student then just bring in your student ID and the tuition fees are waived. I can give you the forms now, if you like.

Exercise B **120** Listen and complete the sentences.

1. Which of these investment vehicles most ....?

2. The service was good, but the food didn't ....

3. You'll need to get .... if you want to leave work early.

4. The whales have now left the area and are .... along the coast.

5. It'll be hard to find a suitable replacement .... we're looking for.

6. There's a fairly secluded internet .... that guests can use.

Canadian English 🇨🇦

Exercise A **121** Listen to this conversation. Notice the speakers' pronunciation.

Woman: Could you tell me about your Life Drawing course, please? I've seen it in your brochure and it looks pretty interesting.

Man: Yes, of course. It runs every Thursday evening for ten weeks, starting next month, from seven till nine. It's for people of any ability, so don't worry if you're a beginner. You're lucky because there's still one place available.

Woman: Oh, I see. And what about the cost? I read something about fees and a charge for materials on top, but I'm a student so would I qualify for any support?

Man: Yes, if you're a full-time student then just bring in your student ID and the tuition fees are waived. I can give you the forms now, if you like.

Exercise B **122** Listen and complete the sentences.

1. A third of the .... on temporary contracts.

2. More .... among public sector employees continues to grow.

3. I didn't realize that New York City ....

4. The composition of this photograph is .... at the same time.

5. Janice Downing is .... tonight's performance.

6. Do you know if a guarantor .... agreement for leases under three years?

Identifying Accents

You will hear this short talk four times. Listen and try to identify each speaker's accent.

Good morning, and welcome to you all. First, let me begin by saying how delighted I am to see so many eager faces. Congratulations on successfully completing the selection process for our Graduate Trainee Program here at Denston. We're expecting great things from you all as you embark upon what will be an intense period of training. Your year here will give you valuable, first-hand experience across many fields, as you rotate between Internal Communications, Finance, Operations, Strategy, Sales, and Human Resources. Of course, you'll be assessed as you go, and on completion you'll be expected to pursue a professional qualification in your chosen area. Myself and the Senior Manager will act as your mentors, and you'll also be assigned a "Buddy" to assist you through your first three months here. This induction week will give you an overview of the company, and help you understand the structure of the business, as well as the culture of success we aim to foster. Now, without further ado, let me hand you over to Karen McNally, our Training Manager, for a more detailed rundown of the week ahead.

	American	British	Australian	Canadian
123 Speaker 1	🇺🇸	🇬🇧	🇦🇺	🇨🇦
124 Speaker 2	🇺🇸	🇬🇧	🇦🇺	🇨🇦
125 Speaker 3	🇺🇸	🇬🇧	🇦🇺	🇨🇦
126 Speaker 4	🇺🇸	🇬🇧	🇦🇺	🇨🇦

Improving Your Accent Recognition

Here are some things you can do to help you become more familiar with the different accents used in the TOEIC test. You will find links to these websites, and many more, on **www.pass-the-toeic-test.com**. Just select FREE ACTIVITIES and go to Improving Your Listening Comprehension.

- Listen to your local English language radio station, or one of these international stations: Voice of America, BBC World Service Radio, Radio Australia, or Radio Canada International.

- Watch programs on TV (news, sports, etc.). Try: CNN, CBS, BBC, ABC, and CBC.

- Watch movies in English, with subtitles if necessary.

- Listen to songs in English. You can listen and read the lyrics, or practice karaoke and sing along! Repeating what you hear is a good way to improve your listening comprehension.

- Go online. There are many great websites with podcasts of native speakers you can listen to.

Word Stress

For words in English that have more than one syllable, at least one of the syllables is pronounced louder or longer than the others. This is called *stress*. Recognizing word stress will help improve your listening comprehension.

Exercise A 127 Listen to these words. Notice how the underlined syllables are stressed.

crowded	factor	journal	license	payment	virus
adapt	consult	enhance	oblige	pollute	subscribe
arbitrate	classify	isolate	merchandise	scrutinize	studio
decision	dramatic	important	profession	strategic	replacement
alternative	complexity	discrepancy	equivalent	luxurious	participant
beneficial	conversation	medication	nomination	pessimistic	systematic

Exercise B 128 Listen to these words. Underline the syllables that are stressed.

agreement	analysis	bulletin	campaign	cancellation	climate
calculate	comparable	compulsory	contribution	critical	deduce
dismissive	dividend	economize	excursion	expectation	forecast
fulfill	incentive	invaluable	itemize	label	original
perform	prevent	priceless	prohibit	reassuring	receipt
receptive	revelation	salvage	sensitive	tenant	transformation

The Schwa

In syllables that are *not* stressed, the vowels are often "reduced" and pronounced /ə/. This is called the *schwa*, and it is the most common vowel sound in English.

Exercise A 129 Listen to these words. Notice the examples of the schwa.

allow	capital	celebrate	doctor	exercise	harmony
level	measure	oppose	protect	support	theater

Exercise B 130 Listen to these sentences. Underline the schwas.

1. Do the inspectors have an appointment to see Mr. Daniels?

2. This stock is to be placed on consignment until further notice.

3. Please don't forget to unlock the fire escape.

4. Thanks to these excellent financial results, we're in profit again.

5. It was such a tough exercise that even the trainers couldn't understand what to do.

6. It has come to my attention that some workers are abusing the overtime system.

7. Can you sign this petition against the government's expansion of the airport?

8. Rangers will continue to protect the forests from illegal loggers and poachers.

Sentence Stress and Rhythm

English is a stress-timed language. This means that syllables are stressed at regular intervals, which gives the language its distinctive rhythm. Usually, the important words (e.g., *nouns*, *verbs*, *adjectives*, and *adverbs*) are stressed, but the stress can change to reflect the speaker's meaning. Listening for words that are stressed can help you identify key information, and improve your listening comprehension score on the test.

Exercise A 131 Listen to these sentences. Notice how the underlined words are stressed.

1. <u>How</u> many <u>people</u> <u>came</u> to the <u>presentation</u> last <u>night</u>?
2. If the <u>parts</u> <u>don't</u> arrive <u>soon</u>, then we'll <u>have</u> to <u>stop</u> <u>production</u>.
3. Let's <u>get</u> some <u>souvenirs</u> and <u>postcards</u> from that <u>store</u> on the <u>corner</u>.
4. <u>Once</u> we've received <u>payment</u> in <u>full</u>, we'll be <u>able</u> to <u>process</u> your <u>application</u>.
5. You'll <u>need</u> to <u>show</u> this <u>pass</u> to the <u>guards</u> at the <u>gate</u>, or they <u>won't</u> let you <u>through</u>.

Exercise B 132 Listen to these sentences. Underline the words that are stressed.

1. We've had a very good response to our appeal for volunteers.
2. The architect said she'll bring the designs when she visits next Wednesday.
3. Why didn't anyone tell me that Gerry has gone on vacation for a week?
4. There are three more candidates to interview, and then we need to make a decision.
5. The next time we have a meeting in Birmingham, let's rent a car instead of taking the train.

Exercise C 133 Listen to this conversation. Underline the words that are stressed.

Man: Have you booked all our hotel rooms for the conference in Milan next month? I spoke to Charlie, but he said he wasn't sure.

Woman: I've hardly had time to even think about it, to be honest. I've been out of the office for most of this week, and now I have a report to finish for Alan before I leave tonight.

Man: I suppose I can phone around a few places, if you like. How about I try The Grand, where we stayed last year?

Woman: No, that was too expensive. But there is one hotel not far away from there I was thinking of calling. I have the card here somewhere. Maybe you could try them?

Exercise D 134 Listen to this short talk. Underline the words that are stressed.

To sum up the advantages of our fiber optic network, we operate at higher speeds, and have a greater bandwidth, than any of our competitors. This means we can carry more information, over longer distances, in less time than anyone else. Our network is also more resistant to interference, and requires less maintenance, offering the security, reliability, and quality our customers demand. Nor should we forget that the cost of transmitting a call over our fiber optic network is a tiny fraction of the cost of transmitting it over copper wire. Of course, components and installation costs are high, but fiber is the future. With our domestic customer numbers currently growing at over 20 percent per annum, for both the home and corporate sector, the extra funding we're asking for today will secure our future as market leaders. Now, I'm happy to take a few questions.

Linking

Because English is a stress-timed language, words are often linked together in order to "keep up" with the rhythm. Common examples of this can be found with contractions (*do not* – *don't*, *he is* – *he's*, *she will* – *she'll*, etc.). Understanding how words join together can help improve your listening comprehension score on the test.

Linking words

Exercise A 135 Listen to these questions. Notice how the sounds change.

1. Where did you /didʒə/ go on your last vacation?
2. Which proposal would you /wudʒə/ recommend we accept?
3. How could you /kudʒə/ tell that the sample was contaminated?
4. Where do you /dʒə/ want to /wonə/ go for dinner tonight?
5. Who are you /əjə/ going to /gonə/ offer the job to?

Exercise B 136 Listen to these questions and count the number of words. Contractions (e.g., *you're*) count as two words.

1. ___   2. ___   3. ___   4. ___   5. ___

Linking consonants and vowels

When a word ending in a consonant sound is followed by a word beginning in a vowel sound, the consonant sound moves forward; for example, *put off* and *look at*.

Exercise A 137 Listen to these sentences. Notice how sounds link together.

1. Please ask at reception if you need any further advice or information.
2. Simon asked us to look at these figures and check if they're accurate.
3. Dinner is at eight so let's hurry up and finish all these invoices or we'll be late.

Exercise B 138 Listen to these sentences. Underline the sounds that link together.

1. The cost of exporting all the tunics was not as high as I'd feared.
2. I asked if Mr. Ho was in his room, but they said he'd already checked out.
3. I'm afraid we're not open on weekends, but if you come back on Monday we'll talk about it then.

Linking vowels

When a word ending in a vowel sound is followed by a word beginning with a vowel sound, they are linked with a /w/ or /j/ sound; for example, *so* /w/ *often*, and *the* /j/ *afternoon*.

Exercise A 139 Listen to these sentences. Notice how the /w/ and /j/ sounds are added.

1. Susan said she /j/ isn't going to /w/ Atlanta until the /j/ end of the month.
2. The /j/ easiest way to /w/ increase your salary is to /w/ ask for a raise.
3. Who /w/ is the /j/ only worker to have won three /j/ awards for excellence?

Exercise B 140 Listen to these sentences. Identify any /w/ and /j/ sounds.

1. Did you see anyone you recognized at the opening ceremony?
2. Let's go over the arrangements for the banquet if you're free on Friday.
3. We agree that there's no other option but to extend the application due date.

Intonation

Native speakers often vary the pitch of their voice in order to express attitude (surprise, frustration, etc.) and to facilitate communication. Understanding intonation can help improve your listening comprehension.

Intonation in *Yes/No* and *Wh-* questions

Intonation in *Yes/No* questions usually rises, whereas intonation in *Wh-* questions usually falls.

Exercise A 141 Listen to these questions. Notice the intonation.

1. Do you want to expand the business? [↑]
2. Did you decide to renew the lease? [↑]
3. Have you been taken on full-time? [↑]
4. Which stocks do you think we should invest in? [↓]
5. Why don't you transfer to a different department? [↓]
6. When do you expect the weather to improve? [↓]

Exercise B 142 Read these sentences. Predict the intonation; then listen and check.

1. Are you thinking about getting a Master's degree?   [↓]   [↑]
2. Who made the decision to delay the shipment to India?   [↓]   [↑]
3. Where did you take the digital camera to be repaired?   [↓]   [↑]
4. Didn't someone say the flight to Shelby was delayed?   [↓]   [↑]
5. How much time is left on the warranty for the printer?   [↓]   [↑]
6. Haven't you been told which supervisor to report to?   [↓]   [↑]

Intonation in question tags

For tag questions, rising intonation indicates a genuine question, while falling intonation asks for confirmation.

Exercise A 143 Listen to these questions. Notice the intonation.

1. The meeting's at ten, isn't it? [↑]
2. You don't work here, do you? [↑]
3. We've never met before, have we? [↑]
4. Mr. Fielding is away today, isn't he? [↓]
5. They'll have some catalogs at reception, won't they? [↓]
6. This office was refurbished recently, wasn't it? [↓]

Exercise B 144 Read these sentences. Then listen and check whether the intonation on each question tag rises or falls.

1. The tall guy standing over there's the mayor, isn't he?   [↓]   [↑]
2. We paid a deposit when we placed the order, didn't we?   [↓]   [↑]
3. That missing security key hasn't turned up yet, has it?   [↓]   [↑]
4. Each refresher course lasts two weeks, doesn't it?   [↓]   [↑]
5. You didn't get a call from Mrs. Wu this morning, did you?   [↓]   [↑]
6. We weren't the only ones to arrive late for the party, were we?   [↓]   [↑]

EXTRA PRACTICE ONLINE

Go to **www.pass-the-toeic-test.com** for advice and useful exercises to help you identify different accents and improve your listening comprehension.

▶ Improving Your Listening Skills

▶ Listening to Different Accents

▶ Recognizing Stress Patterns

Tips on Taking the TOEIC® Test

Here are some tips you might find useful to help you prepare for the TOEIC test.

Before the test…

- **Make sure you know the directions**

  If you are familiar with the format of each section, you can focus more on the questions. Take as many Practice Tests as you can to prepare you for the test. Go to **www.pass-the-toeic-test.com** to register for your two free online TOEIC Practice Tests.

- **Plan your study effectively**

  Practice your listening and reading comprehension skills. Identify what your strengths are, and focus on improving any weaknesses.

- **Expand your vocabulary as much as possible**

  Read as widely as you can. Make a note of all the new words you learn, and test yourself regularly.

In the test…

- **Time yourself**

  Keep a watch in front of you and check the time regularly. Make sure you know how long you should take on each part. Don't fall behind and run out of time! After marking your answer, quickly move on.

- **Stay alert and concentrate**

  The test lasts two hours, and it is easy to become distracted during this time. Make sure you focus all your energy on the test.

- **Never leave a blank**

  Always make a guess if you don't know the answer. You are not penalized for wrong answers, so you have nothing to lose.

- **Eliminate answer choices whenever you can**

  Your chances of guessing the correct answer increase if you first eliminate any answer choices you think are incorrect.

- **Be aware of distractors**

  Make sure you know the common traps used in the test, and avoid them.

- **Trust your instincts**

  Don't waste time changing your mind. Answer a question, and move on.

- **Use effective test-taking techniques**

  Don't forget to use the strategies you have covered in this book to help you achieve the best possible score. Make time to preview the questions whenever you can. Try to predict the answers. Remember that skimming and scanning are effective reading skills.

Go to **www.pass-the-toeic-test.com** for more advice, tips, and lots of practice exercises to help you prepare for the test.

Pass the TOEIC Test – *Advanced Course* Track List

Part 1

1. Overview – Example
2. Mini Test – Previewing Photographs
3. Avoiding Errors: Photograph 1 – Exercise A
4. Avoiding Errors: Photograph 2 – Exercise A
5. Avoiding Errors: Photograph 3 – Exercise A
6. Avoiding Errors: Photograph 4 – Exercise A
7. Avoiding Errors: Photograph 5 – Exercise A
8. Avoiding Errors: Photograph 6 – Exercise A
9. Mini Test – Avoiding Errors
10. Steps to Success – Practice 1
11. Steps to Success – Practice 2
12. Steps to Success – Practice 3
13. Review Test

Part 2

14. Overview – Example
15. Question Types – Exercise A
16. Question Types – Exercise B
17. Question Types – Exercise C
18. Question Types – Exercise D
19. Questions with *What*
20. Questions with *When* or *Where*
21. Mini Test – Questions with *What*, *When*, or *Where*
22. Questions with *Who*, *Whose*, *Why*, or *Which*
23. Questions with *How*
24. Mini Test – Questions with *Who*, *Whose*, *Why*, *Which*, or *How*
25. *Yes/No* Questions
26. *Choice* Questions
27. Mini Test – *Yes/No* Questions and *Choice* Questions
28. *Tag* Questions
29. *Negative* Questions and *Embedded* Questions
30. Mini Test – *Tag* Questions, *Negative* Questions and *Embedded* Questions
31. Statements – Exercise A
32. Statements – Exercise B
33. Mini Test – Statements
34. Avoiding Errors – Exercise A
35. Avoiding Errors – Exercise B
36. Mini Test – Avoiding Errors
37. Steps to Success – Practice 1
38. Steps to Success – Practice 2
39. Steps to Success – Practice 3
40. Review Test

Part 3

41. Overview – Example 1
42. Overview – Example 2
43. Overview – Example 3
44. Overview – Example 4
45. Mini Test – People, Times, and Offers
46. Mini Test – Topics, Reasons, and Advice
47. Mini Test – Locations, Feelings, and Suggestions
48. Mini Test – Activities, Requests, and Problems
49. Mini Test – Plans, Opinions, and Inferences
50. Understanding Inference and Implied Meaning - Exercise A3
51. Mini Test – Understanding Inference and Implied Meaning
52. Mini Test – Conversations Including a Graphic
53. Previewing Short Conversations
54. Previewing – Conversation 1
55. Previewing – Conversation 2
56. Previewing – Conversation 3
57. Previewing – Conversation 4
58. Mini Test – Previewing Short Conversations
59. Steps to Success – Practice 1
60. Steps to Success – Practice 2
61. Steps to Success – Practice 3
62. Steps to Success – Practice 4
63. Review Test

Part 4

64. Overview – Example 1
65. Overview – Example 2
66. Mini Test – Speakers, Opinions, and Inferences
67. Mini Test – Locations, Reasons, and Requests
68. Mini Test – Purpose, Problems, and Suggestions
69. Mini Test – Audience, Advice, and Plans
70. Mini Test – Topics, Times, and Sequences
71. Mini Test – Short Talks Including a Graphic
72. Previewing Short Talks
73. Previewing – Business Talks
74. Previewing – Recorded Announcements
75. Previewing – Advertisements
76. Previewing – Public Announcements
77. Previewing – News, Weather, and Traffic Reports
78. Previewing - Short Talk Including a Graphic
79. Mini Test – Previewing Short Talks
80. Steps to Success – Practice 1
81. Steps to Success – Practice 2
82. Steps to Success – Practice 3
83. Steps to Success – Practice 4
84. Review Test

Listening Comprehension Test

85. Listening Test – Part 1
86. Listening Test – Part 2
87. Listening Test – Part 3
88. Listening Test – Part 4

TOEIC Word List

89. A
90. B
91. C
92. D
93. E
94. F
95. G
96. H
97. I
98. J
99. K
100. L
101. M
102. N
103. O
104. P
105. Q
106. R
107. S
108. T
109. U
110. V
111. W
112. XYZ

Understanding Accents and Spoken English

113. Comparing Accents - Exercise A
114. Comparing Accents – Exercise B
115. American English – Exercise A
116. American English – Exercise B
117. British English – Exercise A
118. British English – Exercise B
119. Australian English – Exercise A
120. Australian English – Exercise B
121. Canadian English – Exercise A
122. Canadian English – Exercise B
123. Identifying Accents – Speaker 1
124. Identifying Accents – Speaker 2
125. Identifying Accents – Speaker 3
126. Identifying Accents – Speaker 4
127. Word Stress – Exercise A
128. Word Stress – Exercise B
129. The schwa – Exercise A
130. The schwa – Exercise B
131. Sentence Stress and Rhythm – Exercise A
132. Sentence Stress and Rhythm – Exercise B
133. Sentence Stress and Rhythm – Exercise C
134. Sentence Stress and Rhythm – Exercise D
135. Linking words – Exercise A
136. Linking words – Exercise B
137. Linking consonants and vowels – Exercise A
138. Linking consonants and vowels – Exercise B
139. Linking vowels – Exercise A
140. Linking vowels – Exercise B
141. Intonation in *Yes/No* and *Wh-* questions – Exercise A
142. Intonation in *Yes/No* and *Wh-* questions – Exercise B
143. Intonation in question tags – Exercise A
144. Intonation in question tags – Exercise B

Practice Test 1

145. Listening Test – Part 1
146. Listening Test – Part 2
147. Listening Test – Part 3
148. Listening Test – Part 4

Practice Test 2

149. Listening Test – Part 1
150. Listening Test – Part 2
151. Listening Test – Part 3
152. Listening Test – Part 4

About the Author

Miles Craven has worked in English language education since 1988, teaching in schools, colleges, and universities around the world. He is the author of several best-selling textbooks, and has a wide range of experience as a teacher, teacher-trainer, examiner, and materials writer. He currently acts as an advisor for Executive Education programs at The Møller Centre for Continuing Education Ltd., Churchill College, University of Cambridge, specializing in the design and delivery of management training programs for aspiring business leaders.

Notes

PRACTICE TESTS

Practice Test 1

This test aims to accurately reflect the TOEIC® test in every way possible. It consists of seven parts, and is designed to be the same level of difficulty as the TOEIC test. The test takes approximately two hours to complete.

Directions:

Allow two hours to complete the test.

Make sure you read the directions for each part carefully.

Mark all your answers on the separate Answer Sheet provided on page 318.

When you finish, you can check your answers in the separate Answer Key. See the Score Conversion Chart on page 320 for a prediction of your score on the TOEIC test.

Listening Test

The Listening Test is an opportunity for you to show how well you understand spoken English. There are four parts, and each part has different directions. You have 45 minutes to complete this Listening test.

Mark your answers on the separate Answer Sheet provided on page 318.

Part 1

145 **Directions:** For each question, you will hear four statements about a photograph. Listen and select the one statement: (A), (B), (C), or (D), that best describes the picture. Then mark your answer on the Answer Sheet. You will hear the statements only once.

EXAMPLE

The best description of the picture is statement (B), "A man's giving a presentation to a small group of people." You should mark answer choice (B) on your Answer Sheet.

GO ON TO THE NEXT PAGE ⮞

1.

2.

3.

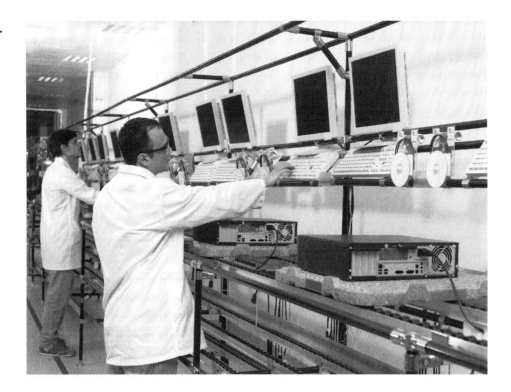

4.

GO ON TO THE NEXT PAGE ▶

5.

6.

Part 2

EXAMPLE

You hear: Would you mind helping me finish this report?

You then hear: (A) That's very kind of you.

(B) I thought you would.

(C) No, not at all.   Ⓐ Ⓑ ⬤

The best response to the question "Would you mind helping me finish this report?" is answer choice (C), "No, not at all." You should mark answer choice (C) on your Answer Sheet.

---

7. Mark your answer on the Answer Sheet.

8. Mark your answer on the Answer Sheet.

9. Mark your answer on the Answer Sheet.

10. Mark your answer on the Answer Sheet.

11. Mark your answer on the Answer Sheet.

12. Mark your answer on the Answer Sheet.

13. Mark your answer on the Answer Sheet.

14. Mark your answer on the Answer Sheet.

15. Mark your answer on the Answer Sheet.

16. Mark your answer on the Answer Sheet.

17. Mark your answer on the Answer Sheet.

18. Mark your answer on the Answer Sheet.

19. Mark your answer on the Answer Sheet.

20. Mark your answer on the Answer Sheet.

21. Mark your answer on the Answer Sheet.

22. Mark your answer on the Answer Sheet.

23. Mark your answer on the Answer Sheet.

24. Mark your answer on the Answer Sheet.

25. Mark your answer on the Answer Sheet.

26. Mark your answer on the Answer Sheet.

27. Mark your answer on the Answer Sheet.

28. Mark your answer on the Answer Sheet.

29. Mark your answer on the Answer Sheet.

30. Mark your answer on the Answer Sheet.

31. Mark your answer on the Answer Sheet.

GO ON TO THE NEXT PAGE

Part 3

147 **Directions:** You will hear thirteen conversations. For each conversation, read the three questions and the four answer choices that follow each question. Select the most appropriate answer: (A), (B), (C), or (D). Then mark your answer on the Answer Sheet. You will hear each conversation only once.

32. Who most likely is the man?
    (A) An accountant
    (B) A personal assistant
    (C) A senior executive
    (D) A technical supervisor

33. What does the woman ask the man to do?
    (A) Print a document
    (B) Check some figures
    (C) Complete a report
    (D) Give a presentation

34. What will the man probably do next?
    (A) Search for information
    (B) Contact the vice president
    (C) Speak with Mei-ling
    (D) Attend a meeting

35. Who most likely is the woman?
    (A) A movie actor
    (B) An advertising executive
    (C) A television repairperson
    (D) A media company executive

36. What can be inferred about television audiences in the 18–49 age group?
    (A) They have been declining in recent years.
    (B) They mostly watch TV on weekends.
    (C) They prefer movies to drama.
    (D) They do not like advertisements on television.

37. What does the woman suggest the man do?
    (A) Interview her again in two months
    (B) Watch more television
    (C) Ask a different question
    (D) Come back at the end of the year

38. What is the man concerned about?
    (A) His age
    (B) His work
    (C) His poor health
    (D) His weight

39. What does the woman mean when she says, "Yes, for sure"?
    (A) She understands the man's inquiry.
    (B) She agrees with the man's judgment.
    (C) She thinks the man looks fit and healthy.
    (D) She is not surprised the man is 58 years old.

40. What will the man most likely do now?
    (A) Have an examination
    (B) Discuss his health problems
    (C) Ask for personal information
    (D) Give the woman his credit card

41. What is the man's occupation?
    (A) Mail carrier
    (B) Bookseller
    (C) Travel agent
    (D) Real estate agent

42. What is suggested about Mr. Ishikawa?
    (A) He is on vacation.
    (B) He prefers living in Japan.
    (C) He lives in an apartment.
    (D) He did not leave a forwarding address.

43. What does the woman ask the man to do?
    (A) Order some more books
    (B) Go to the nearest post office
    (C) Contact Mr. Ishikawa urgently
    (D) Check if a delivery has arrived

44. Where are the speakers?
   (A) In a store
   (B) In a parking lot
   (C) At a train station
   (D) At a movie theater

45. What is the problem?
   (A) The line is too long.
   (B) The woman forgot to buy a ticket.
   (C) The woman has lost her purse.
   (D) The woman is unable to find her ticket.

46. What will the woman most likely do now?
   (A) Wait in line
   (B) Buy a ticket
   (C) Open her purse
   (D) Look in her pocket

47. Who most likely is the woman?
   (A) A teleworker
   (B) A telecommunications engineer
   (C) A support technician
   (D) An accountant

48. What is the problem?
   (A) The woman's headset is faulty.
   (B) A computer has stopped working.
   (C) Some figures are incorrect.
   (D) A product is no longer available.

49. What does the man ask the woman to do?
   (A) Phone him immediately
   (B) Change the computer settings
   (C) Work in a different office
   (D) Test a piece of equipment

50. Where does this conversation take place?
   (A) At a restaurant
   (B) At a hotel
   (C) At an airport
   (D) At a travel agency

51. What is implied about the man?
   (A) He did not make the reservation himself.
   (B) He has been in the area for ten days.
   (C) He has not eaten breakfast.
   (D) He usually wakes up early.

52. What will happen at 5:30 A.M. the next day?
   (A) The man's flight will depart.
   (B) The reservation system will be updated.
   (C) The man will receive a phone call.
   (D) The conference will begin.

53. In what industry does the woman work?
   (A) Printing
   (B) Publishing
   (C) Electronics
   (D) Shipping

54. What does the man mean when he says, "It's hopeless"?
   (A) There is no chance of improvement.
   (B) The product is very difficult to use.
   (C) The situation is extremely desperate.
   (D) It is impossible to solve the problem.

55. What does the woman promise to do in the afternoon?
   (A) Contact the production department
   (B) Speak to the printers
   (C) Send a package to the man
   (D) Provide a name and address

GO ON TO THE NEXT PAGE

56. Who most likely is the man?
    (A) A cashier
    (B) A plumber
    (C) An accountant
    (D) A business owner

57. What is the problem?
    (A) They cannot pay their bills.
    (B) The boiler has broken down.
    (C) Sales have fallen unexpectedly.
    (D) Staff salaries are too high.

58. What does the man mean when he says, "I'm not going to be beaten now"?
    (A) He is sure to succeed.
    (B) He is not willing to give up.
    (C) He feels safe and secure.
    (D) He would prefer a delay.

59. What are the speakers mainly discussing?
    (A) An office relocation
    (B) A security system
    (C) A training program
    (D) A product guarantee

60. Who is Jason Vickers?
    (A) A factory worker
    (B) A security guard
    (C) A staff manager
    (D) An installation engineer

61. Why does the woman say, "If you wouldn't mind"?
    (A) To make a request
    (B) To accept an offer
    (C) To query a decision
    (D) To suggest a compromise

Weather forecast		
City	Saturday 16	Sunday 17
Barcelona	24 degrees	25 degrees
Madrid	35 degrees	35 degrees
Milan	23 degrees	22 degrees
Rome	32 degrees	31 degrees

62. Why does the man suggest taking a city break?
   (A) He wants to celebrate the woman's birthday.
   (B) He has been given a promotion at work.
   (C) He recently won an online competition.
   (D) He received some money unexpectedly.

63. What do the speakers plan to do while they are away?
   (A) Sunbathe
   (B) See the sights
   (C) Go to a museum
   (D) Shop for clothes

64. Look at the graphic. Where will the couple most likely go?
   (A) Barcelona
   (B) Madrid
   (C) Milan
   (D) Rome

GO ON TO THE NEXT PAGE

65. Look at the graphic. Which room will the man go to first?
   (A) 212
   (B) 223
   (C) 304
   (D) 317

66. What does the woman ask the man to do after delivering the room-service items?
   (A) Help out in the kitchen
   (B) Wait for further orders
   (C) Serve in the restaurant
   (D) Check in a group of visitors

67. Why is the woman concerned?
   (A) There is a 20-minute delay.
   (B) Understaffing is causing problems.
   (C) One waiter is unreliable.
   (D) Some visitors have complained.

---

68. Look at the graphic. How much does the man pay for the tickets?
   (A) $20
   (B) $30
   (C) $40
   (D) $50

69. What does the man say about the park?
   (A) It is well-advertised.
   (B) It is extremely popular.
   (C) It received good reviews.
   (D) It has many good rides.

70. What does the woman advise the man to do?
   (A) Keep the tickets in a safe place
   (B) Be patient as the park is very busy
   (C) Come back within one year
   (D) Go first to the roller coaster

Belview Hotel

Room-service order number	Room
Mediterranean crab salad	212
Club sandwich	223
Avocado & tuna salad	304
Cheeseburger and fries	317

50% DISCOUNT!

SUNNY STATE FUN PARK

Please present this coupon to the Sunny State Fun Park Admissions Center to receive half price admission on a standard ticket for one adult or senior citizen.

Offer not valid with pre-purchased tickets. Offer cannot be combined with any other offer or discount. Coupon Code 8145.

Part 4

148 **Directions:** You will hear ten short talks given by a single speaker. For each short talk, read the three questions and the four answer choices that follow each question. Select the most appropriate answer: (A), (B), (C), or (D). Then mark your answer on the Answer Sheet. You will hear each short talk only once.

71. What is this report mainly about?
    (A) Contaminated medical drugs
    (B) A strike at a pharmaceutical company
    (C) The outbreak of an infectious disease
    (D) The publication of a health report

72. What has LixoPharm done about the problem?
    (A) Published a report
    (B) Written to patients
    (C) Issued a product recall
    (D) Called an emergency meeting

73. What should people who take the drug Mydoxovin do?
    (A) Consult with their family doctor
    (B) Change to another medication
    (C) Contact LixoPharm as soon as possible
    (D) Check the expiration date on the packets

74. Who is the audience for this talk?
    (A) Outdoor enthusiasts
    (B) Social club members
    (C) A group of elderly tourists
    (D) Wildlife conservationists

75. What are listeners reminded to do today?
    (A) Pay for an excursion
    (B) Sign a card
    (C) Visit the local hospital
    (D) Register for a fitness class

76. What will take place in July?
    (A) An annual convention
    (B) A pleasure trip
    (C) A seasonal event
    (D) A health conference

77. Where is this announcement being made?
    (A) At a hospital
    (B) At an airport
    (C) At a theater
    (D) At a college

78. What is the announcement about?
    (A) A fundraising event
    (B) A blood drive
    (C) A theatrical performance
    (D) A health examination

79. What are listeners advised to do?
    (A) Apply for travel insurance
    (B) Schedule an appointment quickly
    (C) Call Extension 752 for further details
    (D) Avoid parking in the staff parking lot

80. Where is this talk taking place?
    (A) In an art museum
    (B) In a palace
    (C) In a cave
    (D) In a zoo

81. What does the speaker imply when she says, "Incredible, isn't it?"?
    (A) One painting is extremely well-drawn.
    (B) Nothing like this has ever been done before.
    (C) The age of the paintings is remarkable.
    (D) It is hard to believe some of the facts.

82. What does the speaker say about the venue?
    (A) It benefits from natural light.
    (B) It is currently being repainted.
    (C) It opened two years ago.
    (D) It will close to the public shortly.

83. What is the main purpose of this talk?
    (A) To introduce a speaker
    (B) To welcome the audience
    (C) To wind up a conference
    (D) To pass on transportation information

84. Who is the audience for this talk?
    (A) Aspiring writers
    (B) Amateur photographers
    (C) Literary agents
    (D) Book publishers

85. What is the audience asked to do next?
    (A) Fill out a form
    (B) Go to a reception
    (C) Attend a presentation
    (D) Take a shuttle bus

86. Where is this announcement being made?
    (A) In an airplane
    (B) At an airport
    (C) At a sports stadium
    (D) At a drugstore

87. What does the speaker ask listeners to do?
    (A) Secure their valuables
    (B) Comply with regulations
    (C) Drink more liquids
    (D) Wear light clothing

88. What are listeners asked to remove?
    (A) Beach shoes
    (B) Hats
    (C) Watches
    (D) Wedding rings

89. Who is this advertisement directed at?
    (A) Industrial energy customers in the US
    (B) Home and business energy users
    (C) Energy suppliers across North America
    (D) Natural gas and electricity consumers

90. What are listeners promised?
    (A) Flexible repayment options
    (B) Capped service fees
    (C) Personalized price plans
    (D) Permanently low rates

91. What does the speaker imply when she says, "Why pay more?"?
    (A) Most users are paying too much for their energy.
    (B) Price increases are never justified.
    (C) Environmental considerations can mean higher prices.
    (D) Listeners can save money by switching to Luminex

92. Who is the speaker?
    (A) A mountaineer
    (B) A landscape gardener
    (C) A tree surgeon
    (D) A fashion designer

93. What is the main purpose of the talk?
    (A) To offer safety advice
    (B) To give time-saving hints
    (C) To recommend a product
    (D) To advise on personal grooming

94. According to the speaker, which item of clothing is optional?
    (A) A helmet
    (B) A jacket
    (C) Boots
    (D) Gloves

95. What problem was Mr. Lopez concerned about?
   (A) The loss of engine oil
   (B) Low tire pressure
   (C) An unusual noise
   (D) The cost of the repair

96. Look at the graphic. How much will Mr. Lopez need to pay for today's work?
   (A) $30
   (B) $80
   (C) $160
   (D) $250

97. What does the speaker say he will do?
   (A) Pick up Mr. Lopez' car
   (B) Leave work by 4 P.M.
   (C) Replace the engine gasket
   (D) Complete the work today

	Price ($)
Oil change	30
Tire (each)	80
Brake pads (per wheel)	160
Engine gasket replacement	250

98. Look at the graphic. On which aisle can shoppers get a 20% discount?
   (A) Aisle 4
   (B) Aisle 6
   (C) Aisle 14
   (D) Aisle 17

99. According to the speaker, what will listeners who buy a barbecue grill receive?
   (A) A complimentary gift
   (B) An $80 discount
   (C) A half price coupon
   (D) A discount on soft drinks

100. How long will the special discounts last?
   (A) Today only
   (B) Until tomorrow
   (C) Over the weekend
   (D) All week

	Aisle
Fish	4
Meat	6
Soft drinks	14
Barbecue grills	17

This is the end of the Listening Comprehension section of the test. Go on to the Reading section.

Reading Test

This Reading Test contains a variety of texts and reading comprehension questions. They are designed to test your ability to read and understand written English. There are three parts. You have 75 minutes to complete this section of the test.

Mark your answers on the separate Answer Sheet provided on page 318.

Part 5

Directions: Read each sentence. You will notice that there is a word or phrase missing. Study the four answer choices and select the one answer: (A), (B), (C), or (D), that best completes the sentence. Then mark your answer on the Answer Sheet.

101. Those residents of Delaware County on low incomes may be _____ to benefits and other financial assistance.
(A) entailed
(B) entered
(C) entitled
(D) entrusted

102. There are several reference books in the storeroom on the shelf, one of _____ will certainly contain the information you are looking for.
(A) these
(B) that
(C) whose
(D) which

103. The Statistics Division has _____ responsibility for gathering economic data and providing financial analysis.
(A) direct
(B) directed
(C) direction
(D) directly

104. TransPower Inc. has been awarded a license for oil and gas _____ off the south coast of Greenland.
(A) explore
(B) explorative
(C) explorer
(D) exploration

105. Dr. Wilkinson claimed to _____ me before at a previous conference, but I had no recollection of this myself.
(A) meet
(B) meeting
(C) have met
(D) be meeting

106. We can schedule the repairs for Tuesday or Wednesday next week; _____ days suit me.
(A) both
(B) each
(C) either
(D) every

107. Please could you confirm whether it is your _____ to return to work after the birth of your child.
(A) rationale
(B) meaning
(C) intention
(D) purpose

108. The management consultant we brought in has put _____ some very interesting suggestions for improving our company's performance.
(A) about
(B) on
(C) forward
(D) toward

109. Dr. Ueyama, our vice president, thinks we should reject the offer of a merger with JVW Engineering, and I am _____ to agree.
(A) inclined
(B) included
(C) incensed
(D) incited

110. During Karl Marshall's four-year _____ as governor, unemployment in the state fell by more than 20 percent.
(A) tenancy
(B) tendency
(C) tenor
(D) tenure

111. Older people usually pay a lot _____ for auto insurance because they are less likely to have accidents than other drivers.
(A) less
(B) lesser
(C) least
(D) fewer

112. Jack and Simon have known _____ for many years as they were at college together.
(A) each
(B) each other
(C) theirs
(D) themselves

113. Lisa Collins resigned as a trustee of the Arts Commission _____ to taking up her seat in government.
(A) before
(B) prior
(C) sooner
(D) already

114. The new policy on data protection and confidentiality is expected to be _____ before the end of the year.
(A) implement
(B) implemented
(C) implementing
(D) implementation

115. Ms. Leung is a fully qualified chemical engineer, _____ obtained her bachelor's degree ten years ago and her Professional Engineer (PE) license four years later.
(A) had
(B) has
(C) have
(D) having

116. Production of the new X10 electric car has been stepped up as there was _____ a positive response when it was unveiled at last month's trade fair.
(A) as
(B) so
(C) such
(D) what

117. One of the finest qualities of our outgoing chairman is that he is a man of his word, who always .... his promises.
(A) does
(B) keeps
(C) makes
(D) answers

118. .... the river divides the city, there are two quite distinct parts, and each has its own character.
(A) As well as
(B) However
(C) Because
(D) Due to

119. Most reports suggest that MFW Enterprises is trading broadly in .... with expectations, and remains debt-free.
(A) check
(B) line
(C) collaboration
(D) touch

120. Following .... of an associate's degree program in nursing, I decided to obtain an entry-level job and work toward my bachelor's degree.
(A) complete
(B) completed
(C) completing
(D) completion

121. At the trial, lawyers for Garnton Construction .... all allegations of wrongdoing during the bidding process.
(A) declined
(B) denied
(C) negated
(D) refused

122. We do not want to delay plans for the provision of a matching 401(k) plan, and our employees do not want it to be delayed ....
(A) either
(B) neither
(C) instead
(D) too

123. The economic crisis has meant that many workers are prepared to accept raises that fall .... of the actual inflation rate.
(A) short
(B) shortage
(C) shorten
(D) shortly

124. Florida Rentals offers vacation villas and furnished apartments that are situated .... the eastern coast of Florida, all with stunning ocean views.
(A) at
(B) in
(C) on
(D) behind

125. Since opening a new office in the capital, Carlton Shipping has embarked on a strong .... strategy and has enjoyed significant growth as a result.
(A) promote
(B) promoting
(C) promotional
(D) promoted

126. Although the digital scanners proved difficult to use at first, doctors and staff soon got .... to the new technology and diagnosis rates improved considerably.
(A) use
(B) used
(C) uses
(D) using

127. Such was the level of interest in the football coach's resignation that there were not .... enough chairs at the press conference for the number of journalists present.
(A) only
(B) very
(C) almost
(D) nearly

128. Antitrust laws can be .... through a civil or criminal action brought by an attorney, or through a lawsuit brought by a private individual.
(A) inflicted
(B) enforced
(C) compelled
(D) obliged

129. Patrons at the theater couldn't help .... when the protagonist accidentally fell while walking onto the stage at the beginning of the second act.
(A) laugh
(B) to laugh
(C) laughing
(D) laughter

130. Any government .... to bring in radical welfare reforms would need to secure a mandate from the electorate.
(A) propose
(B) to propose
(C) proposed
(D) proposing

GO ON TO THE NEXT PAGE

Part 6

Directions: Read each text. You will notice that there are four blanks. These are places where a word, phrase, or sentence is missing. For each blank, study the four answer choices and select the one answer: (A), (B), (C), or (D), that best completes the text. Then mark your answer on the Answer Sheet.

Questions 131-134 refer to the following memo.

MEMO

To: All Employees
From: Board of Directors
Re: Loss of Hanro Medical Contract

The sudden loss of a major contract can often lead to ....**131**........ about the future.

Hanro Medical's decision not to renew our healthcare management contract for Providence General Hospital, I know, has caused some nervousness and, inevitably, some rumors about what is going to happen within the company. ....**132**........

I can promise you that business will continue as usual. ....**133**........ the disappointing news, and the tough economic conditions, the board still expects to achieve the targets set last year. Moreover, several other major proposals ....**134**........ in due course, and we are confident of a positive outcome in at least one case and hopefully more. In the meantime, if you have any questions or concerns, please speak to any board member.

---

131. (A) speculate
     (B) speculative
     (C) speculation
     (D) speculators

132. (A) Allow me to provide some reassurance.
     (B) Thank you all for your concern.
     (C) This company was founded in 1985.
     (D) Future events can be hard to predict.

133. (A) Although
     (B) Despite
     (C) Regardless
     (D) Whereas

134. (A) will submit
     (B) have been submitted
     (C) are submitted
     (D) will be submitted

August 4

Ms. Julia Gomez
8426 Mast Boulevard
Santee, CA 92071

Dear Ms. Gomez:

We are pleased to inform you that your application for admission to Guadalajara Institute's International Graduate Program on Advanced Science and Technology has been accepted. You are hereby ....**135**............ admission to the PhD program starting next semester.

............**136**............ The International Student Guide and the Guadalajara Institute Fee Policy contain important information for your attention. Note that your tuition fees are due and payable ....**137**............ the date shown.

As you have been accepted into the preparatory program, we look forward ....**138**............ you on campus in the spring. Should you have any queries or require further information prior to your arrival, please do not hesitate to contact the Graduate Admissions Office.

Sincerely,

Maria Hernandez

Associate Dean of Graduate Studies

135. (A) approved
   (B) granted
   (C) consented
   (D) given

136. (A) May I congratulate you on achieving this qualification.
   (B) All programs are listed in our prospectus.
   (C) We are most grateful for your support.
   (D) Please take time to review the enclosed information.

137. (A) by
   (B) at
   (C) in
   (D) for

138. (A) seeing
   (B) to see
   (C) to seeing
   (D) see

GO ON TO THE NEXT PAGE

AutoMax reports a year-on-year surge in profits

The automotive parts manufacturer AutoMax, ...**139**............... fortunes have fluctuated erratically over the past decade, has reported an increase of almost 40 percent in its profits for the last fiscal year. Net profit amounted to $25.4 million, a 38.8 percent year-on-year increase.

Commenting on the results, company C.E.O. Victor Deng said: "Our continued ....**140**............... on providing our customers with better automotive components that match their evolving needs has helped us maintain our position as the automotive industry's top-performing company. These excellent results ....**141**............... achieved despite the extremely challenging economic climate last year. ....**142**............... We therefore expect to see even more improvement in our sales going forward in this fiscal year."

---

139. (A) who
(B) whose
(C) which
(D) that

140. (A) focus
(B) goal
(C) priority
(D) objective

141. (A) are
(B) had
(C) will be
(D) have been

142. (A) However, I believe this recession is finally over.
(B) Those were very difficult times indeed.
(C) I admit we were in trouble at one stage
(D) All companies were equally impacted by this.

Eastern Rail would like to .... **143** .... passengers that car parking at Turncroft station will be reduced from Monday, 17 March until Sunday, 30 April.

Work is taking place to expand Bramhall Main Line, as part of the electrification of the line northwards towards Market Harborough, Kettering and Corby. This will provide a quieter and cleaner railway for passengers and those living nearby.

.... **144** .... , the bridge north of the station needs to be demolished and reconstructed 300m further up the line. Eastern Rail engineers .... **145** .... two cranes in the car park at Turncroft station to allow this upgrade work to be carried out. .... **146** .... Parking for disabled passengers will not be affected.

143. (A) remind
(B) prompt
(C) announce
(D) reveal

144. (A) In this regard
(B) Afterwards
(C) Successively
(D) As a result

145. (A) have used
(B) will be using
(C) are used
(D) had been using

146. (A) We appreciate your continued participation.
(B) Permission must always be obtained in advance.
(C) There will therefore be a reduction in parking spaces.
(D) This construction requires hard work and perseverance.

GO ON TO THE NEXT PAGE

Part 7

Directions: Read the texts. You will notice that each text is followed by several questions. For each question, decide which of the four answer choices: (A), (B), (C), or (D), best answers the question. Then mark your answer on the Answer Sheet.

Questions 147–148 refer to the following notice.

Lake County
Curbside Recycling Collection

Electrical Items

Please remove all batteries and place small electrical items in this bag, or in any regular-sized plastic shopping bag clearly labeled "electrical items." Put batteries in a separate, clear plastic bag. Leave all bags with your other waste on your regular trash collection day.

Yes, please ✓	No, thank you ✗
• small household electrical appliances • clocks and watches • calculators • flashlights • cameras • cell phones • power tools • small electronic toys	• nonelectrical items • fluorescent light bulbs and tubes • electronics containing refrigerants (e.g., air conditioners) • heavy or bulky items (e.g., ranges or microwave ovens) • disassembled TVs and monitors

Batteries can also be taken to any recycling center listed on the county hazardous materials and waste disposal website at www.lakecountyrecycles.org.

---

147. Who is this notice intended for?
(A) Recycling managers
(B) Public sector employees
(C) Residents of Lake County
(D) Garbage truck drivers

148. According to the notice, what items are NOT suitable for recycling in this way?
(A) Alarm clocks
(B) Hair dryers
(C) Camcorders
(D) Dishwashers

Questions 149–150 refer to the following live chat discussion.

| **Chris** from UChoose | 1:52 P.M. |

Hello again, Philip. Welcome back to our site. How may I help you?

| **PhilipT** | 1:53 P.M. |

I just received the Karlssen dinner service (Item KDS768), but there was hardly any packaging in the box and three plates are cracked. Very disappointed.

| **Chris** from UChoose | 1:55 P.M. |

I am so sorry about that. We'll take care of this for you right now. Would you be able to send back the three cracked plates so we can replace these for you?

| **PhilipT** | 1:59 P.M. |

Thanks, but I'd rather return the lot. They're not as well-made as I was looking for anyway, and they are smaller than I thought.

| **Chris** from UChoose | 2:00 P.M. |

That's fine, Philip. Our returns policy allows you to return unwanted or faulty items within 28 days. You just need your receipt, and shipping is free. You can print out a returns label via the Web site.

| **PhilipT** | 2:02 P.M. |

Can you send me a link to that page?

| **Chris** from UChoose | 2:03 P.M. |

Sure. But before I do, is there anything else I can do for you today? Maybe I can help you choose a replacement to make up for this problem?

| **PhilipT** | 2:04 P.M. |

That's OK. I have to go out in 5m.

---

149. What is NOT mentioned as a reason for returning the goods?

(A) Size
(B) Price
(C) Condition
(D) Quality

150. At 2:04 P.M., what does Philip mean when he writes, "That's OK"?

(A) He is satisfied with the outcome.
(B) He would rather decline Chris' offer.
(C) He accepts the apology for the problem.
(D) He is agreeing to Chris' suggestion.

GO ON TO THE NEXT PAGE

Invoice

Shipment date: August 14

From: Andrews Automotives, 1225 Johnson Street, Santa Fe, NM 87503

....

Ref: Joseph Tang, Purchasing Department

....

Ship to: Metallido Inc., Avenida de Colombia, Buenos Aires, Argentina

Phone: 011-54-11-5555-0163

Description of goods	No. units	Unit weight	Total weight	Unit value (US$)	Value (US$)
Defective motor vehicle parts	5	12kg (26lb)	60kg (132lb)	1,100	5,500

Country of origin of shipment: USA　　　　Total value: $5,500　　　　Waybill No. 88755900/04

NOTE: No commercial value – goods not for resale. Value declared for customs purposes only. Contents of this shipment are being returned to the manufacturer. Nonhazardous goods.

I certify that the information on this declaration is true and correct to the best of my knowledge.

Name: Joseph Tang　　　　　　Signature: *J. Tang*

---

151. Where were the goods listed on the form manufactured?
(A) Argentina
(B) Colombia
(C) Mexico
(D) USA

152. Who does Joseph Tang work for?
(A) A shipping company
(B) US Customs and Border Protection
(C) Andrews Automotives
(D) Metallido Inc.

153. What can be inferred about the goods?
(A) They violate import regulations.
(B) They have been poorly manufactured.
(C) Their resale value is very low.
(D) They pose a risk to the environment.

Questions 154–156 refer to the following information.

Fungumin® lotion contains an active ingredient that is clinically proven to penetrate the skin between the toes and kill the fungus right where it started. It provides effective relief from itching, redness, and irritation. Improvement should be visible within 1–2 weeks.

Apply a thin coat to clean and dry affected areas twice a day with clean fingers. Use as directed. Do not swallow, and do not touch the eyes after applying the lotion. If you are currently taking any medication, please inform your physician that you are using Fungumin®.

Fungumin® is not suitable for:

- new and expectant mothers
- children under 12
- anyone with a milk allergy

154. For which part of the body is Fungumin designed?
(A) Eyes
(B) Feet
(C) Hands
(D) Mouth

155. How is the medication administered?
(A) It is inhaled through the nostrils.
(B) It is injected into the affected area.
(C) It is drunk in liquid form.
(D) It is applied directly onto the skin.

156. Who should avoid using this medication?
(A) Teenagers who are intolerant to gluten
(B) People who are allergic to nuts
(C) Pregnant women
(D) Anyone taking other medication

GO ON TO THE NEXT PAGE

Questions 157–158 refer to the following text message chain.

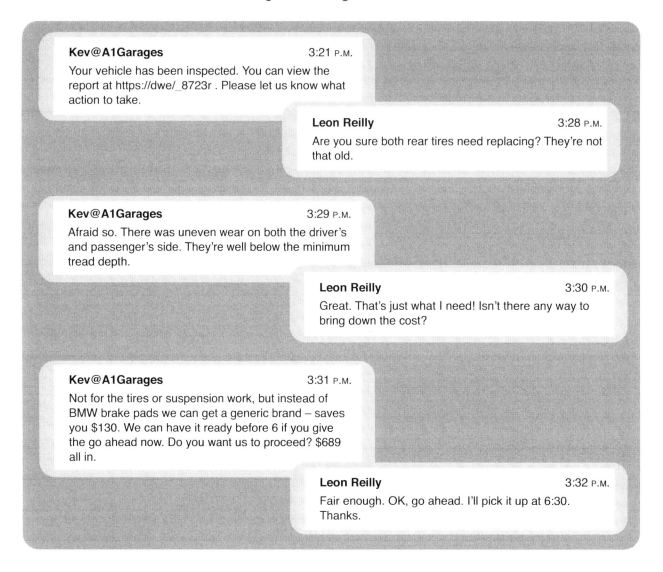

Kev@A1Garages   3:21 P.M.

Your vehicle has been inspected. You can view the report at https://dwe/_8723r . Please let us know what action to take.

Leon Reilly   3:28 P.M.

Are you sure both rear tires need replacing? They're not that old.

Kev@A1Garages   3:29 P.M.

Afraid so. There was uneven wear on both the driver's and passenger's side. They're well below the minimum tread depth.

Leon Reilly   3:30 P.M.

Great. That's just what I need! Isn't there any way to bring down the cost?

Kev@A1Garages   3:31 P.M.

Not for the tires or suspension work, but instead of BMW brake pads we can get a generic brand – saves you $130. We can have it ready before 6 if you give the go ahead now. Do you want us to proceed? $689 all in.

Leon Reilly   3:32 P.M.

Fair enough. OK, go ahead. I'll pick it up at 6:30. Thanks.

---

157. At 3:30 P.M., what does Mr. Reilly mean when he writes, "Great. That's just what I need!"?

(A) He wants the minimum work done.

(B) He is disappointed at the news.

(C) He is happy the inspection met his needs.

(D) He thinks the analysis is exactly right.

158. What is suggested about Mr. Reilly?

(A) He had a traffic accident recently.

(B) He owns a very old classic car.

(C) He is a regular client at A1 Garages.

(D) He thinks the repair cost is reasonable.

Questions 159–161 refer to the following table of contents.

159. Who is this book intended for?
(A) Business students
(B) College professors
(C) Telephone operators
(D) Company employees

160. Advice on which topic would most likely NOT appear in this book?
(A) Customer retention
(B) Courteous behavior
(C) Customer base erosion
(D) Measuring customer service

161. On which page can advice on greeting customers most likely be found?
(A) 8
(B) 13
(C) 24
(D) 30

GO ON TO THE NEXT PAGE

VeriLex Reveals Plans for Recovery

Favorable tax rates and the increasing popularity of home computers were not enough to rescue VeriLex from a disappointing year. ---[1]--- The company's focus on inkjet printers and supplies significantly impacted its revenue, given the falling cost of laser printers, which are now the preferred choice of more and more small businesses and home users. ---[2]---

While VeriLex received a boost from the sale of its factory in Johor Bahru, Malaysia, the company's net earnings showed a year-on-year decrease of 9 percent. ---[3]--- At a press conference yesterday, Chief Executive William Lam was cautiously optimistic about the company's prospects for the forthcoming year. ---[4]--- He used the opportunity to announce a number of measures that the company plans to implement. These include a workforce restructuring plan, consolidation of existing manufacturing facilities, and changes to employees' contractual terms and conditions. Mr. Lam promised that generous severance packages would be offered to all those wishing to take early retirement.

162. In which position marked [1], [2], [3], and [4] does the following sentence best belong?
"This has led to rumors of more closures ahead."
(A) [1]
(B) [2]
(C) [3]
(D) [4]

163. What can be inferred about VeriLex?
(A) It is going through a difficult time.
(B) It manufactures computers.
(C) Its headquarters are in Malaysia.
(D) Its net earnings increased last year.

164. What will the company most likely do next year?
(A) Encourage voluntary retirement
(B) Decrease the retirement age for its employees
(C) Close more manufacturing facilities
(D) Increase production of laser printers

MEMO

To: All staff
From: Vicky Mendoza

We have Sameer Khan, Senior Purchasing Manager at Trent Harlow Clothing, visiting our office tomorrow at approximately 1:15 P.M., initially for a quick tour of the building, followed by a presentation by senior management in the boardroom.

Trent Harlow is a major wholesaler and we want to do everything we can to impress Mr. Khan while he is here. I know that you will all make him welcome when you see him, but can I ask you to ensure that your workstation and surrounding area is clear and tidy, there are no sewing machine or computer cables trailing across the floor, and any fabric bolts, samples, finished garments, etc., are safely stored away?

Vicky

165. Why was this memo written?
- (A) To welcome a new employee
- (B) To invite staff to a presentation
- (C) To make a request of staff
- (D) To warn of a factory inspection

166. Who most likely is Vicky?
- (A) A cleaning contractor
- (B) An office manager
- (C) Mr. Khan's secretary
- (D) A health and safety inspector

167. The word "trailing" in paragraph 2, line 4, is closest in meaning to
- (A) sagging
- (B) hauling
- (C) laying
- (D) shifting

Global Parking Rates on the Rise

The cost of parking increased almost everywhere in the world over the past 12 months. Only the United States did not follow the trend. That's the conclusion of a report published this week in *Business Car User* magazine, which listed two "Top Tens" of the most expensive cities for parking, depending on whether you pay for parking your car on a daily or monthly basis.

No single global region dominates the "Top Ten" lists of most expensive places to park your car. ---[1]--- Cities in North America, Europe, and the Asia-Pacific region appear on both lists. ---[2]--- Latin America is the only region not represented, although parking rates in all major South American cities increased by between 10 and 20 percent.

For the fourth year in succession London comes out on top for monthly parking rates by a margin of more than 20 percent. Zürich replaces Hong Kong in second position, because of last year's dramatic rise in the value of the Swiss franc. Zürich monthly parking costs were $765 (705 Swiss francs)—no change in local currency, but an increase of over 30 percent in US dollars. ---[3]--- Two Australian cities—Sydney and Melbourne—made the top ten.

Things look slightly different on the list of daily parking rates. European cities dominate in this category, with London, Copenhagen, Stockholm, Geneva, Zürich, and Vienna all being beaten for the top spot by Oslo. The only non-European cities on the list are Sydney, Tokyo, and Toronto. Wherever you live in the world, the report predicts that parking is bound to become a bigger expense as time goes on. ---[4]---

168. In which position marked [1], [2], [3], and [4] does the following sentence best belong?
"The hike in charges shows no sign of slowing."
(A) [1]
(B) [2]
(C) [3]
(D) [4]

169. Which city has the highest daily parking rates?
(A) Hong Kong
(B) London
(C) New York
(D) Oslo

170. According to the report, where did parking rates NOT increase?
(A) Asia-Pacific
(B) Australia
(C) Europe
(D) The United States

171. What can be inferred about monthly parking rates in Zürich?
(A) They are similar to rates in Sydney.
(B) They are cheaper than Hong Kong rates.
(C) They are subsidized by the Swiss government.
(D) They are the same as a year ago.

Questions 172–175 refer to the following information.

REALREVIEWS4YOU.COM

Vacation Report

Resort	Days Open Last Year	Visitors' Comments
Alpine Falls	157	• Challenging terrain • Soaring peaks • Slow lifts • Minimal cell phone reception
Crystal Valley	245	• Pricey • Great scenery • Terrific variety of ski areas • Exhilarating slopes • Accessible runs • Fun town, but very crowded
Eglantine	145	• Long runs, some very challenging • Fast and efficient lift system • Heavenly views • Good transportation connections; not hard to get to
Santa Jose	131	• Great variety of terrain • Great training for beginners • Friendly staff • Family-friendly • Good restaurants on the mountain and in town
Willow Creek	192	• Relatively uncrowded • Quaint and charming town • Two major ski circuits • Hard to get to

Real reviews from real travelers. You won't find a more genuine or more reliable source of information on the web.

Why not contribute your own review? Good or bad, we want to read about your experiences. Add your comments below.

SUBMIT

172. What is stated about Crystal Valley?
(A) It is not worth the cost.
(B) Accommodations are easy to find.
(C) It is less busy than Alpine Falls.
(D) It has the longest season.

173. Which place is described as especially good for people with children?
(A) Alpine Falls
(B) Crystal Valley
(C) Eglantine
(D) Santa Jose

174. What can be inferred about Willow Creek?
(A) It is a bustling and lively town.
(B) It is a good destination for families.
(C) It is situated in a remote location.
(D) It is open for less than six months of the year.

175. What is implied about the reviews?
(A) They are trustworthy.
(B) They are written by journalists.
(C) They are up-to-date.
(D) They are very popular.

GO ON TO THE NEXT PAGE

PRACTICE TEST 1   373

Palmsville Business Networking Chapter

Helping you grow your business

- Gain new business leads
- Increase your client base
- Generate referrals for your business
- Improve your networking skills
- Share ideas and referrals with like-minded business professionals

The Palmsville Business Networking Chapter is a networking and referral organization for local small business owners in Palmsville. We're a friendly bunch of men and women of all ages and guarantee you a warm welcome.

The Palmsville Business Networking Chapter is an "exclusive" referral organization, which means that only one member per trade category is allowed. That means no competition for you!

We meet for a very convivial lunch on the second Thursday of every month at the Bounty Steakhouse, 1441 Elysian Way, Palmsville. We invite a guest speaker to speak on a topic of interest to members six times a year. Our meetings begin at 12:30 P.M. and conclude at 2:00 P.M.

There are no fees to join. Why not come along to our next meeting? You'll be happy you did!

To:	contact@palmbus.org
From:	cano@dalecounty.net
Date:	October 4
Subject:	Membership inquiry

Dear Sir/Madam,

I am writing because I would like to join the Palmsville Business Networking Chapter. My friend Natalie Bowman is one of your members and recommended your group very highly. Natalie and I met when we were both attending Rayleigh School of Floral Design six years ago and now we both have florist shops in Palmsville. Even though she opened her shop only two years ago, a year after I opened mine, her business is far more successful, and she says that this is in large part thanks to your organization. This is why I, too, would like to join. I would be a reliable member—Thursday is a good day for me—and would be willing to serve on one of your committees, or help out in any other way.

Please send me an application form, or tell me how I should go about applying for membership.

Thank you.

Paula Cano

Owner, Artistic Flowers of Distinction

176. How frequently does the Palmsville
Business Networking Chapter meet?
(A) Once a week
(B) Twice a week
(C) Once a month
(D) Once every two months

177. Which of the following benefits of
membership does the flyer NOT mention?
(A) Gaining customers
(B) Meeting people
(C) Getting advice on public speaking
(D) Meeting in a friendly atmosphere

178. How long has Paula Cano been in her
current business?
(A) One year
(B) Two years
(C) Three years
(D) Six years

179. Why will Ms. Cano's application for
membership most likely be turned down?
(A) She is unable to attend every meeting.
(B) She does not live in the area of Palmsville
covered by the chapter.
(C) She cannot offer a sufficient number of
referrals per month.
(D) She has a business that is similar to
another member's.

180. In the flyer, the word "convivial" in paragraph
3, line 1, is closest in meaning to
(A) friendly
(B) intimate
(C) businesslike
(D) practical

FOUR CORNERS

The Cultural and History Tour Specialists
3650 O Street NW
Washington, DC 20057

www.fourcornerstours.com

Spotlight Chicago, April 23–25

This new "Spotlight" tour represents a departure from our usual weeklong tours and travel experiences. This inaugural two-night tour offers an extraordinary palette of color and creativity from all eras and from all traditions. Not only will we be visiting the world-famous Art Institute of Chicago, but during the weekend we will also visit the Museum of Contemporary Art Chicago and the National Museum of Mexican Art. The tour is led by Dr. June Rubenstein, currently senior lecturer in art history at the Chicago Institute of the Creative Arts. The weekend begins with a lecture, accompanied by slides, given by Dr. Rubenstein, and she will then escort us around the museums with her expert commentary.

Price: $240 per person. (Based on two people sharing. Single supplement: $60.)

Included in price
Accommodations: 2 nights with continental breakfast at the Heppleton Hotel on Michigan Avenue ("The Magnificent Mile").

Services of Dr. June Rubenstein.

Optional (not included)
Shuttle bus from O'Hare International Airport to the hotel on Friday evening. Please state when booking whether you require this service.

Please reserve your place by visiting our website (www.fourcornerstours.com). Alternatively, call our team of travel advisors at 202-555-0190. If you prefer, you can book by letter, enclosing a check for the full amount or your credit card information. Please include the tour reference number, CHI75T.

Please note that this tour is moderately strenuous. Participants should be physically fit and able to stand and/or walk for up to 90 minutes at a time.

March 2

Four Corners
3650 O Street NW
Washington, DC 20057

To Whom It May Concern:

Please reserve a single room on your two-night Chicago weekend next month, ref. CHI75T. I enclose a check for $240, as requested. Please note that I am fit and healthy, and have no special requirements. I will not need to take advantage of the shuttle bus service from the airport. I will be reporting on the Athletic Trials taking place at the University of Chicago for my paper all that week, and will be staying in another hotel downtown, so will not have far to come.

Sincerely,

Lisa Gonzales

181. Who would most likely be interested in the tour?

(A) Historians

(B) Sports fans

(C) Art lovers

(D) Senior citizens

182. What is stated about the tour?

(A) All meals are included in the price.

(B) Some lectures are optional.

(C) Most participants are from Chicago.

(D) It may not be suitable for some people.

183. What can be inferred about the company, Four Corners?

(A) It has never offered a two-night tour before.

(B) This is the first time it has arranged a trip to Chicago.

(C) It only recently engaged the services of Dr. Rubenstein.

(D) It organizes cultural tours and vacations in many countries.

184. What most likely is Ms. Gonzales' profession?

(A) Athlete

(B) Artist

(C) Journalist

(D) Professor

185. What mistake did Ms. Gonzales make?

(A) She did not give her credit card number.

(B) She paid the wrong amount.

(C) She did not telephone in advance.

(D) She forgot to reserve the shuttle bus service.

GO ON TO THE NEXT PAGE

Questions 186–190 refer to the following information from a Web page, letter, and e-mail.

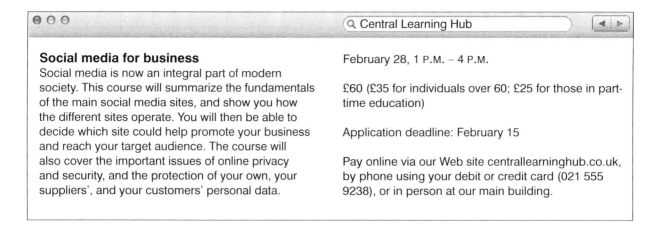

Social media for business
Social media is now an integral part of modern society. This course will summarize the fundamentals of the main social media sites, and show you how the different sites operate. You will then be able to decide which site could help promote your business and reach your target audience. The course will also cover the important issues of online privacy and security, and the protection of your own, your suppliers', and your customers' personal data.

February 28, 1 P.M. – 4 P.M.

£60 (£35 for individuals over 60; £25 for those in part-time education)

Application deadline: February 15

Pay online via our Web site centrallearninghub.co.uk, by phone using your debit or credit card (021 555 9238), or in person at our main building.

---

4 Cherry Court
Blandford Avenue
Birmingham
B33 4QJ

February 12
Central Learning Hub
North Street
Birmingham B2 4JJ

Dear Sir/Madam,

Please enrol me in the Social Media for Business course on February 28. I enclose a cheque for £25 to cover the cost of the course.

I tried but failed to enrol via your website, as it would not accept payment from my card. Anyway, for your records and for any future communications, please use my e-mail address b.bennet@bennet.co.uk.

Yours truly,
Barbara Bennet
Barbara Bennet

E-mail	
From:	admin@centrallearninghub.co.uk
To:	enrolment@centrallearninghub.co.uk
Date:	February 25
Subject:	URGENT: class time change

Dear Students,

Due to a burst water pipe and ongoing safety issues, some classrooms at the Central Learning Hub's main building in North Street are out of use for the remainder of this week. Electricians and plumbers are working on the ground floor and the disruption is too great to allow classes nearby to continue. Consequently, the following classes will now take place in Classroom 14 on the second floor. Please also note that because the morning classes on this floor run until 1 P.M., these rescheduled classes will start 30 minutes later than advertised:

Wednesday February 26: Getting started in social media
Thursday February 27: Introduction to online marketing
Friday February 28: Social media for business

If you have any questions, please contact our admin office by replying to this e-mail, or telephone 021 555 9200.

We are sorry for any inconvenience caused.

Sincerely,
Jamila Roe
Central Learning Hub

---

186. According to the Web page, what will NOT be covered on the Social Media for Business course?
(A) Computing skills
(B) Data protection
(C) Information privacy
(D) Internet security

187. In what way has Ms. Bennet failed to follow the enrolment guidelines?
(A) She supplied incorrect personal details.
(B) She did not submit her application in person.
(C) She applied after the deadline date.
(D) She used an ineligible form of payment.

188. What can be inferred about Ms. Bennet?
(A) She is a student.
(B) She owns a business.
(C) She is in debt.
(D) She lacks online access.

189. What is suggested about the Central Learning Hub?
(A) There was a security breach.
(B) There has been flooding.
(C) Protesters have caused damage.
(D) The building is being refurbished.

190. At what time will the Social Media for Business course now start?
(A) 1:00 P.M.
(B) 1:15 P.M.
(C) 1:30 P.M.
(D) 2:00 P.M.

GO ON TO THE NEXT PAGE

ATTENTION ALL RESIDENTS

In light of the theft of Ms. Young's bicycle from the lobby area this past September, it was suggested at the Residents' Meeting on December 12 that we update our entry security system. Currently, residents have to manually open the main entry door to let in their visitors, and this is inconvenient, especially for the residents of Apartments 5-8 on the second floor, who need to come all the way down the stairs. As a result, the main entry door is usually left unlocked, with obvious security implications.

After some discussion, Mr. Lucas of Apartment No. 8 offered to research suitable video entry systems, which would enable occupants of all apartments to view visitors via a monitor installed in their apartment and open the door electronically. Some residents were concerned about the cost of such systems, and it was decided to set the maximum budget at $600 per apartment. Mr. Lucas will report his findings to fellow residents before the next Association meeting in March of next year, so that they can be discussed at the meeting.

Video Intercom System

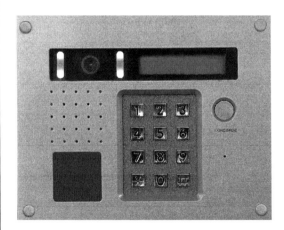

Uses a keypad door station with proximity card access

Includes: digital touch screen monitors, swipe tags, and related products to complete a full installation.

Ideal for builders and property developers looking for a high-quality apartment video intercom system at a competitive price.

Suitable for apartment buildings with up to 4 apartments

Kit Includes:
4 x 7" Monitor – white
4 x Swipe tags
1 x Apartment door entry station with Keypad and proximity card reader
1 x box for mounting the door station
2 x Lithium batteries
Installation manual

12 months Warranty
[Instructions for use available online]

E-mail

From:	j_lucas@mymail.net
To:	E-mail group: all residents
Subject:	Proposed video entry system

Dear all,

I have now had a chance to look into suitable entry security systems for our building. I've done extensive research and have identified what I think is the best option for us. At our last meeting in December, several people were worried about cost, and rightly so, as these systems are expensive. However, I think I have a fair and equitable solution (see manufacturer's Web page here).

It will involve minimal disruption, as the monitors can either be easily attached to the wall or they can be free-standing on any surface. More importantly, if you accept my solution, this system is within our budget.

Please do not bombard me with questions or comments now. All discussion can wait until the Residents' Association meeting next month, when we are all together.

Thanks,
Joe Lucas
Apartment #8

191. What is indicated about the apartment building?
(A) It has been burglarized.
(B) It is fitted with an elevator.
(C) It is in a crime hotspot.
(D) Its occupants have a low income.

192. In the e-mail, the word "bombard" in paragraph 3, line 1, is closest in meaning to
(A) frustrate
(B) overwhelm
(C) inspire
(D) support

193. What is NOT included in the video entry system?
(A) A user guide
(B) A warranty
(C) A video screen
(D) Batteries

194. In which month did Mr. Lucas write the e-mail?
(A) September
(B) December
(C) February
(D) March

195. What most likely is the 'solution' Mr. Lucas refers to?
(A) Each resident should choose if they want the security system.
(B) Residents do not have to attach the monitors to their walls.
(C) Some residents should contribute more towards the cost.
(D) Only apartments on the second floor should have the system.

MEMO

Date: September 6
Subject: Visit by Mr. Fumio Kato (Japanese Trade Organization)

Next Tuesday we will host a visit by Mr. Kato, Chairman of the Japanese Trade Organization. This is very important for Rainford Clinical Packaging, since we are hoping to grow our operations in the Far East. We must therefore leave Mr. Kato with a very good impression of our company.

Final go-ahead from Tokyo is still pending, so we are not sure how long Mr. Kato can spend with us. However, this is the program as it currently stands:

10:30 – 11:00   Welcome (in my office). I will give Mr. Kato a general overview of our company.

11:00 – 12:00   Tour of factory and other facilities including; bottle-filling, syringe-assembly, pumps and sprays, blister packs, as well as the labeling department, and research laboratories. Mr. Kato will be introduced to workers in each of these departments, who have been briefed already.

12:00 – 12:45   Lunch (45m – the quickest the chef can do) in the Board Room with members of the Board, and members of the Workers' Consultation Committee.

12:45 – 13:30   Visit to warehouse, followed by visit to Quality Control (if time).

13:30 – 14:00   Official photos (in my office). Board members to attend. Refreshments.

We will have to be flexible on the day. If Mr. Kato has to cut short his visit, we can postpone lunch by up to thirty minutes and extend the morning tour until 12:15 or 12:30 to include a visit to the warehouse.

Thank you all in advance for your cooperation. I will keep you updated on details of this visit.

Verna Mondi

CEO

E-mail

From:	s_watanabe@jto.jp.org
To:	v.mondi@rainfordclinicalpackaging.com
Date:	September 7
Subject:	Visit on September 12

Dear Ms. Mondi:

This e-mail is to inform you that, due to being required to attend important Ministry discussions next week, Mr. Fumio Kato will not be able to visit your company as planned, on Tuesday September 12. In his place will be Ms. Akemi Matsumoto, the Executive Vice President of our organization. Ms. Matsumoto speaks excellent English, and is very much looking forward to her visit to your factory and meeting as many of your employees and managers as possible. She has heard a lot about what you do there, and is eager to see for herself.

Due to another commitment that afternoon Ms. Matsumoto has asked me to tell you that she will need to leave Rainford Clinical Packaging premises after lunch at 1:00 P.M. An embassy driver will be taking Ms. Matsumoto to her appointments next week. Could you please arrange for a parking space to be available for the duration of her visit?

Thank you.

Sachiko Watanabe
Executive assistant, Japanese Trade Organization

PRESS RELEASE

FOR IMMEDIATE PUBLICATION

September 13 Rainford Clinical Packaging yesterday welcomed Ms. Matsumoto, Executive Vice President of the Tokyo-based Japanese Trade Organization, at its factory in Arrington Business Park. Ms. Matsumoto visited Rainford as part of a nationwide tour of companies with business interests in Japan. She visited the manufacturing areas where Rainford's state-of-the-art packaging is made, and also saw the bottling and other packaging areas where Rainford packages liquid and solid medicines on behalf of its pharmaceutical clients. Mr. Matsumoto met board directors, departmental managers, workers, and trade union representatives. Verna Mondi, CEO of Rainford Clinical Packaging said that Ms. Matsumoto's visit had been a great success, confirming that she had been very impressed with Rainford's facilities, and that the company hoped to strengthen its ties with Japan in the future.

196. What is indicated about Rainford Clinical Packaging?
(A) It manufactures medicines and clinical drugs.
(B) It is seeking to expand its business in Asia.
(C) It does not currently export its products abroad.
(D) It employs an international workforce.

197. What is true about Ms. Matsumoto?
(A) She speaks several foreign languages fluently.
(B) She has visited Rainford on a previous occasion.
(C) She works for a government trade organization.
(D) She will drive to the factory in the morning.

198. In the memo, the word "pending" in paragraph 2, line 1, is closest in meaning to
(A) to be confirmed
(B) imminent
(C) unresolved
(D) approaching

199. What time will lunch most probably be served?
(A) 11:45 A.M.
(B) 12:00 P.M.
(C) 12:15 P.M.
(D) 12:30 P.M.

200. Which department was omitted from Ms. Matsumoto's visit?
(A) Bottling
(B) Research
(C) Labeling
(D) Quality Control

This is the end of the test. If you finish with time to spare, you may go back to Parts 5, 6, and 7 to check your answers.

Practice Test 2

This test aims to accurately reflect the TOEIC® test in every way possible. It consists of seven parts, and is designed to be the same level of difficulty as the TOEIC test. The test takes approximately two hours to complete.

Directions:

Allow two hours to complete the test.

Make sure you read the directions for each part carefully.

Mark all your answers on the separate Answer Sheet provided on page 319.

When you finish, you can check your answers in the separate Answer Key. See the Score Conversion Chart on page 320 for a prediction of your score on the TOEIC test.

Listening Test

The Listening Test is an opportunity for you to show how well you understand spoken English. There are four parts, and each part has different directions. You have 45 minutes to complete this Listening test.

Mark your answers on the separate Answer Sheet provided on page 319.

Part 1

149 Directions: For each question, you will hear four statements about a photograph. Listen and select the one statement: (A), (B), (C), or (D), that best describes the picture. Then mark your answer on the Answer Sheet. You will hear the statements only once.

EXAMPLE

The best description of the picture is statement (B), "A man's giving a presentation to a small group of people." You should mark answer choice (B) on your Answer Sheet.

GO ON TO THE NEXT PAGE

1.

2.

3.

4.

GO ON TO THE NEXT PAGE ➤

5.

6.

Part 2

150 **Directions:** Listen to these questions and statements. After each question or statement, you will hear three responses. Select the most appropriate response: (A), (B), or (C). Then mark your answer on the Answer Sheet. You will hear each question or statement, and the responses, only once.

EXAMPLE

You hear: Would you mind helping me finish this report?

You then hear: (A) That's very kind of you.

                    (B) I thought you would.

                    (C) No, not at all.

The best response to the question "Would you mind helping me finish this report?" is answer choice (C), "No, not at all." You should mark answer choice (C) on your Answer Sheet.

---

7. Mark your answer on the Answer Sheet.

8. Mark your answer on the Answer Sheet.

9. Mark your answer on the Answer Sheet.

10. Mark your answer on the Answer Sheet.

11. Mark your answer on the Answer Sheet.

12. Mark your answer on the Answer Sheet.

13. Mark your answer on the Answer Sheet.

14. Mark your answer on the Answer Sheet.

15. Mark your answer on the Answer Sheet.

16. Mark your answer on the Answer Sheet.

17. Mark your answer on the Answer Sheet.

18. Mark your answer on the Answer Sheet.

19. Mark your answer on the Answer Sheet.

20. Mark your answer on the Answer Sheet.

21. Mark your answer on the Answer Sheet.

22. Mark your answer on the Answer Sheet.

23. Mark your answer on the Answer Sheet.

25. Mark your answer on the Answer Sheet.

25. Mark your answer on the Answer Sheet.

26. Mark your answer on the Answer Sheet.

27. Mark your answer on the Answer Sheet.

28. Mark your answer on the Answer Sheet.

29. Mark your answer on the Answer Sheet.

30. Mark your answer on the Answer Sheet.

31. Mark your answer on the Answer Sheet.

GO ON TO THE NEXT PAGE ➤

Part 3

151 **Directions:** You will hear thirteen conversations. For each conversation, read the three questions and the four answer choices that follow each question. Select the most appropriate answer: (A), (B), (C), or (D). Then mark your answer on the Answer Sheet. You will hear each conversation only once.

32. What is the man's occupation?
    (A) Company accountant
    (B) Sales executive
    (C) Property manager
    (D) Maintenance technician

33. What is the subject of the conversation?
    (A) Payment arrangements
    (B) The cost of services
    (C) Room requirements
    (D) Rental of equipment

34. What does the woman request?
    (A) Group rates
    (B) More time to pay
    (C) A 5 percent discount
    (D) Separate invoices

35. Who is the woman speaking to?
    (A) A coworker
    (B) A journalist
    (C) A website designer
    (D) A marketing manager

36. What are the speakers mainly discussing?
    (A) A technical manual
    (B) A company website
    (C) A magazine article
    (D) A new product

37. What will the man do later today?
    (A) Copy a document
    (B) Contact a personal trainer
    (C) Go sightseeing
    (D) Travel on public transportation

38. Where does this conversation take place?
    (A) At a bus terminal
    (B) At a gas station
    (C) In a coffee shop
    (D) On the street

39. What does the man plan to do?
    (A) Get some refreshments
    (B) Buy a map
    (C) Find the restroom
    (D) Exchange some money

40. What does the woman advise the man to do?
    (A) Use an alternative route
    (B) Take a short break
    (C) Change his plans
    (D) Have some coins handy

41. Where does the man probably work?
    (A) In a mail room
    (B) In a call center
    (C) In a laboratory
    (D) In a gym

42. What does the man mostly talk about?
    (A) His coworkers
    (B) His role and responsibilities
    (C) Training opportunities
    (D) The work hours

43. What can be inferred from the conversation?
    (A) The woman has a hearing difficulty.
    (B) The man has just started a new job.
    (C) The woman is unemployed.
    (D) The man and woman are married.

44. Why did the woman call Mr. Robertson?
    (A) To resolve a dispute
    (B) To provide reassurance
    (C) To ask about production
    (D) To place an order

45. According to the conversation, what is the problem?
    (A) Some supplies are missing.
    (B) A delivery is late.
    (C) A staff member has resigned.
    (D) Some employees are on strike.

46. What does Mr. Robertson ask the woman to do?
    (A) Send written confirmation
    (B) Issue a press release
    (C) Forward a document
    (D) Inform the management

47. Who most likely is the woman?
    (A) A machine operator
    (B) A travel agent
    (C) A fashion designer
    (D) An artist

48. When will the speakers meet again?
    (A) Next week
    (B) In two weeks
    (C) At the end of the month
    (D) Early next month

49. What will the woman do before the next meeting?
    (A) Take a short break in Milan
    (B) Contact the man by e-mail
    (C) Hire two more staff members
    (D) Prepare some clothing samples

50. Why does the woman say, "That would be great"?
    (A) To accept an offer
    (B) To agree to a suggestion
    (C) To predict an outcome
    (D) To recommend a solution

51. What is implied about the speakers?
    (A) They are employed by the same company.
    (B) They have worked together previously.
    (C) They are experienced market analysts.
    (D) They meet on a weekly basis.

52. What does the woman say she will do in the afternoon?
    (A) Meet with coworkers
    (B) Review the decision
    (C) Present an award
    (D) Apply for a position

53. Where does the conversation take place?
    (A) At an air cargo terminal
    (B) At a border crossing
    (C) At a travel agency
    (D) At an export company

54. What is the man's final destination?
    (A) Alaska
    (B) British Columbia
    (C) San Francisco
    (D) Seattle

55. Why is the man upset?
    (A) He has lost some money.
    (B) He has failed an examination.
    (C) He risks falling behind schedule.
    (D) He is in trouble with his employer.

GO ON TO THE NEXT PAGE

56. What are the speakers mainly discussing?
    (A) Additional discounts
    (B) Staffing levels
    (C) Payment terms
    (D) Delivery arrangements

57. What did the man's secretary most likely forget to do?
    (A) Pass on a message
    (B) E-mail the woman
    (C) Sign the bid on time
    (D) Confirm the cost

58. What will the woman do later today?
    (A) Consult a coworker
    (B) Make a purchase
    (C) Telephone the man
    (D) Deliver some goods

59. Why is the man calling?
    (A) To check rental costs
    (B) To confirm a reservation
    (C) To ask for information
    (D) To discuss travel plans

60. What is the woman concerned about?
    (A) The potential risks to children
    (B) The lateness of the man's call
    (C) The unseasonably cold weather
    (D) The chance of accidental damage

61. What does the man imply when he says, "That's too bad"?
    (A) He is sorry to hear about the accident.
    (B) He may decide to make a complaint.
    (C) He is dissatisfied with the response.
    (D) He probably will not make a booking.

62. What is the man's problem?
    (A) He has a toothache.
    (B) His stomach is painful.
    (C) He has food poisoning.
    (D) He has a sore throat.

63. Look at the graphic. Which product does the man buy?
    (A) Calm-o-Quick
    (B) Bizmophenyl X
    (C) LactoMild
    (D) CureFast

Helix Pharma

Product	Format
Calm-o-Quick	Soluble tablet
Bizmophenyl X	Capsule
LactoMild	Liquid
CureFast	Lozenge

64. What does the woman say is important?
    (A) Drinking lots of water
    (B) Sleeping on the side
    (C) Taking enough rest
    (D) Following the directions

65. Look at the graphic. Which dish is not on the menu this evening?
    (A) Moroccan-spiced vegetables
    (B) Quiche Lorraine
    (C) Mediterranean crab
    (D) Roast leg of lamb

66. What does the man offer to do?
    (A) Speak with Mike
    (B) Finish setting the tables
    (C) Check the refrigerator
    (D) Open a little later

67. What time does this conversation take place?
    (A) 5:50 P.M.
    (B) 6:00 P.M.
    (C) 6:20 P.M.
    (D) 6:30 P.M.

Tonight's Specials

Moroccan-spiced vegetables
Quiche Lorraine
Mediterranean crab
Roast leg of lamb

GO ON TO THE NEXT PAGE

WOMEN (no. of repetitions)	20-29	30-39	40-49	50-59	60+
Above average	23+	22+	18+	15+	13+
Average	12-22	10-21	8-17	7-14	5-12
Below average	below 12	below 10	below 8	below 7	below 5

68. Who most likely is the man?
    (A) A medical doctor
    (B) A school teacher
    (C) A personal trainer
    (D) A professional athlete

69. Look at the graphic. How many repetitions did the woman most likely complete?
    (A) 8
    (B) 14
    (C) 17
    (D) 19

70. What is the woman probably going to do next?
    (A) Take a break
    (B) Return to work
    (C) Go over the results
    (D) Continue exercising

Part 4

152 **Directions:** You will hear ten short talks given by a single speaker. For each short talk, read the three questions and the four answer choices that follow each question. Select the most appropriate answer: (A), (B), (C), or (D). Then mark your answer on the Answer Sheet. You will hear each short talk only once.

71. Who is the speaker?
    (A) An academic administrator
    (B) A structural engineer
    (C) A college dean
    (D) A university lecturer

72. Why is the speaker concerned?
    (A) There has been a traffic holdup.
    (B) A cell phone has been stolen.
    (C) A lecturer has not arrived.
    (D) She cannot find an address.

73. What is mentioned about Dr. Chang?
    (A) He is an engineering student.
    (B) He went home earlier today.
    (C) He was taken ill suddenly.
    (D) He has not visited the college before.

74. Where is this talk taking place?
    (A) On a boat
    (B) On a bus
    (C) In a hotel
    (D) On the street

75. How long will the tour last?
    (A) About one hour
    (B) About an hour and a half
    (C) About two and a half hours
    (D) About three hours

76. What does the speaker imply when he says, "They're awesome"?
    (A) The boat tours are very impressive.
    (B) Staff at the hotel do an excellent job.
    (C) Parts of the castle are worth visiting.
    (D) The opera singers have an excellent reputation.

77. What is the purpose of the speech?
    (A) To present an award
    (B) To open a conference
    (C) To inaugurate a building
    (D) To launch a company

78. Who is making the speech?
    (A) An ambassador
    (B) An architect
    (C) A businessman
    (D) A politician

79. What will listeners do next?
    (A) Go sightseeing
    (B) See a show
    (C) Take a tour
    (D) Have some food

80. What type of business is being advertised?
    (A) A car dealer
    (B) An auto manufacturer
    (C) An auto repair shop
    (D) A car rental agency

81. What is indicated about the promotion?
    (A) A $3,000 cash prize can be won.
    (B) Refinancing may be possible.
    (C) Some customers may not be eligible.
    (D) The offers are not yet available.

82. How are listeners asked to respond?
    (A) By registering online
    (B) By visiting in person
    (C) By calling a sales rep
    (D) By mailing an application

83. Where does the speaker probably work?
   (A) At a furniture restorer's
   (B) At an auction house
   (C) At a carpentry shop
   (D) At a department store

84. What item is the speaker describing?
   (A) A cabinet
   (B) A chair
   (C) A table
   (D) A sculpture

85. According to the speaker, what is unusual about the item?
   (A) Its color
   (B) Its carvings
   (C) Its shape
   (D) Its material

86. Where is this announcement being made?
   (A) At a supermarket
   (B) At a garden center
   (C) At a department store
   (D) At a function hall

87. What does the speaker mean when he says, "you'll find that very difficult to believe"?
   (A) Nancy looks young for her age.
   (B) Few elderly people still have jobs.
   (C) 50 years is a long time to work for the same company.
   (D) It is unusual to work on your birthday.

88. What are listeners encouraged to do?
   (A) Sing a song
   (B) Speak to a manager
   (C) Release a balloon
   (D) Have refreshments

89. What sort of organization is Skills and Thrills?
   (A) A puppet theater
   (B) A dance troupe
   (C) A circus
   (D) A concert orchestra

90. What can be inferred about the organization?
   (A) It was founded three years ago.
   (B) Its fortunes have recently declined.
   (C) It is financially successful.
   (D) It employs about 200 people.

91. According to the report, what is scheduled to take place at the end of the month?
   (A) A press conference
   (B) A new production
   (C) A move to new premises
   (D) Employee layoffs

92. How many lectures will there be in all?
   (A) Five
   (B) Six
   (C) Nine
   (D) Ten

93. Which topic will be covered in week 6 of the course?
   (A) Consumer behavior
   (B) Business ethics
   (C) Strategic marketing
   (D) Retail management

94. According to the speaker, what will the course assessment consist of?
   (A) A single exam
   (B) A single assignment
   (C) An exam and an assignment
   (D) Two assignments

95. Who most likely are the listeners?
- (A) Business executives
- (B) Medical students
- (C) Town councilors
- (D) A foreign delegation

96. Look at the graphic. Which department will the group pass on the way to their destination?
- (A) Pharmacy
- (B) Laboratory
- (C) Eye clinic
- (D) Nursing

97. What are listeners asked to do?
- (A) Be as quiet as possible
- (B) Stay together as a group
- (C) Reduce their visiting time
- (D) Check in at reception

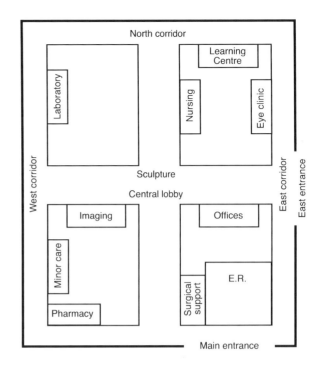

98. According to the speaker, which group of passengers should board now?
- (A) First-class ticket-holders
- (B) Family groups
- (C) Airline personnel
- (D) Those needing help

99. What are the remaining passengers asked to do?
- (A) Prepare their documentation
- (B) Switch off their cell phones
- (C) Listen for their row number
- (D) Return to their seats quickly

100. Look at the graphic. Where is the plane flying to?
- (A) Atlanta
- (B) Charlotte
- (C) Toronto
- (D) Dallas

Flight number	Destination	Time of departure
AA589	Atlanta	7:20 A.M.
UA985	Charlotte	7:20 A.M.
UA575	Toronto	7:25 A.M.
AA595	Dallas	7:30 A.M.

This is the end of the Listening Comprehension section of the test. Go on to the Reading section.

Reading Test

This Reading Test contains a variety of texts and reading comprehension questions. They are designed to test your ability to read and understand written English. There are three parts. You have 75 minutes to complete this section of the test.

Mark your answers on the separate Answer Sheet provided on page 319.

Part 5

Directions: Read each sentence. You will notice that there is a word or phrase missing. Study the four answer choices and select the one answer: (A), (B), (C), or (D), that best completes the sentence. Then mark your answer on the Answer Sheet.

101. Any employee who is interested .... taking part in the company's annual charity Fun Run should contact Vanessa Lee, the Social Responsibility Manager.
    (A) at
    (B) in
    (C) on
    (D) for

102. If either party rejects the compensation sum offered by the insurance company, the case will have to .... through the courts.
    (A) pursue
    (B) be pursued
    (C) have pursued
    (D) have been pursued

103. Some hormones can be administered orally, ... others, including insulin, must be injected directly into the bloodstream.
    (A) whereas
    (B) likewise
    (C) namely
    (D) further

104. It was years since the city's hockey team ....the final round of the tournament.
    (A) has reached
    (B) had reached
    (C) is reaching
    (D) was reaching

105. Keeping tires properly inflated will improve fuel .... by up to 3 percent.
    (A) economy
    (B) economics
    (C) economize
    (D) economical

106. The community garden project receives no government funding, so the general public's support is .... essential to sustain its work.
    (A) exclusively
    (B) conclusively
    (C) likely
    (D) absolutely

107. Mr. Martinez, training manager at Stormont Electrical, was disappointed when two young recruits gave .... their apprenticeships after just a few months.
    (A) away
    (B) in
    (C) out
    (D) up

108. Wider aisles on airplanes may not eliminate congestion while passengers are boarding, but they might reduce ....
    (A) one
    (B) it
    (C) them
    (D) theirs

109. The inquiry concluded that the reorganization of the Consumer Standards Department was not as smooth as it .... have been.

(A) could
(B) would
(C) ought
(D) must

110. The Business Information Systems course will .... between classroom-based lectures and practical sessions at various local companies' workplaces.

(A) alteration
(B) alternate
(C) alternative
(D) alternatively

111. The band members originally teamed up at college, when they discovered that they had the same .... in music.

(A) hearing
(B) like
(C) sense
(D) taste

112. Talks with the firefighters union have broken off for the weekend, but discussions will .... on Monday.

(A) assume
(B) consume
(C) presume
(D) resume

113. Fast-growing technology companies need to have flexible management structures in place so that they can .... quickly to new economic or market conditions.

(A) adapt
(B) alter
(C) fit
(D) suit

114. The fourth-story apartment is in the popular Maple Park neighborhood, and was recently redecorated and newly carpeted ....

(A) therein
(B) thereabouts
(C) through
(D) throughout

115. Your first choice of room cannot be guaranteed, but our staff will .... their best to accommodate individual wishes.

(A) do
(B) act
(C) achieve
(D) make

116. Despite the claims of the manufacturer, users quickly found that the new desktop publishing software was .... but easy to use.

(A) everything
(B) something
(C) anything
(D) nothing

GO ON TO THE NEXT PAGE

117. The warehouse foreman was injured in an accident involving a forklift truck, as a result of .... he was hospitalized for three weeks.
(A) which
(B) what
(C) that
(D) it

118. Before drawing conclusions from this focus group on our new line of vegetarian products, it is worth .... that respondents were paid for participating.
(A) note
(B) to note
(C) of note
(D) noting

119. The decision to move to new offices in Wakefield .... as a surprise to the entire workforce at Lorimer Engineering.
(A) came
(B) took
(C) was
(D) went

120. A Phoenix County Police Department spokesperson said that a fire that caused $100,000 in damage to a hardware store on Aurora Street yesterday appears to .... by faulty wiring.
(A) be caused
(B) been caused
(C) have caused
(D) have been caused

121. The Academy's singing teacher recommends that students devote at least an hour every day to .... basic musical scales.
(A) practice
(B) practicing
(C) practiced
(D) practices

122. The marketing director confirmed that she .... work on the new advertising campaign as soon as the budget had been approved.
(A) begins
(B) will begin
(C) would begin
(D) has begun

123. As far as can be .... from Broadfield Inc.'s annual report, the cash flow problems that plagued the company over the last fiscal year have now mostly been resolved.
(A) summoned
(B) surveyed
(C) surmised
(D) surprised

124. The aviation commissioner informed journalists at the press conference that final details for the airport upgrading project had .... not been finalized.
(A) yet
(B) already
(C) before
(D) still

125. If Mr. Park keeps on working as hard as he .... up to now, then it is very likely that he will soon be promoted to sales manager.
(A) does
(B) was
(C) has been
(D) had done

126. An article in last week's edition of *Theater News* .... about the upcoming Broadway season.
(A) enthused
(B) enthusiasm
(C) enthusiastic
(D) enthusiastically

127. A deadly virus transmitted by parasitic mites has been .... in the recent global decline of honeybee colonies.
(A) implicated
(B) implied
(C) inferred
(D) insinuated

128. Onions are easy to grow and are popular with gardeners .... their hardiness and resistance to frost.
(A) besides
(B) because of
(C) despite
(D) seeing that

129. Bond prices and interest rates are generally said to be .... related since, when bond prices rise, interest rates fall, and vice versa.
(A) conversely
(B) diversely
(C) inversely
(D) universally

130. Had it not been for the backing of the city's largest newspaper, Mr. Garcia .... the mayoral election.
(A) lost
(B) had lost
(C) would lose
(D) would have lost

GO ON TO THE NEXT PAGE

Part 6

Directions: Read each text. You will notice that there are four blanks. These are places where a word, phrase, or sentence is missing. For each blank, study the four answer choices and select the one answer: (A), (B), (C), or (D), that best completes the text. Then mark your answer on the Answer Sheet.

Questions 131–134 refer to the following newspaper article.

Life Is Sweet for Toltzis Inc.

The family behind the Juicy Joy and Fruity Fizz brand names is enjoying a $5,000,000 windfall after a good year of trading last year. Toltzis Inc., the Seattle-based group controlled by the Toltzis family for more than 50 years, saw its pre-tax profits _____131_____ by more than 60 percent.

Analysts attribute the company's success to a warmer than usual summer, _____132_____ stimulated demand for the company's chilled drinks and popsicles.

_____133_____ The company's shareholders _____134_____ more than $2,000,000 in dividends, up from $750,000 the previous year.

---

131. (A) exceed
     (B) soar
     (C) plummet
     (D) hit

132. (A) what
     (B) when
     (C) whose
     (D) which

133. (A) The family confirmed that sales would be revised following an internal review.
     (B) Many believe the unseasonal weather was due to climate change and global warming.
     (C) In fact, most companies across the chilled drinks sector performed remarkably well.
     (D) The Toltzis family were not the only beneficiaries of last year's bonanza.

134. (A) were awarded
     (B) have awarded
     (C) had awarded
     (D) had been awarded

What to Expect from the Interview Process

If you are a professional ....135........ for a senior position, you may be asked to attend a series of interviews, in which you meet individually with various representatives of the company. In the initial interview, the interviewer usually wants basic information regarding your personal skills and managerial abilities. In ....136........ interviews, the focus is on the match between you and the company's goals and objectives. When all the interviews are completed, the different interviewers convene to discuss you and your qualifications for the job. Sometimes unsuitable candidates are screened out at each stage in the process, meaning that ....137........candidates are interviewed in the later stages than in the earlier ones. ....138........

135. (A) apply
    (B) applies
    (C) applied
    (D) applying

136. (A) exclusive
    (B) conducting
    (C) popular
    (D) subsequent

137. (A) less
    (B) least
    (C) fewer
    (D) few

138. (A) By these means, organizations hope to hire the best candidate for the job.
    (B) The first interview is scheduled for the day you start training.
    (C) Interviews in the later stages focus on more senior roles.
    (D) We hope that you decide to apply for a position shortly.

GO ON TO THE NEXT PAGE

To: taylor@capro.net
From: patronnotices@marshalllibrary.org
Date: June 4
Subject: Courtesy notice – library materials due soon

Dear Sally Taylor,

This is a courtesy notice that the following item(s) will be due shortly. To avoid incurring overdue charges, please _____139_____ these item(s) to any library branch, renew them at

http://marshalllibrary.org/patroninfo, or call 269-555-0150 on or _____140_____ the due date.

Please do not reply to this automated message. _____141_____ Please do not hesitate _____142_____ us at 269-555-0152 if you require assistance.

1 Wildflowers of the Indian Subcontinent
Item ID: C0946002743

Circulation Department
Marshall City Library

139. (A) recur
(B) return
(C) reserve
(D) recall

140. (A) unless
(B) until
(C) before
(D) while

141. (A) Our computer system is running slow.
(B) No response from you is needed.
(C) This e-mail box is not monitored.
(D) All books must be returned in person.

142. (A) contact
(B) contacting
(C) to contact
(D) having contacted

This week's movie review: *The Marshan Monsters Meet the Omegans*

The latest movie in the *Marshan Monsters* series is even more ......**143**...... than the first three.

The plot is far-fetched and completely predictable; the Monsters get lost in space and land on the hostile planet Omega—and mayhem ensues from there. In line with previous installments in this movie franchise, the script is lackluster and the jokes are corny. ......**144**......, the special effects are breathtakingly spectacular, and the Marshan Monsters are as likeable as ever. Yes, the Marshan Monsters and their escapades are ludicrous, but we just can't help loving them! *The Marshan Monsters Meet the Omegans* is sure to please the younger members of the family, if not everyone, so why not ......**145**...... the kids this weekend? ......**146**......

---

143. (A) adventurous
     (B) ridiculous
     (C) absorbing
     (D) touching

144. (A) Besides
     (B) On the contrary
     (C) Likewise
     (D) Nevertheless

145. (A) take
     (B) to take
     (C) taking
     (D) taken

146. (A) There are so many reasons why not!
     (B) Tickets are unavailable on Saturdays or Sundays.
     (C) They are bound to enjoy it, and you might too.
     (D) In short, it only lasts 90 minutes.

GO ON TO THE NEXT PAGE ➡

Part 7

Directions: Read the texts. You will notice that each text is followed by several questions. For each question, decide which of the four answer choices: (A), (B), (C), or (D), best answers the question. Then mark your answer on the Answer Sheet.

Questions 147–148 refer to the following notice.

Danville Street—Water Main Replacement

Construction work will begin on Danville Street between Hopkins Drive North and Huntington Avenue on April 14. Old fire hydrants will be removed and aging water pipes will be replaced, resulting in improved water delivery service to the neighborhood. ---[1]---

Until this date, this portion of Danville Street may be closed to traffic for brief periods during each day of construction to allow contractors' vehicles unimpeded access. ---[2]---

Public parking will be prohibited every day between 8:00 A.M. and 5:00 P.M., unless work has not commenced by noon, in which case public parking will be permitted for the rest of that day. ---[3]---

We apologize for any inconvenience this may cause. ---[4]--- Please contact the Public Utilities Department at 555-0130 for further information, or to report problems. Our hours are Monday through Friday from 9:00 A.M. until 4:30 P.M.

---

147. In which position marked [1], [2], [3], and [4] does the following sentence best belong?
"The target completion date is May 5."
(A) [1]
(B) [2]
(C) [3]
(D) [4]

148. According to the notice, what will be the main benefit of the project?
(A) There will be more parking spaces.
(B) Traffic flow will be improved.
(C) The water supply will be updated.
(D) Community services will be enhanced.

Calling All Musicians!

The Humberton Players are actively recruiting. Strings and harp particularly welcome. No audition, but standards are high. We have a wide repertoire, including classical music, and themes from movies and Broadway shows. We give two concerts a year at City Hall. Rehearsals every Tuesday evening at Humberton Community Center.

149. Who most likely placed this advertisement?
  (A) A local orchestra
  (B) A choral group
  (C) A music store
  (D) A theater company

150. Who would be most interested in the advertisement?
  (A) Songwriters
  (B) Violinists
  (C) Conductors
  (D) Vocalists

GO ON TO THE NEXT PAGE

Uncertain Times Ahead for Smartphone Manufacturer

Bagnoli posted profits of $762 million in the final quarter of last year, marking a 54 percent increase over the previous year. Nevertheless, Bagnoli's stock price slumped by 4 percent on the stock exchange after the company predicted a downturn in smartphone sales for the current year. A company spokesperson said that last year's growth spurt in smartphone ownership could not be maintained indefinitely. Rather, the expectation is that prices of Bagnoli's bestsellers would be driven down by a flood of new products on the market. Moreover, the many new entrants to the smartphone market seem happy to accept lower profit margins. Over the next two quarters Bagnoli also expects a slowdown in demand for smartphones in developed countries. Although analysts predict that sales in emerging economies will escalate, thanks to the increasing affordability of smartphones, this will be unlikely to make up for any shortfall.

151. What is this report mainly about?
(A) Bagnoli's flotation on the stock market
(B) One company's performance and prospects
(C) Global trends in smartphone sales
(D) An upcoming new product launch

152. What is indicated about Bagnoli?
(A) It has reduced its dividends.
(B) Its profits have decreased.
(C) Its share price has fallen.
(D) Its sales have declined.

153. According to the report, what is likely to happen in the future?
(A) More companies will be manufacturing smartphones.
(B) Demand for smartphones will continue to rise in the West.
(C) Bagnoli's phones will be more expensive than now.
(D) There will be an economic downturn in emerging markets.

⚓ Sagacity Cultural Experiences ⚓

Mr. Stephen Chadwick
31 Kingston Road
Manchester
M33 7VW

November 26

Confirmation of Payment Received

Tour name: The Golden Age of Seafaring
Tour code: GOLD-CR-02
Tour dates: May 28-May 31

Passenger Names

Mr. Stephen Chadwick

Booking Costs

Base Price	1	£375.00
Single supplement	1	£85.00
	Booking Total Value	£460.00
	Deposit paid (November 15)	£120.00
	Balance due by April 15	£340.00

Additional Notes

The price covers three nights in the four-star hotel Star of Solent in Portsmouth, with breakfast and dinner. Entrance to museums, dockyards, and other places of interest on the itinerary is also included. Tour guests are advised to take out a travel policy. Participants travel to Portsmouth under their own steam.

---

154. What is the purpose of this form?
(A) To quote a price
(B) To request payment
(C) To acknowledge a deposit
(D) To claim expenses

155. What sort of organization is Sagacity Cultural Experiences?
(A) A tour operator
(B) A hotel chain
(C) A shipping line
(D) A travel agency

156. What is NOT included in the cost?
(A) Accommodations
(B) Two meals per day
(C) Tourist attractions
(D) Insurance coverage

GO ON TO THE NEXT PAGE ▶

Questions 157–159 refer to the following e-mail.

	E-mail
To:	Undisclosed recipients
From:	Kenneth Marsden
Date:	March 15
Subject:	Price changes

Dear Partners,

This e-mail is to advise you of an upcoming price increase of 8 percent on our reinforcing bar couplers and other reinforcement products. The increase will become effective on August 1 of this year.

---[1]--- We do not want to lose any existing customers, and must therefore reassure them that Steel Force prices remain competitive in the marketplace and that the quality of our service remains unbeatable. As the frontline staff providing customers' first point of contact with Steel Force, you have a very important role to play in explaining why we are taking this action.

We have not increased our prices for more than two years, but rapidly increasing fuel and shipping costs over recent months have had a significant impact on our own costs. ---[2]--- Please reassure customers that our recent investment in the latest state-of-the-art machinery and technology will help ensure that our prices remain as low as possible in the future. These price increases will enable us to continue to maintain the high standards for which we are well known throughout the construction industry, and to continue to employ a large team of professionals like yourselves to offer excellent face-to-face service to our customers. We do not anticipate any further price increases for the next calendar year unless the price of steel or other raw materials rises unexpectedly.

Your regional managers will shortly be contacting you with details of a meeting which will explain the new pricing structure to you, so that you will be equipped to discuss its implications with your customers. ---[3]--- To summarize briefly here, orders received after August 1 will reflect the price increase. The price charged for orders received between now and August 1 will depend on delivery date. Orders or quotations for products to leave our factory on or after August 1 will reflect the price increase. Orders or quotations for products to leave our factory before August 1 will be honored at current prices. ---[4]--- You will need to evaluate preexisting or regular orders on an individual basis, as the price will depend on the shipping and delivery dates.

If you have any questions before this meeting, please contact your regional sales manager.

Sincerely,

Kenneth Marsden

Sales Director, Reinforced Products Division

157. In which position marked [1], [2], [3], and [4] does the following sentence best belong?

"We realize that some of our customers will be disappointed at this news."

(A) [1]

(B) [2]

(C) [3]

(D) [4]

158. According to the e-mail, what is the reason for the price increase?

(A) Raw materials are more difficult to import.

(B) Transportation costs have escalated.

(C) Steel Force has invested in new machinery.

(D) Demand for steel is outstripping supply.

159. Which of the following statements is true?

(A) Orders placed today are guaranteed at current prices.

(B) Prices will not rise any further in the following year.

(C) The prices for existing quotations will be honored.

(D) Repeat orders will need to be renegotiated.

GO ON TO THE NEXT PAGE

Questions 160-162 refer to the following text message chain.

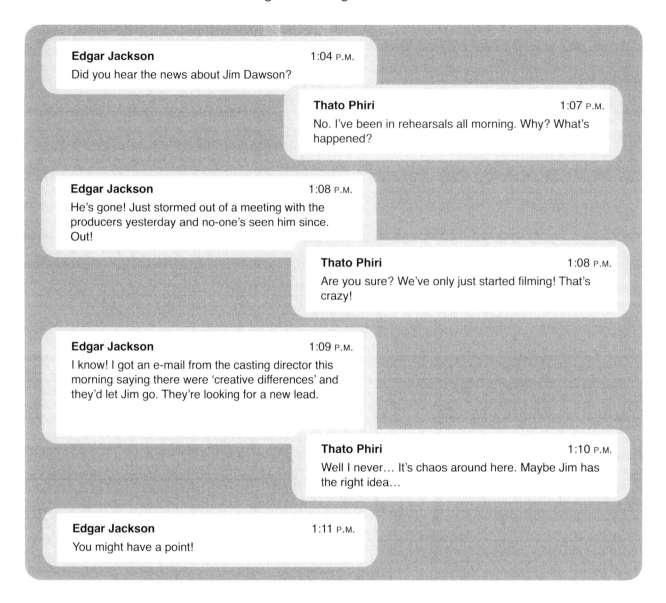

Edgar Jackson   1:04 P.M.
Did you hear the news about Jim Dawson?

Thato Phiri   1:07 P.M.
No. I've been in rehearsals all morning. Why? What's happened?

Edgar Jackson   1:08 P.M.
He's gone! Just stormed out of a meeting with the producers yesterday and no-one's seen him since. Out!

Thato Phiri   1:08 P.M.
Are you sure? We've only just started filming! That's crazy!

Edgar Jackson   1:09 P.M.
I know! I got an e-mail from the casting director this morning saying there were 'creative differences' and they'd let Jim go. They're looking for a new lead.

Thato Phiri   1:10 P.M.
Well I never... It's chaos around here. Maybe Jim has the right idea...

Edgar Jackson   1:11 P.M.
You might have a point!

160. At 1:10 P.M., what does Mr. Phiri mean when he writes, "Well, I never"?
(A) He is very surprised indeed.
(B) He hadn't heard the news.
(C) He never met Mr. Dawson.
(D) He didn't receive the e-mail.

161. What kind of industry do the men most likely work in?
(A) Movie
(B) Theater
(C) Music
(D) Art

162. What is suggested about Mr. Phiri and Mr. Jackson?
(A) They both know Mr. Dawson very well.
(B) They work in the same department.
(C) They have known each other for a long time.
(D) They may consider leaving their employment.

The Psychology of Color

Your staff spend hours in the workplace, so it's worth choosing carefully the colors you surround them with. Some colors stimulate, while others are relaxing. The right color can enhance productivity, and improve workers' moods and entire well-being. Do clients or patients visit your office? The colors you choose say a lot about you, so make sure you are giving the right impression.

Colors have their own individual personalities:

Blue Pale blue is a favorite with every kind of business. It's calming and soothing and helps workers stay focused for long periods.

Gray Neutral and easy to keep clean, but in a study most workers found it depressing and demotivating.

Green Restful and good for promoting harmony. Green is an excellent choice for eco-companies or those working in the environmental field.

Beige Neutral with a calming effect on the senses. Good for offices of all sizes.

Orange Energizing and uplifting. Helps keep people alert and motivated and reduces fatigue.

Pink Has a relaxing and soothing effect. Good for calming distressed workers and clients.

Bear these psychological features of the color palette in mind when you next paint your walls, or choose new curtains, carpets, and furniture. Keep to your chosen color scheme when it comes to packaging and logo design. You'll be building a strong brand and setting firm foundations for a successful and profitable business.

If you don't want to "feel blue" because your bank balance has gone "into the red," use your "gray matter" to pick the perfect color for your decor. Your competitors will be "green with envy."

---

163. Who is this article intended for?
(A) Textile designers
(B) Psychologists
(C) Interior decorators
(D) Business owners

164. According to the article, which color aids concentration?
(A) Green
(B) Gray
(C) Blue
(D) Orange

165. What is NOT indicated about color in the article?
(A) It forms the basis of an effective healing therapy.
(B) It is an important element in the branding mix.
(C) It has the power to influence people subconsciously.
(D) It can have an impact on staff productivity.

GO ON TO THE NEXT PAGE

Questions 166-167 refer to the following online chat discussion.

Ono, Minoru	9:32 A.M.

Hi everyone. Let's get started. Helena, where are we on the UniChem project. All on schedule?

Rosafio, Helena	9:33 A.M.

So far so good. I'm waiting for a quote from Nelson Brothers for the concrete. We need 8 cubic meters per day for the first three weeks, so that'll be two trucks each delivery. Once I get that I should be able to finish our stage 1 costings so we can sign off with their project manager. It might be a day to two.

Ono, Minoru	9:35 A.M.

OK. Send Kevin Richardson an e-mail to let him know. They are our most important client we don't want them thinking we're dragging our feet on this.

Rosafio, Helena	9:36 A.M.

Will do. Brian – are you sure all that timber will be there by the 24th?

Michelson, Brian	9:36 A.M.

Absolutely. The supplier I'm using is very reliable, and they know it's critical.
And the bricks are already at the warehouse.

Ono, Minoru	9:37 A.M.

That's great, Brian. Alberto – is that crane on its way?

Grassi, Alberto	9:38 A.M.

It should be. I haven't heard from Taylors yet, but it's due to arrive a couple of days before we break ground.

Ono, Minoru	9:38 A.M.

Get onto them to confirm, will you? Tell them to deliver it to the Ellis Rd yard. We'll keep it there with the diggers.

Rosafio, Helena	9:39 A.M.

And ask them to send the paperwork to me, please Brian. I don't have a quote from them yet.

Ono, Minoru	9:40 A.M.

OK, guys. Well done. This is a huge project, but I'm confident we haven't bitten off more than we can chew. Onwards and upwards!

166. At 9:40 A.M., what does Mr. Ono mean when he writes, "we haven't bitten off more than we can chew"?
(A) The costs are within budget.
(B) It is a significant undertaking.
(C) The project is achievable.
(D) He trusts his coworkers.

167. Who most likely is Mr. Richardson?
(A) A senior employee of UniChem.
(B) A building materials contractor.
(C) An accounts clerk at Nelson Brothers
(D) A supplier of construction equipment.

Questions 168–171 refer to the following announcement.

Guidelines Concerning Exposure to Noise

It is the legal responsibility of your employer to ensure that your workplace is free of hazards, including excess noise.

State regulations require employers to ensure that workers are exposed to a maximum of 90 decibels per working day, averaged over an eight-hour period. These noise levels may be higher if workers are exposed for fewer hours (see chart below). Employers may not always be aware of day-to-day conditions on the shop floor, and in such instances they will need to liaise with shift supervisors or other line managers.

Hours of Exposure	Sound Level (Decibels)
8	90
5	95
4	97
3	100
2	102
½	105
¼ or less	110

Exposure to impulse noise (sudden sharp surges such as bangs, explosions, and electromagnetic interference sounds) must never in any circumstances exceed 135 decibels. Anything over 160 decibels can damage hearing, and exposure to over 180 decibels can damage internal organs.

If noise exposure exceeds the levels in the table above, employers have a choice of actions to take. They can introduce "engineering controls," i.e., they can make changes to the physical working environment, or they can implement "individual employee controls," such as issuing workers with protective ear coverings. If you have any concerns about the noise levels that you are exposed to, and if you feel that the appropriate controls have not been implemented, you should speak to your union representative, who will raise the matter with management on your behalf.

Note that protective devices are a temporary or short-term measure, and are not an appropriate permanent solution. They may be uncomfortable to wear, and they impede communication, which, in itself, may cause other hazards.

168. Who is this notice intended for?
(A) Shift supervisors
(B) Factory workers
(C) Sound engineers
(D) Business owners

169. According to the article, what is the absolute maximum noise level that people may safely be exposed to?
(A) 100 decibels
(B) 135 decibels
(C) 160 decibels
(D) 180 decibels

170. What is indicated about protective ear coverings?
(A) They can sometimes pose risks.
(B) Workers object to wearing them.
(C) They are completely soundproof.
(D) They are suitable for long periods.

171. Which of the following measures would be considered an "engineering control"?
(A) A requirement to wear hard hats
(B) A reduction in shift hours
(C) The installation of a quieter machine
(D) The commissioning of a report on noise levels

✳ OUR TOP MODELS ✳

Panel Light 420X

* Lightweight and stylish
* Comes in white, gray, or black
* Energy-saving mode
* Wall-mountable (mounting kit included)

Glowbird

* Oil-filled—never needs refilling
* Portable
* Modern, sleek design—choice of white or light gray
* Lower energy consumption— automatically maintains optimal temperature

Cheerbox

* Adjustable thermostat—avoids wasting energy
* Push-button controls with digital display
* 24-hour timer with remote control
* ideal for larger rooms

InfraTemp

* Suitable for patio use—pole fits through standard two-inch patio table umbrella hole
* Steel and aluminum construction
* Instant warmth—three settings
* Save up to 25 percent on energy bills

172. Which product may be used outdoors?
- (A) Panel Light 420X
- (B) Glowbird
- (C) Cheerbox
- (D) InfraTemp

173. What is indicated about the Panel Light 420X?
- (A) It offers good value for the money.
- (B) It can be fixed to a vertical surface.
- (C) It is made of aluminum.
- (D) It is operated by remote control.

174. Which product feature is NOT mentioned in the announcement?
- (A) Efficiency
- (B) Portability
- (C) Dimensions
- (D) Visual appeal

175. In the Glowbird description, the word "sleek" is closest in meaning to
- (A) elegant
- (B) homely
- (C) unusual
- (D) innovative

GO ON TO THE NEXT PAGE

Fall semester starts the third Monday in September. All classes begin at 7:30 P.M and end at 9:30 P.M.

Monday	Tuesday	Wednesday	Thursday	Friday
Getting the Best out of Your Camera Instructor: Chandra Patel **Bookkeeping for Small Businesses** Instructor: Elaine Williams	**Accounting for All** Instructor: Lee Kwan **Beginners French** Instructor: Marie Dupont	**Digital Photography (Beginners)** Instructor: Chandra Patel **Intermediate French** Instructor: Marie Dupont	**Taking Better Photos** Instructor: Ken Hui **Italian for Beginners** Instructor: Luisa Cavelli	**Art History** Instructor: Dr. Sally Bancroft

Waterside Community College

850 9th Avenue North • Myrtle Beach, SC 29578
Tel: 843-555-0160 • www.waterside.edu

September 3

Dear Student:

Thank you for enrolling in a course at Waterside Community College. We are looking forward to seeing you later this month.

All classes will commence the week beginning Monday, September 15, except for Madame Dupont's classes, which will begin one week later due to illness.

You will be issued a student ID card on the first evening. This card will be valid for your entire period of study and entitles you to park in the campus garage, borrow books from the library, and enjoy other privileges of Waterside Community College students (see our website for a full list). Please bring a small, full-face photo for your card.

Your instructor will tell you at your first class meeting which books or other study materials you need to purchase. There are a limited number of lockers available for student use, and students wishing to rent one for the semester should bring a sturdy padlock. We regret that we cannot guarantee all students a locker.

If you have any questions, please contact me or one of my colleagues at the Student Registration Office at the telephone number above. The office will be open the week prior to the start of the semester, beginning September 8.

Sincerely,

Stacey Ellington

Stacey Ellington

176. What is the main purpose of the letter?

- (A) To explain a schedule
- (B) To promote a college
- (C) To provide information
- (D) To respond to a request

177. Who most likely is Stacey Ellington?

- (A) A senior instructor
- (B) A college student
- (C) An administrative worker
- (D) A marketing manager

178. What date will the Intermediate French course begin?

- (A) September 8
- (B) September 15
- (C) September 17
- (D) September 24

179. What should all letter recipients bring for their initial meeting?

- (A) Photographic identification
- (B) A student ID
- (C) A combination lock
- (D) Textbooks

180. What can be inferred about Waterside Community College?

- (A) It specializes in the humanities.
- (B) It is aimed at part-time students.
- (C) It has a well-stocked library.
- (D) It is open around the clock.

GO ON TO THE NEXT PAGE

❧A Full Table❧

Winner of Seattle's "Fresh and Local" award

Runner-up in the Hospitality category of
King County's "Independent Food Purveyor of the Year" competition

Award-winning company supplies delicious sit-down meals and buffets for all your events, including:

Corporate functions	board meetings	*Private functions*	birthday parties
	working lunches		weddings
	conferences		funerals
	seminars		
	receptions		

Buffet Menu A: $18.50 per person
Cocktail sausages
Sandwich platter
Potato salad
Green salad
Assorted breads and cheeses

Buffet Menu C: $22.50 per person
Roasted chicken breast, glazed with spicy barbeque sauce
Shredded beef tacos
Rice salad
Green salad
Rustic Italian and sourdough bread

Buffet Menu B: $20.25 per person
Cheese ravioli
Vegetable lasagna
Roasted asparagus
Mixed salad
Rustic Italian bread

Buffet Menu D: $23.50 per person
Platter of cold turkey and roast beef
Greek chicken salad
Medley of Greek olives
Marinated mushrooms
Assorted breads and cheeses

We supply serving staff, and all tableware and glassware. Rental of tables and chairs, if required. We can also recommend a photographer and musicians or other entertainers.

No travel fees for events held within 20 miles of our downtown Seattle main office.

Harrington & Family Insurance

Suite 17, Crown Buildings ◆ 250 Sunset Way ◆ Bellevue, WA 98052

February 19

Ms. Dolores Moreno
A Full Table
101 Melrose Avenue
Seattle, WA 98133

Dear Ms. Moreno:

Thank you for your time and help yesterday. Thanks particularly for letting me sample a range of your signature dishes—they were all delicious. It was hard for me to choose which menu to opt for, but I can now confirm that I would like to order Menu D for our event on April 25. Mr. Petridis, in whose honor our event is being held, is very fond of meat, and given that he was born and grew up in Greece, I am sure that he will appreciate the Greek dishes on that menu. I expect there to be about 30 people present, but I will confirm the exact figure for you a week beforehand. The buffet will be held in the boardroom at our Crown Buildings offices.

I enclose a deposit of $200, as requested, and will pay the balance when all the details are finalized.

We did not discuss desserts yesterday, but I think it might be a good idea to round off the buffet with some sweet dishes, even though we will be providing a special cake to be cut and eaten at the party. Mr. Petridis has worked with Harrington & Family Insurance for over 40 years, and will be sorely missed. We want to give him a rousing send-off. Could you suggest some options that will complement our savory menu, plus give me prices?

I look forward to hearing from you.

Kind regards,

Patty Lopez

Patty Lopez

181. What sort of business is A Full Table?

(A) A restaurant

(B) A catering firm

(C) A delicatessen

(D) An event planner

182. Which menu would be most suitable for a vegetarian?

(A) Menu A

(B) Menu B

(C) Menu C

(D) Menu D

183. What type of function does Ms. Lopez refer to in her letter?

(A) A retirement party

(B) A board meeting

(C) A new business pitch

(D) A birthday party

184. What does Ms. Lopez request in her letter?

(A) A breakdown of costs

(B) A party cake

(C) A Full Table's recipes

(D) Food recommendations

185. Which of the following will NOT be served at Ms. Lopez's function?

(A) Dairy products

(B) Vegetables

(C) Poultry

(D) Pasta

○○○ 🔍 http://www.plantersandpots.com ◀ ▶

Planters & Pots Garden Center

All of the seeds and plants we sell are suitable for growing in this locality, which is categorized as Hardiness Zone 5. Hardiness zones, also called planting zones, are determined according to the usual minimum winter temperature in the region.

ON SALE NOW: spring-flowering bulbs and other plants. If you want a colorful garden next spring, plant NOW, to give your plants a good 6 – 8 weeks of growing time in the soil before the first frosts appear and the ground freezes.

Daffodil	These highly popular, golden yellow flowers are easy to grow and provide spectacular drifts of color in early spring when planted in groups. Low maintenance.	Exposure: Full sun, partial sun Height: Grows 12-20 inches tall Soil type: Chalk, clay, loam, sand Soil pH: Acid, alkaline, neutral Soil drainage: Well-drained
Tulip	These attractive, vibrantly colored flowers are welcome additions to any garden. Low maintenance.	Exposure: Full sun Height: Grows 12-20 inches tall Soil type: Chalk, loam, sand Soil pH: Acid, alkaline, neutral Soil drainage: Well-drained
Lily of the valley	A very fragrant flower, with dainty, small, white, bell-shaped flowers. Spreads rapidly. Ideal for shady areas. Requires little maintenance.	Exposure: Shade Height: Grows 6-12 inches tall Soil type: Clay, loam Soil pH: Acid, alkaline, neutral Soil drainage: Moist, but well-drained
Freesia	Noted for their sweet fragrance, these elegant flowers are ideal for borders. They are usually grown for use as cut flowers. Very low maintenance.	Exposure: Full sun, partial sun Height: Grows up to 12 inches tall Soil type: Chalk, loam, sand Soil pH: Alkaline, neutral Soil drainage: Well-drained
Hosta	Hostas, also known as plantain lilies, are shade-loving perennials with attractive foliage. This very low-maintenance foliage plant is easy to grow.	Exposure: Shade Height: Grows 6-24 inches tall Soil type: Clay, loam Soil pH: Acid, neutral Soil drainage: Moist, but well-drained

INVOICE

From: Planters & Pots Garden Center
Cheshire Lane, Alstead, NH

2 x 50 count bag daffodil bulbs @ $36.50	$73.00
1 x 50 count bag tulip bulbs @ $36.50	$36.50
2 x 25 count bag freesia bulbs @ $13.50	$27.00
3 x jumbo bare root hosta plants @ $3.95	$11.85
--	
Total	$148.35

E-mail

From:	j_wright@homecall.net
To:	thomasjackson@mailme.com
Subject:	New plants

Dear Dear Mr. Jackson,

I took your advice after our conversation last week and I have now purchased the plants you recommended. Unfortunately, the garden center had sold out of lily of the valley, which you recommended for the bed under the kitchen window, but the assistant suggested a good alternative.

The plants and bulbs are now outside the shed waiting for you. Any time works for me, so come at your convenience. I'll be at home most days this week, but if I'm not, that doesn't matter – you know where to find the spare backyard gate key.

Sincerely,

Joanna Wright

186. Which plant is not known for its flowers?
- (A) Daffodil
- (B) Lily of the valley
- (C) Freesia
- (D) Hosta

187. At what time of year did Ms. Wright most likely buy the plants?
- (A) Early spring
- (B) Mid-summer
- (C) Early fall
- (D) Mid-winter

188. What is suggested about the flowerbed under Ms. Wright's kitchen window?
- (A) It is sheltered from the sun.
- (B) It has alkaline soil.
- (C) It covers a small areas
- (D) The soil there is sandy.

189. Who most likely is Mr. Jackson?
- (A) An assistant at a garden center
- (B) A delivery driver for a local company
- (C) A gardener at a private residence
- (D) A member of Ms. Wright's family

190. In the e-mail. The phrase "at your convenience" in paragraph 2, lines 1-2, is closest in meaning to
- (A) as soon as possible
- (B) whenever it suits you
- (C) at the usual time
- (D) by appointment only

Agricultural Management Certificate – Level 4

Students will develop knowledge and understanding of plant and animal production, and will gain associated skills. Students will acquire their knowledge in the classroom, in the laboratory, on school grounds, and on commercial farms. The certificate leads to multiple opportunities and pathways to employment in the farming and agriculture sector, and provides considerable academic credit for a degree at several Australian universities.

Learning Modules	Elective modules (worth 20% of the overall mark) Choose ONE of the following elective modules
• Management of the farm as a business • Farm case study • Marketing strategies • First aid • Agricultural technology • Commercial plant production systems • Managing plant production • Plant pests and weeds • Animal nutrition • Animal growth and development • Animal pests and diseases • Animal ethics and welfare	• Fiber and fuel technologies • Farming in a changing climate • Biotechnology in farming

Station Hand Required

Young, energetic, and reliable station hand required for an isolated, family-owned cattle station in Queensland. Must have horse and/or motorbike mustering experience. All aspects of cattle processing required, along with other station duties. Some mechanical knowledge is preferable. Successful applicant must have a desire to learn and a willingness to work in a team or individually. Wage negotiable, depending on experience. Accommodation available. Immediate start. Please e-mail resume and references to: stationboondog@outback.net

E-mail	
From:	jason.moore@freeserve1.co.au
To:	stationboondog@outback.net
Date:	March 23
Subject:	Job advertisement - station hand

Dear Sir,

I am interested in the Station Hand position advertised on the Great Outdoors Web site. I attached my resume, which includes references. I spent my childhood on my parents' cattle station in New South Wales and therefore have extensive experience in cattle management and processing. I grew up on horseback, but I also have a motorbike driving license, as well as a tractor-driver's license. In addition, I have some mechanical skills when it comes to vehicle engines. I gained the Agricultural Management Certificate (Level 4) at Tocal Agricultural College last year. I am a reliable, hard-working team-player.

I am currently traveling in Europe and will be returning to Australia in early May. I would welcome the opportunity to discuss this opportunity with you then.

I look forward to hearing from you.

Regards,

Jason Moore

---

191. What is indicated about the Agricultural Management Certificate?
(A) All modules are mandatory.
(B) Practical experience can be gained.
(C) Course participants will earn a degree.
(D) Successful students are offered employment.

192. What is stated in the advertisement about the cattle station?
(A) It is expanding its operations.
(B) It pays competitive wages.
(C) It is the state's largest station.
(D) It is in a remote location.

193. Which module on the Agricultural Management Certificate is most applicable to the advertised job?
(A) Marketing strategies
(B) Managing plant production
(C) Animal nutrition
(D) Fibre and fuel technologies

194. What does Mr. Moore imply in his e-mail?
(A) He had a pet horse as a child.
(B) He is a confident horse rider.
(C) His family did not own any cattle.
(D) He prefers horses to motor bikes.

195. Why will Mr. Moore's job application most likely be rejected?
(A) He has insufficient experience.
(B) He does not have a driving license.
(C) He cannot start work immediately.
(D) He failed to supply references.

Questions 196 to 200 refer to the following Web page, e-mail, and comment form.

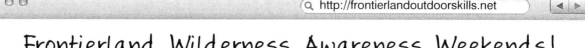

Frontierland Wilderness Awareness Weekends!

Join us for a FUN weekend, where you will be immersed in nature and gain skills in outdoor survival, animal tracking, and much more.

Our Family Wilderness Awareness Weekends offer two days packed full of fun and adventure. You will learn the following skills:

Wildlife tracking learn how to read signs left by animals. This activity involves a fair amount of walking and hiking.

Fire-making discover how to make a fire without matches

Shelter-building build a warm shelter out of naturally occurring materials you find

Eating for free forage for edible plants and berries – and cook them on your fire!

Invisibility skills find out how to camouflage yourself, and how to stalk.

Fish-trapping practice catching fish by hand, and using a home-made trap.

PLUS ... primitive games, bird-watching, tree-climbing and much, much more!

Suitable for ages 8+. Children must be accompanied by a responsible adult at all times.

Make new friends! Learn new skills! Have some awesome fun!

E-mail

From:	Gina Davies
To:	Joe Jones, Rita Park, Sam Khan
Cc:	Chuck Davies
Date:	July 12
Subject:	Upcoming Kids' Wilderness Awareness Weekend

Hi all,

I'm just confirming that the Kids' Weekend will be going ahead at the end of this month – we're fully booked, which is great news.

You all indicated to me last week that you were free that weekend and you have let me know which sessions you'd be happy to lead, so I've planned the program around your responses.

Sam is to lead the fish-trapping and fire-making sessions.

Joe will lead the wildlife tracking session each day.

Rita will run the shelter-building session and will organize the primitive games.

I will cover the remaining sessions.

Please arrive by 8 P.M. on Friday 28, the evening before the first day. If any of you can make it earlier, I'd be very grateful, as Chuck and I could use some help setting up.

Sincerely,

Gina Davies

Co-owner, Frontierland Outdoor Skills

My husband, my children and I all had a great weekend at Frontierland; although I am absolutely exhausted. My sons loved the camouflage and shelter-building activities – I'll never be able to find them now. My daughter has never been particularly adventurous, but I was bowled over at how enthusiastic she was. I can't believe she actually climbed a tree and caught a fish! I must thank Joe for being so patient with her. She absolutely adored his sessions – she can't stop talking about them. We will definitely be back next year! Thank you all so much.

Lisa Godfreys

196. What is stated about the Wilderness Awareness Weekend?
(A) Children of any age can take part.
(B) No child can be left unsupervised.
(C) Participants receive a certificate of attendance.
(D) It covers all day Saturday and Sunday morning.

197. In the comment form, the phrase "bowled over" in paragraph 1, line 5, is closest in meaning to
(A) thrilled
(B) shaken
(C) mystified
(D) astonished

198. Which of these activities did Ms. Davies lead?
(A) Eating for free
(B) Fire-making
(C) Wildlife tracking
(D) Shelter-building

199. What is indicated about Ms. Godfreys?
(A) She is married with two children.
(B) She attended the event previously.
(C) She intends to return in the future.
(D) She is a co-owner of Frontierland.

200. Which activity did Ms. Godfreys' daughter particularly enjoy?
(A) Shelter-building
(B) Wildlife tracking
(C) Tree-climbing
(D) Fish-trapping

This is the end of the test. If you finish with time to spare, you may go back to Parts 5, 6, and 7 to check your answers.

Printed in Great Britain
by Amazon